EASTERN EUROPE
AND THE
THIRD WORLD

Studies of the Institute on
East Central Europe,
Columbia University

EASTERN EUROPE AND THE THIRD WORLD

East vs. South

Edited by
Michael Radu

PRAEGER SPECIAL STUDIES • PRAEGER SCIENTIFIC

Library of Congress Cataloging in Publication Data

Main entry under title:
Eastern Europe and the Third World.

    Includes bibliographical references and index.
    1. Europe, Eastern--Foreign relations--Underdeveloped
areas. 2. Underdeveloped areas--Foreign relations--
Europe, Eastern. I. Radu, Michael.
DJK50. E16   327.470172'4   80-27494
ISBN 0-03-058648-8

Printed in the United States of America

Published in 1981 by Praeger Publishers
CBS Educational and Professional Publishing
A Division of CBS, Inc.
521 Fifth Avenue, New York, New York 10175 U.S.A.

© 1981 by Praeger Publishers

123456789   145   987654321

Printed in the United States of America

FOREWORD

There are at least two reasons why East-South relations have been less carefully studied than East-West or West-South. One is the common practice of using the term North-South relations when the user really means West-South relations. A second is that East-South relations, when they are considered at all, are often treated as incidental to the competition between the major powers when it spills over into the less developed countries.

The dozen or so countries of the "East" and the more than 100 countries that make up the world's "South" exhibit a variety of bilateral relations that call for description and analysis in their own right. Better understanding of the mosaic of East-South relations can no doubt lead to better decisions in the West regarding West-South relations, but this pioneering volume is not an exercise in advocacy.

Michael Radu has provided a framework for systematic inquiry, and he and his associates have made a substantial beginning by examining country by country the relations of the Communist states of Eastern Europe with the South. Because he and some other contributors are former students of mine, I have both personal and professional reasons to welcome the publication of the papers brought together here.

William T. R. Fox

Bryce Professor Emeritus of the
History of International Relations
Columbia University

v

PREFACE

This volume is the result of a symposium on Eastern Europe and the Third World sponsored by the Institute on East Central Europe of Columbia University in May 1980. None of the chapters included here have been published before, and the book itself represents the first attempt to analyze relations between a large group of Communist states and the developing countries as a whole.

Because of its pioneering character, this volume does not pretend to be an exhaustive examination of East-South relations or even of the East European aspects of those relations. The main aim of the contributors is less to provide hard-to-come-by data or to draw definitive conclusions than it is to encourage further research on the topic and to provide a tentative framework for such research. For this reason the contributors have tried to offer as broad a range of approaches and as wide a geographical scope as possible.

The common basic premise for all the contributors is that the Eastern European states do not constitute a monolithic group, and that each one of them has, to a greater or lesser extent, its own motivations and interests in pursuing particular policies with respect to the developing countries. Beyond that common ground, however, there is a degree of disagreement among the contributors as to the scope and importance as well as the limits of those particular policies. For some of the authors, the main goal pursued by countries such as Poland, Hungary, and the GDR is to secure reliable and stable sources of raw materials, especially oil, as possible alternatives to shrinking Soviet sources. The political aspects of those countries' ties with the South are considered to be more a result of internal considerations, such as the respective regimes' needs of legitimization, than an expression of their close ties with the Soviet Union or any obligation to support Soviet geostrategic goals. For other contributors, however, some Eastern European countries, especially Czechoslovakia, Hungary, and the GDR, have geared their entire policy toward the developing countries primarily to the pursuit of what are essentially Soviet national goals, and economic factors are considered to be relatively less important than the advancement of Marxist-Leninist revolutionary goals through the South. Yugoslavia, Albania, and, to a significantly lesser extent, Romania, are generally considered to be in a more complicated position because of their characteristic ideological and political position in Eastern Europe and in relation to the Nonaligned Movement.

Throughout this volume the terms "Third World" and "South" are used interchangeably, with some contributors favoring the latter term because of its nonhierarchical and nonneutralist connotations. For those who prefer to underline the differences between the developing countries and either the West or East the term "Third World" is considered more appropriate. In either case, however, Cuba, Vietnam, Laos, and Kampuchea are not considered to be members of either the Third World or the South.

ACKNOWLEDGMENTS

The editor wishes to express his deep gratitude to the following for their support in the preparation of the present volume: Professor Harold Segel, Director of the Institute on East Central Europe, Columbia University, for his encouragement throughout; Dr. Jane Curry, Senior Research Associate, for her advice in the initial stages of the project; Mr. Robert Scott, Research Associate, for his help in the preparation of the manuscript; Professors William T. R. Fox and Charles Gati of Columbia University, for their willingness to read and comment on the manuscript; Dean Harvey Picker of the School of International Affairs, Columbia University, for his sponsorship of the initial symposium; and the Ford Foundation, for its partial funding of that symposium.

CONTENTS

Page

FOREWORD   v

PREFACE   vi

ACKNOWLEDGMENTS   viii

LIST OF TABLES   xiv

LIST OF ACRONYMS   xviii

PART I: EAST VS. SOUTH: THE GENERAL FRAMEWORK

Chapter

1   EAST VS. SOUTH: THE NEGLECTED SIDE OF
    THE INTERNATIONAL SYSTEM
        Michael Radu   3

    The Structure of a Relationship   6
    Policy Dimensions   14
    Types and Levels of Eastern Involvement   22
    The Ideological Dimension   32
    Trends and Implications for the International System   37
    Notes   47

PART II: INDIVIDUAL EASTERN EUROPEAN STATES
            AND THE THIRD WORLD

2   ALBANIA AND THE THIRD WORLD:
    IDEOLOGICAL, POLITICAL, AND ECONOMIC ASPECTS
        Elez Biberaj   55

    Albania's View of the Third World   58
    Albania's Political and Economic Involvement
        in the Third World   64
    Albania: A "Model" for the Third World?   67
    Notes   74

3   CZECHOSLOVAKIA AND THE THIRD WORLD
         Vratislav Pechota   77

      Prewar Ventures   78
      Renewed Ties   79
      Economics or Ideology?   80
      Nongovernmental Offensive   82
      Influence Through Arms Supply   83
      Trade and Aid Offensive   85
      Years of Heavy Engagement   87
      The Period of Reassessment   90
      Keeping a Low Profile   92
      A Decreasing Share of Third World Trade   93
      Technical Assistance   96
      Multilateral Arrangements   99
      The Future   100
      Notes   103

4   THE GDR AND THE THIRD WORLD:
      SUPPLICANT AND SURROGATE
         Michael Sodaro   106

      The GDR as Supplicant: The Quest
         for Diplomatic Recognition   107
      The GDR and the Third World: A Theoretical Overview   109
      Trade and Aid   111
      Methods of Influence   114
      The GDR and Black Africa   116
      The GDR and the Middle East and North Africa   123
      The GDR and South and Southeast Asia   130
      The GDR and Latin America   132
      Functions of the GDR's Third World Engagement   134
      Notes   137

5   EAST GERMAN SECURITY POLICIES IN AFRICA
         Jiri Valenta and Shannon Butler   142

      External Factors   145
         The GDR–Soviet Alliance   145
         East Germany's Post-1968 Overshadowing
            of Czechoslovakia   146
         The Soviet Union as a Mature Superpower and
            Increased Opportunities in Africa in the 1970s   147
      Internal Factors   148

Chapter		Page
	The NVA and SSD	148
	Economic Needs	150
	The German Inferiority Complex	151
	Case Studies: The 1970s	152
	Angola	152
	Shaba I and II	153
	Ethiopia and South Yemen	155
	Prospects for the Future	162
	Notes	165
6	HUNGARY AND THE THIRD WORLD: AN ANALYSIS OF EAST-SOUTH TRADE	
	Scott Blau	169
	Hungary, the Bloc, and the Third World	169
	Types of Involvement	170
	Goals	171
	Industry and Power in Hungary	172
	The Maturing Bloc System	173
	Scope of Trade with the Third World	176
	Identifying the Main Regions	176
	Composition of Trade	179
	Sub-Saharan Africa	182
	The Middle East and North Africa	186
	Asia	190
	Latin America	192
	Conclusion	195
	Notes	197
7	POLAND AND THE THIRD WORLD: THE PRIMACY OF ECONOMIC RELATIONS	
	Howard Frost	200
	Introduction and Background for the Evaluation of Polish-LDC Relations	202
	Basic Polish Foreign Policy Perceptions	202
	Recent Internal Developments	203
	Conduct of Polish-Third World Relations	205
	Foreign Policy Instruments	205
	General Perceptions and Evaluation of Interaction with LDCs	209
	Dynamics of Current Polish-LDC Relations	212
	Conclusions	228

Notes   229

8   ROMANIA AND THE THIRD WORLD:
    THE DILEMMAS OF A "FREE RIDER"
        Michael Radu   235

    Background on Romania's Foreign Policy   236
    The Ideological Framework   239
    Political Relations   244
    Economic Ties   252
    Conclusions   266
    Notes   269

9   YUGOSLAVIA AND THE THIRD WORLD
        Michael M. Milenkovitch   273

    Approaches to Assessing the Nonaligned Movement   275
    Yugoslavia's Motives for Nonalignment   280
    The Yugoslav Role and Impact upon the Nonaligned
        Movement   286
    Yugoslav Trade with Nonaligned Countries   291
    In Lieu of a Conclusion   293
    Notes   297

PART III: PATTERNS OF EASTERN EUROPEAN INVOLVEMENT

10 PATTERNS OF EASTERN EUROPEAN ECONOMIC
    INVOLVEMENT IN THE THIRD WORLD
        Roger Kanet   303

    The Political Environment of Relations Between
        Eastern Europe and the Developing Countries   305
    Economic Relations Between Eastern Europe
        and the Developing Countries   310
    Some Concluding Remarks   325
    Notes   326

11 POLICY PATTERNS OF EASTERN EUROPEAN
    SOCIALIST COUNTRIES TOWARD THE THIRD WORLD
        Janos Radvanyi   333

    Policy Patterns in the Khrushchev Era   335
    Reevaluation in the Brezhnev Era   336

Chapter   Page

    Summary and Conclusion   341
    Notes   343

INDEX   345

ABOUT THE EDITOR AND CONTRIBUTORS   356

LIST OF TABLES

1. 1   The South's Share in the Foreign Trade of China
and the Soviet Union, 1960-78   29

2. 1   Increase in Albanian Economic Indicators   71

3. 1   Czechoslovak Trade with Developing Countries,
1948-53   80

3. 2   Exports of Arms from Czechoslovakia and the Soviet
Union to the Third World, 1954-73   85

3. 3   Czechoslovak Trade with the Developing Countries,
1955-65   88

3. 4   Czechoslovak Foreign Trade, 1965-78   93

3. 5   Czechoslovak Foreign Trade with India, 1965-78   95

3. 6   Czechoslovak Foreign Trade with Iran, 1965-77   96

3. 7   Share of Domestic Resources in the Overall
Consumption of the Czechoslovak Economy   101

4. 1   Principal Third World Trade Partners of the
GDR, 1970 and 1978   112

4. 2   Countries with Wide Fluctuations in Trade Turnover
with the GDR   113

4. 3   GDR Foreign Trade with the Third World as a
Percentage of Total Foreign Trade Turnover   114

4. 4   Total Number of High- and Secondary-Level
Meetings Between GDR Officials and African Leaders   118

4. 5   GDR Trade Turnover with Selected African Countries   122

4. 6   Sources of GDR Petroleum Imports   124

4. 7   GDR Trade Turnover with Selected Middle
Eastern Countries   126

4. 8   GDR Trade Turnover with Non-Communist
Asian States   132

Table		Page
4.9	GDR Trade Turnover with Selected Latin American Countries	134
5.1	East Germany's Relations with Africa in 1968	143
5.2	Warsaw Pact Military Expenditures	147
5.3	GDR High-Level Visits to Africa, 1975–79	156
6.1	Eastern European Trade with Major Regions in 1975	174
6.2	Hungary's Trade with Major Third World Regions	177
6.3	Composition of Hungary's Trade with Major Third World Regions in 1978	180
6.4	Value and Shares of Trade with Africa	183
6.5	Composition of Trade with Africa in 1977	185
6.6	Value and Shares of Hungarian Trade with the Middle East	187
6.7	Composition of Trade with the Middle East in 1978	189
6.8	Value and Shares of Trade with Asia	190
6.9	Composition of Trade with Asia in 1978	191
6.10	Value and Shares of Trade with Latin America	193
6.11	Composition of Trade with Latin America in 1978	194
7.1	Polish Imports from Selected Developing Countries of Asia	214
7.2	Polish Imports from Selected Developing Countries of Africa	215
7.3	Polish Imports from Selected Developing Countries of Latin America	216
7.4	Polish Exports to Selected Developing Countries of Asia	217

Table   Page

7.5   Polish Exports to Selected Developing Countries
        of Africa   218

7.6   Polish Exports to Selected Developing Countries
        of Latin America   219

7.7   Polish Imports from Selected Developing Countries,
        by Industrial Group and Country of Sale, in 1979   220

7.8   Polish Exports to Selected Developing Countries,
        by Industrial Group and Country of Sale, in 1979   222

7.9   Polish Imports by SITC Commodity Classes   226

7.10   Polish Exports by SITC Commodity Classes   227

8.1   Romania's Trade with Main Middle Eastern Partners,
        1960-78   254

8.2   Romania's Trade with Main Partners in Asia and
        Latin America, 1960-78   258

8.3   Romania's Trade with Main Sub-Saharan Partners,
        1960-78   260

8.4   Romania's Trade with Selected Communist Countries,
        1960-78   262

8.5   Romania's Trade with Main Western Partners,
        1960-78   264

10.1   Ratio of Exports of Eastern European CMEA
        Countries to Total National Income   304

10.2   Arms Sales and Deliveries of the Soviet Union and
        Eastern Europe to Non-Communist Developing
        Countries   308

10.3   Trade of Eastern European States with the Non-
        Communist Developing Countries   312

10.4   Bilateral Commitments of Capital by Eastern Euro-
        pean States to Non-Communist Developing Countries   314

Table   Page

10. 5   Soviet and Eastern European Credits and Grants
         Extended to Non-Communist Developing Countries   316

10. 6   Net Development Assistance Dispersed, by Groups
         of Countries   320

10. 7   Soviet, Eastern European, and Cuban Economic
         Technicians Working in Non-Communist Developing
         Countries   321

10. 8   Technical Personnel from Developing Countries
         Receiving Training in the Soviet Union and
         Eastern Europe   322

10. 9   Academic Students from Developing Countries
         Being Trained in Communist Countries   323

LIST OF ACRONYMS

ANC	African National Council of South Africa
APL	Albanian Party of Labor
ASEAN	Association of South East Asian Nations
CMEA	Council of Mutual Economic Assistance
CPSU	Communist Party of the Soviet Union
EEC	European Economic Community
ELF	Eritrean Liberation Front
EPLF	Eritrean People's Liberation Front
ECOWAS	Economic Community of West African States
FLEC	Frente de Libertação de Enclave de Cabinda
FLNC	Front de Libération Nationale du Congo
FNLA	Frente Nacional de Libertação de Angola
FRELIMO	Frente de Libertação de Moçambique
GATT	General Agreement on Tariffs and Trade
IMF	International Monetary Fund
IBRD	International Bank for Reconstruction and Development
IOJ	International Organization of Journalists
MESAN	Mouvement de l'Évolution Sociale de l'Afrique Noire
MLSTP	Movimento de Libertação de São Tomé e Príncipe
MPLA-PT	Movimento Popular de Libertação de Angola-Partido de Trabajo
MPR	Mouvement Populaire de la Révolution
NIEO	New International Economic Order
OAPEC	Organization of Arab Petroleum Exporting Countries
OAU	Organization of African Unity
OAS	Organization of American States
OPEC	Organization of Petroleum Exporting Countries
OTRAG	Orbital Launch and Rocket Firm
PAIGC	Partido Africano Para Independencia de Guiné e Caso Verde
PLFO	People's Liberation Front of Oman
PLO	Palestine Liberation Organization
POLISARIO	People's Organization for the Liberation of Saguia el-Hamra and Rio de Oro
RCP	Romanian Communist Party
SED	Socialist Unity Party of Germany
SWAPO	Southwest African People's Organization
UNITA	União Nacional para a Independencia Total de Angola
WTO	Warsaw Treaty Organization
ZANU	Zimbabwe African National Union
ZAPU	Zimbabwe African People's Union

PART I
EAST VS. SOUTH:
THE GENERAL FRAMEWORK

1

EAST VS. SOUTH:
THE NEGLECTED SIDE OF
THE INTERNATIONAL SYSTEM

Michael Radu

In December 1979, Soviet troops intervened in Afghanistan in support of a faltering Marxist-Leninist regime that had come into power through a bloody coup in 1978. The invasion took the West by surprise, and when the president of the United States declared that the events had changed his perception of the Soviet Union he was in effect expressing a much more general misperception of Soviet policy toward the developing countries. President Carter's confession of surprise was tantamount to admitting that he was unaware of the radical shift that had taken place in Soviet attitudes toward and goals in what is generally referred to as the "Third World." The invasion of Afghanistan was only the latest and most obvious expression of that change.

The events that began with the coup of April 27-28, 1978, in Kabul and ended with the invasion are highly symbolic for East-South relations as a whole and for the changes they have undergone during the past decade. They contained in essence most of the basic trends of that period.

As became apparent almost immediately after the initial Afghan coup of 1978,[1] the new regime was Marxist-Leninist and pro-Soviet, supported chiefly by the two factions of the Afghan Communist party and by the officer corps. The previous regime, installed in 1973 with similar support, had since shifted to a conciliatory policy toward its neighbors, Iran and Pakistan, had opened up the country to more Western influence, and had attempted to establish a policy of nonalignment with respect to the Soviet Union, the Islamic states, and the West. These moves away from a previously pro-Soviet policy had given rise to discontent among the Communists and the Soviet-trained and indoctrinated military leadership and ultimately resulted in the 1978 coup.

3

The post-coup leadership soon proved to be divided and unable to cope with a growing large-scale popular insurgency. As a result of this deterioration, Soviet troops, whose numbers had been increasing steadily since 1978, staged a new coup, were provided with reinforcements, and, since December 1979, have undertaken the suppression of the insurgency on behalf of a new leadership in Kabul. Afghanistan, meanwhile, has applied for membership in the Council of Mutual Economic Assistance (CMEA), adopted the ruble as the official currency, signed a 20-year treaty of friendship and cooperation with the Soviet Union, and provided military bases for the Red Army.

On a more general level of analysis, these developments reflect a developing country's shift from nonalignment of the pro-Soviet variety to a short-lived attempt at nonalignment of the neutral variety to de facto and de jure alignment with the Soviet Union along both ideological and political lines. At the same time, the Soviet position in Afghanistan has shifted from influence (pre-1978) to domination (1978-79) to control (since December 1979). The symbolic importance of Afghanistan lies precisely in these shifts in position within the international system, a trend which has come to characterize more and more developing countries and to have an influence on the "South" as a whole.

Since all of the countries that constitute what is usually called the "Third World" are or were at one time in one of these stages (to which one may add the pro-Western type of nonalignment), it is perhaps conceptually more accurate to use the term "South" in describing them as a group, rather than "Third World." Unlike the latter term, which has a neutralist connotation, the former term simply denotes economic underdevelopment and a geographical location more or less to the south of the Soviet Union and the developed countries of NATO. Although none of these criteria are applicable to all the states of the South, they are still more useful than a purely negative definition describing the South as those countries which are neither Western democracies nor full-fledged Communist regimes. On the other hand, the clearest, though the least objective, criterion for distinguishing the South from either the West or the East may very well be the well-proved perception of the Southern elites that they are different from both. However, as long as the South continues to search for an identity, a comprehensive scholarly definition of it will continue to be an illusory goal. As for the term "East," it is used here to describe states with centrally planned economies ruled by Marxist-Leninist parties self-described as "vanguard" parties of the proletariat and subscribing to the Leninist principles of democratic centralism and international proletarian solidarity. According to these criteria, there are 16 states that together constitute the Eastern subsystem of the international system: Albania, Bulgaria, the People's Republic of China, Cuba, Czechoslovakia, East Germany, Hungary, Kampuchea (Cambodia), Laos, Mongolia, North Korea, Poland, Romania, the Soviet Union, Vietnam, and Yugoslavia.

The problem of Western perception of the East-South relationship is closely related to the way that the West in general, and the United States and France in particular (as the Western powers most actively involved in the South), react to developments in the South. The prevailing notion among both scholars and policy makers in the West is that the South is only a secondary, albeit important, part of an international system still dominated by the East-West competition, and any possible impact the East may have on the developing countries should be viewed in this light. In more concrete terms, the Soviet, or Cuban, successes in various parts of the South are interpreted as a piecemeal or global attempt to deprive the West of essential raw materials or of the control of strategic sea lines. For other Western analysts with a different ideological orientation, such as the "dependency" theorists, the South is seen as being underdeveloped and poor because of its historic and contemporary links with the capitalist West, a view which, like the previous one, also neglects or even denies any East-South dimension in explaining developments in the South. In this specific aspect, the dependency theorists are, ironically, close to those of their opponents who argue that the economic and political problems of the developing countries would wither away if only they would adopt a free enterprise economic system. In both cases the West-South ties are deemed the predominating factor in explaining and ultimately in solving the problems of the South. On the political level, the implied and often explicit Western attitude is that the South should be left to choose its own path of development and should be influenced only through trade and aid, if at all, while as a group it should be encouraged and helped to "remain" nonaligned. If the West would refrain from intervening militarily or politically in the South and would provide enough economic support, the argument goes, the reasons for Eastern involvement would be eliminated or limited and the South would prosper in a state of permanent detente.

Following this line of argument, which is especially prevalent in Washington, diplomatic ties and trade concessions to the developing countries are expected to prevent the establishment of anti-Western regimes. Where such regimes already exist, recognition as well as aid should be extended, on the undemonstrated premise that these regimes will thereby be steered toward some form of nonalignment. The many voices in the United States demanding increased aid to the Sandinistas in Nicaragua, recognition of the MPLA-PT (Movimento Popular de Libertação de Angola-Partido de Trabajo) regime in Angola, and continuing diplomatic relations with the government in Kabul all reflect this point of view. Moreover, some Western policy makers also tend to believe that it is in the interest of the West as well as its "moral duty" to "take the side of progress" by backing "liberation" movements or by supporting opposition groups in countries ruled by anti-Marxist authoritarian regimes, as well as by making more significant economic concessions within the framework of the New International Economic Order (NIEO). All these voices, as well as those of their ideological opponents supporting resistance to such moves and a more vigorous Western riposte to the East's military involvement in the South, have one thing in common: all seem to neglect both Southern autonomy and the East-South side of the triangular international system. To clarify some of these misperceptions is the topic of this essay.

The main problem facing the would-be student of East-South relations is the limited scope of existing scholarship in the field. Most scholars interested in relations between Communist and developing countries have focused their attention almost exclusively on Soviet and Chinese involvement in the South. However, this approach is both incomplete and misleading. It is incomplete because the Soviet Union and the People's Republic of China are not the only Eastern actors involved in the South, and East-West or Moscow-Beijing rivalries, important though they may be, are not a sufficient basis for explaining variations in the type, scope, and level of Eastern involvement in the South. It is misleading because, like West-South relations, East-South relations are not a one-way proposition, with the developing countries at the receiving end. Rather, they exist within a framework of complex and previously established political and economic conditions in both the East and the South. Shifts in the types of interaction between the two subsystems occur very often and to neglect them is to ascribe to both the East and the South a uniformity of goals and interests that they do not have and to oversimplify a very complex relationship.

For all these reasons a comprehensive analysis of East-South relations has to begin with a clear definition of the actors on both sides. By "actors," in this case, one should understand state actors rather than transnational or international actors.

THE STRUCTURE OF A RELATIONSHIP

A definition of state actors within the Southern and Eastern subsystems involves both a description of their individuality and an analysis of their relative position at a subsystemic level and within the framework of the relationship between the two subsystems. The subsystemic position of various actors has changed dramatically in many instances due to factors pertaining to the international system as a whole and to modifications in the relative distribution of power in both the East and the South. The position of the actors within each subsystem also reflects the basic characteristics of the group and its partic-

ular dynamics. For these reasons, the main criteria used in this description and definition of the actors involved must be both their subsystemic position and their position in the East-South relationship as
a whole.

As a subsystem of the international system, the South may be
defined as an ideologically, politically, economically, and culturally
heterogenous group of states having some structural similarities and
a number of common interests with respect to other parts of the international system. Institutionally, the South expresses those common
interests on an economic level through the Group of 77 and on a political level through the Nonaligned Movement. Regional and cross-re-
gional organizations such as the Organization of African Unity (OAU),
the Organization of American States (OAS), the Islamic Conference,
and the Arab League also play a role in providing some limited regional consensus among countries of the South.

The first type of Southern actors, henceforth referred to as
Group A, includes states like Brazil, Mexico, Nigeria, India, Libya,
Tanzania, Egypt, Saudi Arabia, Iraq, prerevolutionary Iran, and
Morocco. Characterized by a much larger population, area, and military or economic power than their neighbors, these states play the
role of regional powers because of their significant influence over
those neighbors. It should be stressed that a developing country is
part of Group A only to the extent that it actively uses its resources
to promote its interests on a regional basis and has the capability of
power projection on a regional basis. Tanzania, for example, ensures
the survival of friendly regimes in Uganda and the Seychelles by providing military support, and Dar-es-Salaam was the main political
force behind the grouping of Frontline states of Southern Africa during
the Rhodesian civil war. Saudi Arabia uses her enormous financial
resources to maintain a friendly status quo in North Yemen, Oman,
and the Western Persian Gulf area. Brazil uses her power to influence
the policies of states like Paraguay, Uruguay, and Bolivia, and it is
clear that political changes in those countries are often related to the
attitude of Brasilia.

Apart from their regional influence and their willingness to
maintain or expand it, Group A actors also share a common interest
in eliminating or at least limiting outside influence in the surrounding
region. As a consequence, they usually support broadly based Southern
policies of an antisuperpower character. It should be noted, however,
that this intrasubsystemic influence does not translate into an ability
to challenge the superpowers directly; whenever Group A actors perceive one or the other superpower supporting regional challengers to
their predominance, they are quite willing to resort to the help of the
other. From an East-West perspective, therefore, Group A actors
play the most important role of any Southern actors, since shifts in

their foreign or domestic policies immediately reverberate throughout a large region.

Because the Southern regions under the influence of Group A
actors are not contiguous, these actors seldom compete for influence
over the same area, and the majority of the Southern actors are not
subject to their influence. The majority are generally small, weak,
and poor, and their security options are limited to variants of what
is usually and vaguely described as "nonalignment." The actual policies pursued by these Southern actors seem to indicate that there are
at least three distinct (and sometimes contradictory) types of "nonalignment."

The Group B states are now a minority in the South, and their
number has decreased steadily during the past decade. Costa Rica,
Sri Lanka, Nepal, and Botswana are some examples of this type of
country, which seeks to ensure its security through South-wide collective measures, which exclude both the East and the West from their
framework. Such countries usually have economic and diplomatic ties
with both the East and the West, are active supporters of a strengthened role for the United Nations, and tend to follow scrupulously the
principles of noninvolvement in internal affairs, the rejection of the
use of force, and the equality of states under international law. Ideologically, these states are neither Marxist nor capitalist, and their
economies are of a mixed type. The Group B actors were predominant
in the Nonaligned Movement during the 1960s. Their common denomi-
nator continues to be political and ideological nonalignment.

The current majority in the Group of 77 and the ineffective majority of the Nonaligned Movement are states whose foreign policies,
while claiming to be as nonaligned as those of the Group B, are in fact
the unstable result of a contradictory set of internal and external factors, pushing them in different directions. At the United Nations and
in regional organizations these countries attempt to follow an equidis-
tant course between East and West by formally supporting the same
principles of nonalignment as Group B, including noninterference in
internal affairs and equality among states, regardless of size or power. They also share some common emotional stands in colonialism,
apartheid, and Zionism and support the NIEO. However, they realize
that changes have taken place in the international system during the
past decade, tend to be ideologically closer to either the East or the
West, and look for their security beyond collective arrangements with
other Southern states to extrasubsystemic actors. Ideologically, these
Group C actors are divided between "Socialist" and "free enterprise"
regimes, with countries like Guinea, Jamaica, Syria, and Libya representing the first group and Kenya, Ivory Coast, and the ASEAN (Association of South East Asian Nations) states representing the second.
Some of them have bilateral security arrangements with Western pow-

ers, especially France (Togo, Ivory Coast, Gabon, Senegal), while others tend to establish such arrangements with Eastern actors, especially the Soviet Union (Syria, Guinea, and, until recently, Sudan and Somalia). The position of Group C within the South best expresses the deterioration of whatever unity may have existed among the countries of the South and the general trend toward the collapse of the neutralist, Group B type of nonalignment, which has been steadily replaced by polarization. The ultimate expression of this polarization is the last group of Southern actors, Group D. Indeed, the diplomatic nonalignment of Group C is further emptied of any but institutional form in Group D, whose members all belong to the Group of 77 and the Nonaligned Movement.

Group D represents, for the time being, a minority in the South, but it is a growing minority. Its members—Angola, Afghanistan, Mozambique, Ethiopia, and South Yemen—are Marxist-Leninist regimes, in which respect they resemble some Group C states, but they also have very close military, economic, and political ties with the East. They have always formalized those ties in treaties of "friendship and cooperation" with the Soviet Union and her Eastern European allies, and the East's share in their foreign trade is significantly higher than the Southern average. In choosing between the principles of nonalignment described above and the interests of the East, they consistently support the latter, and their regimes' loyalty is offered to the principles of "Socialist solidarity" or "international proletarian solidarity." For all practical purposes, these countries are closer to the intrasubsystemic relationship of the East than to the limited and changing consensus in the South.

A concrete expression of the relative position of the Southern states toward the Soviet Union and the principles enshrined in the Nonaligned Movement's documents ever since 1961 was provided in January 14, 1980, on the occasion of the United Nations General Assembly vote on the invasion of Afghanistan. The general lack of consensus was clearly expressed by the avoidance of any direct reference to the Soviet troops, while the four groups of Southern actors voted according to their perceived interest in either nonalignment or "international antiimperialist solidarity." Afghanistan, Angola, Grenada, Mozambique, Ethiopia, and South Yemem—all Group D actors—voted against the resolution, thus taking the side of the Soviet Union against both the West and the vast majority of the South. Group C states of radical orientation, with the exception of Somalia and St. Lucia, did not vote, were absent, or abstained, demonstrating that, from their viewpoint, it was not possible to choose between the East and nonalignment. The list of these states can perhaps be seen as a list of potential additions to Group D: Benin, Congo, Guinea, Guinea-Bissau, Madagascar, Nicaragua, São Tomé e Príncipe, Cape Verde, Dominica, and the Seychelles.

With a few accidental exceptions, all Group A and B states supported the resolution. It is interesting to note that Iraq, a close friend of the Soviet Union for years and a major customer for Soviet weapons, followed its interest as a Group A actor and voted against the Soviet Union.

Ironically, the Eastern actors manifested less unity than did the Group D actors in supporting the Soviet Union. Not only did Yugoslavia, China, and the Khmer Rouge representative vote against the Soviets, but Romania also failed to support them by absenting itself from the vote. This vote demonstrated that the East itself is far from homogenous with regard to the South and that it also has to be regarded as a divided subsystem.

But divided as it is, the East as a subsystem of the international system still preserves a higher degree of ideological and economic unity than either the West or the South; that unity simply is not reflected at the political level. The political differences between various Eastern actors as far as their policies toward the South are concerned are such as to allow a distinction between actors in most relevant policy areas. Although there is an inner core of Eastern actors organized along hierarchical lines with the Soviet Union at the top, even that inner core is clearly fragmented when viewed from the perspective of East-South relations. A majority of the Eastern actors are closer to the Southern average per capita GNP than to that of the most advanced among them. It is important to note that the following division of Eastern actors takes into consideration their specific policies toward the South and their relative level of economic development, as well as their position toward the inner core.

The first group of Eastern actors, henceforth referred to as Group I, are the two Communist great powers, the Soviet Union and the People's Republic of China (China). Within the Eastern subsystem, and as perceived from the South, they may be considered to be the Eastern superpowers, and in many respects they do act as such. To begin with, they alone among Eastern actors have an overall Southern policy with long-range goals and the capability to implement most of those goals. The obvious differences between their economic and military strength notwithstanding, both the Soviet Union and China manifest the same global type of interests, albeit most of the time opposed in their goals, and the generally small amount of resources needed for the implementation of policy goals in the South tends to offset the inferior level of China's capabilities. For both, the South is an arena of political and ideological competition, and both are attempting to provide the South with a model of development and are able and willing to invest significant amounts of political and economic resources in order to prevail. While it is true that the Soviet Union was able to provide much larger amounts of aid to friendly Southern regimes (in at least three

cases—Indonesia before 1965, Ethiopia in 1977-78, and India in 1980—
it offered more than $1 billion in long-term military or economic aid
to an individual Southern country), China was also able to provide significant support to countries it considered significant for her Southern
strategy, Tanzania, Ghana, and Mali being the most important examples. Even more importantly, they both proved able to limit or eliminate the influence of the other in selected areas of the South. However,
China was unable to provide timely support to Southern regimes friendly to her when they were internally or externally challenged, and as a
result they collapsed. The regimes of Sukarno-Subandrio in Indonesia
in 1965, Ali Soilih in the Comoros in 1978, and Pol Pot in Kampuchea
in 1979, all former Group D regimes aligned with China, were unable
to survive, unlike those which, by receiving extensive support from
the Soviet Union or her allies, have managed, at least temporarily, to
secure their control, as happened in Angola, Ethiopia, and Afghanistan.
Moreover, mostly for domestic reasons, China did not demonstrate the
continuity in her Southern policy as did the Soviet Union, with damaging
results for China's overall Southern goals.

Independent Albania and Yugoslavia form Group II of Eastern actors, characterized by their ability to act as separate policy-making
centers with their own long-range policy goals and the capabilities to
implement them. In both cases, national interest is similar in regard
to the South, different ideological claims notwithstanding, and both
Tirana and Belgrade look at the South as an important factor in securing their independence and in preventing their reabsorption into the inner hierarchical core of the Eastern subsystem. For this reason both
tend to adopt Southern policies at variance with those of Group I, although their short-range goals may coincide with those of one or another of the two Group I actors.

Unlike the first two pairs of Eastern actors, the members of
Group III, North Korea and Romania, are not independent decision-
making centers, but they do have a significant degree of autonomy in
their Southern policy. This autonomy and their position between China
and the Soviet Union in intrasubsystemic relations reinforce each other
to such an extent that these two actors may well be defined as "free
riders." Because of their autonomy and because of the confusion about
the "true" notion of nonalignment prevailing among the developing countries, both Bucharest and Pyongyang enjoy a large degree of acceptance
among all groups of Southern actors, to the extent that North Korea is
a full member while Romania has observer status in the Nonaligned
Movement and both are members of the Group of 77. Insofar as their
short-range policy goals are concerned, the two Group III actors may
adopt stands in open contradiction with one or another of the Group I
actors according to their national interest and circumstances, but their
long-range goals, particularly that of preserving their present status within
the East, can never come into conflict with both China and the Soviet

Union, on a consistent and comprehensive basis. Thus, North Korea may train Zairean troops used to fight the Cubans and their pro-Soviet MPLA allies in Angola, a gesture appreciated by Beijing, but they also fly Libyan planes provided by the Soviet Union and train pro-Soviet Palestinians. Romania, on the other hand, did recognize and give limited support to all three Angolan movements in 1974-75, thus attempting to please both China and the Soviet Union, but in areas of vital importance to the latter, such as the Eastern Mediterranean, it has initiated diplomatic overtures highly favorable to Moscow. Both Group III actors, as small countries adjacent to one or both Eastern superpowers, share a number of vital economic, ideological, and political interests with them and are in a highly unstable and delicate position, their "free rider" status being constantly in danger of shifting toward that of Group V, with a much lesser likelihood of moving closer to Group II.

The fourth type of Eastern actors is in an even closer relationship with the South than Groups II and III. The two members of this group are Cuba and Vietnam, both members of the Nonaligned Movement and the Group of 77. Although both are members of the Soviet-dominated inner hierarchical core of the Eastern subsystem, members of the CMEA, and signatories of treaties of alliance with other Eastern actors, the Group IV members enjoy a high degree of legitimacy as Southern actors, as was demonstrated by the election of Fidel Castro as chairman of the Nonaligned Movement in August 1979. The two most important reasons for that acceptability are their state of underdevelopment, very similar to that of most Southern states, and the emotional perception of them as Davids who have defeated the U.S. Goliath. Moreover, alone among the Eastern actors, their foreign policy is almost totally Southward-oriented. The latter characteristic allows them to allocate proportionally more resources to their Southern policy than can other Eastern actors and thus allows them to have a stronger impact on the South than their overall resources would allow. Moreover, their own limited national resources are greatly supplemented by huge subsidies and security guarantees from the rest of the inner hierarchical core. In both cases, most of the military needs of Group IV are satisfied, almost free of charge, by the Soviet Union, while the economic aid they receive from the Soviet Union and her Eastern European allies amounts to millions of dollars per day. Their long-range goal is support for revolutionary change in the South in order to increase their own international influence and legitimacy and to enhance their security. Regarding the latter aspect, it should be pointed out that the establishment of radical and therefore friendly regimes in their region is even more important for Havana and Hanoi because they are geographically isolated from the rest of the inner core. This main policy goal, these actors' very weak economic base, and their location within Southern areas have combined to give a predominantly military and security-oriented character to their overall involvement in the South. Together, they have more than 300,000 troops deployed outside their borders, but while, for the time being at least, Vietnam's role is more to maintain the stability of the inner hierarchical core and the integrity of the Eastern subsystem as a whole (in Laos and Kampuchea), Cuba's actions provide potential additions to the subsystem, as has been demonstrated in Angola, Ethiopia, Grenada, South Yemen, Mozambique, and Nicaragua. By their "Trojan horse" position in the South, both Havana and Hanoi play a very significant role in encouraging shifts from the Southern groups B and C toward Group D, both by direct intervention and by fanning domestic and subsystemic polarization in the South.

Although the Group IV actors are much more dependent on one of the Eastern superpowers than are Group III or V, they do enjoy a degree of freedom in selecting their own short-range goals and target areas in the South that is significantly higher than that of the latter and only slightly less than that of the former. Their input in the decision-making processes of the Eastern inner core is reflected in the priority temporarily given to one or another target in the South. Once the decision is taken, in accordance with the interests of the inner core as a whole as is usually the case, the tendency is for all its members to act uniformly. When dissidence arises, as it did with Cuba's support for guerrilla groups in Latin America during the 1960s, the dissident is sooner or later brought back into line, as with Castro after Guevara's failure and death.

Group V—Bulgaria, Czechoslovakia, East Germany (GDR), Hungary, and Poland—is made up of relatively developed countries linked directly to the Soviet Union through CMEA and the Warsaw Pact; all of them are part of the inner hierarchical core, in which they occupy a middle-ranking position. While their Southern policies are directly subordinated to the long-range goals of the inner core, they do have a significant degree of autonomy in the allocation of resources toward the implementation of those goals. The resources they possess and the share they are willing or able to allocate for their Southern policies are factors in distinguishing varying patterns and levels of involvement from one country to another and from one period to another. These particular patterns and the common characteristics of Group V actors will be analyzed throughout this volume as well as later on in this chapter. The close relationship between Group V actors and the Soviet Union and the close coordination of their Southern policies with those of Moscow may allow the analyst to describe them as the "loyal five."

The last and least important group of Eastern actors in terms of their impact on the South are those which are under the total control of the inner core or of one of its member actors and which may be accurately described as satellites—Laos, Kampuchea, and Mongolia. All these actors lack the capability and the autonomy for making any significant policy decision, be it domestic or external, and all three are under direct military occupation, thus constituting the lowest level of the inner core of the Eastern subsystem. The relevance of Group VI for the student of East-South relations is their potential role as models for future additions to the subsystem. Until their incorporation into the subsystem they were "typical" developing countries, with Laos and Kampuchea among the Group B actors. As a model they are characterized by a number of common features: their internal order and stability are ensured by foreign troops; their external trade is overwhelmingly Eastward-oriented; their political and economic bureaucracies are both small and thoroughly penetrated and "doubled" by foreigners; their economies are planned and managed by foreign advisers; and their education, media, and cultural life are under the control of foreign experts. Aside from their potential importance as models for Group D Southern actors and the limited significance they may have as United Nations members (Kampuchea does not even have this attribute of sovereignty, given her peculiar U.N. status), the most important impact that Group VI actors, especially Laos and Kampuchea, have is to drain some of the military and political resources that the Eastern inner hierarchical core might otherwise allocate toward the implementation of different policy goals. Moreover, the inner core's policy toward Laos and Kampuchea has sharpened even further the already well-defined demarcation line between itself and other members of the Eastern subsystem. Albania, China, North Korea, Romania, and Yugoslavia strongly opposed the occupation of Cambodia by Vietnam, as did a majority of Southern actors with the natural exception of Group D, thus temporarily isolating the inner core. It is important to mention that, while the Eastern actors did so for reasons having to do with intrasubsystemic relations—mostly fear for their own security and status preservation—the Southern actors did so in the name of solidarity of the Nonaligned Movement, of which both Laos and Kampuchea continue to be members.

POLICY DIMENSIONS

The forms of actual interaction between the various Southern and Eastern actors depend on their different capabilities, goals, policy-making processes, and relative importance for each other. All these factors have to be considered in order to obtain a clear idea of both the development and present state of East-South relations.

For most Southern actors, establishing diplomatic and economic relations with Eastern actors has long been taken as a concrete proof of independence from the West, without necessarily being a gesture with ideological implications. Even strongly anti-Marxist regimes like Chile, Brazil, and Argentina have established or maintained relations with at least some Communist countries and have even expanded their trade with the East. In all these cases, the military regimes felt strong and secure enough—and annoyed enough by Washington—to demonstrate their independence from it, while in the latter two cases that demonstration has proved to be highly profitable in economic terms as well. [2]

For Group A actors, relations with the East may provide additional means for increasing their regional influence, especially since some of those countries, while stronger than most of their neighbors, are still developing and therefore in need of modern weaponry, industrial equipment, technology, and markets for their products. When India successfully negotiated a $1.6 billion arms contract with the Soviet Union in 1980, it did so mostly because the conditions offered by the West were less favorable. However, more than economics is involved in this kind of agreements (similar ones had been made previously by the Soviets with Egypt, Somalia, and Libya) that may encourage a developing country to seek them. India and Libya, as well as pre-1972 Egypt, were all regional powers with their own interests and goals, but in all these cases at least some of those interests coincided with the Soviet Union's. India has been a strong proponent of the transformation of the Indian Ocean into a "zone of peace,"[3] a position which, until recently, was also espoused by Moscow. Should such a plan materialize, India would become the strongest power in the entire northern basin of the Indian Ocean, and the exclusion of the United States and France from the area would greatly enhance Soviet security and weaken the West. However, as the Soviet Navy obtained more and better bases in the Indian Ocean than ever before, the Soviet Union became less interested in the Indian idea, and the Ethiopian events of 1977-78 and Iranian developments of 1978-80 did nothing to increase the chances of the Indian demands. On the contrary, the Soviet Union has actually been attempting to expand its presence in the area and is now looking for new bases in the Maldives and the Seychelles. [4] At one time, however, there was a clear case of similarity and coordination of policies between Moscow and New Delhi. Likewise, the similarity between Libya's attempts to obtain the "demilitarization" of the Eastern Mediterranean and Bulgarian and Romanian initiatives toward the same goal are another example of a local and temporary community of interest between Eastern and Southern actors acting autonomously.

In both cases described above, Eastern actors supported Group A states' goals with a negative regional and strategic impact on the West. Even when such a result is not necessarily intended by a given Southern actor, the ultimate impact could be similar. Brazil's relations with the East and Group D states are a good example in this respect. Immediately after the Angolan civil war, Brasilia extended recognition to the Cuban-installed MPLA regime in Luanda and began to expand trade and cultural links with all five former Portuguese colonies in Africa, links facilitated by a common language. The fact that all those new states are more or less radical and friendly to the Soviet Union did not prevent the conservative Brazilian government from looking on them as potential members of a loose Lusitanian community to be dominated by Brazil. Both the Soviet Union and Cuba encouraged closer ties between those countries and Brazil as a means of providing additional international legitimacy to the new regimes, especially that in Angola. The first Brazilian venture into political relations across ideological lines was paralleled by increased trade with the "loyal five" and, since the U.S. grain embargo, with the Soviet Union as well. While dissatisfaction with U.S. human rights policies and Washington's opposition to the construction of a Brazilian nuclear facility increased the likelihood of Brazil's defying the United States, there were also strong nationalistic and economic incentives for that country to develop closer ties with both the East and its friends in the South. Those ties hardly enabled the Soviet Union or the Eastern Europeans to increase their influence in Brazil, but they certainly reinforced the centrifugal tendencies of the previously cohesive anti-Communist front in the Western Hemisphere. On the other hand, it is highly significant that Brazil consistently rejected Soviet offers of credits while accepting similar Eastern European offers. Thus, while the Soviet Union provided Brazil with $88 million in credits between 1954 and 1978, East Germany alone extended credits amounting to more than $200 million in 1978.[5] Moreover, the Eastern Europeans have provided most of their total of $621 million in export credits to Brazil since 1976, the date of Brasilia's rapprochement with the radical Portuguese-speaking African states, while the Soviet Union provided its small credits long before.[6] In other words, Brazil's openness to the East involved a relative willingness to negotiate some mid-term agreements with the Eastern Europeans but not with the Soviet Union or China, preferring cash or barter arrangements in the latter two cases. This cannot but be interpreted as a political decision to avoid too close a relationship with the dominant Eastern powers. However, in both economic terms, by allowing the Soviet Union to circumvent the U.S. embargo and by easing the Eastern European pressure on Soviet natural resources such as iron, and political terms, by allowing an increased Eastern presence in an area previously hostile and by the legitimacy Brazil gave to Group D states, these relations have enabled the Soviet Union to draw significant advantages from the anti-Marxist military government of Brazil.

While Group A sectors may or may not favor close political ties with various Eastern actors—and there is no clear pattern that would permit any generalization—they all have at least some ties with the East. To expand relations to include as many different kinds of states as possible is an integral part of their ambition to create a strong and significant role for themselves in the international system as a whole. It is interesting to note that their relations with the East usually include ties with both Group I actors and that in some cases China may be in an even better position than the Soviet Union regarding these states because it is perceived as less of a potential threat to their regional influence. However, the greater the discrepancy between the regional ambitions of a Group A state and its military or economic power, the greater the chances that it will move closer to the Soviet Union. Libya and Tanzania are the two most obvious examples where the size and level of development of a regional Southern power impose severe limitations on their political ambitions. As a result, they have sought to expand their capabilities through links with the East. As long as these additional resources are economic, China may play an important role, as it did and still does in Tanzania, but China cannot compete with the Soviet Union in the field of military aid. As a result, both Tripoli and Dar-es-Salaam depend on Soviet weaponry for the pursuit of their regional goals. In both cases, as well as that of India, ideological affinity with the East is limited or even nonexistent, but hostility toward the West or Western-supported challengers in their respective regions is perceived as a far more important factor. Insofar as hostility toward the West is a dominant factor in their foreign policy, these countries tend to support other anti-Western movements and governments and so ultimately coincide de facto with Eastern policy goals. Even more important, the impact of such Group A actors on small developing countries may actually be greater than that of the East, which still may be perceived as dangerous in some areas of the South. Libya's support of Idi Amin's Uganda, Grenada, and Jamaica, for example, is perceived as less of a threat to Western interests than is direct Cuban support to the same countries, even though the impact is ultimately the same: the strengthening of pro-Eastern regimes and/or the weakening of pro-Western ones. Moreover, these states encourage the trend toward polarization in the South, another important goal of the Eastern inner hierarchical core. This latter development is obvious in the case of a country like Tanzania, which supported Cuban and Soviet intervention in the Angolan civil war yet strongly opposed French and Moroccan support for the government of Zaire, Nyerere's claims of "true" nonalignment notwithstanding. The impact of such policies and Tanzania's influence in Africa have resulted in an increasingly deep cleavage within the OAU which has paralyzed that organization's already limited ability to keep the superpowers out of Africa.

While Group A actors directly or indirectly tend to promote polarization in the South because of their particular goals, for Group B actors, increased polarization is often the result of their own weakness, in terms of both domestic affairs and external security. One reason why this weakness, which is not a new development, has recently resulted in an increasing number of Group B actors moving away from the collective security they sought during the 1960s is that the spectacular growth of Eastern power-projection capability combined with the appearance of a growing number of Group D states closely tied to the East has brought Group B actors into increasingly direct contact with the East. Under these circumstances, small nonaligned countries have been forced to reassess their security needs toward more realistic and immediate arrangements, especially as the United Nations and the Nonaligned Movement have proved to be no substitute for powerful friends. Moreover, Group B states are too much in need of aid to be able to obtain it exclusively from such international institutions as the International Bank for Reconstruction and Development (IBRD) or the International Monetary Fund (IMF), which can provide it with no political strings attached. While it is true that such multilateral aid increased in absolute terms from $1.5 billion in 1973 to $7.0 billion in 1977, it has remained much smaller than bilateral aid. [7] Moreover, all multilateral aid comes from either the West or the Organization of Petroleum Exporting Countries (OPEC), and there is little incentive for either to increase it greatly and thereby lose whatever political capital they may gain in return for bilateral aid (this explains the general Eastern support for increased multilateral aid, since such support not only strengthens its image as a protector of developing countries' interests and independence but also helps to minimize Western influence in the South.) In addition, free of political strings though it may be, multilateral aid, and especially IMF loans, often requires painful domestic economic readjustments, as demonstrated by the experiences of Zaire and Jamaica during the late 1970s.

All of these developments, to which may be added the increased role and number of Group A states with their potential threat to smaller Group B actors, make it more and more difficult for the latter to maintain a truly "neutral" type of nonalignment. For a country like Sierra Leone, for instance, membership in the Commonwealth and close economic relations with China[8] and the West may help to alleviate some of her development and security problems, but they cannot solve them in the long run. The Economic Community of West African States (ECOWAS) may provide more economic help in the long run, but the record of Southern integration is far from impressive, and the role of Nigeria in that organization is hardly reassuring for the small West African states. The result has been that some of them, Ivory Coast and Upper Volta in particular, have looked to France for their security

and economic aid, while Benin has attempted to balance Nigerian and
French influence through an increasing ideological and security dependence on Cuba and the Soviet Union. In short, all are moving away
from their former Group B status and toward Group C or even D. As
a result of factors like these, the number of Group B states and their
influence is declining throughout the South.

A common characteristic of almost all Southern actors is their
perception of the West as being responsible for most of their problems.
That perception may or may not be supported by facts in all instances,
but it is increasingly pervasive. Its impact on East-South relations is
very difficult to measure precisely but it clearly seems to be important. As East-South relations on a large and generalized scale are
fairly recent, the developing countries have had no comparable experience with a prolonged Eastern presence to provide a more balanced
view. However, this has begun to change as the experiences of Somalia, Sudan, Egypt, Indonesia, and Chile have demonstrated that overly
close ties with the East can present serious dangers, too. The main
problem here is that it will take a relatively long time for the developing countries to go beyond the prevailing opinion that such experiences have been isolated or irrelevant.

While sharing some of the perceptions and problems of Group
B, the actors in Group C are a step closer toward choosing between
West and East. However, whatever their ideological or economic preferences, they continue to attempt a balancing act intended to insulate
them from the most dangerous aspects of East-West competition. They
usually do so by favoring ties with smaller actors from the two subsystems rather than with the United States or the Soviet Union themselves and by trying to expand their relations with other Southern actors. Two radically different neighbors in West Africa, Guinea and
Ivory Coast, are very good examples. Guinea, a "Socialist" country
once on the threshold of becoming a Group D actor, subsequently cooled her relations with the Soviet Union, reestablished normal ties with
her pro-French neighbors Senegal and Ivory Coast, and greatly expanded her already excellent ties with China and Romania, while developing new trade relations with both France and the United States.
The Ivory Coast, on the other hand, pro-French and pro-free enterprise in orientation, while condemning the Cuban and Soviet intervention in Africa, invited president Ceausescu of Romania to Abidjan in
1977, [9] and has a significant trade with Romania. The shifts in both
Conakry's and Abidjan's policies converged to a large extent and had
an impact on other states in the region such as Cape Verde and Guinea-
Bissau, both of which also moved a step away from their earlier proximity to Group D. Indeed, both these countries successfully sought to
establish better ties with France and the United States, and Cape Verde
pushed her newly found pragmatism so far as to allow South African

planes to land for refueling on the island of Sal, contrary to OAU recommendations.

The developments described above cannot obscure the fact that, by their very ideological proximity to and security arrangements with either Western or Eastern actors, Group C states are likely to reinforce the growing polarization of the South along political lines. The ultimate result of such polarization is the growth of Group D.

Like those Group C actors ideologically oriented toward the East the members of Group D perceive Marxism or, even more frequently, Marxism-Leninism, as the only way of solving the developmental and political problems confronting them. Unlike the former, however, their regimes are unable to come into or remain in power on their own. Thus, the major difference between Guinea or Guinea-Bissau, on the one hand, and Angola or Ethiopia, on the other, is that while Sékou Touré or PAIGC proved capable of taking power and institutionalizing their rule, the MPLA in Angola and the Derg in Ethiopia would almost certainly be defeated by internal opposition without outside help. The very fact that it took tens of thousands of Cuban troops, thousands of Soviet and Eastern European military advisers, and billions of dollars in weapons to ensure a still precarious stability in those countries is a clear demonstration that their regimes depend on the East for their very survival and not simply, as in the case of Group C governments, for additional resources toward the implementation of particular policy goals. While Angola, Ethiopia, Afghanistan, and South Yemen are Group D actors which, for the reason described above, should be considered as being on the threshold of becoming Group VI Eastern actors, countries like Mozambique and Grenada may in time shift toward Group C because their dependence on Eastern military support is more limited and their economies are not yet predominantly Eastern-oriented. Indeed, their trade is still primarily with the West, and there are only uncertain indications of change in the opposite direction. Internal opposition to the ruling FRELIMO and New JEWEL (Joint Endeavor for Welfare, Education, and Liberation) parties is not yet very significant or well organized, but the regimes are dependent on the East for external security.

The differences between radical Group C actors and Group D actors, significant as they are, should not obscure the fact that the similarities between them are also clear and have large implications for the West. As an increasingly cohesive cluster these latter actors have a much larger impact on the stability of the international system than their individual capabilities would otherwise allow. Together and with Group C radicals, however, they have a decisive impact on the leftward shift within the Nonaligned Movement, and, even more importantly, they have begun to play regional roles very similar to those of Group A, with the essential difference that the goals they pursue are those of the Eastern actors who control or dominate them. Moreover, their very existence tends to push former Group B actors toward the kind of bilateral security arrangements characterizing Group C actors. Thus, since FRELIMO came into power in Mozambique, Malawi, and Swaziland, formerly nonaligned, have moved closer to South Africa in both economic and security matters because of the perceived threat from Mozambique-supported opposition groups. At the same time and in the same region, Zambia has strengthened and expanded her ties with Cuba and the Soviet Union, while Botswana and Lesotho have decided that it may be wise to establish such ties. Even tiny Grenada, after the pro-Cuban regime of Maurice Bishop came into power in 1979, immediately began to train "revolutionaries" from all over the Caribbean, set out a mini-alliance with similarly oriented regimes in St. Lucia and Dominica, and scared the governments of Barbados, Trinidad, and St. Vincent into seeking immediate military support from the United States and Great Britain.[10] The fact that these developments were stirred up by Grenada, a country with 100,000 inhabitants and a per capita GNP of $600, clearly demonstrates that the impact of Group D actors on a regional level goes far beyond their individual strength, given their role as de facto extension of Eastern capabilities in the South. Their impact is even more enhanced when one considers the minimal amount of resources necessary to change the political orientation of many a developing country and, by implication, its role in the Southern subsystem as a whole. Events like those in the Comoros in 1977, when a group of 50 mercenaries overthrew the pro-Chinese regime of Ali Soilih, in Liberia and Surinam in 1980, where a few dozen noncommissioned officers took power in presumably stable countries, or in Grenada itself, where the 1979 coup was undertaken by a similarly small number of people, seem to indicate that the possibility of further such actions is very real and that they may be undertaken by the East as well as by radical developing countries—the Comoros were the exception, not the rule—resulting in a further increase in the number of Group D actors. It was not without significance, in this respect, that Libya and Ethiopia were among the first of the small group of states immediately to recognize the new regime in Liberia[11] and to offer support, financial in the first case and political in the second, to Bishop's regime in Grenada. It is precisely this reinforcing character of the radical cluster in the South that significantly increases the impact it has on the international system, a phenomenon which also demonstrates the important role of ideology.

In addition to the vulnerability that results from the small size of many developing countries is a proneness to sudden and radical changes of regime and to increasing reliance on external actors for preventing them because of the usual absence of domestic mechanisms for change. It is very significant to point out that decidedly unpopular regimes like those of Idi Amin, Pol Pot, Macias Nguema, Bokassa, and Ali Soilih have invariably been overthrown only by direct or scarcely veiled external intervention and never by domestic opposition. This may help to explain both why the East has been so successful in so many such instances in the South and also why it is likely to continue to be so. Indeed, it could be argued that the East has only to take advantages of the opportunities provided by such circumstances, but this would hardly explain why such opportunities seem to have multiplied at the same pace as the overall Eastern involvement in the South. The type of that involvement may provide a better explanation, especially when considered in conjunction with the previously mentioned conditions prevailing in so many developing countries. Moreover, at least some aspects of that involvement seem to encourage actively the maintenance or even deterioration of those conditions.

TYPES AND LEVELS OF EASTERN INVOLVEMENT

It is generally admitted that underdevelopment, domestic ethnic and cultural cleavages, and the resulting political instability are common characteristics of most if not all Southern countries. It is also generally assumed that the skewed internal distribution of wealth and the growing gap between rich and poor are reasons for radicalization in the developing countries. It is on this set of assumptions that the West's policies toward those countries has been increasingly based. The once fashionable "human needs" approach to aid and development and the concessions made by the industrialized countries to the South's demands for NIEO or, as in the cases of Lomé I and II, concessions to a particular group of developing countries, including price stabilization arrangements, are all aspects of the widespread conception that economic development in the South depends on aid and internal redistribution of resources. There is no need to deny that the South as a whole does not provide opportunities for economic equality or for political democracy, but it may be questioned whether these realities are related to the increasingly obvious shift to the left throughout the South. Indeed, while it is clear that economic and political inequality both produce instability, it is less clear why most of this instability should be resolved by radical regimes coming into power. There are no grounds for arguing that Marxist-Leninist or even "Socialist" regimes in the South have been any more capable of ensuring development, economic equality, or political freedom than non-Marxist regimes, and there are many cases that point to the opposite conclusion. The real reason behind the leftward drift in the South has much more to do with the character of the international system as a whole, and at a more particular level, of the elites in the developing countries than with widespread popular discontent and misery. Viewed from a nonemotional and less morally loaded viewpoint, it becomes clear that the radical groups in the South always come from and are limited to those already in a privileged social and economic position: a relatively small group of students within a largely illiterate population; a relatively well-paid corps of army officers; a small number of industrial workers with relatively secure and well-paid jobs in a society consisting largely of subsistence farmers. These elites are exceedingly small in absolute numbers and also exceedingly influential in relationship to their numbers. The type of training they have received has an excessive impact on their political inclinations, and regardless of those inclinations they tend to see the growth of the state sector— typically the largest employer by far in practically all developing countries—as always in their best interest. Indeed, a successful individual in a typical developing country is more often than not a powerful bureaucrat, a senior (or often a junior) army officer, and seldom a successful businessman. The power and economic well-being of such an individual depend on his close relationship with the state bureaucracy, into which he has been admitted because of his relatively high level of education. This pattern, while true to some extent of most developing countries, is especially true of Africa.

Seen from this perspective, the large and rapidly growing number of individuals from developing countries who have been trained in the East, and particularly the number of military trainees, has special significance. Moreover, the lack of expertise so common among developing countries is also increasingly compensated for by the employment of Eastern civilian and military experts. Significantly, a majority of Southern trainees in the East have come from Africa— 23,500 out of a total of 45,265 academic trainees in 1978—followed by the Middle East with 12,155. [12] They have come from approximately 60 developing countries, but the majority have been from Groups C and D. For instance, the largest contingents of African students in the academic field in the Soviet Union have been from Ethiopia, Nigeria, Benin, Congo, Equatorial Guinea, Sudan, and Tanzania, [13] and a majority of military trainees have been from Ethiopia, Guinea, and Somalia. [14] China has trained students primarily from Sudan, Tanzania, Togo, and Senegal [15] and military personnel from Congo, Guinea, Sudan, and Tanzania. [16] However, it should be noted that only 10 percent of the students trained in China were in the academic fields, compared with 30 percent of those studying in the Soviet Union. [17] However, China has trained only about 7 percent as many military students and 2 percent as many academic students from the South as have been trained in the Soviet Union, and China trails Eastern Europe (not including Albania and Yugoslavia) as well. [18] This great difference has been only partially offset by China's greater concentration on Africa, from which 88 percent of those it has trained have come, compared with 30 percent in the Soviet Union and 23 percent in Eastern Europe. [19]

Although in absolute terms the number of Southern military trainees in the East has not been too large, it is second only to France with regard to African trainees and surpasses the number in any other country as far as the Middle East and Southwest Asia are concerned. Furthermore, its impact is much more important than these figures would suggest, especially considering the usually very small size of the armies of African countries. Moreover, Marxist countries sending students for military training to the East invariably do so after they have become Marxist, with the important exception of Afghanistan, so the actual concentration of trainees in a brief period has been more intense than the broader period mentioned above (1954-78) would suggest. Also, when a country like Congo, with a regular army of 7,000, has 850 people militarily trained in China, Eastern Europe, or the Soviet Union, quite obviously the impact is very significant. In most such cases, when the next military coup has come it has almost invariably represented a further shift leftward, even when, as in Congo, Ethiopia, and Benin, the previous regimes have themselves been radical. In other words, the growing number of elites indoctrinated in the East has had a decisive impact in institutionalizing Marxism-Leninism at home, even when such elites have been unable to establish their own rule as a particular group. Indeed, at least in Congo and Benin, changes of regime or attempted changes have been the result of various Marxist factions trying to impose their own interpretation of Marxism rather than conflicts between opposing ideologies. [20] In those countries where "liberation" movements have come into power at the moment of independence, such as Algeria or the former Portuguese colonies, the elites have been predominantly Eastern-trained, and there have been no real counter-elites; thus the continuing influence of Marxism and close ties with one or another Group I actor are very likely to persist. Moreover, the fact that some African elites have been trained in Eastern-oriented African countries (Tanzania, Nkrumah's Ghana) and the internationalist character of Marxism-Leninism also explain the willingness of these new ruling elites to support one other. [21] Such a willingness has been demonstrated by Congolese, Mozambican, and Guinean troops fighting on the side of the MPLA in Angola, South Yemeni troops fighting for Ethiopia against fellow Eritrean Moslems, and Ethiopians dying for South Yemen on the border with North Yemen.

The Eastern training of elites has not been the most important reason why so many of those elites have chosen Marxism as their ideology, but it certainly has played an important and insufficiently studied role in the taking of such decisions. A similar role was played by those Southern elites trained in the former metropolises under the strong influence of local Communist parties, such as the French and Portuguese ones. The latter, besides giving a direct and essential support to Marxist movements in the former colonies of Portugal, also provided an infusion of its cadres to the MPLA in Angola. However, there is more than that direct influence through training that makes Southern elites choose the Marxist way to development. When Maurice Bishop of Grenada described the "new respect" with which his delegation was received at the Havana Conference of the Nonaligned Movement in 1979, expressed in his election as a member of the bureau and vice president of the conference, [22] that statement reflected not only the degree of deterioration of the Nonaligned Movement but also a feeling shared by the leaders of many small developing countries desperately seeking legitimacy and equality with more powerful actors in the international arena.

Important as the Eastern training of Southern elites and the legitimacy it confers on them at the international level after they come into power are, they are still less important than the economic and military involvement of the Eastern actors in the South in providing an explanation for the leftward shift and increasing polarization there. Both types of involvement have changed in emphasis and importance from period to period and from region to region and have varied from one Eastern actor or group of actors to another.

From the beginning of their rivalry in the late 1950s and early 1960s and until China's Cultural Revolution, the Soviet Union and China pursued similar but mutually exclusive goals in the South. Until the fall of Khrushchev, Moscow pursued a policy of support for a variety of developing countries through economic aid, in many cases without paying too much attention to their ideological orientation as long as they belonged to and had influence in the Nonaligned Movement, a group seen by the Soviet Union as weakening Western influence. Soviet aid was concentrated in those Southern states which played a leading role in the movement and indicated "anticapitalist" intentions: India, Egypt, Sukarno's Indonesia, and Burma. [23] This aid was offered on an irregular basis, in larger amounts until 1961, less between 1961 and 1963, and again in increasing amounts after 1963. [24] As has been pointed out, [25] the new offers of Soviet aid after 1963 were largely in response to the increased Chinese competition for influence in the South. The highest point in that competition came in 1965, with plans for a Chinese-sponsored Second Afro-Asian Conference to be held in Algiers. At the same time, China was assiduously working to forge an East Asian alliance with Indonesia, Kampuchea, and Burma. Both these Chinese initiatives came to naught after Ben Bella was overthrown in Algeria and Sukarno's control of Indonesia came to an end, for all practical purposes, with the anti-Communist military coup of Septem-

ber 1965. The period that ended then was the only time China effectively competed with the Soviet Union in the South on a large scale,
allocating comparable resources. Moreover, at that time much more
than since then, both Eastern superpowers extended aid to the same
group of developing countries: Algeria, Tanzania, Ghana, Pakistan,
Kampuchea, and Afghanistan. [26] Since then and especially since the
Cultural Revolution, Chinese aid to the South has declined continuously
and has concentrated on those countries or areas where Soviet influence is smaller or where China's has deeper roots. The Soviet Union,
on the other hand, has shifted her aid more and more toward Africa,
the Middle East, and Southwest Asia, especially since 1967. [27] While
before 1965 most of the military trainees in the Soviet Union and the
bulk of Soviet technicians in the South were from or in Egypt and Indonesia, [28] most of the Soviet and Group V countries' efforts by 1978
were concentrated in Africa and the Middle East. These same two
areas also had the largest share of Soviet and Group V technicians,
67 and 29 percent, respectively, with the rest being allotted to East
Asia and Latin America. [29] China's technicians were now concentrated
in Africa south of the Sahara (88 percent of the total). [30] In terms of
economic aid, from the position of quasi-equality it had enjoyed with
the Soviet Union in 1965, China had fallen behind both the Soviet Union
and Eastern Europe by 1978, accounting for only 20 percent of total
Eastern aid to the South. [31]

The concentration of aid by countries is also significant for understanding the types of Southern actors a given Eastern actor or group
of actors consider as most important and throws light on the reasons
for that specific order of priorities. The largest five recipients of aid*
from the Soviet Union, Group V (plus Romania), and China, respectively, for the period between 1960 and 1978 were as follows: India,
Morocco,† Egypt, Afghanistan, and Iran;[32] Syria, Egypt, Iran, Brazil, and Algeria; and Pakistan, Tanzania, Zambia, Nepal, and Somalia. [33] The total number of recipients of significant importance was
46, 38, and 41, respectively, with the five leading recipients accounting for 57 percent of total aid in the case of the Soviet Union, 47 percent in the case of the "loyal five," and 37 percent in the case of Chi-

---

*The term "aid" is generally misleading and is even more so in
the case of the Communist countries. There is practically no grant
content in their aid but mostly import credits or mid- to long-term,
low-interest loans.

†Soviet "aid" to Morocco is composed exclusively of a $2 billion
credit for the exploitation of phosphates, to be paid back in phosphates.
The agreement was concluded in 1979.

na. [34] Of a total of 49 developing countries receiving aid from one of these sources, only 26 received it from all three of them, thus demonstrating a relative "specialization" among the three largest Eastern donors. A comparision of the lists of recipients of aid from the three Eastern donors is instructive. China provided most of her aid and, in most instances, more than either the Soviet Union or Eastern Europe when it was not the only Eastern donor) to the following developing countries: Tunisia, Botswana, Burundi, Cameroon, Central Africa, Chad, Gabon, Gambia, Guinea-Bissau, Liberia, Madagascar, Mauritius, Mozambique, Niger, Rwanda, São Tomé e Príncipe, Senegal, Seychelles, Sierra Leone, Tanzania, Togo, Upper Volta, Mauritania, Zaire, Guyana, Malta, Nepal, and Laos (until 1976). [35] It is instructive to note that the majority of sub-Saharan recipients of Chinese aid are also recipients of even more substantial French aid.

The Southern countries receicing more Eastern European aid than either Chinese or Soviet or receiving only Eastern European aid, were Mauritania,* Tunisia, Angola, Congo, Gabon,* Mozambique, Nigeria, Senegal,* Sudan, Zambia,* Burma, Indonesia, Phillippines,* Argentina, Brazil, Peru, Ecuador, Guyana, Jamaica, Mexico, Venezuela, Cyprus, and Syria. [36]

The Soviet Union provided the largest part of the Eastern aid to Algeria, Morocco, Guinea, Kenya, Bolivia, Chile (under Allende), Colombia, Uruguay, Egypt, Iran, Iraq, North Yemen, South Yemen, Afghanistan, India, Bangladesh, and Pakistan. [37]

The same fragmentation of effort and divergent concentration of resources visible in the distribution of aid is demonstrated by the distribution of Eastern economic and military advisers throughout the South. The Soviet Union and the Eastern Europeans (excluding Albania and Yugoslavia) had in 1978 more than 1,000 economic advisers in each of the following developing countries: Algeria, Libya, Angola, Afghanistan, Egypt, India, Iran, Iraq, South Yemen, and Syria; China had more than 100 in Algeria, Ethiopia (since then it has been vastly outnumbered there by Cuba, the Soviet Union, and East Germany), Guinea, Liberia, Nepal, Pakistan, Mali, Mauritania, Somalia, Sudan, Tanzania, Iraq, North Yemen, and Sri Lanka; Cuba had over 100 in South Yemen, Iraq, Tanzania, Jamaica, Angola, Ethiopia, and Libya. [38] The military advisers were distributed as follows: Pakistan, Bangladesh, Mozambique, and Equatorial Guinea (until the August 1979 overthrow of the pro-Eastern dictatorship of Macias Nguema) had more than 50 percent of all Chinese military advisers in the South;

---

*Most if not all the Eastern European aid to these countries was provided by Romania.

the Soviet Union and the East Europeans had more than 200 each in Algeria, Libya, Afghanistan, Angola, Ethiopia, Mozambique, Iraq, South Yemen, and Syria; and Cuba had more than 100 each in Libya, Angola, Equatorial Guinea, Guinea, Guinea-Bissau, Mozambique, Iraq, and South Yemen, for a total much higher than China's.[39]

In all of these areas, as well as with regard to academic trainees[40] and military trainees, the Soviet and Eastern European list of chief aid recipients in the South coincide, and they also coincide with Cuba's, but only a few developing countries have received such support from China or Group II actors: Tanzania and Mozambique are two of those. Even countries on China's top priority list, such as Sudan, Guinea, and Tanzania, have more military advisers from the Soviet Union and Eastern Europe or even Cuba than from Beijing. The same holds true in the case of military trainees in the case of Mozambique, for example. China has more military advisers than the Soviet Union only in Pakistan and Bangladesh, although it also had more in Equatorial Guinea (but still fewer than Cuba). It has trained more military personnel than the Soviet Union in the case of Cameroon and Congo (but less than the Soviet Union and Eastern Europe combined), Sierra Leone, Togo, Zaire, Zambia, and Pakistan[41] and has had more economic advisers than the Soviet Union in Mauritania, Gabon, Gambia, Liberia, Madagascar, Mali, Mauritius, Niger, Rwanda, Saõ Tomé and Príncipe, Senegal, Sierra Leone, Somalia (after the Soviets had left), Sudan, Tanzania, Zambia, Malta, Burma, North Yemen, Bangladesh, Nepal, and Sri Lanka.[42] While China has been unable to compete with the Soviet Union and her allies in terms of personnel training and sending experts, her lack of resources to challenge Soviet goals in the South is even more obvious in the area of military aid and sales of weapons.

The difference was clear throughout the entire 1954-78 period, and the gap between Chinese and Soviet or even Eastern European military sales and aid steadily widened. During the 1954-62 period, the Soviet Union concluded military agreements with developing countries amounting to $5,505 million, compared with China's $250 million; between 1968 and 1978 the figures were $27,260 and $660 million, respectively.[43] Although the proportion of actual deliveries as compared with the amount initially agreed upon has been somewhat higher in the case of the Chinese, the absolute differences remain extremely large. Moreover, China's military aid and sales to the South was less than one-third as much as that of Eastern Europe throughout the same period.[44] In terms of yearly amounts, the Soviet deliveries since 1970 have never fallen under $1 billion, while China's record in 1975 was a poor $80 million. The East Europeans as a group, on the other hand, have remained constantly above $120 million since 1972, and their deliveries have increased ever since.[45]

The same Soviet and East European ability to outspend China in the South is clear when one compares the amount of economic aid provided during the past ten years. Although between 1972 and 1974 China did extend more aid than Eastern Europe, it has fallen behind ever since and has never been able to provide more than one-fifth or one-third as much as the Soviet Union. [46] However, in strictly economic terms, the South is more important to China than to either the Soviet Union or the Eastern European countries, with the exception of Romania. Thus, the South's share in the foreign trade of China and the Soviet Union between 1960 and 1978 was as shown in Table 1.1.

TABLE 1.1

The South's Share in the Foreign Trade of China and the Soviet Union, 1960-78 (percentages)

	1960	1970	1975	1976	1977	1978
Soviet Union						
Imports	9.7	10.8	11.2	9.8	10.0	8.1
Exports	6.3	15.6	14.2	13.7	15.4	15.6
China*						
Imports	N.A.	13.3	11.7	11.7	19.5	12.5
Exports	N.A.	21.7	24.7	23.4	23.4	23.1

*Trade with Hong Kong and Macao not included; 1960 figures for China not available.

Source: CIA, Handbook of Economic Statistics, 1979 (Washington, D.C., 1979), Table 60 for the Soviet Union, Table 63 for China.

These figures not only demonstrate that the South has a larger share in China's trade than in the Soviet Union's (in imports as well as in exports) but also indicate that in both cases there are fluctuations from one year to another and that the South is more important as a market than as a source of goods. It should be mentioned that the latter pattern is true for all the Eastern actors. Moreover, with the exception of Albania, China, and, to a much lesser extent, Romania, the main commodity that the East imports from the South is oil, which may explain the particular importance the Middle East has for most Eastern actors, although this is not the only explanation.

From the data presented in the previous pages a set of patterns

of political and economic interaction between East and South begins
to emerge. The patterns described below do not elaborate on the Eastern Europeans' place in them; this will be analyzed in depth throughout
this volume.

Unlike China, the Soviet Union has tended to concentrate her
efforts in the South on Group A states through economic aid and the
training of personnel and military support, and among those states
the greatest attention has been paid to Middle Eastern countries. In
all of these cases, the ideological affinities between the Soviet Union
and her main Southern trade partners have been limited, although the
their regional goals have usually if not always overlapped. In all of
these cases, any form of Southern detachment from or hostility to the
West has been encouraged, even if it has not meant a concomitant move
to the left. Soviet national interests seem to prevail over ideological
commitments here. Among radical Group C states and especially a-
mong Group D actors, however, the Soviet Union has tended to link
the relative amount of all types of aid to the degree of ideological
proximity. The neutralist type of nonalignment supported during the
1960s in the case of Group A states is actively discouraged among
small Group C and D states.

China, on the other hand, has tended to provide most of her aid
to neighboring countries, such as Nepal, Burma, Pakistan, and Bangladesh, and to Group B and C actors. In the latter case, the obvious
goal was and remains the strengthening of neutralist, anti-Soviet, and,
perhaps less important after Mao's death, anti-Western tendencies.
While the attention given to neighboring countries has had more to do
with China's own security, the support Beijing is giving to the second
group of developing countries—such as Togo, Mauritania, and Sierra
Leone—coincides with Western support to the same group. This coincidence between Chinese and Western, primarily French, goals in
Africa has become increasingly obvious during the 1970s. Most of China's friends in sub-Saharan Africa are Francophone states, some of
which also have defense arrangements with Paris. During the two
Shaba episodes of 1977 and 1978, Zaire was decisively aided by a combination of French, Moroccan, Chinese, and Egyptian support. Those
episodes had demonstrated not only Mobutu's well-known diplomatic
ability to an ever greater extent, but also, that the West and China were
equally interested in stopping the spread of Soviet and Soviet-sponsored
influence across the continent. Less spectacular but as significant as
the Shaba episodes is the role both Beijing and Paris have had in helping the three small Portuguese-speaking states of West Africa—São
Tomé e Príncipe, Guinea-Bissau, and Cape Verde—to remain free
from the total dependence on the East that characterizes Angola. All
three of them receive aid from France, China, and some other pro-
Western African countries, such as Gabon and Ivory Coast, and since

1979 they had begun to participate in the annual Franco-African summit meetings. Once again, China supported and encouraged such moves, which were aimed at strengthening Groups B and C and against the increased polarization of the South encouraged by the Soviet Union and her allies.

Group IV, and especially Cuba (since Vietnam is too deeply involved in Indochina to be a very active actor in other areas of the South), has concentrated all its efforts in the South on radical regimes, mostly Middle Eastern regional powers such as Iraq, Algeria, and Libya, on small Group C radical actors, and on Group D actors. Although small and unable to provide economic aid to the developing countries, Cuba has a very large impact on the South, especially among smaller radical countries both in Africa and in the Caribbean basin, an area of only limited direct Soviet activity. In addition to having a very significant role in furthering the polarization of the South through armed interventions and training of guerrilla and terrorist groups, Havana also uses the institutional tool of the Nonaligned Movement toward the same goal. More than any other Eastern actor, Cuba also has had a decisive impact on the expansion and preservation of the emerging cluster of Marxist-Leninist regimes in the South. Cuban presence in all of those countries, the specific aggressivity of the Castro rhetoric, all combine to provide a superficial unity to what is otherwise a very heterogeneous group. By presenting herself as a developing country and by being able to send blacks overseas as her representatives, thereby strengthening her image as just another Southern country, Cuba is the most valuable instrument of the inner hierarchical core for the implementation of its Southern policy goals. While Vietnam has had and still has a significant role in the preservation of the integrity of the inner core through its control over Laos and Kampuchea, Cuba has a similar role in the preservation of the radical cluster in the South as well as in its growth through new additions. By using the division of the Communist political socialization in Eastern Europe elaborated by Herspring and Volgyes[47] and by extrapolating it to radical Group C and to Group D Southern actors, one may conclude that Vietnam's role in Laos and Kampuchea is that of establishing the "forcible resocialization" indigenous forces are unable to establish, while Cuba, although it does play that role in Angola and Ethiopia, undertook the responsibility for the implementation of the second phase—"power consolidation"—in those countries as well as others, such as South Yemen, Congo, Benin, and Mozambique. According to Herspring and Volgyes, that phase is characterized by extensive politicization aimed at the internationalization of the body politic. Cuba's training of tens of thousands of Angolan, Ethiopian, and Congolese youths and the huge infusion of Cuban teachers in radical developing countries are all intended to provide those countries with

a new type of elite totally loyal to the principles of "international proletarian solidarity" and able to perpetuate and develop Communist
systems in the South.

THE IDEOLOGICAL DIMENSION

Ideology is the best and usually the earliest indicator of significant shifts in the policy of any Eastern actor because it is the clearest
and most comprehensive public expression of national goals and the
means of implementing them. Detectable changes occur in a particular country's definition of the tenets of Marxism-Leninism as a result
of a decision to reallocate resources and reassess priorities. For
these reasons, a brief discussion of the ideological changes in various Eastern actors' perceptions of the South is necessary here, even
though this is one of the few well-studied aspects of East-South relations. As is usually the case, ideological changes may come before
policy changes are detected, but they are the result of already decided
changes in policy. One has therefore to distinguish between ideology
as a theoretical framework for political decision making and ideology
as a language into which the decisions are expressed.

Emotionally and politically, the Chinese have always considered
themselves to be an intermediary between East and South, and this
perspective should always be kept in mind when analyzing Beijing's
relations with the South. Even before the Sino-Soviet break, Mao expressed his belief that China had a privileged position with respect to
the developing countries and a better understanding of them than did
the Soviet Union. China therefore had the right and internationalist
duty to pursue an independent Southern policy. After the break with
China, the Soviets began to accuse her of giving primacy to underdevelopment and race as unifying factors in the South rather than to the
class struggle. [48] In fact, such "accusations" were unfounded until after the Cultural Revolution and especially after Mao's death, when
Beijing did indeed pursue Southern policies often devoid of a clear
ideological orientation, consistent only in their aim of thwarting Soviet plans. However, the Chinese have not always seen this nonideological approach to the South as contradicting their own earlier calls
since the early 1960s for the "world villages," by which they mean
the developing countries, to defeat the "world cities," defined as the
Western and Eastern European developed countries, including the Soviet Union. Even during the Cultural Revolution there were pragmatic
and nonideological sides to China's Southern policies. [49]

During the 1970s China's approach to the problems of the Nonaligned Movement in general and its basic definition in particular has
been extremely close and has been growing closer to those of Group

B and nonradical Group C states. Indeed, the Chinese have called for the Nonaligned Movement to avoid both "hegemonist" and "imperialist" temptations, a position which, for all practical purposes, is quite similar to that adopted by Tito at the Havana Conference of the Nonaligned Movement in August 1979 and stated by the Yugoslavs before and after that meeting. As Belgrade has put it, it is the duty of the nonaligned countries to "exert maximum efforts to help the emancipation of nations and countries which resist power politics, imperialism and colonialism, hegemony, interference, and military intervention"[50] (emphasis added). North Korea took a very similar stand at Havana, and in a position paper published a month before the conference it warned the Nonaligned Movement against both imperialism and "dominationist forces" (meaning the Soviet Union). [51] Romanian President Ceausescu, in his message to the same Havana conference, also warned the participants to act against "the continuation of the old imperialist policy of force and domination, the intensification of tendencies towards a redivision of zones of influence and domination"[52] (emphasis added), a clear allusion to both the United States and the Soviet Union. As shown elsewhere in this volume, Albania's position is also oriented toward solidarity among the developing countries against the United States, the Soviet Union, and China, that is, in support of eliminating any superpower influence in the South. What the similar approach taken by all the Eastern actors who are not members of the inner hierarchical core of the subsystem seems to indicate is that their ideological rationalization of their national policies toward the South tends to converge in the common goal of countering or limiting the polarization process encouraged by the Soviet Union and the subordinate members of the inner core. That there has been a convergence in this sense among China, Yugoslavia, North Korea, and Romania is also indicated by the increasingly close relations among them, reflected in the increasing number of summit meetings between their leaders and the concrete coordination of their stands on such issues as Kampuchea's representation at the United Nations and at the Nonaligned Conference and the invasion of Afghanistan. More important from the standpoint of overall East-South relations is the de facto and, as expressed in the wording of the political section of the Final Resolution of the Havana Conference, the de jure convergence between their understanding of the basic concepts of nonalignment and that of the majority of Groups B and C of Southern actors.

On the other hand, the same Havana meeting witnessed a clear coordination of the efforts of Groups D, IV, and VI, with the Soviet Union looming large in the background. Cuba, supported by Ethiopia, Angola, Grenada, South Yemen, and Afghanistan, as well as by Vietnam and Laos, pushed hard to have the Final Resolution declare the East and its inner hierarchical core in particular (given Castro's repeated attacks on China) the "natural ally" of the South,[53] and, while they did not succeed in having those precise words introduced into the document, they did manage to give an overall anti-Western and, hidden behind terms like "peace-loving, democratic, progressive states," pro-Eastern tone to the document. A few weeks after Havana, however, the realities of polarization in the South reasserted themselves again, with a majority of states siding with China, Yugoslavia, Romania, and the West on the issue of Kampuchean representation at the United Nations, and against the Soviet and Cuban stands. But while Castro did not succeed completely in institutionalizing the leftward shift of the Nonaligned Movement he did succeed in sharpening the ideological divisions within the movement. Judging from both the actual Soviet policy toward the South and Soviet ideological stands toward the developing countries, it is clear that this polarization is exactly what the inner Eastern core intends.

Yugoslavia, Romania, and North Korea[54] all see the present division between Southern countries as a development contrary to their own and the developing countries' best interests. In the opinion of these three Eastern actors, the unity of the developing countries is their biggest asset in preventing superpower encroachments in the South and in ensuring a fair chance for an international atmosphere favorable to their security and developmental needs. On the contrary, the Soviet Union, Cuba, Vietnam, and the "loyal five" see Southern divisions as a natural development to be encouraged and welcome the sharpening of the conflict between "progressive" and "reactionary" forces on both internal and subsystemic levels in the South. Their ideologists claim to detect a series of changes in the general Southern ideological climate, changes which they profess to believe are the result of the shifts in the balance of power between the Soviet Union and the United States in favor of the former.

Most important among those changes is the appearance of "revolutionary democracies" in the South and, in some cases (Angola and Mozambique are most often mentioned) the building of "people's democracies" similar to those of Eastern Europe in the late 1940s and early 1950s. [55] In Africa in particular such changes have created conditions favorable to the "deepening of the revolutionary process,"[56] mostly through increasing class polarization that has arisen since independence within the African societies and was also expressed in new relations among African states. The forces of the left, according to this view, are coming even closer to Marxism-Leninism, while the right-wing forces are gravitating toward the "imperialist" position. [57] Among the countries moving toward Marxism-Leninism are the African people's republics—Benin, Congo, Angola, Ethiopia, and Mozambique—as well as Afghanistan and South Yemen. An approach similar to the Soviet one about the character of Southern "revolutions" and

their chances of only later becoming armed with the theoretical framework of Marxism-Leninism, is that of the Cuban theoreticians, demonstrated in their analysis of the Ethiopian situation. As Raúl Valdéz
Vivó, a member of the Cuban Communist party's Central Committee,
put it, "Ethiopia shows something else, as well: without the way being
prepared openly by ideology, in Ethiopia the people first made their
Revolution—using the means created to prevent it (that is, the old
army)—and then their revolution began to discover itself and its ideology."[58] It is interesting to note that the Cubans have very good
grounds to consider that a Southern revolution which may start as a
nationalist enterprise may or should become Marxist-Leninist after
its success, as their own revolution was the first to fit this very pattern. This is also quite a likely explanation of their being so adept in
helping other developing countries to follow that same pattern.

What is also instructive is to see how both the Soviet and the
Cuban theoreticians have managed to "solve" the tricky problem of a
revolution without a Marxist-Leninist vanguard party later becoming
a "Socialist revolution": they have managed to confer "revolutionary
legitimacy" on more or less radical military coups in the South. According to this new ideological explanation, these coups and pseudo-
revolutions—and the military men staging them—"found their ideology"
later, and that ideology is, of course, the only "truly" revolutionary
one: Marxism-Leninism. Where various radical parties are in power,
after such "revolutions" they are considered, for the time being, to
be "vanguard revolutionary-democratic" in character, even though
they are not Communist.[59] However, as they expand their ties with
the "international working class and Communist movement,"[60] they
move closer and closer toward becoming true Marxist-Leninist parties. This approach, which gives foreign factors an importance never
accepted by Marx or Engels, tries to solve the other thorny theoretical problem facing any Marxist analysis of political change in the
South, namely that the ruling parties, radical as they may claim to
be in their rhetoric, are not and cannot be "vanguard parties" of a
proletariat which does not usually exist, at least not in Marx's definition. This dilemma becomes even more obvious when one considers
the fact that Ethiopia is only now, after the "revolution" trying to establish a revolutionary party, in total contradiction with the Leninist
principle that such a party is essential for the very success of a revolution. As for radical Southern rhetoric, Soviet analysts choose to
take it seriously, primarily by drawing a distinction between "pure"
Marxist-Leninist and "scientific socialist" ideology and a merely
"Socialist" one, which does not accept some of the Leninist tenets. In
this respect it is significant that the Soviets perceive the establishment of a Confederation of African Socialist States, proposed by countries like Zambia, Senegal, and Tanzania, as a threat, a reflection of

the "right-wing social democracy of Europe,"[61] that is, of the Socialist International, of which Senegal is a member.

The Soviet interpretation of the theoretical problems posed by Southern radicalism has had an immediate and decisive impact on the diplomatic and international political level as a result of its rationalization of the so-called Brezhnev doctrine's expanded scope to include Southern states, as demonstrated in Afghanistan, and implied in the arguments used to "legitimize" the Cuban interventions in Angola and Ethiopia. Once the Kremlin proclaims its duty to support "revolutionary accomplishments" in various developing countries directly or through other Eastern actors, it signals the West that it considers to have as much a stake in the survival of Group D actors as in the preservation of its Eastern European security area, thus correspondingly raising the risks faced by potential challengers. If one considers the limited and ineffective Western response to any circumstance when this happened, from Angola to Ethiopia to Afghanistan, it becomes obvious that those risks are considered too high in Washington.

This Soviet approach to the growing Southern radicalism, although completely elaborated only after 1974-75, can be discerned as early as 1966, when Brezhnev declared that Soviet support for "the peoples' struggle for final liberation from colonial and neocolonial oppression" is an "internationalist duty" of the CPSU (Communist Party of the Soviet Union), and the ties between "the communist and revolutionary democratic organizations in Asian, African, and Latin American countries" were defined as "fraternal."[62] The Soviet-dominated Conference of Communist and Workers' Parties in 1969, while mentioning the "noncapitalist path" followed by some developing countries, also called for a coalition of "peasants, democratic army circles, students, urban middle strata,"[63] which the Soviets then considered to be a kind of Southern version of the Eastern European coalitions that paved the way for Communist takeovers in the late 1940s.

By 1971, Brezhnev was able to declare that the "national liberation struggle has begun to grow into a struggle against both feudalism and capitalism,"[64] thus clearly demonstrating that the Soviet notion of and reasons for supporting "liberation" movements did not coincide at all with that of the Nonaligned Movement, for which they were groups struggling to implement the movement's basic principle of the right to self-determination in a strictly political sense. For the Soviet Union, however, as Brezhnev's words made clear, those movements, or at least those dependent on Soviet support, were considered vehicles for social revolution at least as much as instruments for political emancipation of colonial peoples. In this interpretation the Soviets had taken a position very similar to that espoused by China in the 1960s and until Mao's death. Indeed, the Chinese also claimed that, under international law, the "liberation" movements should be treated as de facto governments of peoples still under foreign domination[65] and should therefore enjoy the same right to make policy for their respective territories, domestically, ideologically, and externally. It is also true, as the Soviets were eager to point out, that the universal right to self-determination was not supported by Beijing in all circumstances, witness the cases of Macao and Hong Kong. [66] However, as China's attitude toward the three Angolan movements indicated, in the second half of the 1970s Beijing moved closer to the prevailing Southern opinion that "liberation" movements are to be supported merely on the grounds that they are struggling for independence, regardless of their ideological outlook. Moreover, the Chinese division of the world along ideological lines has also changed since Mao's death, shifting toward a more political approach. Indeed, while for Mao the "three worlds" were those of the two superpowers, the lesser capitalist and Communist developed countries, and the developing countries including China, the 1978 division of tasks among the Chinese leadership suggests a change toward the generally accepted division into a "first world" of capitalist states, Deng Hsiaoping's area, a "second world" of Communist states, Hua Gaofeng's, and a "third world" of the South, Li Hsien nien's. [67]

TRENDS AND IMPLICATIONS
FOR THE INTERNATIONAL SYSTEM

In light of the different and sometimes conflicting ideological and political approaches of various Eastern actors toward the South, what are the discernible trends in East-South relations, especially in terms of Eastern policy, the most active side of the relationship? What impact do intrasubsystemic relations have on the Eastern actors' Southern policies? What is the impact of the East on the South and what trends may be discerned in that respect? Finally, what is the role of Eastern European states in the overall framework of East-South relations?

Obviously, no definitive answers to these questions can be provided by this study, which is really the first attempt to introduce East-South relations as an autonomous field in the study of international relations. The data and preliminary conclusions this volume offers are partial, focusing as they do on the Eastern European actors only, and are only intended to be a starting point for a more comprehensive examination of the problem.

On the basis of the preliminary and incomplete data presented here, however, some trends can be discerned in the East-South relations during the 1970s. The first such trend, and the most important for the international system as a whole, has been the inner hierarchical core's successful and consistent attempt to sharpen the ideological and political polarization in the South. Behind this overall approach, which was and still is intended as a means rather than a goal, a more significant goal may be discerned: a reassessment of the possibility of implementing the historic goal of worldwide revolution on the basis of Marxism-Leninism.

The Soviet perceptions and their actual political implementation in this regard were closely related to the Marxist-Leninist break-through that occurred in the South since the 1974-75 events in Portugal, former Portuguese Africa, and Indochina. Soviet goals since then shifted from a strategy of denial of resources and of influence over entire Southern areas to the West to an increasingly clear realization that such areas which could be separated from the West could also be added to the Eastern subsystem. Soviet support for the Nonaligned Movement in the 1960s was based on a defensive strategy oriented toward limiting Western strength more than toward the more expensive and risky strategy of expansion. Soviet support for leaders like Sukarno, Nehru, and Nasser during the Khrushchev era was intended to strengthen anti-Western groupings in the South rather than to create new communist states, even if, as in the cases of Egypt and Sudan, [68] this meant sacrificing ideological goals by allowing the ruling regimes to crush local Communist parties.

The two events that more than anything else convinced the Soviet Union that a reassessment of its own goals in the South is needed were the Portuguese coup of April 1974 and the collapse of the Indochinese resistance to the victorious North Vietnamese and Khmer Rouge armies one year later. In the first case, the power vacuum created by the hasty withdrawal of the leftist regime in Lisbon from Africa, to which one may add the open, and not so open, direct support Portugal gave to the most radical groups in its former colonies, was rapidly filled by radical regimes, two of which—Angola's and Mozambique's—were strategically located close to South Africa, the richest, most developed, most anti-Communist, and most powerful state in Africa. Moreover, the new regime in Luanda was virtually installed into power by the application of direct Eastern force, the first such case in a Southern country, and a very successful one at that. It may be a matter of speculation to decide if the Soviet Union and Cuba were more encouraged into repeating the means used in Angola by Western indecision or by the supreme confusion demonstrated by the OAU or, for that matter, by countries like Yugoslavia, a recognized spokesman of the Nonaligned Movement, at least at that time. Indeed, in the case of Angola, Belgrade actively participated in the imposition of the MPLA as the sole ruler of Angola. In this sense, the Angolan episode of 1975-76, with the subtle use of racist sentiments in Black Africa (the South African intervention in itself, regardless of its geopolitical merits, was the reason for nonradical African states automatically to support the MPLA, Nigeria being the best and most important example) and disarray in the West, was a masterpiece of diplomacy combined with the most brutal use of force. In the atmosphere of confusion following the Portuguese coup and due to the vague character of the Western perception of the principle of self-determination, countries like Cape Verde and São Tome e Príncipe, where no meaningful anti-Portuguese struggle ever occurred, became independent under radical regimes, thus adding to the Eastern gains obtained through a limited use of resources in Angola. Similarly, after the collapse of South Vietnam, little or no attention was paid anymore to the Vietnamese occupation of Laos, although that country was supposed to be neutral. In Angola and South Vietnam and Laos, direct military occupation was used to impose a basic reorientation of an entire society, and that pattern was later expanded to Kampuchea.

After two decades of patient investment of economic and political resources in the South, the Eastern inner hierarchical core finally decided, based on the circumstances of 1974-75, that the time had come to draw the ultimate conclusion, which was that establishing a presence and building influence in the South is not a sufficient guarantee of obtaining strong assurances of their permanence.

Indeed, the two decades of East-South relations starting with Khrushchev's coming into power witnessed the formulation and successive implementation of four distinct Eastern intermediate goals of an increasingly resolute Southern strategy. These were the establishment of a presence in as many developing countries as possible, regardless of ideological considerations, followed by the building of influence in those Southern states where conditions are favorable, the expansion of that influence toward domination, and, finally, after 1974-75, the permanent consolidation of that domination into outright control. These intermediate goals have not necessarily been implemented consecutively in all developing countries or areas but have often been carried out simultaneously. In other words, there is no automatic transformation of presence into influence or of influence into domination and control in the same Southern country, but some of these intermediary goals are conditioning the implementation of others.

The combined impact of the implementation of these intermediate goals on the South as a whole has become increasingly decisive and, while it was initially enhanced by previously existing instability and sources of conflict in the South, it itself has now become a factor in the creation of conflict and has played a role in changing the character of that conflict. In this sense, the widely held interpretation of Soviet, Cuban, and other Eastern successes in the South as a result of favorable circumstances offering attractive opportunities can be considered correct only if it is applied to the events in Angola and Indochina. Since then, the selection of areas of preexisting instability as favorable targets by the inner hierarchical core has been increasingly replaced by attempts to create such instability throughout the South, which have resulted in a multiplication of the number of accessible targets. The appearance of Group D states since 1975 has had the practical result of greatly expanding the areas of direct contact between East and South and thereby has provided the political and military basis necessary to take advantage of the new conflicts produced by the very existence of those new states. The security of Group D states requires friendly neighbors, and, in an atmosphere of growing ideological polarization in the South, "friendly" has come increasingly to mean similarly oriented regimes. Moreover, these Group D states consider it their internationalist duty not only to help each other, as described above, but also to aid "fraternal" opposition groups in neighboring countries. In these circumstances, internationalist goals and external and domestic security needs have coalesced to create a very active policy of revolutionary expansion.

The role of the four intermediate goals of the Southern policy of the various Eastern actors varies according to the extent of those actors' real interest in the South, their relative needs for domestic legitimization, their security needs, and their place within the Eastern subsystem. It also depends on the circumstances surrounding their initial involvement in the South.

Eastern presence in the South takes the form of the establishment of diplomatic and trade relations with various developing countries. In this respect, Romania and Yugoslavia, given their favorable image in the South as independent or struggling minor Eastern actors, have a distinct advantage over the "loyal five," widely perceived as too closely associated with the Soviet Union. Both have relations with almost all developing countries, and their avoidance of any attack on the governments of those countries distinguishes them from other Eastern European states, which make a sharp distinction between "reactionary" and "progressive" regimes. North Korea, which has relations with over 80 developing countries, is in a rather peculiar situation in this respect; until the early 1970s it refused to have any ties with states recognizing Seoul. Cuba has relations with most Southern actors, but it draws a sharp distinction between strictly state-to-state relations and her activism in support of radicals, which continues to limit her acceptance among Group B and nonradical Group C states. The presence of Vietnam and the "loyal five" has long been even more limited, largely as a result of their limited interest or resources to aid the South. Moreover, the latter are increasingly perceived as developed countries and therefore often required to provide an amount of aid they are both unable and unwilling to extend. Also, their close ties with the Soviet Union may, in some case, limit their acceptance as partners, especially among the anti-Communist regimes in the South. East Germany combines the problems of North Korea with those of Cuba, to which one may add the fact that is also the most developed Eastern European state. Once again, the collapse of the Hallstein doctrine balances the perception of East Berlin as a Soviet satellite, even with such anti-Marxist regimes as those of Brazil or Argentina.

The Soviet Union and China also have a presence in a large number of developing countries, although not in as many as either Yugoslavia or Romania, a fact which reflects their character as Eastern superpowers and their relatively abundant resources. While they have expanded their diplomatic relations with most if by no means all Southern countries, they still are perceived as potentially dangerous partners. That holds true especially for the Soviet Union, although detente did play a large role in eliminating some of the ideological obstacles in the way of antiradical Southern states' acceptance of Moscow as a normal trade and diplomatic partner. The new pragmatism of Beijing after Mao's death and its de facto dumping of extreme left groups in Southern areas such as Latin America, groups which to some extent are now inherited by Tirana, had a similar effect.

The "loyal five" tend to have a presence in the same group of developing countries; in some cases, such as Panama, this presence reflects those Southern governments' continual reluctance to take the step of establishing ties with the Soviet Union herself. Those same countries, however, have less problems in establishing such ties with either Cuba or China or both. For all these Eastern actors, as large a presence as possible in the South serves to increase their own legitimacy on the international arena, and in the case of the "loyal five" and, to a lesser extent, China, to provide the essential minimum degree of communication needed to develop trade ties.

Influence, as defined by Rubinstein, [69] is one actor's ability to orientate effectively the policy goals of the subject actor toward an increasing similarity with their own through nonmilitary means. This similarity would increase the ability of the influencing actor to implement its national goals. As was clearly demonstrated in the cases of Chile, India, and Indonesia, the establishment of influence by an Eastern actor (Cuba, the Soviet Union, and China, respectively) is a highly unstable endeavor and may not produce a long- or even mid-range commonality of interests. It may also prove dangerous, with the ever-present possibility of a backlash on the part of the Southern actor and a potential for long-lasting damage to the interests of the Eastern actor, as was spectacularly demonstrated in Indonesia after September 1965 and in Chile after August 1973.

Domination is usually the result of a long-lasting influence and is also related, as a rule, to a long-lasting presence and influence. In this case, there is a convergence between the policy goals of the subject and object actors, and those goals are closely related to vital national interests. Although it is usually more difficult for the object actor to detach itself from this type of relationship, it is possible and has been done in the cases of Egypt in 1972, Sudan in 1974, and Somalia in 1977-78. Given the high cost of establishing domination for the subject actor, the ending of such a relationship represents a significant loss for it. The Soviet Union, for instance, lost much more than a substantial say in Egyptian affairs when Sadat expelled Soviet and "loyal five" personnel from Egypt, more than a chance to use Cairo as an intermediary for the implementation of Soviet goals in the Middle East. It also lost invested resources, both financial and political, as well as prestige throughout the South. It was precisely because of the highly risky nature of domination of a Southern country or area that the Soviet Union has attempted in the cases of Group D actors to move one step further, to the establishment of long-lasting control, that is, to make permanent the convergence of goals and ensure a continuing capacity to enforce it.

The establishment of complete control over a distant policy may be defined as the successful subordination of the polity's decision-making process, means of policy implementation, and formulation of long-range policy goals. The West did establish such control over its former colonial dominions, but it seldom allowed the formal attributes of sovereignty to remain, although it did so in such cases as Morocco, Egypt, and China. The East in general and the Soviet Union in particular, on the other hand, seem to prefer retaining formal trappings of sovereignty; this strategy has the advantage of providing an ideal means for the eventual institutionalization of control within the subordinate state. Once that is realized, the subordinate actor tends to become part of the self-regulating network of the Eastern subsystem, and patterns of domination—that is, the temporary or discrete use of force sufficient to ensure the preservation of subordination—reappear to replace the more brutal and direct force initially used to establish control. Eastern Europe has reached the point to which Soviet interests and Marxist values are socialized deeply enough to ensure a fair degree of stability to the ruling regimes and, as a result, a limited degree of autonomy for them in their foreign policies. Once that point was reached, the political returns for the Soviet Union were impressive enough to compensate for whatever drain of military and economic resources was needed to establish initial control. Mutatis mutandis, the initial Soviet investment in Group D countries, especially when it was done through proxies, Cuba in particular, and with the exception of Afghanistan, is expected to provide similar if not proportionally larger political and even economic returns. The only case where those returns are already apparent seems to be South Yemen, where the political socialization of the new Soviet-introduced values is advanced enough to allow Moscow to encourage autonomy. After the staunchly pro-Soviet president Abdul Fattah Ismail was replaced, with Soviet connivance, by the less rigid but by no means less loyal Ali Nasser Mohammed, [70] the impression was created that the new ruler in Aden is less subservient to Moscow, an impression reinforced by his overtures to Saudi Arabia and North Yemen.

Angola, Ethiopia, and especially Afghanistan are all still in the stage of imposition of Eastern control. There are more East German, Soviet, and especially Cuban troops and military advisers in Angola than the 30,000-man Angolan army, and two or more times more Soviet troops as Afghan soldiers defend the rulers in Kabul. In Ethiopia, the ratio is "only" about two to one in favor of the national army over the Cuban, Soviet, East German, and South Yemeni troops stationed there. Moreover, in all these cases, the highest echelon of the military command is under Eastern control. Ethiopian planning is done mostly by East Germans, as is Afghanistan's by Soviet and Angola's by Cuban advisers. Education, health services, and factory management are all under direct Eastern supervision, and the very fact that education is controlled by Easterners or else takes place in Cuba, [71] the Soviet Union, or Eastern Europe demonstrates the long-term goals of the East regarding the Group D actors. Treaties of friendship and cooperation concluded, as a rule, for periods of 20 years, may or may not include military provisions, but they certainly formalize a long-range unity of political goals. While it is true that such treaties also exist between Group C radical states and Eastern actors, their significance is completely different from that of Group D states, where the survival of the dependent actor's regime is guaranteed exclusively by external support. The friendship and cooperation treaties provide plausible legal grounds for the application of the Brezhnev doctrine to Group D actors, at least as plausible as its application was in the case of Czechoslovakia. Even if non-Eastern actors might not be persuaded, such treaties could certainly provide a valuable instrument for Eastern actors in convincing their own people of their right and duty to intervene in defense of "revolution" in Southern states. Afghanistan again seems to be a good example, insofar as the Soviet population is more or less supportive of the intervention there.

For Southern actors willingness to accept an Eastern presence is usually a reflection of a desire to demonstrate independence with respect to the West, hope for possible aid, a desire to help build bridges between East and West to increase the chances of peace, and hopes for trade benefits. Once an Eastern presence has been established—and in some cases it has been established before a Southern actor has gained independence, usually through the vehicle of "liberation" movements—there is not necessarily any impetus for it to evolve into influence or, even less so, control. Only when a developing coun-

try's foreign or domestic policy goals are unattainable through domestic resources alone and immediate goals are in accord with those
of a given Eastern actor or set of actors can conditions favorable to
the establishment of Eastern control or influence develop. Somalia,
with her essential national goals of reunification of the Somali people
now living in three other countries, is too weak and small to reach
that goal, and therefore it had to seek additional military support from
the East as the only possible source. When that support developed into
domination and the Somali goal was not significantly advanced, conflict
became inevitable. However, the statement that Somalia "threw the
Soviets out" in 1977 should not be taken too literally; those developments do not necessarily prove that domination is easily reversible.
The bitter hostility between Ethiopia and Somalia and the clearly
greater advantages the Soviet Union could reap from Addis Ababa in
fact have made the Soviet Union willing to abandon Somalia, especially
as there was no certainty that a radical change of direction in Mogadishu could be ruled out. The nature of Eastern penetration of Ethiopia, on the other hand, seems to suggest that no such change may be
expected there in the foreseeable future.

What all these patterns of Eastern involvement in the South during the 1970s portend for the international system as a whole may be
defined as dysfunctional for all three subsystems and as having a large
role in the radical modification of the character of the system.

In the South, further polarization between pro-Eastern and pro-
Western countries should be expected to advance, accompanied by the
de facto decline of the Nonaligned Movement and its ever growing inability to provide collective security to its members, especially the
small and medium-sized ones. The disappearance of many of the unifying goals of the Southern majority—anticolonialism, antibloc stands,
and support for self-determination—and the increasingly sharp differences between the rates of growth, level of industrialization, and general level of development of different Southern countries will probably
continue to reinforce the present trend toward more and more conflicts
between them. The appearance of a large and growing number of Group
D actors with limited prospects for development (if the experience of
Groups IV and VI actors has any relevance) but with a strong military
and political impact would further hinder the development of the South
as a whole, while increasing the gap between rich and poor Southern
countries. One of the main reasons for this development is the necessary reallocation of resources toward military spending throughout the
South. At an intrasubsystemic level, a growth in numbers and relative
strength of Group A actors, matched by an even larger increase in the
number of Group D actors, will increase the likelihood that Group B
will further erode and that Group C will gravitate increasingly toward
either East or West for reasons of security and economic necessity.

In the East, the trend will probably be toward new additions to the inner hierarchical core, as more and more Group D countries will become undistinguishable from Group VI actors, with a consequent strengthening of the Soviet geopolitical position but, at the same time, it will imply a possible overextension of the inner core's capabilities. The "loyal five" will probably become more involved in the South for their own as well as intrasubsystemic reasons, in search of markets and, increasingly, raw materials. At the same time, though, this involvement will add to the overall capability of the inner core to influence, control, or dominate Southern actors. For those Eastern actors outside the inner core, the mid- or even long-term goal in the South will probably be aimed increasingly at limiting the effects of ideological and political polarization, and, in this sense, they may develop a more consistent coordination. They may also move even closer to those radical Group C actors aware of the dangers of Eastern domination and control, thereby extending Eastern subsystemic ideological and political conflicts into the South.

For the West, a failure to come to grips with the realities of Southern polarization could result in a continuing inaccurate allocation of resources in the South, with aid and political support given indiscriminately to developing countries, regardless of their orientation and role in the polarization process. The huge amounts of funds flowing to Libya for her oil, the fact that Tanzania, one of the Group A actors most closely coordinating its policies with the East, is also the recipient of the highest per capita grant aid in Africa (mostly from the Scandinavian countries), and the continuation of Western aid to Mozambique, Congo, and Benin are all examples of an unrealistic distribution of Western resources in the South. As long as the West persists in its belief that it can counterbalance Southern polarization through aid and concessions, it will continue to provide incentives to radicals for moving further to the left and not enough incentives to nonradicals to avoid such moves.

The effects of Eastern-encouraged and exacerbated polarization in the South could also confront Western military planners with the necessity of allocating increased resources into Southern areas where Group A and D actors are increasingly challenging Western interests with Eastern backing. Moreover, the more Group D becomes assimilated to Group VI of the Eastern subsystem, the greater the risk of confrontation with the Soviet Union should a Western actor attempt to prevent that process from developing further.

For the West, this raises the following kinds of issues: can it allow the South to come under increasing Eastern influence, domination, or control, without irreparable damage to the entire international balance of power and the prospects for peace? Might it not be more appropriate to strongly challenge Eastern inroads into the South, ideologically, politically and militarily?

The most rational approach Western policy makers could adopt under these circumstances, assuming that they begin to realize the depth of Southern polarization, the radically changed goals of the Eastern inner core in the South, and the East's growing ability to implement those goals, could be to reinterpret the very notion of detente. It is not only inaccurate but also illogical to claim that the Soviet Union and her allies are violating the spirit of detente by their expansion in the South because neither the East nor the South ever considered detente to apply to East-South relations. * To assume that a reduction of tensions between East and West should automatically apply to the South as well is to dismiss unrealistically the Southern subsystem's autonomy and to consider the developing countries as a natural geopolitical appendage of the West, which they certainly are not anymore. If the West intends to expand detente to the South, it should also expand its deterrent capabilities into that area by reorganizing its entire defense system and taking a more global approach. Western military and economic aid to the South should be oriented toward a limitation of polarization, but it cannot be successful unless the West recognizes the strong probability that it may only be able to prevent further shifts leftward rather than reverse the trend toward polarization in general.

For the international system as a whole, the changes resulting from increased Eastern impact on the South seem to be the cause for

---

*S. Rajaratnam, Singapore's deputy prime minister and longtime foreign minister, a representative voice for many nonradical developing countries, made the following revealing observations regarding the future of the South in the 1980s, and the Southern perception of detente:

> The indications are that in the eighties, if the global crisis is left unresolved, civil wars, small nation-wars, and proxy wars will spread further in the Third World. . . . All these are ripe for conversion into great-power proxy wars. Though I welcome the detente between the great powers, we in the Third World should be aware of the dangerous implications it has for us. The detente is an understanding that under no conditions will the great powers wage war directly against one another. . . . But nowhere does detente repudiate the rivalry between great powers or their practice of resorting to proxy wars. Thus it is inevitable that the Third World provide the arenas for these wars. [72]

a shift away from what seemed for a time to be tripolar world during the heyday of the Nonaligned Movement in the 1960s and toward a renewed bipolarity. This trend does not signify a return to the type of bipolarity that characterized the 1950s but to one in which security for all actors can be ensured only by realignment with either West or East, despite the probable persistence of economic and even ideological differences within both groups. This return to bipolarity could mean a sharp increase in the number and level of conflicts, most of them in the South.

A second probable impact of the return to bipolarity could be the diminishing role of international or regional organizations, such as the United Nations or the Arab League, and even more so in the case of the OAU, as more and more states lose any confidence in those organizations' role as conflict-solving actors or as protection against superpower rivalries.

Finally, the new bipolarity could have a profound influence on the subsystems of the international system on the level of political culture, economic development, and ideology. Southern solidarity, weakened as it already is, could further wane, and so probably would Eastern cohesion, ideological unity, and formal adherence to similar goals. All these developments may be expected to increase the probability of systemic and intrasubsystemic conflicts and to destabilize further the international order.

NOTES

1. Hannah Negaran, "The Afghan Coup of April 1978; Revolution and International Security," Orbis (Spring 1979): 93-114.
2. "Soviets Look for New Supplies in South America," and "Soviets Buy Brazilian Sugar Because of Cuba's Poor Harvest," News World, May 4, 1980; for data on Soviet meat and grain imports, worth $800 million, from Argentina, see Time, July 7, 1980, p. 59.
3. Stephen P. Cohen and Richard L. Park, India: Emergent Power? (New York: Crane, Russak, 1978), pp. 40-41.
4. Business Week, June 2, 1980, pp. 62-63; "Seychelles: New Outpost for Russians?" U.S. News & World Report, March 24, 1980, p. 36.
5. CIA, Handbook of Economic Statistics (Washington, D.C.: 1979), table 75.
6. Ibid.
7. Ibid., table 69.
8. Michael Kamara, "The East Europeans in West Africa: Perspectives from Nigeria, Ghana, Sierra Leone and the Ivory Coast" (Paper presented at the symposium on Eastern Europe and the Third World, Columbia University, May 2, 1980).

9. For the Romanian comments on that occasion, see Scinteia, March 1, 1977.

10. "Grenada: A Tiny Exporter of Revolution?" Newsweek, March 31, 1980, p. 44; Tad Szulc, "Radical Winds in the Caribbean," New York Times Magazine, May 25, 1980, pp. 16-73.

11. New York Times, June 1, 1980; ibid., June 17, 1980.

12. CIA, National Foreign Assessment Center, Communist Aid Activities in Non-Communist Developing Countries, 1979 (Washington, D.C., 1979), table 8.

13. Ibid.

14. Ibid., table 4.

15. Ibid., table 8.

16. Ibid., table 4.

17. Ibid.

18. Ibid., tables 4, 8.

19. CIA, Economic Statistics, table 80.

20. For a perceptive description of these developments in Benin and the Congo, see Samuel Decalo, Coups and Army Rule in Africa: Studies in Military Style (New Haven: Yale University Press, 1976), pp. 39-86; also Decalo's "Ideological Rhetoric and Scientific Socialism in Benin and Congo/Brazzaville," in Socialism in Sub-Saharan Africa. A new assessment, ed. Carl G. Rosberg and Thomas M. Callaghy (Berkeley: Institute on International Studies, University of California, 1979), pp. 231-64; for the institutionalization of radicalism in other developing countries, see also Helen Desfosses and Jacques Levesque, eds., Socialism in the Third World (New York: Praeger, 1975).

21. For such an impact, see Miles D. Wolpin, "Marx and Radical Militarism in the Developing Nations," Armed Forces and Society 4, no. 2 (Winter 1978): 245-64.

22. Maurice Bishop, "Grenada: Revolution in the Caribbean," Political Affairs 59 (March 3, 1980): 37-38.

23. Marshall I. Goldman, "Soviet Foreign Aid Since the Death of Stalin: Progress and Problems," in Soviet Policy in Developing Countries, ed. Raymond W. Duncan (Waltham: Ginn-Blaisdell, 1970), p. 32, table 1.

24. Ibid., p. 36.

25. Ibid., pp. 37-38.

26. Ibid., p. 38, table 2.

27. Leo Tansky, "Soviet Military Aid, Technical Assistance, and Academic Training," in Duncan, Soviet Policy in Developing Countries, p. 47.

28. Ibid., pp. 45-46.

29. CIA, Economic Statistics, table 81.

30. Ibid.

31. Ibid.

32. Ibid. , table 76.

33. Ibid.

34. Compiled from Ibid.

35. CIA, Communist Aid Activities, table 5.

36. Ibid.

37. Ibid.

38. Ibid. , table 7.

39. Ibid. , table 4.

40. Ibid. , table 3.

41. Ibid. , table 4.

42. Ibid. , table 3.

43. CIA, Economic Statistics, table 75.

44. Ibid.

45. Ibid. , table 74.

46. Ibid.

47. Dale R. Herspring and Ivan Volgyes, "The Military as an Agent of Political Socialization in Eastern Europe," Armed Forces and Society 3, no. 2 (Winter 1977): 250-53.

48. For an interesting and revealing analysis of the Soviet view on China's policies in the South, see Beorge Ginsburgs, "The Soviet View of Chinese Influence in Africa and Latin America," in Soviet and Chinese Influence in the Third World, ed. Alvin Z. Rubinstein (New York: Praeger, 1975), pp. 197-220.

49. Ibid. , p. 199.

50. Veselin Djuranovic, "Non-Aligned Policy the Bright Side of International Relations," Yugoslav Information Bulletin 3-4 (1980): 8; a useful collection of Tito's remarks on various aspects of the non-alignment concept, in Tito and Non-Alignment (Beograd: STP, 1979).

51. Samuel S. Kim, "Pyongyang, the Third World, and Global Politics," in Korea and World Affairs 3, no. 4 (Winter 1979): 455-56.

52. "Message Addressed by the President of the Socialist Republic of Romania, Nicolae Ceausescu, to the Sixth Summit Conference of the Non-Aligned in Havana," Romania and the Developing Countries (September 1979): 4.

53. For a full English text of the Havana Final Declaration, see Review of International Affairs 30 (Belgrade), (September 20, 1979): 18-67.

54. Kim, "Pyongyang," passim.

55. Anatoly Gromyko, "Anti-Imperialist Struggle in Africa," Political Affairs 59 (February 1980): 12.

56. Ibid. , p. 10.

57. Ibid.

58. Raúl Valdéz Vivó, Ethiopia's Revolution (New York, International Publishers, 1978), p. 33.

59. Gromyko, "Anti-Imperialist Struggle," p. 14; for an inter-

esting comparison between present and older Soviet views on the possibility of Communist takeovers in the developing countries, see the relevant chapters in Thomas T. Hammond, ed. , The Anatomy of Communist Takeovers (New Haven: Yale University Press, 1975); also Hammond's analysis of present Soviet opinions on the matter, in "Moscow and Communist Takeovers," Problems of Communism 25 (January-February 1976): 48-67.

60. Gromyko, "Anti-Imperialist Struggle," p. 14.

61. Ibid. , p. 16.

62. "Excerpts from the Report of the CC CPSU to the Twenty-Third Congress of the CPSU, Delivered 29 March 1966, by Leonid Brezhnev, First Secretary of the CC CPSU," in Jeffrey Simon, Ruling Communist Parties and Detente: A Documentary History (Washington, D. C. : American Enterprise Institute for Public Policy Research, 1975), p. 61.

63. Reproduced in Simon, Ruling Communist Parties, p. 101.

64. Ibid. , p. 119.

65. Suzanne Ogden, "The Approach of the Chinese Communists to the Study of International Law, State Sovereignty and the International System," in China Quarterly, no. 70 (June 1977): 318-19.

66. Ginsburgs, "The Soviet View of Chinese Influence," p. 201.

67. Eric Chou, "South-East and East Asia: China's Big-Power Policies," in Annual of Power and Conflict, 1978-79, ed. Brian Crozier (London: Institute for the Study of Conflict, 1979), p. 433.

68. For the Soviet readiness to sacrifice the local communist parties in order to accommodate important Third World leaders, specifically Nasser and Nimeiri, see Hammond, "Moscow and Communist Takeovers,"; for the new Soviet approach to the possibility of Marxist-Leninist takeovers in the South, defined as "counter-imperialism," see Richard Lowenthal, "Soviet Counterimperialism," in Problems of Communism (November-December 1976): 52-63.

69. Alvin Rubinstein, "Assessing Influence as a Problem in Foreign Policy Analysis," in Rubinstein, Soviet and Chinese Influence in the Third World, pp. 3-10.

70. For the extent of Soviet control over South Yemen, see Pranay B. Gupte, "Soviet Activity Found Growing in Aden Region," New York Times, June 10, 1980; Pranay B. Gupte, "South Yemen Seeks to Widen Arab Ties," New York Times, June 12, 1980; also, Newsweek, May 5, 1980.

71. For a series of analyses on Cuba's involvement in the Caribbean, especially in small states in the area, see Caribbean Review (Winter 1980); for East Germany's role in the stabilization and development of "proto-Leninism," see Melvin Croan, "A New Afrika Korps?" Washington Quarterly (Winter 1980): 29-32.

72. S. Rajaratnam, "The Crisis of the Third World," Washing-

ton Quarterly (Winter 1980): 15-16; a similar perception of the dangers of proxy wars for the South—and it should be admitted that the East is much more often behind such wars than is the West—is that of the Yugoslavs, such as Dusan Dozet, "Contemporary Wars by Proxy," Survey 4 (1979): 205-15.

PART II
INDIVIDUAL
EASTERN EUROPEAN STATES
AND THE THIRD WORLD

2

ALBANIA AND THE THIRD WORLD: IDEOLOGICAL, POLITICAL, AND ECONOMIC ASPECTS

Elez Biberaj

The People's Socialist Republic of Albania (PSRA) has followed a unique policy toward the Third World: its scope, nature, and level have differed substantially from those of the other Eastern European countries. The developing countries of Africa, Asia, and Latin America have witnessed an extensive political, economic, and military involvement by the Eastern European Communist states. These nations have provided substantial economic and military assistance to many developing states and pro-Communist national liberation movements and have participated in joint economic ventures with some Third World states.

Of all the Eastern European countries, Albania has been least involved politically and economically in the Third World. It has not been in a position to provide economic or military assistance to any developing country or to any Third World national liberation movement. Similarly, Albania has neither made any investments in the Third World nor engaged in joint economic ventures with any developing state. While the PSRA has conducted trade with some Middle Eastern and a few selected African, Latin American, and Asian states, its trade with the Third World has comprised only a small portion of its foreign trade.

Albania's policy toward the Third World has been determined by

The author is grateful to Professors Nicholas C. Pano and Peter R. Prifti for their insightful comments on an earlier draft of this chapter. The author, of course, assumes sole responsibility for any remaining errors.

several interrelated factors: ideology, political, and economic considerations, and perceptions of the developing nations. The ruling Albanian Party of Labor (APL) has been strongly committed to promoting revolution at home as well as abroad. The APL has perceived the Third World as the weakest link of the "imperialist" system and, therefore, ripe for revolution. Albania has supported revolutionary movements and Marxist-Leninist parties throughout the Third World. However, Albania's propagation of revolution has come into conflict with the ever growing importance of political and economic factors in its policy toward the Third World. At times these competing objectives have led to an inconsistency in Tiranë's propaganda and policies regarding the Third World. The need to maintain visibility in the international arena, legitimacy at home, and new markets for its exports, have, however, caused Albania to enter into political and economic relations with many Third World states without regard for their sociopolitical systems.

The PSRA differs substantially from most developing nations in the level of its economic development, political and economic systems, size, culture, and ideology. Nevertheless, it shares important similarities with these states, such as a common heritage of foreign domination and subjugation, weakness and insecurity, lack of economic viability, and a fierce nationalism. Throughout most of its modern history, Albania has been subject to domination and insult by hostile and more powerful neighbors and other foreign countries. When it gained its independence in 1912, Albania, like many a Third World nation, was unjustly partitioned among its neighbors by the great powers. More than half of its territory and about 40 percent of its people were excluded from the boundaries of the new Albanian state. Close to 2 million Albanians still live in neighboring Yugoslavia, mainly in the province of Kosovë.

Since independence in 1912, Albania's sovereignty and territorial integrity have often been seriously threatened. This fact has made the preservation of Albanian independence the primary objective of its foreign policy. The PSRA is a small and weak country, with a population of 2.7 million people in 1979. Threatened by its neighbors, weak and security-conscious, Albania has not been in a position to ensure its security by relying on its own forces and thus has had to rely on friendly great powers and favorable international developments for its protection.

Like most Third World states, Albania has lacked economic viability. This factor has played an important role in Albania's political alignments and realignments. Economic dependence has usually led to political dependence and loss of decision-making autonomy. Albania has had to deal with the task of preserving its political independence while at the same time being dependent on foreign assistance for its economic survival and development. Foreign aid has been accompanied by high political costs, which have served as constraints on Albania's foreign policy.

Albania's foreign dependence has, in the past, made it highly vulnerable to pressures, threats, and interference in its domestic affairs and has seriously threatened its independence. Reliance on Italy during the interwar period led to outright annexation of Albania in 1939. After World War II, the PSRA has had the unique distinction of having aligned and broken, in turn, with three major centers of international communism—Yugoslavia, the Soviet Union and the People's Republic of China.[1] Tiranë's alliance with Belgrade nearly led to Albania's absorption into the Yugoslav federation, and that along with Moscow led to interference in domestic affairs and foreign policy compliance. In the early and mid-1970s, ideological and political divergences emerged between Tiranë and Beijing, mainly due to Albania's opposition to the U.S.-Sino rapprochement. China applied economic pressure on the PSRA by delaying the signing of trade agreements and reducing trade and credits. Then, in July 1978, China cut off all economic and military aid to the PSRA and withdrew its technicians.

Albania's highly negative experience with its former allies has contributed to the development of a siege mentality among its leaders and has reinforced attitudes of resentment and mistrust of foreigners. To this day, Albania's traditional fears of partition, dismemberment, and foreign domination and subjugation persist. The present Albanian leaders believe that their country has suffered humiliation, partition, and foreign domination because of its political, economic, and military weakness. In order to escape further humiliation as well as foreign exploitation and domination the Communist regime of Enver Hoxha has given top priority to the preservation of Albania's political independence at the expense of all other factors, including more rapid economic development. Convinced that political independence cannot be preserved without achieving economic independence, the Albanians have adopted a strategy of independent economic development based on self-reliance.

Tiranë has perceived the developing countries as facing the same struggle of preserving their political independence as Albania. The PSRA has portrayed itself as a "model" for the developing countries of Africa, Asia, and Latin America in their struggle to eliminate or reduce their foreign dependence and become truly independent.

This chapter will seek to analyze Albania's view of the Third World, its political and economic interaction with the developing nations, and, finally, the applicability of Albania's development strategy as a "model" for the developing states in their attempts to strengthen their independence and promote their economic development.

ALBANIA'S VIEW OF THE THIRD WORLD

The most salient ideological aspects of the PSRA's foreign policy have been its division of the world into two opposing systems, two-front struggle against the hegemonistic tendency of the two superpowers, and promotion of revolution through armed struggle. These principles have been embodied in Albania's 1976 constitution. According to article 4, the PSRA is committed "to ensuring the final victory of the socialist road over the capitalist road, at achieving the complete construction of socialism and communism." Albania's global revolutionary objectives have been reflected in article 15, which states that the PSRA "supports the revolutionary movement of the working class and the struggle of the peoples for freedom, independence, social progress and socialism."[2] It is in this context that national democratic revolutions and national liberation movements in many developing nations have received Albanian political and moral support.

In keeping with its Marxist-Leninist ideology, the PSRA has sought to classify various countries according to their socioeconomic order. According to this criterion, there are only two systems or "worlds," the Socialist system, where the proletariat rules, and the capitalist system, where the bourgeoisie rules. Since capitalism has allegedly been restored in the former Socialist countries, the Soviet Union, the Eastern European states, and China since 1978 are no longer considered Socialist states. Albania has portrayed itself as the only truly Socialist country in the world and the defender of the purity of Marxism-Leninism. Tiranë has maintained that the Socialist camp still exists and is represented by the PSRA, which is "successfully building socialism."[3]

Albania has followed a highly militant foreign policy reminiscent of the Cold War period, which is based on an uncompromising struggle against the two superpowers. The United States and the Soviet Union have been characterized as the biggest and most dangerous "imperialist" powers in the history of the world. The two superpowers are seen as cooperating and competing, simultaneously, in the "imperialist" strategy for world domination. China's rapprochement with the United States and the Chinese notion that the United States represented less of a danger to China and the world proletariat than did the Soviet Union were vigorously opposed by Albania, and this was one of the major factors leading to the Sino-Albanian break. Albania regards the United States and the Soviet Union as equally dangerous. At the Sixth Congress of the APL in November 1971, the Party's First Secretary Enver Hoxha warned China that it could not rely on one "imperialism," that is, the United States, to oppose the other, the Soviet Union, and called for the continuation of a two-front struggle against both superpowers.[4]

Hoxha has continued to maintain that the two superpowers are

equally dangerous, adding that they represent "the main enemy of socialism and the freedom and independence of nations, the greatest
force defending oppressive and exploiting systems, and a direct threat
that mankind will be hurled into a third world war. "[5] The PSRA is apparently the only country in the world that does not maintain diplomatic relations with the two superpowers. However, contrary to official
Albanian declarations, the PSRA does conduct trade with the United
States. Since 1975 the volume of U. S.-Albanian trade has shown a remarkable increase, and in 1979 it reached an estimated $20 million. [6]
Following the break with Beijing, Albania's propaganda machine has
given China the same polemical treatment as the United States and
the Soviet Union. Hoxha has declared that China also aspires to become a superpower and therefore it is as dangerous as the other two
superpowers and thus must be opposed. [7]

In contrast to other countries, Albania has rejected such concepts as "nonaligned countries," "First, Second, and Third Worlds,"
"developing nations," and "North and South." According to Hoxha,

All these terms, which refer to various political forces
acting in the world today, cover up and do not bring out
the class character of these political forces, the fundamental contradictions of our epoch, the key problem
which is predominant today on a national and international scale, the ruthless struggle between the bourgeois-
imperialist world on the one hand, and socialism, the
world proletariat and its natural allies, on the other. [8]

The "nonaligned" movement has come under especially harsh
Albanian criticism, primarily due to Yugoslavia's role in that movement. Yugoslavia has been considered a U.S. ally and has been accused of "faithfully" serving American "imperialism" through the
propagation of "nonalignment."[9] The main object of Tiranë's attack
on "nonalignment" has been as follows:

The aim of this "theory" is to achieve one of the goals of
imperialism in the political plan. By reaching the group
with a supposedly neutral stand . . . this "theory" is intended to deflect the peoples from the real struggle against
imperialism, the superpowers and local lackeys in their
service. [10]

An important issue in the Sino-Albanian conflict was the differ-
ence between the two former allies in their approach toward the Third
World. At the Sixth Special Session of the U.N. General Assembly in
April 1974, China proclaimed its now famous "theory of three worlds,"

according to which the two superpowers make up the First World; the developed nations, the Second World; and the developing countries of Asia, Africa, and Latin America, the Third World. The chairman of the Chinese delegation, Deng Xiaoping, declared that the countries of the Third World "constitute a revolutionary motive force propelling the wheel of world history and are the main force combatting colonialism, imperialism, and particularly the superpowers."[11] Furthermore, Deng added that China, a Socialist and a developing country, was a member of the Third World.[12]

Tiranë rejected the "theory of three worlds," and Hoxha accused Beijing of disregarding "international class struggle and the internal class struggle of unliberated nations." Upon his return from the UN General Assembly, Deng received the Albanian ambassador and told him that the "theory of three worlds" represented "the basic direction of the foreign policy of our party at the current stage."[13] However, Deng failed to win the backing of the Albanians. An editorial in the daily organ of the Central Committee of the APL on July 7, 1977, explained Albania's opposition to the "theory of three worlds." The editorial characterized the theory as "antirevolutionary" and "a flagrant departure from the teachings of Marxism-Leninism" because it allegedly preaches social peace and collaboration with the "bourgeoisie," covers up class contradictions, ignores the principal contradiction between capitalism and socialism, and is intended to curb the revolution and defend capitalism. The Chinese "theory of three worlds" was also criticized for failing to make a distinction between "the genuine anti-imperialist and revolutionary forces in power" in many Third World countries and for being guided by the same anti-Marxist policy and ideology as the Yugoslav theory of "nonalignment."[14]

Hoxha also rejected the Chinese characterization of the Third World as "the great motive force which is driving the wheel of history forward." He maintained that such a role could not be played by a diverse group of states, a majority of which were ruled by the "bourgeoisie," "feudal lords," "reactionaries," and "fascists." Only the proletariat, according to Hoxha, could play such a role.[15]

Albania has also rejected other concepts concerning the Third World, such as "developing nations," the "South," and even the concept of a New International Economic Order. These concepts have been characterized as elements of a "reactionary strategy" whose aim is to preserve the status quo, the revolution and national liberation movements, and perpetuate the domination and exploitation of many Third World nations by the "imperialist" powers.[16]

Tiranë considers the Third World in general as an extension of the single world "imperialist" system dominated by the two superpowers. According to Hoxha,

Few states in the "third world" can be called independent,
because in fact, each of them is dependent on this or that
imperialist power in one way or another. Even if it is called politically independent, it is economically dependent,
and according to the teachings of the classics of our Marxist-Leninist science, if you are dependent economically you
cannot be independent politically. [17]

The PSRA makes a distinction between revolutionary and reactionary Third World countries. The first group includes radical Third
World states such as Algeria, Iraq, Tanzania, and Mexico, which have
been sympathetic to Albania. The second group includes all those countries ruled by "feudal landlords, kings, and fascist dictators," such
as Saudi Arabia, Zaire, and Chile. In Hoxha's view, the leaders of
this latter group follow policies that are contrary to the interests of
the proletariat, the revolution, and national liberation movements
and therefore hinder the struggle against "colonialism, imperialism,
and the two superpowers."[18] Albania has urged the peoples of Third
World nations to wage a resolute struggle against "imperialism,"
"neocolonialism," and the local "bourgeoisie" in order to gain their
national independence and freedom. Revolution is seen as "the sole
means of transforming the world, the only road to escape the yoke of
national and social bondage."[19]

Hoxha considers the present international situation highly revolutionary and maintains that the revolution for the overthrow of "the
bourgeois-landowner order and the liquidation of imperialist dependence" is the order of the day. Therefore, the duty of all revolutionaries, progressives, and patriots in the Third World is to organize
and mobilize the people into a "liberation struggle."[20] Tiranë has
maintained close links with many Marxist-Leninist parties, primarily
in Latin American and African states. In the 1960s, China and Albania
sponsored the establishment of splinter Marxist-Leninist parties in
Western Europe and the Third World. These parties played an important propaganda role in China's conflict with the Soviet Union. As a
result of the Sino-Albanian conflict in the mid-1970s, the Marxist-
Leninist movement split into pro-Tiranë and pro-Beijing factions.

The PSRA has continued to show a great interest in the propagation and support of the Marxist-Leninist movement. Third World
Marxist-Leninist party delegations representing Brazil, Argentina,
Ceylon, Ecuador, Indonesia, Bolivia, Colombia, Peru, Chile, Paraguay, Uruguay, Philippines, and the Dominican Republic attended the
Seventh Congress of the APL in November 1976.[21] Seven delegations
from Latin America, representing Argentina, Bolivia, Brazil, Colombia, Chile, Ecuador, and Uruguay, held a joint meeting in Tiranë,
and soon afterward issued a joint declaration, clearly taking Albania's

side in the Sino-Albanian conflict. [22] These and a few other Marxist-Leninist parties from the Third World have denounced the Chinese "theory of three worlds" and have held the same ideological stand as Albania on the Third World and other important international issues. In many respects, Tiranë has become the leading center for these parties. Marxist-Leninist party delegations have visited Tiranë regularly for consultation with the APL as well as for instructions and financial assistance. The Albanian media has given them wide publicity, although in their respective countries these parties do not seem to enjoy any significant backing among the people.

In October 1978, the Institute of Marxist-Leninist Studies in Tiranë, organized a "scientific session" on problems of current world development. Most of the papers presented at the session dealt with the propagation of revolution and the role of Marxist-Leninist parties. These parties were characterized as "the leaders of the revolutionary and liberation struggle of the masses of the people" and as the decisive subjective condition for the proletarian revolution. [23] The session was attended by six delegations representing Third World Marxist-Leninist parties from Brazil, Chile, Ecuador, Iran, Mexico, and Venezuela. Speeches by the representatives of these parties emphasized armed struggle as the highest form of revolutionary struggle and the important role that Albania plays in the promotion of the revolution. The general secretary of the Peasants and Workers Party of Iran declared that the PSRA "represents the center of socialism and revolution. The duty of all communists and Marxist-Leninist parties is the defense of this center of socialism and revolution. "[24] Albania's support and propagation of Marxist-Leninist parties is a useful propaganda tool against China and the Soviet Union. It is also important for internal consumption to show that the PSRA is not isolated and that it has the support of "the Marxist-Leninist movement" in its conflict with China and for its foreign policy line in general.

Albania's advocacy of worldwide revolution has been met with opposition by the Chinese leaders. Huang Hua, China's foreign minister, in a secret speech to an assembly of senior political, military, and party cadres on July 30, 1977, expressed China's dissatisfaction with Albania's policy:

> There are certain leading comrades of the Albanian Party
> of Labor who, like other fervent opportunists, are fran-
> tically advocating the advent of a revolutionary high tide,
> but fail to see what is the tide of the times. They want to lead
> blindly and adventurously, the present stage of revolu-
> tion to the realm of socialist revolution. They want to
> lead the proletarian revolutionary rank and file, a power-
> ful force now in the formative stage, to an adventurous
> offensive which would only cause the revolution to suffer
> another setback and retreat. They oppose the theory of

the Third World, which is tantamount to opposing the
struggle of the proletariat to rally and unite the majority
of the masses. [25]

Tiranë has also supported various national liberation movements
in the developing countries, such as the Palestine Liberation Organization (PLO) and movements in Zimbabwe, Namibia, South Africa,
Burma, Malaysia, the Philippines, Indonesia, and other countries.
The PLO and the Arab countries have received unreserved support
from the PSRA in their conflict with Israel. In the United Nations and
other international bodies, Albania has consistently supported the A-
rabs and has repeatedly called on the Arab people to unite and wage
an armed struggle for the liberation of the occupied territories. Only
"a strong militant unity" among the Arabs, according to Hoxha, can
ensure a triumph against Israel. The PSRA maintains ties with the
PLO, and Palestinian delegations have been welcomed in Tiranë. Albania has demanded that the Palestinians be granted their "national"
rights, including their own independent state. The Camp David accords
have been opposed, and Egypt has been accused of having adopted a
narrow nationalist stand in reaching a separate peace with Israel. [26]
The PSRA was also sympathetic to the national liberation movement in Zimbabwe. An Albanian delegation headed by the vice minister
of foreign affairs, Ksenofon Nushi, attended Zimbabwe's independence
celebrations on April 18, 1980, and the two nations have established
diplomatic relations. [27]
Tiranë has supported revolutionary movements in many developing countries, including Nicaragua and Iran. Its attitude toward the
Islamic revolution in Iran is especially interesting. In 1967, Albania
proclaimed itself the world's first atheist state and has followed a
highly repressive antireligious policy. While it has played down the
role of religion in the Iranian developments, Tiranë has nevertheless
acknowledged that the Shiite religious sect has played a positive role
in the overthrow of the Shah. [28] Iran's conflict with the United States
has been given wide publicity in the Albanian media and has been portrayed as a determined struggle by Iran to stand up to U.S. threats,
pressures, and intimidation. An Albanian government delegation headed by Professor Sofokli Lazri attended the proceedings of an Iranian-
sponsored conference on "the verification of American interventions
in Iran" in June 1980. [29] In the wake of the Soviet intervention in Afghanistan, which has been denounced as a "fascist" invasion of a sovereign state, [30] Albania has warned Iran to be vigilant against the other superpower, too, that is to say, the Soviet Union. The Iranian revolution has been characterized as "an inspiring example also for the
other Moslem peoples" to free themselves from domination by the superpowers. Arab and other Moslem nations have been urged by Tiranë
to support Iran firmly in its conflict with the United States. [31]

The APL has used ideology as a guide and justification for its actions. Its concepts of a worldwide revolution and a two-front struggle against the exploitation and domination by the two superpowers have permitted Albania simultaneously to support Third World Marxist-Leninist parties, national liberation movements, national democratic revolutions, and any developing nation involved in a conflict with the superpowers. The APL has justified its support of these distinct revolutionary movements by considering them as parts of the same revolutionary process— the world proletarian revolution.

ALBANIA'S POLITICAL AND ECONOMIC INVOLVEMENT IN THE THIRD WORLD

Like all Communist party states, Alabania makes a distinction between its party-to-party and state-to-state relations. Despite its rhetoric, ideological considerations have not, in general, served as a constraint on the expansion of state-to-state relations between the PSRA and the developing states. Prior to the early 1970s, the PSRA gave low priority to its relations with the Third World. But the Soviet invasion of Czechoslovakia in 1968, and the Sino-American rapprochement a few years later caused Albania to reassess its foreign policy.

The first development caused the Albanians to appreciate the threat posed to them by the Soviet Union and their unrealistic reliance on distant China. The second development convinced them that their ally China had embarked on a policy reorientation that ran counter to Albania's perceived national interest and ideological line. Thus it became extremely important for Albania to expand its ties with other nations. As a result of this policy reassessment, PSRA's relations with the Third World assumed greater importance. Albania's goal has been to develop good political and economic relations with friendly developing states. This objective has become especially important in light of Tiranë's break with Beijing and has taken precedence over APL's global revolutionary objectives.

In the early 1970s, the PSRA launched a diplomatic offensive of expanding its ties with other nations. As its differences with China intensified, by the mid-1970s Albania made a breakthrough in its relations with the developing nations. By July 1980, the PSRA had established diplomatic ties with some 90 states, a majority of which were Third World nations. Tiranë has declared its readiness to establish relations with all developing nations, regardless of their sociopolitical systems. While it criticized China for collaborating with "reactionary" regimes in the Third World, the PSRA itself established and maintained good relations with such countries as Iran during the Shah's rule, the Central African Empire during Bokassa's rule, Morocco,

Brazil, Kuwait, and many others. In such cases, Albania's political as well as economic considerations have taken precedence over its ideological considerations.

Within the Third World, Albania has displayed the greatest interest in improving its ties with the Middle Eastern countries. It has diplomatic relations with Algeria, Egypt, Lebanon, Libya, Iraq, Kuwait, Morocco, Sudan, Syria, Tunisia, and the two Yemens. Albania's second greatest area of interest has been Africa, where it maintains relations with some 20 states, followed by Latin America and Asia. Tiranë has essentially relied on a people-to-people diplomacy, preferring to exchange delegations with social, cultural, and political organizations from Third World nations sympathetic to APL's domestic and foreign policy orientation. This preference has been reflected in the type of delegations that have participated at the congresses of the Trade Unions and the Women's Union of Albania. At the Eighth Congress of the Trade Unions of Albania in June 1977, nongovernmental trade union delegations representing Chile, the PLO, the African National Union of Zimbabwe, Algeria, Tanzania, Zambia, Burundi, Iraq, and Madagascar attended the proceedings. [32] The Eighth Congress of the Women's Union of Albania was attended by delegations representing Brazil, Benin, Iran, Chile, Mali, Mexico, the PLO, Tanzania, the African National Union of Zimbabwe, and so on. [33] Albania has also exchanged governmental delegations with the developing nations, but these exchanges have usually involved low-level officials. In August 1978 a Tanzanian agricultural delegation paid a visit to Albania. [34] A year later, an Iraqi governmental delegation headed by the minister of state for foreign affairs, Hamid Alwan, visited Albania. Alwan and PSRA foreign minister Nesti Nase held talks on the further expansion of relations between the two states. The Iraqi foreign minister also held talks with Nedin Hoxha, minister of foreign trade, on the possibilities of further trade expansion between Iraq and Albania. Before leaving Tiranë, the Iraqi delegation was received by Adil Çarçani, first deputy chairman of the Council of Ministers. [35]

Albania's economic interaction with the Third World has been limited, and the economic factor in Tiranë's Third World policy has been of secondary importance. This has been a reflection of Albania's economic capabilities and needs, its economic reliance on China until 1978, and better trade opportunities in Eastern and Western Europe. At the end of 1979, the PSRA maintained trade relations with only 45 states worldwide, including almost all the European countries. [36] Of the developing nations, the PSRA regularly conducts trade with most Middle Eastern states, such as Egypt, Libya, Iraq, Sudan, and Syria, as well as with Algeria, Tanzania, Zambia, Mexico, Guinea, and a few other African, Asian, and Latin American states. In 1970, Albanian exports to Egypt amounted to $3 million, and imports amounted to $1.6 million. In other years, Albania's exports amounted to an average of $0.5 million per year. [37] The 1977 agreement, however, provided for a total trade between Albania and Egypt of $7 million. [38] Albania's exports to Zambia in 1970 amounted to $0.6 million, and exports to Libya in 1974 rose to $1 million, while imports from both of these countries remained relatively small. However, Albania's imports from Morocco increased from $0.7 million in 1971-73, to $3.6 million in 1974, and $5.7 million in 1975. [39]

In early 1977, Albania proposed to Iran the negotiation of a barter trade and payments agreement, with a view of developing long-term trade exchanges. In February 1977, an Iranian trade delegation, headed by Khosrow Fazel, director general of the Ministry of Trade for European Countries, paid an official visit to Albania. Talks were held with the Albanian foreign trade minister and an agreement on trade and payments was signed. Through this agreement Albania hoped to secure a new market for its exports of raw materials, foodstuffs, cement, and timber and to purchase industrial goods from Iran. [40]

Albania does not publish data on its international trade. Also, most developing nations that trade with Albania do not provide statistics because of the insignificant amount of this trade. Thus, it is difficult to determine the exact volume of Albania's trade with the developing nations. But taking into account Albania's total trade with Eastern European and Western states, which can be calculated from statistics provided by these states, it can be concluded with some degree of certainty that Albania's Third World trade has not represented a significant percentage of the total volume of its foreign trade. However, since the break with China, political and economic considerations have come to play a greater role in Albania's policy toward the Third World, and prospects seem to be good for a further expansion in relations. Traditionally Albania has carried on the bulk of its trade with its foreign assistance donors. For more than a decade, China was Albania's major trading partner. During the last phase of this alliance, Albania's trade with China accounted for 35 to 40 percent of its total trade. [41] The economic break with China and China's subsequent refusal to trade with Albania has caused a major reorientation in Albania's foreign trade. While for the most part Albania has turned toward its trade partners in Europe, it is very likely that in the future the PSRA will display greater interest in improving trade relations with the Third World and particularly with the Middle Eastern states.

The political climate is favorable for better relations between the PSRA and the developing nations. For the first time in its modern history, Albania finds itself without a foreign protector. At odds with both the Eastern and the Western blocs, unaligned Albania has much in common with many developing states. In the wake of the Soviet invasion of Afghanistan, the APL's emphasis on the ever present Soviet menace to Albania and uncertainties concerning the foreign policy orentation of post-Tito Yugoslavia make Albania's association with the Third World all the more important for political as well as psychological reasons.

ALBANIA: A "MODEL" FOR THE THIRD WORLD?

Like most developing countries, the PSRA has been dependent on other countries for economic assistance. Between 1945 and 1978, Albania had run a continuous balance-of-payments deficit, which was covered by foreign assistance from Yugoslavia (1945-48), the Soviet Union (1949-61), and China (1962-78). This foreign aid, however, has been accompanied by high political costs, a serious compromise of decision-making autonomy, and, in the case of the alliance with Yugoslavia, a near loss of independence and sovereignty. Albania's historical experience with its aid donors has led to a perception that reliance on foreign assistance leads to economic dependence, which eventually compromises a nation's political independence. The Albanians believe that the best method of achieving economic independence and thus preserving political independence is through a policy of self-reliance.

Tiranë has recommended its principle of self-reliance to the developing nations as a feasible policy to eliminate their foreign dependence and achieve or strengthen their political independence. Developing countries have been warned against the dangers of excessive reliance on foreign assistance, joint economic ventures, foreign investments, and involvement by multinational corporations. According to Tiranë, these represent "nothing else but disguised forms of neocolonialism."[42] As one high-level Albanian official has observed,

> The "aid," credits, capital investments, joint companies of imperialists and social imperialists, are not a contribution to the development and progress of the backward countries. They are new shackles to enslave them, instruments to suck their blood, to plunder their wealth, to subjugate them and bring them to their knees. In the interest of world capital, wars and conflicts among peoples are fanned up, as has occurred and is occurring in the Middle East, Southeast Asia, Africa, and other regions of the world. [43]

Since World War II, Albania's foreign economic relations have followed its alliance pattern. Albania's political stance has determined its economic policy, and its economy has had to operate under politically imposed constraints. PSRA's economy has been characterized by a highly centralized economic management, with the APL exercising direct influence in all economic decisions. The primary economic objective of the APL has been to make Albania economically self-sufficient in as many sectors as possible and thus reduce or end its foreign dependence. In line with a typical Stalinist model of economic development, Albania has followed an ambitious policy of rapid industrialization, emphasizing heavy industry at the expense of the other sectors of the economy.

The Albanians began to stress the principle of self-reliance in the mid-1960s. However, it was only in the mid-1970s, when China sharply reduced its assistance, that self-reliance became the main element in Albania's economic development program. This policy was very unpopular with Albania's economic establishment. High-level economic officials seem to have recommended that the PSRA increase its trade with the West and abandon the policy of self-reliance. Hoxha, however, rejected this recommendation and initiated a purge of the top echelons of the economic establishment, which resulted in the political demise of such prominent officials as Abdyl Kellezi, chairman of the Planning Commission, Koço Theodhosi, minister of heavy industry and mining, and Kiço Ngjela, minister of trade. [44] As a result of this policy, Albania's trade with the West, which had shown a remarkable increase in the early 1970s, decreased sharply. Compared to 1975, in 1976 Albania's imports from West Germany declined by 71 percent, from Italy by 18 percent, and from Yugoslavia by 50 percent. [45]

PRSA's policy of self-reliance is based on rejection of foreign assistance, reliance on internal manpower and material resources, and the implementation of a strict savings regime. The PSRA is probably the only state in the world that has a constitutional provision prohibiting its government from seeking foreign aid and credits. Article 28 of the 1976 constitution states:

> The granting of concessions to, and the creation of foreign economic and financial companies and other institutions or ones formed jointly with bourgeois and revisionist capitalist monopolies and states as well as obtaining credits from them are prohibited in the People's Socialist Republic of Albania. [46]

The self-reliance policy also has its political and psychological aspects. The APL has sought to create the illusion that Albania has no alternative to an inward orientation because as the only truly Socialist state in the world, it is surrounded and blockaded by "imperialist" and "revisionist" states that are allegedly bent on its destruction. A psychology of siege has been created and is maintained by an extensive mass media campaign. In his report to the Seventh Congress of the APL, Mehmet Shehu, the chairman of the Council of Ministers, dwelt on Albania's alleged encirclement:

> To have a proper understanding of the situation of encir-
> clement and of personal responsibility to cope with this
> situation, to really think, work, and fight as in a state
> of siege, this is the primary condition to cope with the
> encirclement successfully.
> . . . The situation of encirclement and blockade is
> a state of war. The people must fight for the fulfillment
> of the state plan just as a military detachment in wartime
> fights to break the encirclement.
> In our conditions, the encirclement and blockade
> cannot be broken if we do not produce our bread at home,
> if we do not produce our spare parts at home, if we do
> not produce our oil at home, if we do not carry out the
> tasks of the state plan. [47] (emphasis added)

In the PSRA, the principle of self-reliance is being applied at all levels of economic activity: national, district, enterprise, agricultural cooperative, and individual. In a speech commemorating Albania's thirty-fifth anniversary of Communist rule in November 1979, Shehu reiterated APL's determination to pursue such a policy:

> When the APL states that it is constructing socialism by
> relying on the forces of the Albanian people, that means
> that Albania will never extend its hand for charity and
> credit to any capitalist or revisionist country. We will
> make do with what we have and, as the Albanian people
> say, we will stretch our legs as far as the blanket per-
> mits. [48] (emphasis added)

The PSRA has built a relative industrial base thanks to the foreign assistance it received from the Soviet Union and China. With the inauguration of such important projects as the hydroelectric station in Fierzë, the metallurgical combine in Elbasan, the autotractor combine in Tirana, the oil refinery in Ballsh, and the iron-nickel mine and upgrading factory in Guri i Kuq, Albania's economy has entered a new phase of development. Albania is close to achieving its objective of processing all its minerals locally. It is now producing its own pig iron and steel, and in the near future it will produce nickel and cobalt. These developments have increased Albania's exporting capacity. Thus, steel, pig iron, and other metal products that used to be imported are now being exported. Machinery and industrial equipment, including complete factories and plants as well as Albanianbrand tractors, are now being produced domestically. [49] The Albanian economy, according to official statistics, provides for more than 85 percent of the needs of its people for consumer goods and about 90 percent of the needs for spare parts and is self-sufficient in bread grains, electric energy, oil, and other products of the chemical industry. [50]

Despite these impressive gains, the Albanian economy is encountering many problems and is far from achieving overall self-sufficiency in the foreseeable future. Albania's economy has been hurt by the cut-off of Chinese economic and technical aid. The completion of many projects begun with China's assistance has been delayed. Resources are being devoted to high-cost industrial projects, and this is causing problems in the other sectors of the economy. In April 1979, Albania was also hit by an earthquake which caused tremendous damages in the northern districts of Shkoder and Lezhë. It was reported that 35 people died, and about 100,000 people remained homeless. In keeping with the spirit of self-reliance, the PSRA rejected all outside aid. After five months of intensive work, which involved nearly 20,000 specialists from all over Albania, close to 15,000 dwelling houses and flats and 165 various economic and socioeconomic objects were built or repaired. The work on the liquidation of the earthquake consequences apparently was a tremendous drain on Albania's resources and manpower. [51]

Despite the fact that the Sixth Five-Year Plan targets are modest in comparison to the preceeding plan, the results achieved so far have been disappointing. As Table 2.1 shows, shortfalls have been reported in the most important sectors of the economy. In January 1980 the Central Committee of the APL held its Seventh Plenum, which dealt with economic problems. [52] Despite the fact that the Albanian economy showed a modest growth during 1979, the overall plan targets were not met, and the Ministry of Heavy Industry and Mining and the Ministry of Food and Light Industry came under attack for problems in their sectors. [53] The governmental shuffle announced on April 27, 1980, may very well be a reflection of the severe economic problems that the PSRA is facing as a result of its implementation of a self-reliance policy. Xhafer Spahiu, the minister of industry and mines, was replaced by Prokup Murra, allegedly for "health reasons," and Kristaq Dollaku, the minister of food and light industry, was replaced by Esma Ulqinaku, for undisclosed reasons. Also, Mehmet Shehu gave up his post as minister of defense, while still retaining his influential position as chairman of the Council of Ministers. [54]

The implementation of self-reliance has necessitated a policy of import substitution. The PSRA is short of hard currency, and it

TABLE 2.1

Increase in Albanian Economic Indicators (percentage)

Indicator	1971–75 Actual	1976–80 Plan	1978 Plan	1978 Actual	1979 Plan	1979 Actual	1980 Plan
Industrial output	52	41–44	8.5	6.0	10.1	8.0	10.2
Agricultural output	33	38–41	28.0	N.A.	30.0	12.0	17.8
Investment	50	35–38	17.8	N.A.	12.0	7.6	7.6
Transport volume	45	30–32	8.2	N.A.	7.0	N.A.	10.4
Retail trade	35	22–25	7.4	N.A.	8.3	4.0	5.6
Labor productivity in industry	21	15–17	3.6	N.A.	9.0	N.A.	6.4
Labor productivity in construction	28	12–13	3.8	N.A.	5.0	N.A.	4.2
National income	38	38–40	12.2	N.A.	15.0	14.0	12.7
Exports	75	N.A.	10.0	N.A.	10.0	N.A.	32.0

Sources: Hasan Banja and Veniamin Toçi, Arritje e Perspektiva të Industrisë në RPS te Shqipërisë [Achievements and Perspectives in Industry in the PSR of Albania] (Tiranä: 8 Nëntori, 1978), pp. 91, 107; Zëri i Popullit, February 21, 1978, February 20, 1979, and February 12, 1980.

has mainly limited its imports to capital goods that will contribute to its achieving self-sufficiency. But in order to proceed with its industrialization the PSRA needs to import production and processing equipment to exploit its reserves of chrome, coal, copper, and iron ores. Albania is placing great emphasis on the expansion of its exports. The 1980 plan projects an export increase of 32 percent over 1979. An attempt is being made to replace exports of raw materials with refined or semi-manufactured products. In 1980, the locally processed goods will reportedly account for 65 percent of the total volume of Albania's exports. [55]

In recent years the PSRA has attempted to achieve economic development based on its own resources and at any price. From the available data on the performance of the Albanian economy it can be concluded with some certainty that the PSRA is in a position to sustain its economic growth by relying on its own forces. It must be pointed out, however, that Albania's self-reliance, such as it is, has been achieved thanks to the massive aid and credits received from the Soviet Union and China. The PSRA received about $5 billion in Chinese aid prior to the Tiranë-Beijing break in 1978. [56] By implementing a self-reliance policy, Albania will have to accept a relatively low rate of growth, which will have adverse consequences for its long-term economic development. Self-reliance is a heavy burden for a developing state such as Albania with a small population, small territory, and relatively limited resources. The cost of such a policy is extremely high and thus make it impractical for a country bent on rapid industrialization. The gap in economic development between Albania and other European nations has widened, and the standard of living, which is already the lowest in Europe, will most likely remain low in the foreseeable future. All these factors are bound to cause dissatisfaction among economic administrators and the population in general, and this dissatisfaction could have an adverse effect on the increase in productivity. The PSRA lacks sufficient experts and administrative cadres to make use of a modern and sophisticated technology, and it will have to rely on its present technological level, which in the long run will contribute to its lagging behind.

The Albanian propaganda machine has portrayed the PSRA as a successful example of "rejecting the practice of borrowing from capitalist or revisionist countries as being alien and unacceptable"[57] and has maintained that self-reliance is the best method to achieve economic independence and thus avoid foreign influence and exploitation. Many developing nations, especially those that have experienced the dangers and consequences of depending on foreign assistance and markets, have been attracted by this policy. Also, changes in world markets, drastic price increases for many essential imports, and the benefits of policy-making independence have made self-reliance an attractive policy option.

Although the principle of self-reliance may be desirable, it is not a practical policy for the less developed countries. The main objective of these nations is to achieve a higher degree of development, usually through industrialization. If these nations were to implement a policy of self-reliance, such as that practiced by the PSRA, it would be highly unlikely that they could achieve their economic objectives. Many developing states, in contrast to Albania, are characterized by large populations, lack of natural resources, high illiteracy, lack of national cohesiveness, and regime instability. These variables make the PSRA a less than ideal model for the developing nations to follow in their development strategy.

Most developing nations are extremely poor and have yet to achieve an industrial base, even on the level of that of Albania. Thus foreign aid is necessary to create the conditions required for economic self-sufficiency before a developing nation can even attempt to embark on a self-reliance policy. Reliance on foreign assistance is not desirable, but it is a more practical policy for economic development than self-reliance. Contrary to Tiranë's insistence, foreign assistance does not necessarily lead to political dependence. The rational use of foreign aid as a supplement to one's own domestic resources will undoubtedly contribute to economic development. Many developing nations that have relied on foreign aid and credits have been able to preserve their decision-making autonomy, and their political independence does not seem to have been seriously compromised.

The implementation of a policy of self-reliance involves autarky and requires radical social reforms. The APL has been able to undertake massive social reforms because of the authoritarian nature of Albania's regime, the grip it holds over the country, and the PSRA's isolation from the rest of the world. Albania has a command-type economy characterized by the abolition of private property, state ownership of the means of production, collectivization, and a highly centralized planning and administrative structure. The political and economic systems of developing nations differ radically from those of the PSRA. A fundamental change would have to take place in their political and economic systems for these states to embark on a policy of self-reliance.

Environmental constraints in many developing nations further preclude the application of Albania's model of self-reliance. The PSRA is relatively rich in natural resources such as chrome ore, copper ore, natural gas, iron ore, lignite, and oil, and in recent years it has become an energy exporting nation. Most developing nations, however, do not have important natural resources. Thus they have no realistic policy options but to rely on foreign aid, credits, and investments. Third World countries lack experienced economic administrators and experts to direct even their present unsophisticated economies; therefore they need technical and administrative assistance. A policy of self-reliance would in the long run impede the economic development of Third World nations. China's abandonment of this policy and the adoption of a more realistic approach toward foreign assistance, investments, and even joint economic ventures testifies to the impracticability of the self-reliance policy. In today's interdependent world, it is unrealistic to follow a policy of going it alone, as the PSRA is attempting to do.

Albania's unique strategy of development has been conditioned by its particular ideological and political considerations as well as the Communist regime's fear of adopting a more realistic policy and ending its isolation from the rest of the world. Albania's extremely repressive internal policies as well as its militant foreign policy have not found much appeal in the Third World. Despite attempts to portray itself as a "model," the PSRA has remained a relatively unimportant source of inspiration or influence for the developing nations.

NOTES

1. For a general review of Albanian developments since 1945, see Nicholas C. Pano, The People's Republic of Albania (Baltimore: Johns Hopkins University Press, 1968); and Peter R. Prifti, Socialist Albania Since 1944: Domestic and Foreign Developments (Cambridge, Mass.: MIT Press, 1978).
2. Kushtetuta e Republikës Popullore Socialiste të Shqipërisë [The Constitution of the People's Socialist Republic of Albania] (Tiranë: 1976).
3. Zëri i Popullit, July 7, 1977.
4. Enver Hoxha, Report Submitted to the 6th Congress of the Party of Labor of Albania (Tiranë: Naim Frashëri, 1971), p. 30.
5. Enver Hoxha, Report Submitted to the 7th Congress of the Party of Labor of Albania (Tiranë: 8 Nëntori, 1976), p. 166.
6. U.S., Department of State, Bureau of Intelligence and Research, Trade of NATO Countries with Communist Countries, 1975-1978, Report no. 1275, November 28, 1979; and Business Eastern Europe 9, no. 11 (March 14, 1980): 85.
7. See Enver Hoxha, Imperialism and the Revolution (Tiranë: 8 Nëntori, 1979); and Reflections on China, vol. 2 (Tiranë: 8 Nëntori, 1979).
8. Hoxha, Report to the 7th Congress, pp. 172-73.
9. Hoxha, Imperialism and the Revolution, pp. 50-61, 326-35.
10. Iro Vito, "The Theory of Nonaligned Countries at the Service of the Superpowers, the Bourgeoisie and Reaction," Bashkimi, February 9, 1979.

11. Peking Review, no. 16 (April 19, 1974): 6-11.

12. Ibid. , p. 11.

13. "Notes on Teng Hsiao-ping's Speech at the 1977 CCP CC Plenum," Background on China (Chinese Information Service, New York), B. 78-006, May 17, 1978, p. 3.

14. "The Theory and Practice of the Revolution," Zëri i Popullit, July 7, 1977.

15. Hoxha, Imperialism and the Revolution, pp. 260-61.

16. Priamo Bollano and Lulxim Hana, "The New International Economic Order—A New Attempt for the Perpetuation of the Enslavement and Exploitation of the Peoples," Rruga e Partisë (December 1978): 48-49.

17. Hoxha, Reflections on China, p. 351.

18. Hoxha, Imperialism and the Revolution, pp. 252-314.

19. Hoxha, Report to the 6th Congress, p. 226.

20. Hoxha, Imperialism and the Revolution, pp. 200, 210.

21. Kongresi VII i PPSH (The Seventh Congress of the APL) (Tiranë: 8 Nëntori, 1977), pp. 8-10.

22. Rruga e Partisë (February 1977): 84-89.

23. Agim Popa, "The Marxist-Leninist Parties—the Leading Force of the Revolutionary Movement Today," in Instituti i Studimeve Marksiste-Leniniste Pranë KQ të PPSH, Probleme të zhvillimit të sotëm botëror (Problems of Current World Development) (Tiranë: 8 Nëntori, 1979), pp. 63, 71.

24. Halil, General Secretary of the Peasants and Workers Party of Iran, "Proletarian Internationalism," ibid. , p. 157. For statements by other Third World Marxist-Leninist parties, see pp. 239-48, and 459-72.

25. "Full Text of Huang Hua's 42,000-Word Foreign Policy Address," Background on China, B. 77-012, December 26, 1977, p. 14.

26. Hoxha, Imperialism and the Revolution, pp. 177-81; and also Hoxha, Report to the 7th Congress, p. 208.

27. Zëri i Popullit, April 15, 22, 1980.

28. Ibid. , February 18, 1979, January 19, 1979.

29. Ibid. , June 6, 1980.

30. Ibid. , January 5, 1980.

31. Ibid. , April 13, 1980.

32. Kongresi i 8-të i BPSH [The 8th Congress of the Trade Unions of Albania] (Tiranë, 1977), pp. 6-7.

33. The 8th Congress of the Women's Union of Albania (Tiranë: 8 Nëntori, 1978), pp. 13-14.

34. Zëri i Popullit, August 23, 1978.

35. Ibid. , August 22, 23, 24, 1979.

36. Albanian Foreign Trade (Tiranë, December 1979).

37. Michael Kaser, "Trade and Aid in the Albanian Economy,"

in East European Economies Post-Helsinki, Joint Economic Committee, Congress of the United States (Washington, D.C.: Government Printing Office, 1977), p. 1331.

38. Quarterly Economic Review of Rumania, Bulgaria, Albania no. 3 (Economist Intelligence Unit, London, 1977): 19.

39. Kaser, "Trade and Aid in the Albanian Economy," p. 1331.

40. Tiranë Domestic Service, in Albanian, 1900 GMT, February 26, 1977, March 3, 1977; Teheran Domestic Service, in Persian, 1030 GMT, February 26, 1977; and Quarterly Economic Review of Rumania, Bulgaria, Albania, no. 2 (1977): 23.

41. Petro Dode, "On the Fulfillment of the Plan and State Budget for 1978, and the Draft Plan and State Draft Budget for 1979," Probleme Ekonomike, no. 1 (1979): 5.

42. ATA (Albanian Telegraphic Agency), in English, 0900 GMT, August 30, 1979.

43. Ramiz Alia, "The Revolution—A Question Put Forward for Solution," in Instituti i Studimeve Marksiste-Leninste Pranë KQ të PPSH, Probleme të zhvillimit të sotëm botëror, p. 15.

44. Nicholas C. Pano, "Albania in the 1970s," Problems of Communism (November-December 1977): 39-40. See also Petro Dode, "The Enemy Group of A. Kellezi, K. Theodhosi, and K. Ngjela and the Struggle for Their Elimination," in Instituti i Studimeve Marksiste-Leniniste Pranë KQ të PPSH, Sesione Shkencore për Luftën e Klasave [Scientific Session in the Class Struggle] (Tiranë: 8 Nëntori, 1977), pp. 167-82.

45. Business Eastern Europe 6, no. 42 (October 21, 1977): 334.

46. Kushtetuta, article 28.

47. Mehmet Shehu, Report on the Directives of the 7th Congress of the Party of Labor of Albania for the 6th Five-Year Plan (1976-1980) of Economic and Cultural Development of the People's Republic of Albania (Tiranë: 8 Nëntori, 1976), pp. 81, 84.

48. Zëri i Popullit, November 29, 1979.

49. Albanian Foreign Trade (November 1978, March 1979, August 1979).

50. Ibid. (February 1979); Zëri i Popullit, September 2, 1979, March 26, 1980; and Dode, "On the Fulfillment of the Plan and State Budget for 1978, and the Draft Plan and State Draft Budget for 1979," p. 6.

51. ATA, in English, 0900 GMT, October 3, 1979.

52. Zëri i Popullit, January 17, 1980.

53. Ibid., February 12, 13, 1980.

54. Ibid., April 27, 1980.

55. Albanian Foreign Trade (January 1978), (June 1979); and ATA News Bulletin, March 19, 1980.

56. New York Times, July 14, 1978.

57. Zëri i Popullit, November 22, 1978.

3

CZECHOSLOVAKIA AND THE THIRD WORLD

Vratislav Pechota

Czechoslovakia is a landlocked country in the heart of Europe with a population of over 15 million and perennial concerns about political and economic survival. Its natural, geographic, demographic, and socioeconomic conditions make its economy heavily dependent on transnational trade. The advanced and structurally diversified processing industry depends to a great extent on imports of primary commodities, fuels and minerals, and on exports of manufactured goods. Imports cover a considerable part of the consumption, especially of foodstuffs as well as consumer goods. This held true in the past and holds true even more at present. Moreover, the growth of the manufacturing sector stimulated by technological progress requires huge outlays for modern machinery and equipment abroad.

Historically the society and its economy have been accustomed to interacting with other economies in a broader transnational framework. Throughout the Middle Ages, the Kingdom of Bohemia was an important part of the loosely federated Holy Roman Empire; its ties to other parts of the empire and to the outside world were extensive. Prague, the capital city, was a bustling trade center habitually visited by merchants from lands as distant as the Levant and North Africa. Ibrahim Ibn Jakub, a tenth-century Levantine merchant, left a vivid account of the traffic at Ungelt, the Prague trading place, referring to it as a place where the West and East meet. [1]

Bohemia and Moravia became the workshop of the Hapsburg Empire in the nineteenth century; the bulk of the Austrian manufacturing industry was concentrated in the cities of Prague, Brno, Plzeň, Ostrava, and Liberec. Austria was the only European power that did not possess overseas colonies; so the access to overseas markets had to be secured through an energetic pursuit of foreign trade. Bohemian and Moravian manufacturers and the Vienna bureaucracy joined forces in establishing the renowned Oriental Academy, whose task was to prepare diplomatic, consular, and trade personnel needed to extend Austria's political and economic presence throughout Asia and Africa.

PREWAR VENTURES

The creation of the independent Czechoslovak Republic in 1918 freed the Czech and Slovak economies of the bureaucratic controls of the Vienna government and gave industry a new impetus. The new democratic constitutional framework and liberal trade regulations spurred the rise of big corporations seeking access to less competitive markets outside Europe. The late 1920s and early 1930s saw the formation of multinational corporations with interests in Asia, Africa, and Latin America, the Baťa Shoe Company in Zlín being an example. By 1939, Baťa's factories and sales outlets had spread over five continents of the globe. In India alone, the Baťa Shoe Company employed several thousand workers in its factory in Batanagar (a town named after the Czech manufacturer). Other corporations heavily engaged in business activities in countries outside Europe included the Škoda Works in Plzeň; the Vitkovické Železárny in Ostrava-Vítkovice, the Českomoravská Kolben-Daněk in Prague, and the První Brněnská Strojírna in Brno. The Škoda Works was one of the foremost arms producers in the world, on a par with Vickers in Great Britain and Schneider-Creusot in France. No wonder, then, that in the 1930s Czechoslovakia occupied second place among arms-exporting nations.[2]

External economic activities were unhindered by government regulations, and matters regarding tariffs and taxation were satisfactorily settled in treaties of commerce and navigation which Czechoslovakia concluded with a great number of countries, including such non-European nations as Afghanistan, Bolivia, Brazil, Ecuador, Egypt, Iran, and Liberia. Treaties with Belgium, France, the Netherlands, Portugal, Spain, and the United Kingdom included clauses according most-favored-nation status in overseas territories to Czechoslovak exporters.

The prewar Czechoslovak Republic had no political ambitions toward what is now called the Third World. As an ally of major European colonial powers (France, Great Britain), it respected the existing structure of political relationship in Africa, Asia, and Latin America, but in its own dealings with these continents it proceeded along the principles of equality and mutual advantage. In this way Czechoslovakia succeeded in creating a reservoir of good will, which became an asset during the tragic years after Munich and in the postwar period.

RENEWED TIES

Unlike other countries of Eastern Europe, postwar Czechoslovakia was no newcomer to cooperation with the various regions of the Third World. It had a background derived from years of commercial experience in Asia, Africa, and Latin America and did not have to experiment at any length in creating a policy toward these continents. It could effectively use the wide network of diplomatic and consular contacts maintained throughout the war by the government-in-exile and build upon its reputation as a loyal and reliable friend of underprivileged nations. Leaders in the developing countries did not associate Czechoslovakia with attitudes of superiority, nor did they yet regard its overtures with the suspicion that it was acting as a surrogate; that issue did not arise until after February 1948. Czechoslovakia could elaborate the principles of its relations with the Third World and credibly employ the vocabulary of self-determination, equality, independence and nonintervention in internal affairs.

At the time when the Soviet Union and most of Eastern Europe were only marginally involved in economic dealings with distant countries, Czechoslovakia succeeded in developing active commercial ties with many parts of Asia, Africa, and Latin America. Its products, including investment goods, found easy access into the hungry postwar markets and made trade with Czechoslovakia attractive, especially to those countries which, like Iran in the early 1950s, were eager to lessen their dependence on the West.

The external economic policy pursued by Czechoslovakia between 1945 and 1948 was predominantly practical and nonideological. It was oriented almost exclusively to trade and did not demonstrate any significant element of aid philosophy. It rested on the prewar treaty foundations and was conceived in traditional terms of reciprocal trade agreements with an assurance of nondiscrimination. Complementing these bilateral arrangements was Czechoslovakia's membership in the General Agreement on Tariffs and Trade (GATT), the International Monetary Fund (IMF), and the International Bank for Reconstruction and Development (IBRD). *

---

*Czechoslovakia signed the General Agreement on October 30, 1947, and has remained a member of GATT. It is the only Socialist country with original and full membership in GATT (Yugoslavia and Poland acceded to the General Agreement in 1958 and 1959, respectively, as members of a special category). Czechoslovakia was an original member of the IMF and the IBRD but terminated its membership in 1954.

ECONOMICS OR IDEOLOGY?

It was only after 1948 that the rationale for Czechoslovakia's policies toward developing countries identified political and ideological motives as constantly dominant. The change was part of the overall shift toward the Stalinist policy of militant "anti-imperialism" occasioned by the February 1948 Communist party takeover. Material motives for cooperation with the Third World were not set aside completely, but ideological objectives clearly underlied the approach to relations with Third World countries. Czechoslovakia's view held that trade constituted a form of development aid and countries that showed greater independence from the West should be given more aid so that no opportunity was missed for encouraging nations to accept economic and political systems that would favor Socialist values.

Ironically, at the very time when the issue of economic relations with the Third World assumed an ideological dimension and aid policy was geared toward winning over the uncommitted nations to a Socialist point of view, the physical volume of the Czechoslovak trade with the potential political allies was steadily declining (see Table 3.1).

TABLE 3.1

Czechoslovak Trade with Developing Countries, 1948-53 (millions of Kčs)

Trade Year	Total Turnover	Index (1948 = 100)
1948	1,536	100
1949	1,305	85
1950	958	63
1951	1,275	83
1952	1,011	66
1953	904	59

Source: Postavení ČSR ve světovém hospodářství (Prague: Orbis, 1957), p. 113.

Aside from the fact that only a handful of developing countries qualified for ideologically motivated cooperation at the time, the decline was due primarily to the isolation in which Czechoslovakia found itself in the wake of the 1948 about-face and also to the increasing tendency to autarky within the Socialist bloc. To justify its isolationist policy, the government put the blame on the "capitalist encirclement" that allegedly forced the country to change its economic and trade patterns and to seek economic security in close cooperation with the Soviet Union. As a result, the Soviet Union became Czechoslovakia's all-purpose purveyor of raw materials, fuels, agricultural produce, and foodstuffs and an insatiable outlet for its manufactures. Its vast industrialization programs in turn created an immense market for the Czechoslovak manufacturing industry, removing all economic incentives for Czechoslovakia to expand its exports to and imports from the developing countries.

When the question of decolonization and self-determination of previously dependent peoples and countries came up on the international agenda in the late 1950s Czechoslovakia was provided with an opportunity to renew its old ties to the Third World and to create new ones. In view of the anticipated needs of its growing industry, Czechoslovakia regarded it essential for the future to establish its economic presence in the newly emerging countries. However, it did not neglect the political and military contacts, which offered a welcome opportunity to play a role in international affairs after a long period of reduced international activity. The role that Czechoslovakia assumed with regard to the Third World in the decade of 1955-65 was both ambitious and significant.

In the political and diplomatic field, Czechoslovakia sought to impress upon the developing countries the idea that the commonality of interests predestined the Socialist and the developing countries to mutual cooperation and informal alliance. Its active involvement in the process of implementing the 1960 United Nations Declaration on the Granting of Independence to Colonial Countries and Peoples[3] served to assure the Third World of full solidarity with its fundamental demands. Specific joint initiatives by Czechoslovakia and Asian, African, and Latin American states in the United Nations show the extent of mutual cooperation. Perhaps most important was Czechoslovakia's proposal in 1962, supported by a group of nonaligned countries, for the elaboration and enunciation of principles of international law concerning friendly relations and cooperation among states. [4] It purported to codify the new international balance created by the emergence of many new states and demanded a fundamental review of basic principles of international law, with a view to bringing them into conformity with the new international realities. Among other things, the Czechoslovak draft declaration affirmed that "peoples have an inalienable right to eliminate colonial domination and to carry on the struggle, by whatever means, for their liberation, independence and free government,"[5] a proposition de lege ferenda which the anticolonial majority in the United Nations was quick to adopt as a doctrine justifying assistance to the liberation struggles in Angola, Mozambique, and Rhodesia and elsewhere in Africa. The Czechoslovak initiative developed into a major item on the U. N. agenda until the General Assembly adopted a declaration on the subject in 1970. [6]

Another Czechoslovak initiative with implications for the Third World concerned an issue of vital interest to the least privileged developing nations, the landlocked countries. In preparation for the First United Nations Conference on the Law of the Sea, Czechoslovakia, together with Afghanistan and Bolivia, proposed to formulate an agreed position among landlocked countries on the law in force relating to access to the sea by countries having no coast of their own. They convened a special preliminary conference in Geneva in February 1958, which drafted an expository code (sometimes unofficially called the "Magna Charta of Landlocked Countries") purporting to become a part of the codified law of the sea. [7] The underlying principle of the document, namely that the landlocked countries are entitled to special rights compensating for the gross inequalities created as a result of their unfavorable geographical position, has had considerable appeal to almost two score of landlocked and geographically disadvantaged countries of the Third World and continues to dominate their current search for preferences in the context of the ongoing negotiations on a new comprehensive regime of the sea. [8]

NONGOVERNMENTAL OFFENSIVE

An important role in the Czechoslovak political offensive in the South has been assigned to nongovernmental organization. In 1962 the Czechoslovak National Front established a Committee of Solidarity with the Peoples of Africa and Asia. Its task was twofold: first, to win the support of the public for political and economic involvement in the Third World; second, to seek direct access to "progressive" organizations and the "masses" in African and Asian countries. The committee organized solidarity campaigns and distributed its publications, including Solidarity—A Monthly Magazine of Czechoslovak-African Relations, throughout Africa.

Closely collaborating with the committee was the Czechoslovak Society for International Relations, a prestigious organization of civic leaders, academics, and men and women of science, arts, and letters. Its specific tasks included developing contacts with nongovernmental institutions in the Third World and encouraging local groups there to establish leagues of friendship with Czechoslovakia; 27 such leagues were in existence in 1964.

The picture would be incomplete without mentioning the activities of Marxist-oriented international organizations. Three of them had their headquarters in Prague and were substantially subsidized by the Czechoslovak government and staffed largely by Czechoslovak personnel. The first, the International Union of Students, concentrated mainly on recruiting Third World students to study in the Socialist countries; it also sought a role in organizing leftist student alliances in the African, Asian, and Latin American countries and exposed them to its influence.

The second, the International Organization of Journalists, served as a channel of assistance provided by Czechoslovak institutions to newly emerging nations in the field of mass information. In 1961, the IOJ sent a team of Czechoslovak instructors to Guinea to run a school for journalists and helped arrange for direct servicing of the local press by the Czechoslovak News Agency (ČTK). In Mali, the IOJ established an office for coordinating aid to the fledgling national communications media. Under its auspices, the Czechoslovak News Agency held courses and seminars for journalists from the Third World and sent its experts to several African countries to advise on the organization of news services.

Still another group, the World Federation of Trade Unions, provided an outlet for spreading Socialist ideas throughout the Third World and for securing a foothold in the labor movement. Hundreds of union officers from Asia, Africa, and Latin America were invited to attend special programs in Czechoslovakia in order to get "first-hand knowledge of a state run by workers and peasants."

Most of these activities were financed by the Czechoslovak treasury, and they put a considerable strain on the government's resources. However, no one was allowed to question the wisdom of the enterprise, and the goal was regarded as politically expedient.

INFLUENCE THROUGH ARMS SUPPLY

Ideological commitments provided an excellent justification to resume Czechoslovakia's traditional role as the world tradesman in arms. The case of the Czechoslovak-Egyptian arms deal in 1955 best illustrates the point. On September 27, 1955, President Nasser announced that an agreement had been signed under which Czechoslovakia would supply arms to Egypt in exchange for such Egyptian products as cotton and rice. He said that the Egyptian government had taken the step "after its repeated failure to obtain arms from the Western countries on conditions compatible with the aims of the Egyptian revolution."[9] Grave concern was aroused in the Western countries and Israel, which on October 4 informed the Czechoslovak government that it regarded the sale of arms to Egypt as an "unfriendly act" and tantamount to abetting aggression. Three Western powers, France, the

United Kingdom, and the United States, expressed their dismay at the huge purchase, which comprised, according to Western estimates, some 300 tanks, 100 artillery pieces, 200 jet fighters, and 60 heavy bombers. [10] It was clear that the Soviet Union was behind the deal and that the step was calculated as the start of Soviet involvement in the Arab-Israeli conflict. In any case, it raised the embryonic arms race in the Middle East to an altogether higher plane. As could have been expected, Israel reacted by claiming that the deal implied a political and military link-up between Egypt and the Warsaw Pact and appealed to the Western powers to supply new weapons to the Israeli Army and to conclude a security pact with the Israeli government. [11]

Of course, Czechoslovakia did not reap the strategic benefits appropriated by Moscow. But the involvement bolstered the spirit of the Czechoslovak government, which took pride in effectively assisting the "world revolutionary process." From that time on, Czechoslovakia has engaged in large-scale deliveries of arms to nationalist governments and revolutionary movements in the Third World. In the same year when it concluded the agreement with Egypt, it offered military assistance to Syria, Iraq, and Indonesia. Quite naturally, it was on the side of the Algerian revolution against the French, and that involvement developed into a serious diplomatic conflict when, in April 1959, a Czechoslovak freighter, the Lidice, with 600 tons of arms on board, was intercepted by the French Navy off the Moroccan coast and taken to Oran. The French authorities alleged that the arms were intended for the "Algerian rebels," while the Czechoslovak government insisted that the act of seizure constituted a flagrant violation of the freedom of the high seas. [12] The French eventually released the ship, but only after having unloaded and confiscated the cargo.

The first significant Czechoslovak arms client in sub-Saharan Africa was Sékou Touré's Guinea. A Czechoslovak military mission arrived in the country in March 1959, and at the same time a cargo of arms, ammunition, and military vehicles was delivered to the newly organized Guinean military establishment. Mr. Telli, Guinea's permanent representative to the United Nations soon afterward stated in New York, "Our army is now fully equipped." [13]

Castro's Cuba also had turned to Czechoslovakia for military assistance before it began to tap the resources of the Soviet Union. At the time, Czechoslovakia was the most self-sufficient of all the Eastern European nations outside the Soviet Union: it produced its own high-quality small arms, crew-served weapons, jet training aircraft, and, under license, tanks and jet fighters. Czechoslovak hardware was a success item of the East-South trade in the 1950s, since its components ideally fitted the needs of middle-size non-European countries. It is interesting to note that the "golden age" of the Czechoslovak-Third World arms trade did not last long. As Table 3.2 shows,

TABLE 3. 2

Exports of Arms from Czechoslovakia and the Soviet Union to
the Third World, 1954–73
(millions of dollars, at constant 1973 prices)

Year	Czechoslovakia	Soviet Union
1954	—	6
1955	43	62
1956	58	145
1957	6	252
1958	23	193
1959	58	108
1960	45	158
1961	5	374
1962	5	773
1963	12	326
1964	7	276
1965	3	398
1966	6	590
1967	9	861
1968	30	571
1969	17	588
1970	24	786
1971	11	1003
1972	10	570
1973	1	1175

Source: SIPRI, Arms Trade Register: The Arms Trade with
the Third World (Stockholm: Almquist and Wiksell International,
1975), pp. 150–51.

exports declined sharply after 1960, as the role of the main supplier
shifted to the Soviet Union (see Table 3. 2).

TRADE AND AID OFFENSIVE

In the economic field, Czechoslovakia soon discovered that the
trade patterns of the past were not applicable to the newly emerging
nations. An analysis of the Czechoslovak economic thrust between
1955 and the early 1960s shows that its reaction to the new realities

in the Third World was prompt and effective. With an eye to the changing balance of political forces in the world, Czechoslovakia seized every opportunity to win the confidence of the new countries and to convince them of the advantages of cooperation with the Socialist countries. Its main ideological argument was that developing countries were necessarily impeded by capitalist-oriented trade in achieving the social and economic goals that socialism would give them more quickly and painlessly. Pointing out that industrialization was the prerequisite for the development of independent national life, it offered assistance in achieving this end. More important, it urged the developing countries to build a state-owned industrial sector, which could become the basis for a planned economy. It argued that an independent state with a viable economy was the most reliable shield against domination by foreign capital. Finally, it stressed the importance of economic cooperation with the Socialist countries as an alternative to Third World dependence on Western capital markets and promised that Czechoslovakia would commit its resources to industrial aid.

Although inspired by ideology, the offensive did not lose sight of the fact that development aid constituted a basic investment in the aiding country's future customers and markets and that the involvement had become imperative in the face of growing international competition among industrialized nations. Well aware of the fact that it could hardly compete with Western exports of capital goods in volume and technological aspects, Czechoslovakia adopted a policy under which the available resources would be directed to the support of countries that experienced difficulties in the Western markets and that could be relied upon both as political friends and suppliers of vital commodities.

A clear expression of this strategy was the concept of "countries of priority interest," which included nations in Asia, Africa, and Latin America that had a strong neutralist, if not anti-Western, tendency and were likely to pursue a noncapitalist path of development, including nationalization of their natural resources. Given the Socialist penchant for constancy, Czechoslovakia believed that its interests would be best served through long-term agreements on trade and payments supplemented, where necessary, by agreements on scientific and technical cooperation and credit arrangements.

It must be noted, in this connection, that the Czechoslovak understanding of development aid never encompassed the charitable notion of transfer of resources without compensation. Development aid has always been viewed as a process of economic cooperation offering advantages to both parties. Although the transfer of resources from the government of one country to that of another should be realized on terms easier than those that can be obtained in the private capital market,[14] the quid pro quo remained an integral element of the relationship.

YEARS OF HEAVY ENGAGEMENT

In the first stage, such agreements were concluded with Burma (1955), Cambodia (1956), Ceylon (1955), Egypt (1955), India (1957), Indonesia (1956), Iraq (1959), Sudan (1955), Syria (1952), and Yemen (1956). The next stage coincided with the "African emancipation years" of 1959-61. Because of its record as a staunch supporter of decolonization and also because of its ties with African liberation movements and many radical leaders during their exile in Europe, Czechoslovakia succeeded in creating a web of treaty relationships extending from North Africa (Algeria) to the Congo Basin. Intimate relations with Guinea had begun in 1958, when the country became an independent republic and rejected participation in the proposed French Community. A treaty with Ghana was concluded in 1960, with the manifest object of helping Ghana accelerate its transformation from an essentially agricultural, tribal society into a modern semi-industrialized state and assist it along "the road to socialism." Strong ties with Mali developed after that country withdrew from the French Community in 1960, and proclaimed its ideological commitment to socialism. The involvement in the Congo (Leopoldville) started in 1960, during the Lumumba period, and culminated in a 1961 treaty with Gizenga. Disappointed by the turn of events in the Congo, the Czechoslovak government joined in the ostracism of U.N. Secretary-General Dag Hammarskjöld and did nothing to prevent violent outbursts by African students in Prague against the Belgian and Swedish embassies. Relations with Algeria became especially close after the country acceded to independence in 1962. Czechoslovak military aid during the revolutionary war paid off, and Prague soon established its presence in the Maghreb. The treaties with Algeria, Tunisia, and Morocco constituted the backbone of an extensive economic, scientific-technical, and cultural cooperation, mostly to fill the void left by France. The first economic mission to visit Cuba after the 1959 revolution and to enter into agreements on trade relations and aid was that from Czechoslovakia. The extent of the Czechoslovak commitment in the first two years of Castro's regime surpassed aid to any other country.

To be sure, other Eastern European countries launched similar programs, but for some years Czechoslovak aid remained the most extensive. It consisted essentially in the supply of investment goods and military hardware; consistently rising from year to year here, however, various forms of technical assistance, especially in training national personnel. This volume of the aid was reflected in the turnover of trade (see Table 3.3).

The fact that exports considerably exceeded imports must, of course, be attributed to long-term credit arrangements. It is estimated that the credits extended to Third World countries over the ten-

TABLE 3.3

Czechoslovak Trade with the Developing Countries, 1955-65 (millions of Kčs)

Trade Year	Total Turnover	Exports	Imports
1955	2,149	1,221	928
1960	2,814	1,535	1,279
1962	2,893	1,642	1,251
1963	3,076	1,628	1,448
1964	3,217	1,796	1,421
1965	3,408	1,901	1,507

Source: Statistická ročenka ČSSR 1966 (Prague: Nakladatelství technické literatury, 1966), p. 426.

year period between 1955 and 1964 reached the sum of $400-500 million and accounted for some 60 percent of all Eastern European financial assistance (outside the Soviet Union) to the Third World.[15] These figures exclude credits made available to Cuba. Some analysts estimate that Czechoslovak financial aid to Castro between 1959 and 1964 amounted to another $430 million.[16]

The loan contracts were geared to particular projects being financed, and their terms were clearly concessional: they usually stipulated an interest rate of 2.5 percent, a grace period, and long periods of repayment. The following examples provide evidence on which to base an evaluation of the credit terms:

1. An agreement with Egypt in September 1957 provided for a grant of aid to the equivalent of £22 million in the form of credit for the supply of capital equipment in connection with Egypt's industrialization program. Egypt was to start repayment of the credits received after five years, in annual installments spread over a 12-year period.[17]

2. The Indo-Czechoslovak Agreement on Economic Cooperation of November 24, 1959, whereby (1) Czechoslovakia made available to India a long-term credit amounting to 231 million rupees, bearing 2.5 percent interest per annum and repayable within eight years. The credit was designated for purchases of Czechoslovak machinery and equipment for a forge plant at Ranchi, machine-tool building and electrical plants, and other projects included in the Indian Third Five-Year Plan. India was to make repayments by deliveries of such goods

as pig iron, chemical products, nonferrous metals, iron and manganese ore, and jute, the proportionate first installment for each project becoming due one year after completion of the final delivery of equipment for the project concerned. [18]

3. Another credit agreement signed on May 11, 1964, whereby Czechoslovakia provided to India a loan amounting to 400 million rupees for the expansion of the Tiruchirapalli Boiler Plant and the Hyderabad Heavy Electricals Plants, as well as for setting up additional foundry and forge facilities at Ranchi. The credit on similar terms as the above was repayable in rupees, which were to be used for the purchases by Czechoslovakia of Indian exports; the repayment period was ten years. [19]

4. An agreement with Indonesia dated July 19, 1959, whereby Czechoslovakia undertook to supply complete factories, industrial equipment, and other capital goods to Indonesia on long-term credit terms to a total value of 12 million rupiah. [20]

5. The Czechoslovak-Iraqi Agreement on Economic Cooperation of October 23, 1959, providing for the construction by Czechoslovakia of oil refinery installations and thermal and hydroelectric plants in Iraq and the granting to Iraq of a Czechoslovak credit of 12 million dinars. [21]

6. By an agreement concluded in 1957, Syria received a loan of 108 million Kčs for the construction by Czechoslovakia of an oil refinery at Homs,* to be repaid within ten years. [22]

7. Pakistan accepted in the fall of 1963 a loan of $40 million on very soft terms to construct cement factories and sugar-refining plants. The terms provided for ten years' maturity and 2.5 percent interest. [23]

The fervor with which Czechoslovakia pursued its aid strategy began losing momentum in the mid-1960s. Some of Czechoslovakia's debtors were experiencing such severe difficulties in servicing their debts that they sought postponement of payments or outright cancellation of the unpaid balance. Czechoslovakia came to realize that it had overextended its foreign aid potential and was no longer able to shoulder the commitments involved. The country's economy went into another round of recession, and future political stability depended largely upon economic growth; any misallocation of resources therefore posed serious long-term threats. As the leading Czechoslovak economist of

----

*The refinery was destroyed by Israeli bombers during the 1973 Arab-Israeli war and a new Czechoslovak loan enabled its reconstruction.

that time, Ota Šik, put it, "For an unbalanced economy even quite
small credits can prove an enormous burden, not to mention the fact
that a less demanding market fails to exert pressure toward profitable
performance."[24] In addition, the public began to raise objections to
aid on the ground that it slackened the economy and reduced the already stagnant rate of progress in the standard of living.

THE PERIOD OF REASSESSMENT

The issue of foreign aid burst into open discussion in 1968. The
context was provided by a critical reexamination of the Czechoslovak
economic policy which many described as a failure. The chief com-
plaint was that the economy operated ineffectively, was constrained
by bureaucratic methods of management, and crippled by a wasteful
wave of investments that were beyond the country's capabilities. The
critics pointed out that to avoid salutory confrontation with competitive markets the Czechoslovak economy let many highly unprofitable
products escape to the less sophisticated markets, which in no way
contributed to stability, if only because such trade was usually conducted on credit and the terms were steadily deteriorating.[25] The informed and concerned public demanded a thorough reform of the economic system based on a market economy, which would end, among
other things, the system of subsidies that had involved substantial government expenditures for price control and foreign economic assistance.[26] Specifically, the commentators criticized heavy involvement
in aid programs at a time when the ailing economy was itself in need
of substantial foreign loans and called for an examination of aid to the
developing countries in the light of "our real possibililities."[27]

To be sure, the criticism was not meant to diminish the importance of Czechoslovakia's relations with the Third World. While the
economic situation required a deemphasis on Czechoslovak aid involvement, political developments brought out demands for a more active
and independent foreign policy, which included a call for strengthening the ties with Yugoslavia and its fellow members of the Nonaligned
Movement. Characteristic of the debate was also a great deal of understanding for the problems of developing countries and a strong
popular support for their striving for political and economic independence.[28] This attitude was reflected also in the statements of government representatives. The foreign minister of the Dubček government,
Jiří Hájek, assured that Czechoslovakia would continue to support developing countries but its material aid was limited by its own economic difficulties and must take the form of scientific-technological and
cultural assistance. He also urged coordination of the policies of the
Socialist states toward the Third World, greater stress on the training

of personnel, and the elaboration of long-term conceptions that would correspond to both developmental trends and Czechoslovakia's possibilities and interests. [29] Political motives were not to play the decisive role, and aid was to be given to countries in real need. At the same time, the government made it clear that it wished to work through U. N. agencies providing development aid on a multilateral basis.

The Soviet military intervention in August 1968 abruptly ended all public discussion and arrested the attempts at a reform of the political and economic system in Czechoslovakia. It had a disastrous effect on every aspect of the life of society. It crippled the economy, inflicted heavy damage on the productive forces, and isolated the country in international relations.

Inevitably, relations with the Third World came under the impact of the new situation. In the political field, countries with a strong attachment to principles of sovereignty and independence lost interest in becoming closely associated with a government that acquired a dubious legitimacy by having come to power as a result of foreign military intervention. In the economic field, it was apparent that Czechoslovakia's depleted resources would not permit it to go on with its extensive programs of development aid. On the other hand, Czechoslovakia had to take into account the coalition interests of the Warsaw Pact countries, which prevented it from vacating positions it had gained in the Third World until other Socialist countries were able to fill its place.

In the process of readjustment, the primacy in the extent of engagement has passed gradually and quite naturally from Czechoslovakia to the German Democratic Republic. Already in the 1960s the GDR—still diplomatically unrecognized—was striving to establish its presence in the Third World. The bulk of East German activities in the developing countries in that period was carried through the intermediary of Czechoslovak diplomatic and economic missions. More than with any other Socialist country, Czechoslovakia shared with the GDR its experience and its connections as well. After gaining diplomatic recognition as a result of East-West detente in 1972-73, the GDR eagerly expanded its relations with the Third World and was prepared to commit vast resources to developmental aid. Because of the similarity of industrial structures of the two countries, the GDR could easily substitute for Czechoslovak assistance in major areas of interest to developing countries, such as investment programs and improvement of defense capability.

The past decade has seen an unprecedented increase in direct Soviet involvement in the Third World, which has made the use of its allies as surrogates practically unnecessary. The Eastern European involvement thus has become complementary to the Soviet Union's own efforts. To some extent, the new situation has enabled the Eastern European countries, including Czechoslovakia, to shape their external economic relations in ways that suit their respective economic needs and political aspirations.

KEEPING A LOW PROFILE

Czechoslovakia's international position and unresolved internal problems have accounted for considerable prudence in its relations with the Third World throughout the 1970s, compared with the period of inflated ideological and political ambitions of the 1950s and 1960s.

In quantitative terms, both contacts and trade have continued to grow, but the growth has been slow in comparison with other Eastern European countries and the world at large. For example, although 80 developing countries have established diplomatic relations with Czechoslovakia, only 23 now maintain diplomatic missions in Prague. Sub-Saharan Africa is represented by two embassies only, those of Ghana and Sudan; other African countries that previously maintained separate missions in the Czechoslovak capital have moved them to Moscow, Warsaw, or Berlin, an indication of a shift in focus on more politically active members of the Socialist bloc. The general lack of initiative with respect to the Third World is one other difference between the policies of individual Eastern European countries that should be noted. While other Socialist countries have shown an evident interest in developing extra-bloc relationships and giving a boost to contacts with the Third World in pursuance of their national objectives, the trauma of 1968 continues to curtail Czechoslovakia's self-confidence. Where Czechoslovakia did undertake politically motivated actions, it almost invariably acted in tandem with the Soviet Union or other Socialist countries. No major political or diplomatic initiative comparable to the diplomatic ventures of the earlier period were in evidence during the 1970s.

While not relenting in the issuance of high-sounding proclamations in support of the struggle against colonialism, neocolonialism and imperialist dictates, Czechoslovak diplomacy has been slow in appreciating the more tangible interests of the developing countries in the postcolonial era. For example, it long resisted their call for declaring the resources of the world sea a "common heritage of mankind" to be used primarily for the benefit of economically and technologically disadvantaged countries. Also, contrary to its interests as a landlocked industrial country, it helps the Soviet Union (and for that matter other maritime powers with an interest in unrestricted exploitation of sea resources) in blocking the establishment of an international authority with sufficient power to ensure equal distribution of benefits accruing from sea mining.

A DECREASING SHARE OF THIRD WORLD TRADE

Although the total volume of Czechoslovak foreign trade has increased nearly four times since 1965, the share of the developing countries has dropped during the same period from 8. 6 to 6. 6 percent. These figures contrast sharply with the steady increase in the share of other Socialist countries. [30] They also compare unfavorably with substantial increase in Czechoslovak trade with the developed Western countries, as can be seen from Table 3. 4.

TABLE 3. 4

Czechoslovak Foreign Trade, 1965-78
(millions of Kčs)

Trade Year	Turn-over	Communist States	Capitalist States	Developing Countries
1965	38,599	28,272	6,919	3,408
Percentage	100. 0	73. 0	18. 4	8. 6
1968	43,793	31,319	8,871	3,603
1970	53,910	37,750	12,069	4,091
1975	97,362	68,775	21,754	6,838
1978	131,683	95,749	21,283	8,651
Percentage	100. 0	72. 7	20. 7	6. 6
Growth 1965-78				
(1965 = 100)	341	338	394	254

Source: Statistická ročenka ČSSR 1979 (Prague: Nakladatelství technické literatury, 1979), p. 441.

This drop in aid has been due mainly to the declining export efficiency of the Czechoslovak economy and, at the same time, its growing demands for imports of Western technology required by programs to upgrade the efficiency of the Czechoslovak manufacturing industry. (Only to a small degree is it due to the fact that since 1973 Cuba has not been included, for purposes of trade statistics, among the developing countries and has been listed as a Socialist country.) Among the factors that account for the declining export efficiency is the relatively high consumption of raw materials, fuels, and energy. A comparison with the industrially advanced countries reveals that Czechoslovakia is showing a 40-50 percent higher material consumption in the overall value of products. [31] As a consequence, the fast rise in the price of raw materials has weighed particularly heavily on the Czechoslovak economy.

More important, however, is the reduced capability to provide large credits. The time of spectacular lending is over. Most of the loans now extended are medium-term credits in connection with exports of complete plants and installations. A special procedure has been established for screening each case carefully. The main criteria for approval of new credits are Czechoslovakia's economic possibilities, specific conditions of economic development and industrialization of the developing country concerned, and the conditions of competition on the world market. [32]

Politically motivated soft-term loans are not only infrequent but also relatively insignificant. For example, when the Comecon countries decided, in March 1971, to provide economic aid to the revolutionary military government of President Velasco Alvarado in Peru, Czechoslovakia offered only $7 million, while the Soviet Union committed $30 million, Poland $10 million, Hungary $15 million, and Bulgaria $10 million. [33] Another rare instance of a concessional loan was a credit in the amount of $3 million extended to Afghanistan shortly after the 1978 revolution overthrowing the government of President Mohammed Daud. It is assumed that additional aid has been forthcoming in view of the strong political commitment to support the revolutionary government.

The obvious limits of Czechoslovak credit capability in the 1970s account for a change in the balance of trade with most important partners in the Third World. Typical in this respect is the case of India. Traditionally, that country was a recipient of huge loans provided at regular intervals, which kept Czechoslovak exports well above imports; the unavailability of new Czechoslovak loans in recent years has reversed the relation (see Table 3.5). [34]

Czechoslovak trade with the Third World is influenced by a curious mixture of ideology and pragmatism. The ideological component purports to play a role in policy decisions concerning the regional distribution of trade, as can be seen from the following statement by the prime minister of Czechoslovakia made at a party congress in 1976:

> In our economic and scientific-technological policy towards the developing countries, especially those which have chosen the noncapitalist road, we shall concentrate not only on expanding trade turnover but also on establishing long-term, stable, and mutually beneficial relations. Thus we shall be also expressing our solidarity with these countries and supporting their efforts toward political independence and economic and social progress. [35]

TABLE 3. 5

Czechoslovak Foreign Trade with India, 1965-78
(millions of Kčs)

Trade	1965	1970	1976	1977	1978
Turnover	594	532	520	540	516
Imports	250	262	249	353	293
Exports	344	270	271	187	223
Balance	94	8	22	-166	-70

Sources: Facts on Czechoslovak Foreign Trade (Prague: Chamber of Commerce, 1978), p. 66; Statistická ročenka ČSSR 1979 (Prague: Nakladatelství technické literatury, 1979), p. 478.

But the slogan of support for "progressive forces" is in many instances a holdover from the vocabulary of more confident days. The care and reticence with which the commitment was defined shows that the notion of "noncapitalist developing nations first" remains just that, a persistent nation but not a reality. One way or another, Czechoslovakia is seeking ways around it. The government's eagerness to expand trade relations with such countries as Saudi Arabia, Kuwait, and Iran proves that pressing needs of the Czechoslovak economy, especially for fuels and energy, and a steadily declining foreign exchange reserve bear more on the selection of partners than any ideological motives. The case of Iran well illustrates the point. The pompous reception of the Shah in Prague in August 1977 sharply contrasted with the concerns of the progressive international public about human rights violations in Iran and with previous Czechoslovak criticism of the monarch's pro-U.S. policy. The main reason for this unprincipled departure from the previous policy was, however, spiraling trade with Iran, which yielded a high foreign exchange surplus (see Table 3. 6).

The perennial problem is how to fit the requirements of the developing countries into a body of Czechoslovakia's own development plans. Entry into agreements for projects extending over many years has been the chief method, and so far Czechoslovakia has concluded such agreement with 60 Third World countries. But the crucial test for Czechoslovakia comes in relation to the adjustment of its economy to the structural development of the Third World. In the 1960s, most developing countries had a traditional structure in which the prevailing sector was agriculture, followed by the service sector and backward industry. On the other hand, Czechoslovakia's economic structure was

TABLE 3. 6

Czechoslovak Foreign Trade with Iran, 1965-77
(millions of Kčs)

Trade	1965	1970	1976	1977
Turnover	100	195	620	922
Imports	55	66	128	405
Exports	45	129	492	517
Balance	-10	63	364	112

Source: Facts on Czechoslovak Foreign Trade (Prague: Chamber of Commerce, 1978), p. 66.

predominantly industrial, with a stress placed on engineering. The mutually complementary structures provided a basis for a relatively fast development of economic cooperation. But with the increasing industrialization of some of its main partners in the Third World (for example, India), Czechoslovakia has encountered obstacles similar to those experienced in trade with the Western nations. In its search for a solution, Czechoslovakia is now placing emphasis on the formation of a new dynamic complementarity, which involves mutual readjustment through long-term plans. It demands that the developing countries display maximum understanding for Czechoslovakia's own needs, strictly observe all commitments ensuing from mutual long-term agreements on structural adjustments, and undertake to ensure not only their permanence but also the stability of mutual relations. [36]

TECHNICAL ASSISTANCE

Czechoslovakia's approach to the problems of the Third World has been based on the belief that an essential engine of their economic growth is the volume of potential energies released by local material and human resources that contribute directly or indirectly to the economic development. This attitude is reflected in the special role that Czechoslovakia assigns in its relations with the developing countries to technical assistance.

In general, Czechoslovakia follows the same pattern that characterizes the policy of other Socialist countries in matters of technical assistance. Transfer of technology under agreements on scientific and technological cooperation, sending of experts on the request of the receiving government, and training of national personnel in developing countries are its main forms. The bulk of assistance is provided on a bilateral basis, and only a small—though by no means negligible—part is channeled through international agencies, principally through various U. N. programs. [37]

In 1979, Czechoslovakia had almost 60 agreements on economic cooperation and 35 agreements on scientific technical cooperation with the developing countries. [38] Some of these arrangements envision advanced forms of industrial cooperation, such as the use of Czechoslovak patents and know-how and assistance in solving technical problems in industrial production, transportation, and agriculture. Their implementation has been pursued vigorously in recent years, and certain goals have already been achieved. For example, agreements have been made with India, Mexico, and Iran to start a joint production of the Czechoslovak motorcycle "Jawa," and India and Iraq manufacture the medium-size Czehcoslovak tractor "Zetor" under a license. Nevertheless, it takes a lot of trial and error to deal with the expansion of economic and technical cooperation with the Third World. Tying cooperative ventures to a normal flow of exports and imports was and still is a headache because of Czechoslovakia's relative inexperience with these modern economic activities.

One field in which Czechoslovakia had and continues to have preeminence, is education and training of national personnel as well as providing expertise to the developing countries.

In 1961 the influx of foreign students prompted a decision to establish the separate University of November 17th in Prague* for the purpose of "assisting the peoples that have liberated themselves from the colonial yoke." [39] Considerable effort and resources were invested in the venture, and expectations as to the impact of the new institution ran very high. Apart from a school of general studies, providing language and other basic skills needed for successful graduate study, the university had two departments: science and technology, and social sciences and humanities. The total enrollment in the peak years (1963-64) was 3,000. Like a similar institution in Moscow, the Patrice Lumumba University of People's Friendship, the University of Novem-

---

*The name of the new institution was related to a tragic event in the history of Czechoslovak universities: on November 17, 1939, the Nazi authorities closed down all Czech institutions of higher education following mass student protests against the German occupation of the country. One student, Jan Opletal, was shot on the spot, and hundreds were sent to concentration camps. After World War II, November 17 was designated International Students Day.

ber 17th offered comprehensive programs of political and professional training for students from Asia, Africa, and Latin America and supervised specialized programs for foreign students at other educational institutions.

In spite of the fairly large number of graduates over the years, the university was not a success. The student body was a mixture of achievers and failures. Many students from a tradition-oriented society had difficulty in dealing with a totally strange Eastern European environment; others, having made the transition, were dissatisfied with the lack of intellectual freedom and general conditions of life in a Socialist country; still others experienced financial problems, despite the relatively generous stipend, and left the university before completing their study program. Moreover, the concentration of foreign students in one place became a pause for anxiety on the part of the government because of the proliferation of spontaneous political activity among them. After 1968, for example, organizations of Asian, African, and Latin American students in Prague continued to praise Dubček's democratization experiment, despite its condemnation by the new pro-Soviet government.

All in all, the compounded difficulties led to the demise of the university in 1972. At present, fixed numbers of students from the Third World are admitted to the existing educational institutions. Greater emphasis is being laid on postdoctoral study, with a view to preparing candidates for advanced academic or professional work.

Relatively high is the number of trainees undergoing practice in Czechoslovak factories and other facilities. In 1963, Czechoslovakia received 27 percent of all trainees sent by the developing countries to Comecon states (including the Soviet Union),[40] and although the relation has changed considerably the country continues to invite up to 1,000 trainees each year. In proportion to other Eastern European countries, its training programs attract more personnel seeking to acquire special skills in industrial production and services.

Conversely, Czechoslovakia continues to send its experts to the Third World in relatively high numbers. It is estimated that in 1978 more than 1,000 specialists, including doctors, geologists, agronomists, technicians, and other professionals, were working in non-European countries.[41] Particularly significant has been the increase of expert geologists: they are now working in Libya, Morocco, Tunisie, Algeria, Nigeria, Kuwait, Burma, Jordan, and Peru.[42] Attempts to recruit larger numbers of experts and advisers have been hindered, however, partly by the difficulty of finding engineers and technologists in needed fields able to communicate in the required languages and partly by the strict screening procedure, which disqualifies candidates who fail to meet Party-inspired criteria of political reliability.

MULTILATERAL ARRANGEMENTS

In general, the Socialist countries discount the effectiveness of aid provided through multilateral channels. They maintain that international institutions, by interposing themselves between donors and recipients of aid, interfere with their proper and desirable close relationship. Although some of the underlying political rationale has lost relevance (for example, U. N. programs have ceased to be predominantly Western-administered), the resentment is sustained by the feeling that the Socialist countries are not sufficiently represented in the administrative bodies and that there exist differences among their members as to how development funds should be distributed.

While generally agreeing with this attitude, Czechoslovakia does not avoid participation in U. N. programs where such participation offers an opportunity for access to developing countries that have so far been little responsive to unilateral offers. Due to the fact that its contributions to various programs administered by the United Nations, UNIDO, UNESCO, ILO, WHO, FAO, and other agencies, are in kind or in nonconvertible currency, Czechoslovakia is able to retain, at least partly, control over the execution of its share in the aid program.

Unlike most other Socialist countries, Czechoslovakia never gave up the use of multilateral instruments in such matters as tariffs and trade preferences. Despite the Soviet disapproval of GATT as a means of preserving the economic privileges of Western industrial countries, Czechoslovakia has continued its membership in GATT and has participated in all major negotiations concerning its application to new countries. The attractiveness of GATT for Czechoslovak trade with the Third World is in that the agreement, which now includes more than 40 developing countries among its parties, displaces bilateral reciprocal trade agreements with an assurance of nondiscrimination as regards tariff rates and other trade barriers. The benefits accruing from a general and unconditional most-favored-nation clause now covering some 65,000 items, including practically all items exported and imported by Czechoslovakia, have been estimated by Czechoslovak experts in the millions of dollars.

To compensate for the "unprincipled expediency," Czechoslovakia supports the developing countries in their effort to spur the exports of both primary commodities and industrial goods through commodity agreements, temporary tariff preferences, and preferential groupings among the exporting countries.

Its support for the integration movement among the developing countries is qualified. On the one hand, Czechoslovakia recognizes that it is "a process in which the developing countries strive to improve their position in the international division of labor, which objectively weakens the positions of world imperialism."[43] On the other

hand, it does not fail to see that "in the economic and political practice, the integration process of the developing countries is under the
strong influence of the economic development in advanced capitalist
countries and in their integration groupings."[44] It urges "a more active approach on the part of the [Comecon] countries to developing
states, more than ever before" and reminds the developing countries
that they and the Socialist states have "identical long-term interests
. . . in the political, economic and social spheres," which "result
mainly from the anti-imperialist orientation of the two processes and
from efforts to remove the injustice and inadequacies of the existing
international division of labor."[45] In other words, the developing countries are admonished not to believe in the method of liberalization of
trade inherent in a capitalist integration but rather to follow the method
of harmonization of plans developed by the Socialist countries associated in Comecon.

While the association between Third World integration groupings
and the European Economic Community is an accomplished fact, cooperation with Comecon remains insignificant. Only two non-Socialist
developing countries, Iraq and Mexico, have so far shown interest in
signing, individually, agreements of cooperation with Comecon as an
integration grouping.[46] However, given their general character, the
agreements should be considered as letters of intent rather than self-
executing provisions for concrete multilateral cooperation. Yet another
qualification expressing current Czechoslovak concern is being attached
to the support for the concept of the "new economic order" propounded
by the Third World. According to Czechoslovak economists, "This order should conceptually include not only development of equitable and
mutually advantageous economic relations between the developing and
the advanced capitalist countries, not only improvement and expansion
of economic cooperation between the socialist and the developing countries, but also development of relations between the socialist and the
advanced capitalist countries" (emphasis added).[47]

THE FUTURE

In a keynote address to the Central Committee of the Czechoslovak Communist Party in November 1974, Gustav Husák, general secretary of the Party, declared:

> Generally, it must be stated that the period in which it
> was possible to obtain fuels, energy, raw materials as
> well as foodstuffs relatively easily and at low prices has
> ended. This is a new important fact which we must draw
> long-term conclusions from in our economic-political
> activities.[48]

In August 1979, in a speech in Northern Moravia, Prime Minister Lubomír Štrougal stated that the Soviet Union alone could not meet the growing needs of the Socialist countries in fuels and that further increase in oil imports after 1980 could be obtained only from non-Socialist countries. [49]

The situation is the more serious owing to the fact that the Czechoslovak economy is heavily dependent upon importation of basic materials. As Table 3.7 shows, only a small part of the consumption of raw materials and fuels can be procured from domestic sources.

TABLE 3.7

Share of Domestic Resources in the Overall Consumption of the Czechoslovak Economy (percentages)

Resource	Share
Iron ore	11
Aluminium	0
Cattle hides	48
Sulphur	60
Grain	70
Cotton	0
Zinc	8
Meat	85
Crude oil	2
Wool	47

Source: Jaroslav Budín, "The Position of Czechoslovakia in the World Economy," New Trends in Czechoslovak Economy 8 (1968): 22.

The above considerations will no doubt dominate Czechoslovak policy toward the Third World. It must be expected that the role of developing countries as suppliers of raw materials and fuels, especially crude oil, will be of decisive importance. Provisions have already been made for increased imports of iron and manganese ores, metals, oil, and natural gas. A 1975 tripartite arrangement among Iran, Czechoslovakia, and the Soviet Union envisions increasing deliveries of Iranian natural gas to the Soviet Union and of Soviet gas to Czechoslovakia and Western Europe. The construction of a pipeline from the Yugoslav port of Rjeka to Bratislava in Czechoslovakia to transport crude purchased from oil-exporting Third World nations is nearing completion. According to some Western estimates, Czechoslovakia will have to acquire at least 5 million tons of crude oil annually beginning in 1980 from sources outside the Soviet Union. [50]

An increase in the volume of Czechoslovak-Third World trade therefore seems imminent. The question remains, however, to what extent Czechoslovakia will be able to match the rising costs of its imports with increasing exports.

Paradoxically, the expansion of cooperation with the developing countries in order to obtain deficient raw materials and fuels depends, in the final analysis, on the stability of East-West relation and on the future of detente. Czechoslovakia cannot expand its trade with the Third World unless it increases the export efficiency of its lagging economy by sizable imports of advanced Western technology required for the modernization of its manufacturing industry.

The favorable market position held by Czechoslovakia prior to the price explosion on the world commodity markets is a thing of the past. The country's foreign trade has been in the red since 1973, and the deficit in the balance of payments is acquiring a threatening proportion. Slackening economic development forced the government to reduce planned targets for 1980. This may foreshadow an economic stagnation for some years to come and a consequent vulnerability for the precarious political balance within the country sustained by the promise of a higher standard of living.

Contingency plans are being prepared to cope with the situation. They envision a more active approach to the developing countries, on both the political and economic planes, and, at the same time, intensification of economic ties with the West. International detente, cooperation, and development emerge as the most important factors bearing upon these goals. Relying on the process of detente, Czechoslovakia expects a substantial increase in economic and scientific cooperation with the Western nations. As regards the Third World, it abhors the idea that the proponents of a "new economic order" might come to an agreement with the West to the detriment of the Socialist countries and seeks to influence the outcome of the current debate on the structure of world economic relations by stirring up anti-Western sentiments among the developing countries, which may appeal to some of them but alienate others. In introducing new measures that Czechoslovakia plans to take in order to attain the goals of its external economic policy, Foreign Trade Minister Andrej Barčák told a session of the Federal Assembly in Prague on April 10, 1980, "The developing countries have become an important force in implementing anti-imperialist policy," and "conditions must be created for external economic activities that aim at strengthening those countries' economic and political independence and at preparing the ground for the practical realization of a new international economic order."[51] He did not, however, disclose any actual proposals to create such conditions.

The terms of a future partnership between Czechoslovakia and the countries of the Third World are yet to be determined. However, one thing seems certain. Czechoslovakia will need the friendship and cooperation of the Third World more than ever in the past. The British philosopher Isaiah Berlin suggests that history consists of changing patterns of liberating ideas. It remains to be seen what new emancipating conceptions will emerge on the Czechoslovak side to break the straitjacket of the present sluggishness, which must be broken at all costs.

NOTES

1. Josef Janáček, Dějiny Prahy (Prague: Nakladatelství politické literatury, 1964), p. 68.

2. According to the estimates of the League of Nations, Czechoslovakia's share in international arms trade between 1929 and 1938 amounted to 12.6 percent. Only Great Britain exported more arms than Czechoslovakia; Germany and France occupied third and fourth place, respectively. See Nakhim M. Stoutzki, The World Armament Race, 1919-1939 (Geneva: Geneva Research Center, 1941), p. 71.

3. Adopted on December 14, 1960, by U.N. General Assembly Resolution 1514(XV).

4. U.N. Document A/C.6/L.505.

5. U.N. Document A/AC.125/L.16.

6. Declaration on Principles of International Law Concerning Friendly Relations among States in Accordance with the Charter of the United Nations. Adopted on October 24, 1970, by U.N. General Assembly Resolution 2625(XXV).

7. United Nations Conference on the Law of the Sea, 1958. Official records: Annex 7 (A/CONF.13/C.5/L.1—Preliminary Conference of Landlocked Countries). Geneva. The joint proposal served as a basis for the adoption of article 3 of the Convention on the High Seas of April 29, 1958. See 450 United Nations Treaty Series (U.N.T.S.), p. 82.

8. John R. Stevenson and Bernard H. Oxman, "The Third United Nations Conference on the Law of the Sea: The 1975 Geneva Session," American Journal of International Law 69 (1975): 784.

9. Xkiesing's Contemporary Archives (1955): 14449A.

10. Ibid., p. 14985A.

11. Ibid.

12. V. Dvořák, "The Interception of a Czechoslovak Freighter, the Lidice, by the French Naval Force on the High Seas from the Point of View of International Law," Právník (1959): 666-70.

13. XII Kiesing's Contemporary Archives (1959): 17325 A.

14. See the definition of foreign aid in Edward S. Mason, Foreign Aid and Foreign Policy (New York: Harper & Row, 1964), p. 11.

15. As data on foreign lending and borrowing are not published in Czechoslovakia, these figures are based on estimates. See, for example, Kurt Müller, "Uber Kalkutta nach Paris? Strategie und Aktivit" ät des Ostblocks in den Entwicklungsländern (Hannover: Verlag fur Literatur und Zeitgeshehen, 1964), p. 185; and Wolf Preus, "Die Entwicklungshilfe der Volksrepublik China," Ausenpolitik, no. 10 (1964).

16. Financial Times (London), July 29, 1964.

17. XI Kiesing's Contemporary Archives (1957): 15906 D.

18. XII Kiesing's Contemporary Archives (1959): 17140 C.

19. XV Kiesing's Contemporary Archives (1964): 20872 A.

20. XII Kiesing's Contemporary Archives (1959): 17597 A.

21. XII Kiesing's Contemporary Archives (1959): 17797 G.

22. Robert F. Lamberg, Prag und die Dritte Welt (Hannover: Verlag für Literatur und Zeitgeshehen, 1965), p. 175.

23. Ibid.

24. Ota Šik, Czechoslovakia: The Bureaucratic Economy (White Plains, N. Y.: International Arts and Science Press, 1972), p. 78.

25. Ibid.

26. H. Gordon Skilling, Czechoslovakia's Interrupted Revolution (Princeton, N. J.: Princeton University Press, 1976), p. 424.

27. J. Hanák, in Reportér (Prague), March 27-April 3, 1968. Quoted in Skilling, Czechoslovakia's Interrupted Revolution, p. 621.

28. It therefore came as a surprise to many Czechoslovaks when in August 1968 some developing countries adopted an attitude which in fact condoned the Soviet occupation of Czechoslovakia. For example, Algeria declared in the U. N. Security Council that the "crisis which is at present shaking the Czechoslovak nation must be set in its European context . . . which is primarily determined by a balance accepted by everybody since the Second World War." Algeria, India, and Pakistan abstained when the council voted on the draft resolution demanding an immediate withdrawal of Soviet occupation forces from Czechoslovakia and restoration of the country's sovereignty and independence. See United Nations, Security Council, Official Records: Twenty-Third Year, 1442nd meeting, 22 August 1968, pp. 27, 29.

29. Nová Mysl (Prague), no. 8 (1968). Quoted in Skilling, Czechoslovakia's Interrupted Revolution, p. 627.

30. In 1978 the average share of the Third World in the trade of Comecon countries was 10 percent; in the case of the Soviet Union, 12 percent. See Ladislav Dvořák, "Hlavní tendence ve vztazích mezi socialistickými a rozvojovými zeměmi," Mezinárodní vztahy 14 (1979): 31.

31. See Miroslav Bursa, "The World and Czechoslovakia," Czechoslovak Economic Digest 4 (1975): 38.

32. Andrej Barčák, "Twenty-Five Years of Czechoslovak Foreign Trade," Czechoslovak Economic Digest 3 (1970): 40.

33. XVIII Kiesing's Contemporary Archives (1971): 24923 A.

34. XXIV Kiesing's Contemporary Archives (1978): 29037 A.

35. "Report on the Main Trends in Economic and Social Development in the Czechoslovak Socialist Republic in 1976-1980," Rudé Právo, April 14, 1976.

36. Alois Holub, "The New International Economic Order—Conditions, Features and Problems," Czechoslovak Economic Digest 3 (1977): 106.

37. For details, see Péter Vas-Zoltan, United Nations Technical Assistance (Budapest: Akadémiai Miadó, 1972), pp. 160-67.

38. Zdeněk M. Veselý, "Acting in Unison for the Developing Countries," Czechoslovak Life 10 (1979): 15.

39. Governmental Decree of September 15, 1961, Collection of Laws and Regulations, no. 108 (1961).

40. Lamberg, Prag und die Dritte Welt, p. 196.

41. Vladimír Mička, "The Role and Importance of External Economic Relations." Czechoslovak Economic Digest 2 (1978): 43.

42. Veselý, "Acting in Unison for the Developing Countries," p. 15.

43. Alois Holub and Jaroslav Foltýn, "Methodical Links between Integration Programmes of Socialist and Developing Countries," Czechoslovak Economic Digest 7 (1975): 42.

44. Ibid.

45. Ibid. , p. 46.

46. The agreements were signed in 1975. They affirm the intentions of the partners to promote cooperation in the fields of economy, science, and technology, subject to the terms of special arrangements between the parties concerned. Otta Henyš, "Mezinárodně politické aspekty třicetileté cesty: Rada vzájemné hospodářské pomoci," Mezinárodní vztahy 14 (1979): 17.

47. Holub, "The New International Economic Order," p. 103.

48. Rudé Právo (Prague), November 24, 1974.

49. Nová Svoboda (Ostrava), September 1, 1979.

50. Czechoslovak Situation Report/4, RFER, February 6, 1980, item 2.

51. Rudé Právo (Prague), April 11, 1980.

4

THE GDR AND THE THIRD WORLD: SUPPLICANT AND SURROGATE

Michael Sodaro

The German Democratic Republic first appeared on the Third World scene as a supplicant. Initially, its primary objective was to secure international acceptance of its claim to constitute a sovereign, independent German state worthy of full-fledged diplomatic recognition. Having finally achieved this long-coveted goal by 1973, following the normalization of its relations with the Federal Republic of Germany and other Western states, the GDR next moved into a new, more active phase of involvement in the developing world, this time as a foreign policy surrogate of the Soviet Union. In this category, the GDR is in many respects the most active of all the Soviet Union's allies in Third World activities with the exception of Cuba (and, quite possibly, Romania, which pursues its own goals in the area). By supplying significant amounts of technology, expertise, and manpower to a select group of Third World nations and national liberation movements, the GDR has provided a vital source of support for Soviet ambitions in Africa, the Middle East, and Latin America across the continent of Asia. The scope of East Germany's contribution to Soviet undertakings ranges from moral support for struggling pro-Communist elements to the supply of important, and occasionally indispensable, economic and military assistance to friendly forces.

I would like to thank the Institute for Sino-Soviet Studies and the German Academic Exchange Service for grants enabling me to conduct research for this study in Germany. I would also like to thank Manfred Ackermann, Johannes Kuppe, Siegfried Kupper and Henning von Löwis of Menar for their helpful assistance.

Interestingly, however, the GDR has recently combined this surrogate role with a renewed appearance in the role of supplicant. This time the object of its importunity is a commodity at least as precious as its cherished diplomatic status: oil. Moscow's decision in 1975 to raise the price and reduce the supply of petroleum exports to its Eastern European allies confronted nearly all of these states with the necessity of seeking new suppliers of primary energy. Thus far, neither the GDR nor any other member of the Warsaw Pact has succeeded in weening itself from almost total dependence on Soviet oil (again, with the exception of Romania), despite earnest attempts to find secure supplies at affordable prices on the world market. In the years to come, it seems certain that this supplicant's demand for diversified sources of oil will color the GDR's relationships with the developing countries at least as decisively as its more assertive posture as a Soviet surrogate, if not more so.

The analysis that follows will attempt to delineate the GDR's activity in the Third World as it relates to these central themes. After first glancing at some of the difficulties encountered by the GDR in its early initiatives toward the developing world, I shall look briefly at the fundamental theoretical postulates that guide the GDR's basic orientation to the panoramic diversity of the Third World's political systems and policies. I shall next survey East Germany's trade and aid policies toward the area as a whole and then mention some of the more political methods the GDR employs in its dealings with certain less developed countries. This will set the stage for a regional analysis of GDR activities, starting with Africa and the Middle East and moving on to Asia and Latin America. * Finally, in the concluding section, I shall point out some of the international and domestic functions of East Germany's Third World engagement, with an eye to foreseeing how they might develop in the future.

THE GDR AS SUPPLICANT: THE QUEST FOR DIPLOMATIC RECOGNITION

Although the post-Stalin leadership of the Soviet Union succeeded in achieving a significant breakthrough in its relations with the Third World as early as the mid-1950s with the windfall of Egypt's opening to the Soviet bloc, the GDR was not able to capitalize on Moscow's

---

*In this essay, the term "Third World" does not apply to the Communist-controlled countries of Cambodia, Laos, Cuba, North Korea, Mongolia, or Vietnam.

good fortune. Ironically, as the Soviets increasingly championed the nascent Nonalignment Movement, the GDR found itself constantly discriminated against by leaders of those very countries, many of whom justified their refusal to recognize the GDR by the principle of nonalignment itself. Both Nasser and Nehru declared that the establishment of de jure relations with East Germany would violate their concept of neutrality, and Nehru was particularly indisposed to accord the GDR diplomatic recognition following the construction of the Berlin Wall in 1961. [1] As the Nonalignment Movement expanded with the wave of newly independent African states in the late 1950s and early 1960s, the GDR suffered additional frustrations of this type. Even erstwhile Soviet client states such as Nkrumah's Ghana and Touré's Guinea held back from granting Moscow's wish for formal recognition of the East German state. The result was a clear victory for West Germany's Hallstein doctrine, which mandated the severing of diplomatic and economic ties with any state that recognized the GDR. [2]

Of course, in many cases it was not merely the principle of neutrality that motivated the nonaligned states to defer to Bonn's position in this matter. A number of the countries in question were recipients of substantial trade and aid benefits from the FRG. Bonn's ability to outspend and outproduce the GDR provided strong economic incentives to quite a few Third World states, significantly reinforcing the diplomatic pressures which Bonn vigorously applied on them to prevent a move in East Germany's direction. In what was perhaps the most blatant example of a widely shared interest in the Third World in retaining Bonn's friendship, in 1971 President Bokassa of the Central African Republic rudely broke off recently established diplomatic relations with the GDR on the grounds that East Germany had not come through with its promised economic favors. [3]

Not even Walter Ulbricht's loudly trumpeted state visit to Egypt in 1965 brought about the desired breakthrough in relations with the developing world. Although this was the first time the leader of the Socialist Unity Party of Germany (SED) had been formally received by a non-Communist government, the trip did not result in the establishment of diplomatic ties. [4] Nor did the revelation that the FRG was supplying arms and reparations to Israel, an action which induced several Arab states to break relations with Bonn in 1965, lead to the hoped-for normalization between these countries and the GDR. It was not until two years after the June War in the Middle East that the GDR scored its first triumphs in this region, gaining recognition by Iraq on May 10, 1969 (only two days after Cambodia became the first non-Communist state to take up diplomatic relations with East Germany). Soon thereafter, formal relations were established with Sudan (June 3, 1969), Syria (June 5), South Yemen (July 10), and Egypt (July 11). (Meanwhile, the Republic of South Vietnam recognized the

GDR on June 20, 1969.) In 1970, seven additional states entered into formal ties with the East German state, but only four more were added to the list by the summer of 1972. Only when negotiations were nearly completed on the Basic Treaty with the FRG (signed in December 1972) was the diplomatic logjam finally broken. India recognized the GDR in October of that year, to be followed a month later by Pakistan. December 1972 proved to be a veritable bonanza, as some 22 countries formally took up diplomatic relations with the GDR, most of them from the Third World. Forty-six additional states recognized East Germany in 1973, and by the end of the decade the GDR maintained relations with a total of nearly 130 states.

In sum, then, the GDR's ties to the Third World up to the end of 1972 were largely contingent upon the "German question," a matter which most Third World states (including some pro-Moscow ones) were generally reluctant to resolve for themselves in East Berlin's favor. With the signing of the Basic Treaty, however, and in the context of detente in Europe, an enormous obstacle was lifted from the GDR's capacity for maneuver in the Third World. Coincidentally, the GDR's new profile as a diplomatic partner of the developing nations emerged just as the break-up of Portugal's colonies provided opportunities for expanded Soviet involvement in Africa. As will be noted shortly, the GDR became quickly embroiled in these African adventures.

THE GDR AND THE THIRD WORLD:
A THEORETICAL OVERVIEW

In its theoretical approach to the phenomena of Third World political and economic development, the GDR tends to stick closely to positions laid out by Soviet scholars and ideologists. Like their Soviet counterparts, East German theoreticians are sensitive to the extraordinary variety of Third World regimes and are generally candid in observing the virtual absence of "real" Socialist systems in the developing world. However, both Soviet and East German writers hasten to note that a number of these states "orient themselves" toward socialism, largely by adopting a "noncapitalist" mode of development.[5] In these cases, according to one authority,

> If one were to regard them in an isolated fashion, there exist neither the objective nor the subjective preconditions for a socialist revolution; however, within the world revolutionary process, in which they are objectively incorporated, they can shorten the way to socialism by avoiding a capitalist development or by overcoming it relatively early.[6]

Institutionally, this process is generally undertaken by what Soviet-bloc theorists call the "national-democratic state." This is a blanket designation applied to a host of structurally differentiated Third World regimes whose common destiny, in the Soviet view, is to manage the transition from colonial rule to "real socialism." Scholars in the GDR have shown a growing interest in the theory and practice of "national-democratic states" in recent years but seldom stray far beyond the propositions formulated on this subject by their Soviet counterparts. [7]

Coupled with this qualified approval of the path taken by certain of these "noncapitalist" countries, however, is a categorical rejection of any attempts by Third World states to construct their own "third way" to economic development, one which is neither "capitalist" nor "socialist," as these terms are understood in the Soviet bloc. This is a problem of considerable concern to the Soviets, as not a few Third World states have come to insist that their rejection of Western capitalism by no means implies their acceptance of the Soviet model of development. East German writers tend to echo Moscow's disapproval of this tendency. [8]

Meanwhile, the GDR seems to be fully aware of the instabilities inherent in one-man rule by charismatic leaders. Several decades of postcolonial experience (especially in Africa) have demonstrated to Soviet-bloc observers the hazards of banking on non-Communist "strong men" with flimsy bases of institutional or popular support. Like the Soviets, the East Germans also recognize that such examples of personalized power, while frequently conditioned by powerful historical forces, are nonetheless "contradictory and problematic." According to GDR experts, one-person rule "is not . . . the decisive factor for the stabilization of the national-democratic state. Ultimately the decisive question is whether the national-democratic state and its leadership enjoy the trust and support of the popular masses and to what degree this support finds an organizational expression."[9] As we shall see, it is precisely in the domain of building such organizational props of power that the GDR is heavily engaged in a number of Third World countries at present.

With respect to recent appeals by Third World states for a "new world economic order," East German theorists generally approve of the slogan but insist that it should not be construed as implying the need for unwarranted economic demands on the developed Warsaw Pact states. They reject the notion of a confrontation between "North" and "South" on the grounds that the Socialist states do not deserve to be equated as fellow "Northerners" with the capitalist countries, which alone must bear responsibility for the economic exploitation of the Third World under imperialism and neocolonialism. Here, too, the East German writers lean heavily on the views of their Soviet colleagues. [10]

These theoretical considerations aside, however, it should be noted that, in practice, the nature of a state's political system has little to do with the GDR's (or the Soviet Union's) willingness to enter into trade or political relations. Neither Moscow nor East Berlin hesitates to engage in trade with regimes regarded as politically objectionable, while both have consistantly courted states that suppress local Communist elements. In short, practical political or economic calculations, not ideological consistency, characterize the Soviet Union's approach to the Third World, and the same goes for the GDR.

Despite this close correlation between East German and Soviet views on the Third World, it should be stressed that the SED's interest in the subject, as reflected in GDR literature, is strong and growing stronger. The number of articles on the developing countries appearing in such journals as Deutsche Aussenpolitik and Horizont seems to be expanding, as is press coverage of the Third World in the SED's daily, Neues Deutschland. In addition, the GDR has a journal devoted entirely to Third World problems (Afrika, Asien, Lateinamerika), as well as quasi-academic establishments concerned with Third World studies (such as the African Institute associated with Leipzig University) or with the training of students and professionals from selected Third World states. It appears quite likely that the GDR's growing involvement in the Third World will continue to be matched by increasing theoretical interest in its problems.

TRADE AND AID

Although the GDR failed to attain diplomatic recognition from the less developed nations until 1969 and thereafter, its trade relations with selected Third World countries gained a firm foothold in the early 1950s. By the end of 1979, the GDR had commercial or other economic relations with 52 Third World countries. [11] Initially, the GDR's chief trading partners were Brazil, India, Egypt, and Iraq. These countries still assume a large share of the GDR's trade with the Third World, which tends to be concentrated in about half a dozen nations (see Table 4.1).

While trade with Brazil, India, and Iraq has risen relatively steadily over the past decade, economic relations with a number of other countries have exhibited fairly wide swings either up or down (or, as is the case with Libya, both up and down). Table 4.2 shows some of the widest fluctuations in the GDR's trade flows with the Third World in recent years. These variations tend to reflect either political vicissitudes (Egypt, Angola, Mozambique) or the GDR's interest in oil imports (Algeria, Iraq, Iran, Libya, Nigeria, Syria).

As a percentage of its total trade turnover, however, East Ger-

TABLE 4.1

Principal Third World Trade Partners of the GDR,
1970 and 1978
(millions of valutamarks)

Trade Partner	1970	Rank	1978	Rank
Egypt	389.7	1	442.2	4
India	276.7	2	472.1	2
Brazil	242.5	3	507.4	2
Turkey	67.3	4	120.3	12
Syria	67.0	5	405.7	5
Colombia	57.6	6	—	—
Peru	50.5	7	157.8	9
Iraq	48.7	8	724.7	1
Lebanon	32.7	9	—	—
Iran	27.4	10	159.5	8
Sudan	25.0	11	—	—
Sri Lanka	20.5	12	—	—
Ethiopia	—	—	316.5	6
Angola	—	—	233.7	7
Argentina	—	—	148.8	10
Mozambique	—	—	130.5	11

Note: The valutamark is the official GDR trade currency. In 1976, 1 VM was equal to 0.72 DM. Dashes indicate country was not a principal trade partner for that year.

Source: Statistisches Jahrbuch 1979 der Deutschen Demokratischen Republik.

many's trade with the developing world is consistently rather low. According to calculations based on official GDR statistics, Third World trade has remained in the range of 3 to 5 percent through most of the 1970s (see Table 4.3). Trade turnover with some 30 less developed countries rose from 1.6 million VM in 1970 to slightly over 5.0 million VM in 1978.[12]

Few precise figures are available on East German aid to the developing world, largely because much of it is hidden in credit agreements or other economic transfer arrangements for which details are rarely made public. It has been estimated, however, that, at least by the late 1960s, East German foreign aid amounted to about 0.02 percent of its national product. This figure has probably increased very little in more recent years. It falls considerably short of the FRG's performance in both the late 1960s (when the Federal Republic spent more than 1. 0 percent of its gross national product on development projects) and the 1970s (when the FRG devoted slightly less than 1. 0 percent of its GNP to development aid.) The average figure for the Comecon bloc as a whole, meanwhile, has been about 0. 04 percent. [13] As a giver of aid, the GDR has at times ranked below Poland and Czechoslovakia when its contributions are measured as a percentage of national income. [14]

Thus, economic relations with the Third World do not appear to take up a large portion of the GDR's annual budget. However, it should be noted that trade with the Third World brings in goods that are considered vital to East German consumers (coffee, tea, fruit, and so on) and industry (for example, petroleum), while providing an outlet for East German industrial products which cannot be sold easily to advanced countries. For its part, aid fulfills important political functions, especially in those areas where Moscow has a large stake. Over

TABLE 4. 2

Countries with Wide Fluctuations in Trade Turnover
with the GDR
(millions of valutamarks)

Country	1973	1974	1975	1977	1978
Algeria			72. 9		324. 0
Angola			0		233. 7
Argentina			26. 4		148. 8
Egypt			639. 6		442. 2
Iran			62. 1		159. 5
Iraq	186. 1	648. 0			724. 7
Libya			12. 1	84. 8	13. 3
Mozambique			0		130. 5
Nigeria			3. 3	19. 3	14. 4
Syria			211. 2		405. 7

Note: The valutamark is the official GDR trade currency. In 1976, 1 VM was equal to 0. 72 DM.
Source: Statistisches Jahrbuch 1979 der Deutschen Demokratischen Republik.

TABLE 4. 3

GDR Foreign Trade with the Third World as a Percentage of
Total Foreign Trade Turnover

Year	Percentage of Total Foreign Trade Turnover
1970	4. 0
1971	4. 1
1972	3. 2
1973	3. 4
1974	4. 9
1975	4. 4
1976	4. 5
1977	4. 9
1978	5. 2

Source: Computed from statistics in Statistisches Jahrbuch
1979 der Deutschen Demokratischen Republik.

the course of the next decade, it can be expected that both imports
from and aid (including military aid) to the Third World will increase,
and both will become increasingly expensive. Ultimately, these growing economic commitments can only have a negative impact on domestic consumption, a fact which the East German authorities endeavor
to conceal when reporting their economic statistics. At a time when
the GDR economy is experiencing rising prices, reduced growth rates,
and mounting shortages of consumer goods, the domestic costs of a
more active Third World policy may be felt all the more acutely at
home, by economic planners as well as the general population. [15]

METHODS OF INFLUENCE

In addition to direct diplomatic ties and trade relations, the GDR
reinforces its links with selected Third World states through a variety
of other mechanisms. Party-to-party contacts, for instance, involving
the SED or other parties in the GDR's "bloc-party system" perform
similar quasidiplomatic functions. The GDR also provides training
and advice for Third World functionaries engaged in economic planning,
constructing state-controlled educational and media systems, or building mass organizations. Various flanking organizations of the SED are
often involved in this process. Thus, the GDR's trade union, the FDGB

assists client states in setting up centrally controlled workers' movements; the GDR's youth organization (the FDJ) sends "friendship bri-
gades" to various Third World countries to work on development projects; East German teachers are engaged in training their counterparts
in states that are particularly friendly with the GDR, and textbooks for
use there are printed in East Germany; and the GDR's Journalists' Union runs a "Solidarity School" for preparing Third World journalists.

It is through activities such as these that the GDR helps establish the "preconditions for socialism" in countries ripe for this type
of development. By educating thousands of "cadres" (expecially young-
er ones) in the techniques of managing centrally directed economic
and political institutions and by inculcating Soviet-style Socialist doctrine in the process, the GDR is seeking to build what may be called
a Marxist-Leninist infrastructure in a number of closely allied Third
World states (such as Ethiopia, Mozambique, and Angola). Whether
these efforts result in the establishment of new elites that are thoroughly committed to Soviet methods of economic development and political control in these countries is a question that only future observers can answer. What is certain at present, however, is that the GDR
is fully dedicated to preparing the next generation of prospective allies
in these states, in the expectation that these individuals will be even
better schooled in the fundamentals of "real socialism" than their
predecessors in the current generation of national liberation movement leaders.

Among the mechanisms employed by the GDR to express its
sympathy for promising Third World causes are a panoply of organizations, campaigns, and festivities, all closely patterned on Soviet
models, designed to advertise East Germany's interest in Third World
problems. Meetings of the World Peace Council, the organization of
"solidarity weeks" and "friendship days" in East Berlin with guests
from selected countries, the establishment of a League for People's
Friendship for the purpose of encouraging people-to-people and cultural contacts with the Third World, and official gestures of support
for Third World campaigns against racism, imperialism, and even
human rights violations are all part of a growing program of propaganda activities serving to link the GDR with the developing nations.
The "solidarity committees" of the GDR are largely responsible for
coordinating many of these efforts. In addition to providing direct financial assistance to selected countries or liberation movements, the
solidarity committees also help provide food and medical assistance
to needy clients and arrange hospital care in the GDR for combatants
wounded in Third World struggles. The committees also hold training
courses for technicians, teachers, doctors, and the like (often with
the cooperation of the FDGB and the FDJ) and engage in a variety of
special activities, such as inviting children from Third World areas

for vacations in the GDR and organizing mass letter-writing campaigns against right-wing Third World regimes. In 1978 alone, the solidarity committees spent approximately 200 million Marks ("thanks to the generous contributions of the population" of the GDR, in the words of the organization's secretary general) and welcomed 180 injured Third World "freedom fighters" into East German hospitals. [16] All of these undertakings proceed from the SED's firm commitment to support states and peoples fighting against "imperialism," a commitment underscored in the GDR constitution and in the SED party program.

THE GDR AND BLACK AFRICA

During the 1970s, Africa stood out as the principal focal point of direct East German involvement in the Third World. By the end of the decade, the GDR maintained diplomatic relations with 46 African states and had economic treaties with 13. Moreover, the enhanced opportunities for intervention in African affairs by the Soviet Union and its allies, which were created by the dissolution of the Portuguese empire and by the revolution in Ethiopia and the acceleration of the black struggle for independence in Rhodesia and Southwest Africa, opened up new possibilities for the East German regime to add its weight to the cause of Moscow's clients (or would-be clients). Much of this assistance has been of a military nature, prompting some Western analysts to describe the GDR's engagement in terms of a new "Afrika Korps."[17] The designation is not entirely facetious, as the contribution to this volume by Jiri Valenta and Shannon Butler amply demonstrates.

The military assistance channeled to Soviet clients in Black Africa in recent years represents an extension of carefully cultivated political relations which, at least in some cases, antedates the final victory of the pro-Soviet forces by several years. [18] Like Moscow, the GDR began establishing ties with a number of "national liberation movements" well before their ultimate success was in view. Angolan leader Agostinho Neto, for example, led an MPLA delegation to the GDR in 1971, but this was a full ten years after the GDR first acknowledged its support for the MPLA by publishing its statutes. (In fact, the SED was the first party in Eastern Europe to establish ties with the MPLA.) Amilcar Cabral of Guinea-Bissau headed a PAIGC delegation in East Berlin in 1972, while the vice president of FRELIMO, Uria T. Simango, brought a group of what was later to become the ruling party of Mozambique on a visit to the GDR as early as 1963. Samora Machel, FRELIMO's leader, addressed the SED's Eighth Party Congress in East Berlin in 1971. [19] In October 1972, the GDR hosted a "Solidarity Week for the Liberation Struggle of Guinea-Bissau, Mozambique and

Angola," one of many manifestations of "solidarity" with specific
Third World movements. Joshua Nkomo met with Erich Honecker in
East Germany in March 1977, a meeting which paved the way for the
opening of a ZAPU office in East Berlin in January 1978, the first of
its kind in the Soviet bloc. The SED has also maintained good ties with
SWAPO and the African National Congress of South America, both of
which opened offices in the GDR in the fall of the same year. [20]

Since 1976, the East German regime has visibly stepped up both
the quantity and the quality of its contacts with favorably oriented African states. Table 4.4 indicates the number of high- and secondary-
level visits by East German delegations to Africa and by African representatives to the GDR. *

The GDR's diplomatic blitz in Black Africa and the Horn intensified in 1977, when the SED Politburo's ill-fated African expert, Werner
Lamberz, made three separate trips to the area. In addition to stopping in Ethiopia on each journey, Lamberz visited Somalia and Mozambique in February, the People's Republic of the Congo and Zambia
in June, and South Yemen in June and December. (The trips to South
Yemen were directly related to the GDR's African policy, as East Germany helped train South Yemeni troops for deployment in Ethiopia's
war against Somalia.) SED Politburo member Konrad Naumann led a
delegation to the Cape Verde Islands in November, and Horst Sinder-
man, a particularly high-ranking SED leader, visited Angola and São
Tomé e Príncipe in the following month. It was during a trip to the
Middle East and North Africa in March 1978 that Lamberz died in a
helicopter crash in Libya, thereby depriving the SED of its foremost
African troubleshooter. [21]

Lamberz's three visits to Ethiopia in 1977 were clearly related
to that country's border conflict with Somalia. Since the resolution of
the conflict in Ethiopia's favor in 1978, a result achieved with considerable East German military assistance, the GDR has solidified its
links with the Derg. In November 1978, Ethiopian leader Mengistu
was grandly received in East Berlin, and Honecker returned the visit
a year later. Mengistu's stopover in the GDR, which followed on the
heels of a visit to Moscow, resulted in the signing of a Declaration of
Principles on Friendship and Cooperation between Ethiopia and the

---

*As defined here, "high-level" contacts include meetings be-
tween SED Politburo members and leading African party or state officials that appear to have a special political significance, whereas
"secondary-level" meetings, while often important, involve GDR
party or government officials in talks with personages other than the
head of the state or party.

TABLE 4.4

Total Number of High- and Secondary-Level Meetings between GDR Officials and African Leaders

Country	1970	1971	1972	1973	1974	1975	1976	1977	1978	1979
Angola	1[a]	1	0	0	1[a]	0	6	4	2	2
Benin	0	0	0	0	0	1	1	2	0	1
Cape Verde	0	0	0	0	0	1	2	0	1	2
Ethiopia	0	0	0	0	0	0	2	7	3	3
Guinea	3	2	1	2	1	1	1	0	1	0
Guinea–Bissau	0	0	1[b]	1	1	1	4	2	0	0
Mozambique	0	1	0	0	1[c]	1	2	3	2	6
São Tomé e Príncipe	0	0	0	0	0	1	1	2	0	0
People's Republic of the Congo	1	0	1	1	1	1	0	6	0	0
Nigeria	0	0	0	0	0	0	1	0	0	0
Zambia	3	1	0	1	0	0	0	2	0	3

[a]Movimento Popular de Libertação de Angola (MPLA).
[b]Partido Africano para Independencia de Guiné e Caso Verde (PAIGC).
[c]Frente de Libertação de Moçambique (FRELIMO).

GDR. [22] The document was patterned on the Treaty of Friendship and Cooperation that Mengistu had just concluded with the Soviet Union. The GDR got the chance to sign a treaty of its own with Ethiopia during Honecker's visit at the end of 1979. [23]

A comparison of these texts and statements made by Honecker at the time of their conclusion with declarations made by Mengistu reveals some interesting differences in the expressed viewpoints of the two leaders on several outstanding issues. Whereas Mengistu referred explicitly to Addis Ababa's struggle against the Eritrean secessionists ("separatist bandits") and to the victory over Somalia ("the expansionist and reactionary regime of Mogadishu"), Honecker passed over the these points in silence. Both he and the documents signed in 1978 and 1979 papered over these issues with ritualistic references to the necessity of upholding the principle of territorial inviolability. Honecker also failed to echo Mengistu's claim that Ethiopia espoused the principles of Marxism-Leninism and "proletarian internationalism."[24] The GDR's reluctance to voice approbation of Mengistu's opinions on these issues reflected Moscow's apparent unwillingness to express public approval of the Derg's operations against the Eritreans as well as its evident desire to avoid aggravating the split with Somalia. The Soviets are also less than enthusiastic about embracing the Mengistu regime as a bona fide example of Marxist-Leninist socialism. Another possible contentious question between Ethiopia and the Soviets centers on Mengistu's tardiness in establishing a Soviet-style Communist party, which still had not been developed by the middle of 1980. It is highly possible that Honecker's negotiating agenda with Ethiopia included a frank discussion of Soviet preferences in these matters. [25]

Despite these nuances, there can be no doubt that Ethiopia constitutes the GDR's most important bridgehead in Black Africa. By 1978, Ethiopia had become the GDR's leading economic partner there, with a total trade of 316.5 valutamarks. This figure for the most part reflected East German exports of agricultural equipment, construction machinery, trucks, textiles, medicines, and food. Ideologically, Mengistu's idiosyncratic interpretations of Marxism-Leninism did not prevent Honecker from joining with the Ethiopian leader in laying the cornerstone for the first "Karl Marx Memorial" on the continent. Even Honecker's failure to mention the Eritrean conflict may simply have been a means of avoiding direct reference to East German military support for the Derg's struggle against the separatist movements there. According to one Eritrean leader, the GDR has provided Mengistu with additional troops and advisers for pursuing the conflict.[26]

Next to Ethiopia, Angola and Mozambique have won the lion's share of East Germany's attentions in Africa. Honecker visited both countries on his first African swing in February 1979. In each case, long-term treaties of "friendship and cooperation" were concluded. [27] A comparison of these two treaties with each other and with the GDR-

Ethiopian treaty reveals some significant variations which may reflect the particular problems and varying degrees of dependence on the Soviet bloc exhibited by these three African states. As Valenta and Butler point out in Chapter 5, the treaty with Mozambique makes the most explicit reference to collaboration in the military sphere. The only reference to military assistance in the GDR-Ethiopian treaty is a veiled allusion to cooperation "in other areas" besides the political, economic, and cultural spheres. This resort to an implicit form of referring to the GDR's military aid to Ethiopia may be an additional example of the Soviet Union's desire to refrain from openly taking the Derg's side with respect to the civil war (an issue of some embarrassment to the Kremlin, which had once supported the Eritreans during Haile Selassie's rule) and to avoid further arousing Somalia's suspicions.

Curiously, however, the treaty between the GDR and Angola contains no references to military cooperation of any kind, either direct or implied. The treaty also omits mention of certain other areas of collaboration with the GDR, such as education, literature, film, the media, and the "training of cadres" (although agreements in some of these areas were concluded subsequently). Cooperation in these fields was explicitly mentioned in the treaties with Ethiopia and Mozambique. Furthermore, the GDR-Angola treaty fails to note that the two countries are working toward the "harmonization" (Abstimmung) of their foreign policies or that there exists a "natural anti-imperialist alliance between the socialist states and the national liberation movements." Statements to this effect were an integral part of the GDR's treaties with Mozambique and Ethiopia. Conceivably, the absence of clauses relating to these forms of cooperation with East Germany may be indicative of Neto's apparent wish to seek a greater measure of autonomy from the Soviet bloc in the period before his death. Meanwhile, in light of Mengistu's efforts to quash the Eritrean independence movements, the GDR-Ethiopian treaty does not include any support for "the people's right of self-determination," a principle staunchly defended in the GDR's treaties with Angola and Mozambique.

These differences present subtle but transparent evidence that the GDR (and the Soviet Union) must be sensitive to the particular interests of their African clients—interests which may not always coincide with those of the Soviet bloc—and to the reluctance exhibited by at least some of these states to being embraced too tightly by their benefactors in the Soviet alliance. In short, there are limits to the Soviet-East German engagement in Africa, a fact discussed at greater length by Valenta and Butler.

This is especially the case with respect to countries that are courted by the Soviets and their allies but are not exactly clients. Tanzania and Zambia represent two examples of African states with which the GDR has at various times sought improved relations but with only modest results. Prior to Tanzania's formation out of Tanganyika and Zanzibar, the government of Zanzibar in January 1964 became the first country in Africa to accord the GDR diplomatic recognition. Several months later, however, the new government of Tanzania under Julius Nyerere broke off relations with East Germany after the FRG threatened to invoke the Hallstein doctrine. Formal relations were not established until December 1972.

Zambia has become a more recent target of East German overtures. Erich Honecker visited the country on his African tour in February 1979. (The fact that the announcement that the SED chief would visit Zambia, Angola, and Libya came on the day of Honecker's departure and several days after his trip to Mozambique was revealed suggests that some difficulties may have been encountered in arranging his stops in these countries. [28]) His talks with Kenneth Kaunda were apparently aimed above all at putting relations between the two countries on a smoother track following the strain they had suffered in 1971, when the Zambian foreign ministry expelled the GDR's trade representative for interference in internal affairs. Zambia eventually recognized the GDR in early 1973, and received Werner Lamberz and his entourage in June 1977. Honecker's mission in 1979 resulted in a joint declaration rather than a formal treaty. Whether the GDR succeeds in drawing Zambia into closer ties remains doubtful, particularly as the Kaunda government relies heavily on trade and aid from the West. More pointedly, Zambia has good economic and political relations with the Federal Republic, as emphasized by Chancellor Helmut Schmidt's visit there in 1978. [29]

Indeed, the economic aspects of the East-West rivalry in Africa offer the most ponderous question about the long-term prospects for the GDR's African engagement. Up to now, most of the GDR's African clients have been engaged in some form of military struggle, whether internally (for example, the MPLA, ZAPU, and SWAPO) or internationally (for example, Ethiopia and Somalia). The GDR has managed to carve out an important role for itself as a supplier of military hardware and know-how to these forces. But what will happen when these struggles are over or lose their urgency and the regimes in question must grapple with the more protracted problems of economic development? Will the GDR turn out to be as reliable a partner for economic resources as it has been for military ones?

As already noted, the GDR's record as a supplier of aid is not exceptional. Between 1969 and 1978, East Germany provided African states with $440 million in development aid, as against $4.2 billion sent by the FRG. [30] Furthermore, the prospects for solidifying ties by expanding trade are not very promising, considering that countries like Ethiopia have little to offer the GDR beyond coffee and fruit. This will scarcely prove sufficient to cover the costs of importing East German technology and industrial machinery. Thus, the GDR's "trade" with many African countries in effect amounts to aid, and East Germany will therefore have to continue to operate at an economic loss there if it is to remain economically useful to them. On the positive side of the ledger, it has been reported that the GDR is importing coal from Mozambique and petroleum and copper from Angola. [31] Figures on these imports, however, have not been published by official East German sources.

In the long run, the GDR may have to rely increasingly on reaping the fruits of its current efforts at building a "Marxist-Leninist infrastructure" in friendly countries in order to ensure its continuing influence there. This, however, can prove to be a task of long duration, with few guarantees for success. Nevertheless, Africa will most assuredly remain a center of East German attentions in the future. It was with this interest in mind that the GDR's deputy foreign minister described Erich Honecker's first visit to the continent in 1979 as "a peak in the history of the foreign policy of the GDR."[32]

TABLE 4.5

GDR Trade Turnover with Selected African Countries
(millions of valutamarks)

Country	1970	1975	1976	1977	1978
Angola				236.0	233.7
Ethiopia	0.6	0.2	0.2	278.2	316.5
Ghana	2.2	17.7	9.1	17.7	15.5
People's Republic of the Congo	0.3	0.1	8.0	3.8	1.0
Mozambique				24.9	130.5
Nigeria	12.9	3.3	19.4	19.3	14.4
Tanzania	6.6	6.3	2.2	2.0	12.0

Source: Statistisches Jahrbuch 1979 der Deutschen Demokratischen Republik. (This source has not published separate figures for imports and exports for most countries since 1973, and it contains no trade data for other Black African countries.)

THE GDR AND THE MIDDLE EAST AND NORTH AFRICA

To be sure, economic factors are assuming a growing importance for the GDR's stake in the Third World, especially with respect to the GDR's need for more diversified energy sources. Nowhere is this more the case than in the GDR's relations with the Middle East. It is on this account that the SED regime is playing a supplicant's role once again, this time as a supplicant for oil. The GDR also plays an active role as a helpmate of Soviet policy in political dealings with favored states and groups such as South Yemen and the Palestine Liberation Organization (PLO). Accordingly, the ensuing analysis of the GDR's Middle East policy will look first at East Germany's relations with oil-exporting countries and next at its more politically oriented ties with Aden and the Palestinians.

East German statistics attest to the country's growing thirst for oil. Even though the GDR presently supplies approximately two-thirds of its energy needs out of domestically produced coal, petroleum imports nearly doubled from 1970 to 1978 (from 10. 3 to 19. 9 million metric tons). [33] The overwhelming bulk of these oil supplies was imported from the Soviet Union. Indeed, at a time when the Soviets themselves are faced with the prospect of dwindling domestic reserves and are urging their Eastern European allies to look elsewhere for oil, the GDR's petroleum dependence on the Soviet Union has actually <u>increased</u> in recent years. In 1975, East Germany imported 88. 8 percent of its petroleum from the Soviet Union; in 1978, the figure was 89. 4 percent. [34]

The GDR's inability to secure major oil supplies from OPEC producers is partly a function of price. Although the Soviets have substantially raised the price of the oil it exports to Warsaw Pact allies since 1975, these prices are still below current world market levels. Thus the GDR has little financial incentive to turn to the OPEC (Organization of Petroleum Exporting Countries) spot market. However, political considerations have also acted to obstruct the GDR's quest for new energy supplies. As Table 4. 6 indicates, Egypt was East Germany's leading petroleum supplier after the Soviet Union in 1970. The consequences of the Arab-Israeli war of 1973 and of President Sadat's subsequent foreign policy turnabout, however, resulted in a drastic setback in Egyptian oil deliveries to the GDR by the mid-1970s. Though trade as a whole continues to be lively between the two countries, official contacts have cooled in the wake of Sadat's Western orientation and the Camp David accords, which the GDR has vociferously condemned. [35] In December 1977, the Egyptian government ordered the closing of East Germany's consulate in Alexandria and two GDR cultural centers.

Iraq next emerged as the GDR's principal oil supplier after the

TABLE 4.6

Sources of GDR Petroleum Imports
(thousands of metric tons)

Country	1970	1975	1976	1977	1978
Soviet Union	9,233	15,097	16,012	17,007.0	17,760.0
Egypt	932	187	180	135.0	179.0
Iraq		1,454	1,576	1,072.0	1,157.0
Syria	18	240	258	301.0	350.0
Algeria				12.7	310.6
Total	10,183	16,978	18,026	18,527.7	19,656.6
Published total*	10,334	16,997	18,036	19,042.0	19,925.0
Unaccounted for in official GDR statistics	251	19	10	514.3	268.4

*The total figure for petroleum imports published. These official totals do not account for the sum of oil imports obtained when the columns indicating oil imports by country are added up.

Source: Statistisches Jahrbuch 1979 der Deutschen Demokratischen Republik.

Soviet Union. The East Germans first began importing oil from Iraq in 1972 (369,000 metric tons), and by 1976, following the conclusion of a long-term oil agreement in the previous year, this amount had nearly tripled. In the second half of the decade, however, the Baghdad government decided, apparently for economic reasons, to expand its trade relations with the West, including the FRG. [36] Trade with the Soviet bloc accordingly declined over the next several years, and by 1977 this tendency was perceptible in the case of the GDR. In that year, East German oil imports from Iraq fell by nearly a third of the previous year's total and continued to fall in 1978. As if to demonstrate its declining interest in doing business with the GDR, Iraq did not attend the meeting of the joint GDR-Iraq Standing Committee for Economic, Scientific and Technical Cooperation scheduled for the first quarter of 1979. The meeting was held only after an SED Politburo delegation under Günther Kleiber visited Baghdad in late April. Kleiber visited the country again in September 1979 for the next meeting of the standing committee. Meanwhile, the Iraqi regime renewed its drive

against local Communists, an action which the GDR criticized while
continuing to address Hussein and his fellow ministers as "comrades."[37]

It must be emphasized, however, that Iraq is one of the GDR's
closest friends in the Middle East. The GDR's political and economic
dealings with the Iraqis go back several years before the establishment of diplomatic relations in 1969. Since then, some 25 high- and
secondary-level exchanges have taken place, including visits to Iraq
in 1971 and 1977 by General Heinz Hoffmann, the GDR's defense minister. (Since 1973, Hoffmann has also been a member of the SED Politburo, in recognition of the political importance of his position.)
Finally, as noted earlier, Iraq is by far the GDR's leading trade partner in the Third World. What the GDR's somewhat disappointing experience in its oil dealings with Baghdad seems to indicate is that, as
a general rule, political friendship is no guarantee of secure petroleum supplies.

Syria has lately become another promising source of petroleum
for the motors of East Germany. Oil imports from Syria have risen
steadily over the last several years, reaching a total of 350,000 metric tons in 1978. However, the GDR's relations with President Assad's
regime, while friendly, are subject to the same tensions that occasionally distrub Moscow's ties with Damascus. Assad has been reluctant
to reduce economic links with the West and has generally sought sufficient room for independent maneuver in Middle East politics to avoid
complete subservience to Soviet wishes. Like a number of Arab states
joined together in the "Steadfast Front" against Israel, Syria calls
for the dissolution of the state of Israel, a cause which the Soviet Union does not share. The limits of Assad's willingness to adopt Moscow's views on a number of issues were apparent during the Syrian
president's visit to East Berlin in October 1978. Assad confined his
remarks primarily to Middle East questions, whereas Honecker addressed issues of European security and condemned the NATO powers
for intervention in Africa and in the Middle and Far East. If diplomatic
salutations are any guide to the degree of intimacy existing between
two states, then perhaps there is some significance in the fact that
Honecker referred to Assad as "Esteemed Comrad," whereas Assad
addressed the SED chief merely as "Esteemed Mr. Chairman Erich
Honecker."[38] The Syrian leader's visit concluded with the signing of
a rather bland Joint Declaration on Friendship and Cooperation between the two countries.[39]

Despite these elements of stiffness in the GDR-Syrian relationship, Syria and the GDR continue to enjoy close relations. Exchanges
of various official delegations began long before Syria formally recognized the GDR in 1969, and they have continued unabated ever since.
The visit of an East German military delegation under General Hoff-

mann in 1971 and meetings involving the GDR's interior minister with his Syrian counterpart in 1969, 1975, and 1976 are clear signs of the GDR's interest in Syrian military and police organizations. In addition, the pace of high-level SED Politburo meetings with Syrian officials has quickened in recent years. Between 1969 and 1973, there were ten secondary-level meetings between officials of the two states and only one high-level encounter. Since 1974, however, there have been eight high-level meetings (including trips to Baghdad by Sindermann in 1974, and Kleiber in 1975 and 1977 and twice in 1979) and seven secondary-level meetings. Moreover, trade with Syria continues to rise (see Table 4.7).

TABLE 4.7

GDR Trade Turnover with Selected Middle Eastern Countries (millions of valutamarks)

Country	1970	1975	1976	1977	1978
Algeria	27.2	72.9	120.3	101.3	324.0
Egypt	389.7	639.6	559.2	546.3	442.2
Iraq	48.7	764.2	779.0	595.0	724.7
Iran	27.4	62.1	96.9	120.8	159.5
Kuwait	8.9	31.0	39.7	42.6	38.0
Lebanon	32.7	58.2	67.9	35.7	55.2
Libya	6.4	12.1	63.3	84.8	13.3
Morocco	20.3	48.6	33.9	47.1	71.2
Sudan	25.0	33.3	47.7	51.3	46.1
Syria	67.0	211.2	348.6	344.4	405.7
Tunisia	10.3	13.4	15.4	29.2	25.3

Source: Statistisches Jahrbuch 1979 der Deutschen Demokratischen Republik. (This source provides no data on trade with South Yemen.)

Algeria has lately blossomed into another source of petroleum supplies. Oil imports rose from a mere 12,700 metric tons in 1977 to over 310,000 in 1978. However, the GDR has not engaged in direct high-level or secondary-level official contacts with Algeria to the same extent as it has with Iraq or Syria. Since establishing diplomatic relations with Algeria in 1970, the GDR has sent Defense Minister Hoffmann to Algiers in 1973, and the SED Politburo's economics ex-

pert, Günter Mittag, in 1977 and 1980. It has also signaled its support
for Algeria's demand for independence for the former Spanish Sahara
region currently contested between Morocco and the POLISARIO liberation movement.

Perhaps the most controversial ties between the GDR and the
Middle East center on Libya and Iran. While both states are known to
have supplied petroleum to the GDR in recent years, the East German
regime has not published statistics on these transactions. (This may
account for the fact that the sum of the oil imports from the countries
listed in Table 4. 6 is less than the official figure for total annual petroleum imports.) Both states represent regimes that are by nature
reprehensible to Soviet-style socialism. Qaddafi's militant Islamic
ideas, while fundamentally anti-Western, include a vehement denun-
ciation of communism, and the Shah's regime was hardly ideal from
Marxist-Leninist point of view. Nevertheless, the GDR began moving
closer to both states in the late 1970s, and in large measure because
of economic considerations.

Libya entered into diplomatic relations with the GDR in June
1973. Following the exchange of three secondary-level delegations
(in 1975, 1976, and 1977) the GDR moved to upgrade the level of its
contacts with Qaddafi's government in the fall of 1977. Politburo member Hermann Axen, responsible for international contacts, visited the
country in October 1977, and was soon followed by Special Ambassador Lamberz, who arrived in Tripoli in December of the same year.
It was on his second trip to Libya that Lamberz was killed in March
1978.

The high points of the GDR-Libyan relationship were reached
when Qaddafi visited East Berlin in June 1978 during a tour of Soviet-
bloc countries and when Honecker went to Tripoli on his African trip
in February 1979. Although friendly words were exchanged, the visits
did not result in any formal friendship and cooperation treaty. The
communiques signed on both occasions contained some clear differences of opinion when compared with Honecker's earlier remarks.
In particular, they did not refer to the SED chief's anti-NATO opinions. [40]

This omission was more than just an oversight. Libya's trade
with the West, and particularly with the FRG, has grown in recent
years, * thus providing Qaddafi with additional incentives to avoid

---

*West German imports from Libya amounted to 3. 4 billion DM
in 1975, 5. 2 billion in 1976, 5. 0 billion in 1977, and 3. 4 billion in
1978. FRG exports went from 1. 3 billion in 1975 to 1. 6 billion in 1978.
In addition, the level of FRG investments is high. Qaddafi has sought

moving too closely toward the Soviet bloc. The latent inter-German rivalry observable in these relationships appears to have worked to the GDR's disadvantage.

The GDR's connections with the Shah were especially intriguing. Sindermann visited Teheran in 1973, and the president of the National Iranian Oil Company, Egbal, met with Premier Willi Stoph in East Berlin in June 1977. Economic cooperation between the two nations intensified as the result of additional meetings between responsible officials. In September 1977, a delegation led by Deputy Prime Minister Rauchfuss met with the Shah and Prime Minister Amuzegar, and two months later Foreign Minister Oskar Fischer came to Iran for another meeting with the Shah. Most importantly, the GDR was on the verge of welcoming the Shah in East Berlin in late 1978, on the eve of his overthrow.

Prior to this event, relations between the GDR and Iran suffered a minor jolt in February 1978, when the GDR arrested a group of Iranian students who had been demonstrating against the Shah in front of the Iranian embassy in East Berlin. After sentencing a dozen of them to jail terms of up to a year, the East German authorities quickly expelled them. (Most had been students in West Berlin.) Iran complained that the students should have been imprisoned and recalled its ambassador on March 2. To calm the situation, a special emissary was dispatched to Teheran in May, bearing a letter from Honecker to the Shah. Matters were sufficiently smoothed over by late summer to enable the GDR to announce on September 9 that the Shah would begin a three-day visit to East Germany on September 14. The announcement was preceded by an interview with the Iranian monarch published in Neues Deutschland on September 6, in which the interviewers praised the Shah's "resolve" in seeking "a new democratic international economic order."[41] However, the revolutionary tumult that erupted in Iran shortly thereafter compelled the Shah to cancel the visit.

In the aftermath of the Shah's fall, the GDR moved cautiously to establish links with the new provisional government in Teheran. One week after his appointment as prime minister, Mehdi Bazargan received a telegram from Erich Honecker on February 13, 1979, which called for continuing cooperation between the two countries. The GDR's ambassador in Iran met with Foreign Minister Zandshabi ten days later to pursue this aim. In late May, the GDR-Iran Standing Committee for Economic, Scientific and Technical Cooperation met for the fourth time since its inception under the Shah. Meanwhile, GDR press com-

---

to improve political relations with Bonn in recent years, concluding an agreement to cooperate in combating terrorism, among other things.

mentary on Iranian events, while showing no great enthusiasm for
Ayatollah Khomeini, offered guarded approval for the revolution and
printed periodic reports of "U. S. threats" against the new regime.
(These reports continued following the takeover of the U. S. embassy
in November 1979.)

In spite of these efforts to maintain a working relationship with
the revolutionary government, the GDR suffered a decline in oil imports from Iran in the aftermath of the fall of the Shah. Although reliable statistics on the extent of this shortfall are not available, it
may be reasonably concluded that, in the wake of Khomeini's cancellation of the second pipeline to the Soviet Union and the general dis-
ruption of Iranian oil production that accompanied the revolution, the
collapse of the Shah's regime brought at least a temporary economic
loss for the GDR. It should be emphasized, however, that this loss
probably involved little more than 1 percent of the GDR's total oil imports.

It is largely strategic and political rather than economic considerations that underlie the GDR's relations with South Yemen and
the Palestine Liberation Organization. With its critical location at
the foot of the Arabian peninsula, the People's Republic of Yemen has
been the object of Soviet-bloc overtures ever since the South Yemeni
regime took an anti-Western turn in 1969. In June of that year, diplomatic relations were established with the GDR, and trade and related
agreements followed in the fall. As was later to be the case in Ethiopia, Angola, and Mozambique, the GDR began providing South Yemen
with credits, agricultural and communications technology, and scores
of economic advisers, propagandists, and teachers. Functionaries of
South Yemen's Socialist party are known to have been trained in SED
party schools. The GDR has been especially active in providing instructors and equipment for South Yemen's army and security police
and may even have trained members of the Aden-based People's Liberation Front of Oman (PLFO). GDR advisers also assisted the Yemeni regime in writing its constitution. [42] More than any other state
in the Middle East, South Yemen has come the closest to allowing the
GDR to attempt to build a Marxist-Leninist infrastructure, although
it is still too early to determine how far this effort has proceeded.

In the second half of the 1970s, high-level contacts between the
two countries increased substantially, culminating in Erich Honecker's
visit to Aden in November 1979. Earlier, State Council Chairman Willi
Stoph and Foreign Minister Oskar Fischer traveled to Aden in 1976,
and Werner Lamberz and General Hoffmann followed suit the following
year. These latter two visits were almost certainly intended to coordinate the GDR's training of Yemeni troops for operations against
Somalia in Ogaden. Honecker's trip resulted in the signing of a Treaty
of Friendship and Cooperation, which confirmed the "harmonization

of foreign policy activities" of the contracting parties for the next 20 years. [43] Although South Yemen is officially regarded in East Berlin as a "national-democratic state," Honecker addressed his host, Abdul Fattah Ismail, as "Comrade" and had words of praise for Islam. [44] He was less enthusiastic than Ismail about the desirability of reuniting North and South Yemen, however, although the final communique expressed the GDR's "satisfaction" with the Kuwait and Sanaa declarations regarding reunification. [45] In sum, South Yemen constitutes the most successful achievement to date of the GDR's activities as a Soviet surrogate in the Middle East.

The GDR's ties with the PLO have also developed significantly in recent years. On the basis of agreements signed in 1973 and 1978, the GDR has provided "noncivilian equipment" and financial assistance to the PLO, which complements considerable propaganda support. [46] Honecker met personally with Arafat on two occasions in 1978, and the PLO leader maintains contacts with East German representatives in Lebanon and elsewhere in the Middle East. In general, the GDR has strictly followed the Soviet line on the Middle East, tempering its support for a Palestinian state and opposition to the Camp David process with reluctance to support the PLO's demand for the destruction of Israel. Here again, the GDR plays a valuable supporting role on behalf of Soviet interests.

THE GDR AND SOUTH AND SOUTHEAST ASIA

Of all the Third World nations of Asia, stretching from the Indian subcontinent to the Philippine Islands, India remains the chief object of the GDR's attentions. Honecker himself underscored East Germany's special interest in India when he led a 167-member delegation there in January 1979. The visit climaxed a series of high-level exchanges between the two countries which received a particular impetus in 1976, when Indira Ghandi became the first non-Communist head of government to make a state visit to the GDR. Earlier in the same year, the ubiquitous General Hoffmann headed a military delegation to India, possibly to coordinate East German training programs for pilots of India's MIG-21s, [47] and Sindermann led a group to New Delhi in 1978.

The GDR's ties with India date from 1954, when the first trade agreement was concluded between the two countries. Over the course of the next decades, the GDR adopted the same positions as the Soviet Union in its stance toward India, voicing support for New Delhi's position in its conflicts with Portugal, Pakistan, and China and expressing "sympathy" for Indira Ghandi's emergency laws. [48] Following her removal from power, political relations cooled somewhat, and this

coolness was reflected in the atmosphere surrounding Honecker's
visit. The communique that concluded the trip was somewhat perfunc-
tory, and neither Prime Minister Desai nor President Reddy expressed
any enthusiasm for Honecker's expressions of solidarity with Vietnam's
struggle in Cambodia or with Brezhnev's proposals for European disarmament of October 1978. It may therefore be assumed that the East
Germans were just as pleased as the Soviets when Ghandi returned to
power.

Afghanistan has assumed a special importance for all Soviet-
bloc states as a consequence of the Soviet invasion of December 1979,
which followed a series of changes in the Afghan leadership. To date
the GDR's role in the wake of the invasion has largely been devoted
to echoing approval of Soviet actions. [49] The first "solidarity aid" to
Afghanistan was dispatched in September 1978 by the GDR's solidariy
committees, and East German hospitals have been caring for injured
Soviet soldiers in the period since the invasion began. Despite this
obligatory backing of the Soviet involvement in Afghanistan, the GDR
may have good reason to feel uncomfortable about some of its consequences. For one thing, the GDR joined with the Soviets in losing face
before the majority of Third World states at the United Nations, where
the invasion was roundly condemned. East Germany's pro-invasion
stance was particularly visible inasmuch as the GDR was taking its
turn as a member of the Security Council when the issue came up for
consideration in late January and used its vote to sustain the Soviet
veto of a resolution denouncing the invasion. For another, East Berlin
has a great deal of economic and other benefits to lose in the event of
a rupture of detente and a reversion to a tenser East-West relationship. As a result, the East Germans have sought to prevent the Afghan
events from damaging their ties with West Germany and other Western
European states.

Most of the GDR's East Asian engagement has been concentrated
in the Communist states of the region. Trade and political relations
with the non-Communist nations of Southeast Asia tend to be considerably less intense than the GDR's involvement in Africa or the Middle
East. The pinnacle of direct high-level contacts in this area was
reached in December 1977, when Honecker led a delegation to the
Philippines. The apparent purposes of the visit, beyond simply demonstrating the GDR's interest in Southeast Asia, were to improve trade
relations and promote Soviet schemes for an Asian collective security
agreement. Although the trip resulted in the signing of a trade agreement, the communique made no mention of the Soviet proposal. [50] The
GDR's relations with other countries in the region are generally limited to trade ties and the usual propaganda support for Communist or
allied forces.

TABLE 4.8

GDR Trade Turnover with Non-Communist Asian States
(millions of valutamarks)

Country	1970	1975	1976	1977	1978
India	276.9	351.4	348.1	339.3	472.1
Indonesia	6.9	22.2	28.5	41.7	39.9
Malaysia		22.8	28.1	48.4	52.9
Pakistan	0.5	17.4	30.3	14.2	11.9
Sri Lanka	20.5	28.7	27.8	14.1	14.8

Source: Statistisches Jahrbuch 1979 der Deutschen Demokratischen Republik. (This source contains no data for trade with other non-Communist Asian states.)

THE GDR AND LATIN AMERICA

Ever since the inauguration of the Allende government in Chile in 1970, the GDR has manifested a widening interest in the problems of Latin America. Earlier, East Germany's presence in the area was confined largely to trade relations with a handful of governments, the most important of which (Brazil) it regarded as politically contemptible. Allende's election brought a decided upsurge in the GDR's economic and political engagement in the region. Between 1970 and 1973, the GDR demonstrated its support for the Allende regime by means of extensive activity on the part of its solidarity committees and vastly increased trade relations. (GDR exports to Chile grew from 3.3 million VM in 1969 to 32 million VM in 1973, while imports increased from 0.2 million VM to 69.2 million in the same years.)[51] Even now some 1,500 Chilean exiles who supported Allende reside in the GDR.[52]

A recent analysis of Latin America by an East German specialist concluded that, despite the success of the "counterrevolutionary violence" exercised by the United States in Chile and elsewhere on the continent, the prospects for "national-democratic and anti-imperialistic revolutions" are improving, thus "clearing the path for socialism." Recent revolutionary developments in Nicaragua and Grenada are singled out as prime examples of this process, and leftist forces in other countries are seen as becoming "strengthened" as a result of efforts to repress them. Meanwhile, Mexico and Venezuela are described as oil-rich states exhibiting "tendencies toward a stronger anti-imperialist consciousness."[53]

While some of this analysis borders on the hyperbolic, it is nevertheless true that events in several Latin American countries have lately opened up new opportunities for the GDR to expand its political and economic undertakings there. Nicaragua is a case in point. In addition to providing rhetorical support for the Sandinistas for several years, the GDR signaled its willingness to help the revolutionary regime by sending Foreign Minister Fischer to Nicaragua in September 1979, barely two months after recognizing the new post-Somoza government. In December an East German plane transported a group of wounded Sandinistas to the GDR for medical treatment,[54] and in early April 1980 a series of agreements on economic, cultural, and scientific cooperation were signed, all "in the spirit of anti-imperialist solidarity."[55] Elsewhere in Latin America, the GDR has sought to improve ties with Guyana (President Burnham met with Honecker in East Berlin in 1978) and Panama (which signed a trade agreement with the GDR in early 1980). In addition, the SED maintains good contacts with established Latin American Communist parties.

Meanwhile, the GDR has also sought to broaden its economic dealings in the area in accordance with its role as an oil supplicant. Mexico, with its newly discovered petroleum reserves, has come to occupy a special place in East Germany's calculations. Honecker sent a special message to President Lopez-Portillo in March 1978, and in November the first meeting of the GDR-Mexico Mixed Government Commission was convened in East Berlin. Most importantly, Günter Mittag visited Mexico in June 1980, and signed trade agreements which foresee a turnover of $250 million by 1982. In addition, Mittag concluded special long-term agreements providing for cooperative undertakings by the state-run industrial sectors of the two countries. These agreements will enable the GDR to take advantage of low production costs in Mexico to manufacture products there for export to North America. For its part, Mexico did not come through with the desired promises of oil deliveries to the GDR, at least until 1983. Clearly, however, the GDR hopes to gain a firm economic foothold in Mexico, with a view to gaining eventual access to its prized petroleum resources.[56]

The GDR has also sought to expand its trade relations with Ecuador and Colombia, both of which welcomed Fischer for talks in 1979, as well as with other traditional trade partners, such as Argentina, Brazil, and Peru (see Table 4.9). Even Pinochet's Chile, despite constant vilification in the East German press, signed a trade agreement in June 1980, following two years of negotiations initiated at the GDR's behest.[57]

In short, Latin America is developing into a fertile area for East Germany's dual activities as Soviet surrogate and economic supplicant. While it by no means occupies the same level of importance for the

TABLE 4. 9

GDR Trade Turnover with Selected Latin American Countries
(millions of valutamarks)

Country	1970	1975	1976	1977	1978
Argentina	11. 3	26. 4	47. 3	169. 9	148. 8
Brazil	242. 5	263. 5	498. 7	462. 9	507. 4
Colombia	57. 6	40. 0	120. 0	153. 1	102. 2
Mexico	13. 8	35. 8	33. 9	44. 2	49. 6
Peru	50. 5	122. 7	126. 3	232. 7	157. 8

Source: Statistisches Jahrbuch 1979 der Deutschen Demokratischen Republik. (This source contains no trade data for other Latin
American countries.)

GDR as does Africa or the Middle East, its potential for development
as a target of future GDR engagement cannot be underestimated.

FUNCTIONS OF THE GDR'S THIRD WORLD ENGAGEMENT

The GDR's activities in the Third World may be viewed as ful-
filling four functions: (1) assisting the Soviet Union's efforts to influence various Third World states or liberation movements; (2) providing the GDR with necessary import goods and export markets; (3) enhancing the international visibility and prestige of the GDR, a goal
which assumes special significance in view of East Germany's continuing rivalry with the Federal Republic; and (4) bolstering the internal legitimacy of the GDR.

Little has been said thus far about the last two functions. Both,
however, are important features of the GDR's Third World engagement. Even though the GDR has normalized its relations with Bonn
and has won diplomatic recognition by nearly all the states of the
world as a consequence, the rivalry with the FRG for prestige and
influence in the Third World remains a live issue. On occasion, the
GDR has gained support among developing nations for its political positions with respect to the "German question. " Certain of the GDR's
"friendship and cooperation" treaties, for example, refer to "Berlin"
as "the capital of the German Democratic Republic, " and some states
(such as Mozambique and Guinea-Bissau) have actually rejected aid
from the FRG owing in part to differences over the status of Berlin. [58]

The East German government has also developed its own version of the "sole representation" theory, presenting itself as the sole custodian of the "good" German traditions of social justice, cultural development, and peace, in contrast to the negative traits of imperialism allegedly characteristic of the Federal Republic.

To be sure, the GDR still perceives itself as engaged in a continuing rivalry with the FRG in the Third World. Articles appearing in East German foreign policy journals periodically denounce Bonn's "neocolonial" designs, which are ostensibly aimed at undermining relations between the Third World and the Soviet bloc and at keeping open the "German question" to the detriment of the GDR's ties with the less developed countries. [59] This view corresponds fully with the GDR's (and the Kremlin's) notion that detente is not indivisible; hence, the diminution of inter-German tensions in Europe does not of itself imply a need for the GDR to abate the "ideological confrontation" in other parts of the world. [60] As a result, the GDR not only keeps up a steady barrage of propaganda assaults at Bonn's Third World policies but has even used its influence in certain client states to obstruct their relations with Bonn. Thus, the GDR was probably responsible for Ethiopia's expulsion of the West German ambassador in 1978 and for the collapse of negotiations between the FRG and Mozambique and Cape Verde in the same year. [61] Moreover, a good deal of East Germany's propaganda and other activities at the United Nations are also directed squarely at the FRG. [62] For its part, the government of the Federal Republic, while holding to its position on Berlin, has been working to avoid direct conflicts with the GDR in the Third World in the interest of maintaining correct, and occasionally even cooperative, inter-German relations there. [63]

As a general rule, however, it is mainly in closely allied client states that the GDR has succeeded in curbing or blocking improved relations with the FRG. Since the leaders of these states, normally a group of self-proclaimed "Socialists," tend to be predisposed against the West anyway, it is perhaps surprising that the East Germans and the Soviets must occasionally use pressure to prevent them from seeking to establish closer economic or political contacts with Bonn. Elsewhere in the Third World, however, the GDR has been less successful in wooing erstwhile "anti-imperialistic" countries into more intimate ties at the expense of relations with the West. In part this failure has been due to political factors (such as commitments by the states in question to real nonalignment or to a rejection of communism), but economic considerations also play a role.

On occasion these economic factors join with political ones in thwarting the GDR's efforts to counter Bonn's influence in the Third World, largely as a result of the FRG's superior economic engagement in Third World countries. GDR writers themselves note that

Bonn allocated 3. 4 billion DM to development aid in 1979 alone and that by 1977 the FRG had exported state and private capital to the developing world in excess of 120 billion DM. [64] The FRG's contributions to such funds as the United Nations Development Program have also substantially exceeded those of the GDR. [65] As we have already seen, certain states courted by the GDR have held back from intensifying their relations with the Soviet bloc at least in part because of their need for Western aid or trade (such as Libya and Zambia). Even the Sandinista regime in Nicaragua, clearly a target of GDR overtures, recently manifested its interest in obtaining economic assistance from all possible sources when it sent separate delegations to the GDR and the FRG to discuss aid requests. Over the long term, the West's substantial economic involvement in the developing countries may prove to be a major factor in countering Soviet-bloc influences in the Third World.

The internal function that is served by the GDR's endeavors in the Third World is clearly regarded by the SED leadership as an important one. Visits to East Berlin by Third World dignitaries and the reception accorded East German leaders abroad have been portrayed with banner headlines and photographs on the front page of Neues Deutschland with growing frequency. The manifest pride the GDR authorities take in these displays of public diplomacy is obviously intended to "rub off" on the citizens of the GDR, with a view to extracting greater popular support for the SED as the legitimate ruling force in a duly recognized state. It should also be pointed out that the GDR's front-and-center involvement in the Third World demonstrably contributes to enhancing its prestige among its Warsaw Pact allies. It may very well be the case that the GDR hopes to make the GDR as indispensable to the Soviet Union in the Third World as it is in Europe.

However significant these last two functions may be, it is the first two that directly underlie the GDR's motivations in the Third World. The role of Soviet surrogate and the role of economic supplicant are unquestionably the most vital functions that East Germany's Third World policies perform. Although the prevalence of one role over the other may vary from country to country, on the whole the GDR is presently both a surrogate and a supplicant in the Third World. But what will the future bring?

As already mentioned, East Germany's interventions in several Third World countries in recent years have involved political, military, and economic support for "Socialist" regimes struggling for internal supremacy or against foreign adversaries. The checkered history of numerous developing nations in the last decades, however, offers ample warnings against the assumption that pro-Soviet clients maintain either their domestic power or their foreign friendships indefinitely. East German writers on the Third World appear to be grimly aware of the unpredictable nature of these realities. Whether the Soviet Union and its allies can "hold on" to countries like Ethiopia (which recently signed a mutual assistance treaty with Kenya) or Angola (which has shown some signs of moving away from excessive reliance on Moscow) thus remains an open question. Furthermore, the economic costs to the GDR of helping to maintain its various clients may prove to be a severe strain on the East German economy, which is already beset with staggering costs and decelerating growth rates. Thus the GDR's successes in the developing world are not without insecurities or liabilities.

In addition, it appears certain that the GDR's future relations with the Third World will also center around its need for petroleum and other raw materials. In this domain, too, success is neither guaranteed nor inexpensive. What is certain is that the price of OPEC oil will impose yet another strain on the East German economic system (as well as on its foreign currency reserves), while the availability of supplies will hinge to no small extent on political decisions that neither Moscow nor East Berlin may be able to influence, no matter how great their political support for the countries in question.

In the end, the GDR's Third World ventures, like the imperialist ambitions of the Eastern powers in an earlier epoch, may prove to bring more burdens than benefits.

NOTES

1. For Nehru's attitude, see Eberhard Schneider, "Südasien," in Drei Jahrzenhnte Aussenpolitik der DDR, Hans-Adolf Jacobsen, et al., (Munich: R. Oldenbourg Verlag, 1979), pp. 703-4. For Nasser's, see Bernard von Plate, "Der Nahe und Mittlere Osten sowie der Maghreb," ibid., p. 681.

2. For an elaboration of the international dimensions of the inter-German conflict in this period, see Heinrich End, Zweimal deutsche Aussenpolitik (Cologne: Verlag Wissenschaft und Politik, 1972).

3. In the period 1950-71, the FRG dispersed some $5 billion in the Third World. Cited in Hans Siegfried Lamm and Siegfried Kupper, DDR und Dritte Welt (Munich: R. Oldenbourg Verlag, 1976), p. 139.

4. Egypt's "invitation" to Ulbricht was actually the result of a letter from the SED leader to Nasser informing him that, for reasons of health, a visit to a warm country would be desirable. See Henning von Löwis, "Das politische und militärische Engagement der Deutschen Demokratischen Republik in Schwarzafrika," Beiträge zur Konfliktforschung, no. 1 (1978): 23.

5. In 1977, an East German writer listed the following states in

this category: Algeria, Angola, Burma, Guinea, Guinea-Bissau, Iraq, the People's Democratic Republic of Yemen, Congo-Brazzaville, Mozambique, Somalia, Syria, and Tunisia. Ethiopia is conspicuously absent from this list. See Martin Robbe, "Die Dritte Welt: Deuting und Fehldeutung," Deutsche Aussenpolitik, no. 3 (1977): 69-70.

6. Ibid., p. 70.

7. See G. Brehme, ed., Der national-demokratische Staat in Asien und Afrika (East Berlin: Staatsverlag der Deutschen Demokratischen Republik, 1976).

8. Robbe, "Die Dritte Welt," pp. 75-78.

9. Brehme, Der national-demokratische Staat, pp. 147, 148.

10. See Helmut Faulwetter and Gerhard Scharschmidt, "Die Forderung der Entwicklungsländer nach einer 'Neuen internationalen Wirtschaftsordunung' im Lichte einiger jüngster Entwicklungstendenzen im kapitalistischen Weltwirtschaftssystem," Deutsche Aussenpolitik, no. 3 (1978): 74-78.

11. Statement by the GDR representative to the U.N. Economic Commission, November 14, 1979. Cited in Deutschland Archiv, no. 12 (1979): 1347.

12. Statistisches Jahrbuch 1979 der Deutschen Demokratischen Republik, Berlin, 1979.

13. Cited in Lamm and Kupper, DDR und Dritte Welt, p. 136.

14. Tadeusz T. Kaczmarek, "Stosunki ekonomiczno-handlowe NRD z krajami rozwijającymi się," Handel Zagraniczny, no. 2 (1979): 16-18. I am indebted to Dr. Heinrich Machowski for providing me with this source.

15. For a discussion of the domestic repercussions of the GDR's current economic predicament and their possible evolution in the 1980s, see Michael J. Sodaro, "Foreign and Domestic Policy Linkages in the GDR" (Paper prepared for the Conference on Eastern Europe in the 1980s, George Washington University, April 4-5, 1980).

16. On the role of the GDR solidarity committees, see Kurt Krüger, "Solidarität der DDR mit den Völkern Asiens, Afrikas und Lateinamerikas," Deutsche Aussenpolitik, no. 10 (1979): 52-64.

17. See, for example, Melvin Croan, "A New Afrika Korps?," Washington Quarterly 3, no. 1 (Winter 1980): 21-37; and Joachim Nawrocki, "Hoffmanns Afrikakorps," Die Zeit, May 26, 1978.

18. For an account of the GDR's early political relations with Africa, see Löwis, "DDR in Schwarzafrika," pp. 5-38.

19. See Ilona Schleicher, "Internationalistische Entwicklung der FRELIMO und ihre Beziehungen zur SED," Deutsche Aussinpolitik, no. 7 (1979): 62-76.

20. See Jürgen Zenker, "Zusammenarbeit der SED mit revolutionär-demokratischen Parteien in Afrika und Asien," Deutsche Aussenpolitik, no. 10 (1977): 93-106. The GDR's consistent support for

Nkomo prior to Zimbabwe's independence in 1980 served to sour its relations with Mugabe's government afterward. For an East German study that glosses over these facts, see Christa Schaffmann, Simbabwe ist frei (East Berlin: Dietz Verlag, 1980).

21. See Henning von Löwis of Menar, "Das afrikanische Erbe von Werner Lamberz," Deutschland Archiv, no. 4 (1978): 348-51.

22. For the text, see Neues Deutschland, November 26, 1978 (hereafter cited as ND).

23. For the text, see ND, November 19, 1979.

24. See, for example, the toasts offered by Honecker and Mengistu in ND, November 27, 1978, and Honecker's speech in ND, November 15, 1979.

25. The GDR's support for Mengistu has not always been consistent. While the power struggle in the Derg was still on, the GDR hinted its support for Teferi Benti, who was subsequently shot by Mengistu himself. See Bernard von Plate, "Aspekte der SED—Parteibeziehungen in Afrika und der arabischen Region," Deutschland Archiv, no. 2 (1979): 144.

26. See the statement by Taha Mohammed of the Eritrean Liberation Front, cited in Henning von Löwis of Menar, "Die DDR als Schrittmacher im weltrevolutionären Prozess," Deutschland Archiv, no. 1 (1980): 44.

27. The text of the GDR-Angola treaty is in ND, February 20, 1979; the GDR-Mozambique treaty is in ND, February 26, 1979.

28. See Johannes Kuppe, pp. 347-52. "Investitionen, die sich lohnten," Deutschland Archiv, no. 4 (1979).

29. Between 1975 and 1978, the FRG imported 983. 2 million DM worth of goods from Zambia and exported goods worth 632. 3 million DM. See Statistisches Bundesamt, Statistisches Jahrbuch 1979 der Bundesrepublik Deutschland.

30. Der Spiegel, no. 10 (1980): 43. Löwis has estimated that the GDR spends more than $250 million per year in Africa, of which $100 million is for military purposes. See "Africa, Expensive Luxury at $250 million a Year," To the Point, September 22, 1978.

31. Der Spiegel, no. 10 (1980): 52.

32. Klaus Willerding, "Zur Afrikapolitik der DDR," Deutsche Aussenpolitik, no. 8 (1979): 5.

33. Statistisches Jahrbuch 1979 der Deutschen Demokratischen Republik.

34. Calculated from figures in ibid.

35. On the GDR's reactions to the Egyptian-Israeli peace process, see Henning von Löwis of Menar, "Geschichte ist ein schneller Reiter," Deutschland Archiv, no. 5 (1979): 461-64.

36. Direct FRG exports to Iraq jumped from 931. 4 million DM in 1974 to 2. 5 billion in 1975. Over the next several years, FRG ex-

ports averaged 1.7 billion DM. Meanwhile, the value of West German oil imports from Iraq went from 285 million DM in 1975 to 386 million DM in 1978. See Statistisches Bundesamt, Aussenhandel mit den Entwicklungländern (Spezialhandel), 1978.

37. See Kurt Seliger, "Solidarität und Staatsraison," Deutschland Archiv, no. 11 (1979): 1195-97.

38. ND, October 2, 1978.

39. For the text, see ND, October 5, 1978.

40. For the texts, see ND, June 29, 1978, and February 19, 1979. See also Kuppe, Investitionem, p. 348.

41. ND, September 6, 1978.

42. See Löwis of Menar, "Die DDR als Schrittmacher," pp. 46, 48.

43. For the text, see ND, November 19, 1979.

44. See Honecker's toast in ND, November 16, 1979.

45. ND, November 19, 1979.

46. See Peter Dittmar, "Uneingeschränkte Unterstützung," Deutschland Archiv, no. 8 (1978): 807.

47. See Johannes Kuppe, "Honecker in Indien," Deutschland Archiv, no. 2 (1979): 120-23.

48. Ibid. See also Lamm and Kupper, DDR und Dritte Welt, for a case study of Indian-GDR relations, and Schneider, "Südasien," pp. 699 ff.

49. For the GDR's reactions to events in Afghanistan, see Karl Wilhelm Fricke, "Der Fall Afhanistan im Spiegel des Neuen Deutschlands," Deutschland Archiv, no. 2 (1980): 123-26.

50. For the communique, see ND, December 9, 1977. See also Joachim Glaubitz, "Ost und Südostasien sowie Ozeanien," in Drei Jahrzehnte Aussenpolitik der DDR, Hans-Adolf Jacobsen, et al. (Munich: R. Olderbourg Verlag, 1979), p. 735.

51. Cited in Heinrik Bischof, "Lateinamerika (Ausser Kuba)," in Drei Jahrzehnte Aussenpolitik der DDR, Hans-Adolf Jacobsen, et. al. (Munich: R. Oldenbourg Verlag, 1979), p. 649.

52. Krüger, "Solidarität der DDT," p. 64.

53. Manfred Uschner, "Neue revolutionäre Erschütterungen in Lateinamerika," Deutsche Aussenpolitik, no. 12 (1979): 43, 45.

54. ND, December 28, 1979.

55. ND, April 2, 1980. No precise figures were cited in this source.

56. Frankfurter Allgemeine Zeitung, June 9, 1980.

57. Der Tagespiegel (West Berlin), June 15, 1980.

58. Der Spiegel, no. 10 (1980): 58-59. See also Löwis of Menar, "Die DDR als Schrittmacher," pp. 40-41.

59. See, for example, Gertraud Liebscher, "Die Politik der BRD gegenüber Entwicklungsländern," Deutsche Aussenpolitik, no. 3

(1980): 47–49. The GDR has also criticized the efforts of the SPD and the Socialist International in support of social democratic movements in the Third World. See Uschner, "Neüe revolutionäre Erschutterungen in Lateinamerika," pp. 51–52.

60. On the GDR's efforts to maintain favorable ties with the FRG in the wake of the Iran and Afghanistan events, see "East Germany Worried About A Confrontation with West over Iran," New York Times, April 20, 1980.

61. von Plate, "Aspekte der SED," p. 141.

62. For an extended treatment of the GDR's role in the United Nations, see Wilhelm Bruns, Die UNO-Politik der DDR (Stuttgart: Verlag Bonn Aktuell, 1978).

63. Der Spiegel, no. 10 (1980): 60–61.

64. Liebscher, "Die Politik der BRD," pp. 52, 53.

65. Between 1976 and 1980 (inclusive), the FRG's contributions to the UNDP totaled $272,054,135, while the GDR contributed $5,651,817. Source: UNDP, New York.

5

EAST GERMAN SECURITY POLICIES IN AFRICA

Jiri Valenta and Shannon Butler

When the German Democratic Republic (GDR) initially became involved in Africa in the late 1950s, its actions were part of an overall effort to achieve international legitimacy and, coincidental with this objective, to use Africa as an arena for countering the Hallstein doctrine. * These efforts were notably nonmilitary in nature, instead involving the formation of economic and cultural ties with various nations to be used as a stepping stone for expanded diplomatic connections and, ultimately, full diplomatic relations.

East Germany gradually became involved in Guinea and Ghana in the late 1950s and in other countries (most notably Egypt, Algeria, Mali, and Tanzania) in the 1960s. The GDR did manage to conclude agreements in various fields which opened the door for subsequent moves into the continent; by 1968, the GDR had a number of varied relations and agreements with 13 African nations (see Table 5.1).

----

*The Hallstein doctrine, named after its originator Dr. Walter Hallstein, a former Common Market president and Konrad Adenauer's first secretary for foreign affairs, was formulated in the late 1950s and proscribed diplomatic ties with any country that recognized East Germany. Implied in the doctrine was the idea that the Federal Republic of Germany (FRG) was the sole legitimate authority capable of speaking and acting for the German nation. Withdrawal of diplomatic ties carried with it withdrawal of all economic ties, a condition which few developing African nations were prepared to accept. Thus, the doctrine served the FRG well in its actions against GDR initiatives in Africa.

TABLE 5.1

East Germany's Relations with Africa in 1968

Country	Consular Relations	Resident Trade Missions	Cooperation Agreements					
			General Economic	Air Transport	Technical	General Cultural	Education, Training	Trade, Payments
Algeria		X[a]		X		X	X	X
Congo–Brazzaville		X	X					
Dahomey						X		X
Ethiopia			X	X				
Guinea		X[a]		X	X	X	X	X
Libya		X						
Mali		X[a]	X	X	X	X	X	X
Morocco		X[a]						X
Sudan		X[a]		X				X
Tanzania	X		X			X		X
Tunisia		X[a]	X			X	X	X
United Arab Republic	X[b]		X	X	X	X		X
Zambia		X						

[a]"Government level," by mutual agreement.
[b]Raised to "mission level" but without diplomatic status in January 1969; to embassy status in mid–1969.
Source: William W. Marsh, "East Germany and Africa," Africa Report 14 (March–April 1969): 60.

Despite these "advances," the GDR encountered the Hallstein doctrine at every bend in the road. For example, when Zanzibar (which had recognized East Germany prior to its union with Tanganyika) merged with Tanganyika in early 1965, the Tanzanian government announced that the East Germany embassy in Zanzibar had ceased to hold embassy status and that its decision to accept the establishment of a consulate-general from the GDR in Dar-es-Salaam was not intended to give or imply diplomatic recognition. [1] Other African governments with which the GDR had agreements were also quick to make it clear to the FRG that these agreements, as well as the establishment of trade missions, in no way meant diplomatic relations had been established with the GDR. It was only in the late 1960s—and then only with the Arab nations of Egypt, Algeria, and Sudan—that the GDR was able to realize full diplomatic relations with any African country, largely as a result of rampant anti-Israeli sentiment following the 1967 war and the implications of the FRG as an arms supplier to the Israelis.

The second stage of East German initiatives in Africa in the 1970s witnessed an increased emphasis on military and security aspects of GDR foreign policy. * The area focus of the GDR's activity also shifted in the mid-1970s, primarily to Angola, Mozambique, and Ethiopia, all three Marxist-Leninist espousing countries, and to the national liberation movements that sprouted in the decade of the 1970s: the Zimbabwe African People's Union (ZAPU) faction of the Patriotic Front, the African National Congress (ANC) of South Africa and the Southwest Africa People's Organization (SWAPO). † Having ridden the roller coaster of Soviet experiences with "nonprogressive" countries

---

*The GDR's military role in Africa actually began in 1969 with its support of FRELIMO forces. There are also unconfirmed reports of East German pilots flying against Biafra during the Nigerian civil war. However, these activities were on a small scale, and it wasn't until about 1973, with the military treaties with Angola and Congo-Brazzaville, that the GDR entered upon the African scene as a force to be reckoned with.

†Since the normalization of the GDR's international status in 1972-74, it has had, of course, varied relations with most African countries. In fact, the GDR includes such countries as Guinea Bissau, Cape Verde Islands, the Congo, Benin, Saõ Tomé e Príncipe in its listing of "progressive" nations. However, the three largest and most attractive countries from an economic and strategic standpoint are Angola, Mozambique, and Ethiopia, and it is upon these three that most attention is lavished.

in the late 1950s and 1960s, the East Germans now seem to believe that a "foot in the door" can more likely become an "open door" with those countries and movements of similar ideological tastes.

East Germany's new role in Africa in the 1970s (particularly in contrast to its earlier failures on the continent in the 1960s), its opportunities and constraints, and a future assessment for an East German role in other areas of the strategic Third World will be the focus of this essay. First, however, it is perhaps necessary to discuss briefly those major external and internal factors which have contributed to the GDR's assertiveness in Africa in the 1970s.

EXTERNAL FACTORS

The GDR-Soviet Alliance

Walter Ulbricht's downfall in 1971, resulting largely from his obstinate refusal to follow Soviet rapprochement with the FRG, marked a turning point in GDR-Soviet relations. With Ulbricht went the notion that the GDR was somehow different from the other Socialist nations. This shift was reflected in the revised constitution of 1974, which no longer spoke of a German nation divided into two states. The GDR was now "a socialist peasant's and workers' state . . . irrevocably allied with the Soviet Union."[2] The changes in the new constitution were followed in quick succession by a new treaty of friendship, cooperation, and mutual assistance, signed in 1975, and by the 1976 party congress, which adopted a new party program and statute. All three have served to underscore the post-Ulbricht era of even closer relations between the two countries—relations which are most notably marked by the GDR's eager willingness to follow the Soviet lead in foreign and domestic affairs. Thus since 1971 the GDR has moved even closer to complete integration with the Soviet Union in all facets of their relationships—military, economic, and politico-ideological. This closeness has, in reality, an air of East German subordination.

In the military sphere, for example, the National People's Army (NVA), which includes ground, air, and naval forces, is the only Warsaw Pact military force directly subordinate to the Soviet-controlled Warsaw Treaty Organization. While the NVA is both well trained and equipped, it is relatively small. The ground forces consist of six divisions, the air force has about 350 fighter-bomber aircraft, and the navy has a small number of limited-range ships which operate primarily in the Baltic. The Soviet Union has not judged (and probably never will judge) it propitious to build up the size of the NVA. Such an act would expose the Soviet Union not only to charges from the West of encouraging German militarism but also would probably have equally sensitive implications for the GDR's Eastern European neighbors, Poland and Czechoslovakia.

In security matters, while details are lacking because of the inherently secretive nature of such activities, it can be reasonably assumed that the GDR's State Security Service (SSD) is closely linked to the Soviet KGB. Further, it is difficult to imagine the absence of close cooperation in this field when security matters play such an important role in the Soviet Union's foreign policy.

Perhaps the most salient feature of East German-Soviet economic relations is the GDR's continued dependence upon Soviet exports of raw materials, particularly oil. East German concern for continuing oil supplies was reflected in the agreement concluded in 1980 on the coordination of the Soviet-GDR five-year plans for 1981-85, which assures Soviet deliveries throughout the period and at a price, which while still high, is below world market prices.

In the politico-ideological arena, the similarity of the organizational structures of the Socialist Unity Party (SED) and the Communist Party of the Soviet Union (CPSU) provides the basis for closely coordinated actions. Political integration is visible not only at the highest Party echelons, but also down through the ranks to at least the district level. Ideologically, the GDR is constitutionally committed to Socialist Internationalism and to the development of all-around friendship and cooperation with the Soviet Union.

While the scope and depth of GDR integration with (and concomitant dependence on) the Soviet Union places constraints upon East Germany's foreign policy, the closeness of this relationship also makes the GDR a valuable asset to the Soviet Union's foreign policy in the Third World. East German expertise in know-how, managerial skills, and military and police matters, as well as a traditional efficiency, are all useful tools which can be easily translated from the regional context (the Warsaw Pact) into the international environment.

East Germany's Post-1968 Overshadowing of Czechoslovakia

Up to 1968, Czechoslovakia played the major role, next to the Soviet Union, in both Eastern European matters and Third World foreign policy. Czechoslovakia had a substantial indigenous arms industry and was able to provide developing countries with considerable numbers and varieties of military equipment. They also acted as a "go-between" for the Soviet Union in arms deals when the situation was deemed sensitive enough to warrant such a scheme (to wit, the Czech-Egyptian arms deal of 1955).

Czechoslovakia's front-running position began to decline in 1968, the year of the Soviet invasion, and it is justifiable to say (at least in terms of defense budgetary matters; see Table 5.2) that since that time, although it still supplies arms to certain African nations, it has been surpassed by the GDR in a variety of military and security-related ways.

TABLE 5.2

Warsaw Pact Military Expenditures

Country	1958	1967	1968	1978
Bulgaria	156 (3.7)	222 (2.4)	238 (2.3)	504 (2.8)
Czecho-slovakia	1089 (4.5)	1232 (4.3)	1322 (4.1)	1885 (3.9)
GDR	521 (2.3)	1137 (3.3)	1521 (4.2)	2636 (4.5)
Hungary	—	275 (2.1)	338 (2.4)	548 (2.4)
Poland	602 (3.0)	1345 (3.8)	1517 (4.0)	2339 (2.9)
Romania	288 (3.1)	412 (1.9)	460 (2.0)	904 —

Note: Figures are in millions of U.S. dollars at 1973 exchange rates and prices. Numbers in parentheses indicate percentage of GNP.

Source: SIPRI Yearbook, 1979, World Armaments and Disarmament (London: Taylor and Francis, 1979), pp. 36-39.

Also adding to the GDR's ascendancy over Czechoslovakia was the decreased confidence the Soviets had in the country and its armed forces after the invasion in 1968. Coincidentally, the GDR's policy of very close politico-ideological alignment with the Soviet Union paid off in terms of Soviet confidence in the reliability of the NVA. Western observers, noting this change, have subjectively evaluated the over-all utility of Warsaw Pact forces to the Soviets in a confrontation with NATO forces and have given the GDR (along with Bulgaria) top ratings, while Czechoslovakia is rated at the bottom. [3] It can be hypothesized that the Eastern European reliability of the NVA can be translated into a concomitant reliability in the Third World.

The Soviet Union as a Mature Superpower and
Increased Opportunities in Africa in the 1970s

Having had its hands burned while practicing premature global-ism in Cuba in 1962, the Soviet Union undertook a gradual military buildup which culminated in nuclear parity with the United States in the early 1970s. The changed correlation of forces was related not only to the spectacular rise in Soviet military might but also to the perceived unwillingness of the United States to counter Soviet moves in the Third World (in the wake of Vietnam). Additionally, Soviet conventional might, particularly its airlift and sealift capability, was greatly expanded, as was illustrated during the 1975-76 Angolan civil war and in the battle for the Ogaden in 1977-78.

Then too, the early years of the 1970s witnessed an intensification of independence struggles by African national liberation movements. The decline of the Portuguese empire in Angola, Mozambique, and Guinea-Bissau, as well as the continued racist policies of the white bastions in Rhodesia and South Africa, sparked increasing resistance from indigenous forces. Further, increased instability in Zaire as a result of economic and political corruption gave renewed vigor to the Front for the National Liberation of the Congo (FLNC), then operating out of Angola. Without exception, all of those groups desired and needed more intensive military and security aid and were willing to accept that aid from any nation offering it.

INTERNAL FACTORS

The NVA and SSD

In light of the NVA's subordination to the Soviet armed forces there appears to be little room for professional military cadres to establish an identity of their own. Melvin Croan has noted, "The matter of identity figures in a number of different ways. One involves the . . . National People's Army (NVA). As an institution, its status is not particularly imposing at home."[4] The NVA's subordinate position apparently led to a morale problem in the late 1960s and early 1970s, as indicated by criticisms in East German military publications, most notably Volksarmee, about the "nationalist tendencies" among the officer corps.

Further, detente and rapprochement with West Germany in the early 1970s apparently had a negative effect upon the NVA, both in terms of combat preparedness and ideological purity. To ensure a high degree of political loyalty in the NVA in the face of a relaxation of tensions, the party sought to reemphasize the importance of the East German commitment to Soviet-led Socialist Internationalism. Combat preparedness, on the other hand, was increased through greater integration with—and hence subordination to—the Soviet armed forces.

The preceding discussion suggests that if the NVA were ever to

improve its prestige and mission it would have to look beyond its domestic frontiers. It ultimately did so, under the dynamic leadership
of General Heinz Hoffmann, the minister of defense and NVA commander who, coincidentally, was elevated to full Politburo membership in
1973. With this rise in status, General Hoffmann's presence in the Politburo might have served as a factor in upgrading the NVA's institutional position in the decision-making process.

Moreover, there appear to be some parallels between late nine-
teenth- and early twentieth-century German exploits in Africa and the
NVA's current role there, as two authors explain:

> The German colonial officer formed a corps d'elite. Ser-
> vice in the colonies was highly sought after at a time when
> the long peace in Europe seemed endless and when the only
> shots heard by the average soldier were those discharged
> on a firing range. . . . Africa . . . had its compensations.
> . . . It was an excellent school for real war, especially
> guerrilla operations; there were plenty of opportunities
> for initiative. [5]
>
> A high proportion of these officers . . . came from
> Eastern Germany . . . Silesia, West and East Prussia,
> Pomerania or the Province Sachsen of the Prussian King-
> dom. [6]

German officers had professional reasons for service abroad in
the past, and African military experience was predominantly a Prus-
sian affair. In a similar manner, perhaps some reasons for late twentieth-century East German military operations in Africa may be viewed in the same light. As in the past, Africa again offered in the 1970s
a unique opportunity to invigorate the morale of the armed forces.

While more difficult to discuss substantially, the SSD under Paul
Verner, GDR secretary for state security, probably also has institutional interests in mind for an assertive role in Africa and perhaps
elsewhere in the Third World. Western analysts of East German foreign policy, in fact, attribute a role in the decision-making process
to the military-security interest group. Then, too, Africa provides
the SSD with abundant opportunities to undermine West German influence and prestige on the continent, as may have been the case in the
exposé on The West German Orbital Launch and Rocket Firm (OTRAG)
operations in Zaire's Shaba province (see below).

The contention here is that the military and security forces provided institutional motivating forces leading to the GDR's new assertiveness in Africa. While they most certainly were not the major factor behind this new role, the interests of the NVA and SSD were probably taken into consideration in the Politburo's decision to expand GDR

activities. In this light, and perhaps reinforcing this argument, it is interesting to note that the Cuban involvement in Africa has been undertaken, in part, to further the institutional interests of the Cuban armed forces. [7]

Economic Needs

As mentioned earlier, the GDR recently signed an agreement with the Soviet Union in which it will be guaranteed continued delivery of Soviet raw materials, particularly oil. While the GDR can pay for some of these imports by exporting its products to the Soviet Union, the price of oil has increased to such an extent that the GDR's terms of trade with the Soviet Union, which began worsening in 1975, are expected to continue to do so unless compensatory measures can be taken. Adding to this dilemma is the high net hard currency debt of the GDR ($5.9 billion in 1977, second only to Poland in Eastern Europe) and the high debt-service ratio. (In 1977, for example, the GDR's debt-service ratio was listed as 40, meaning that unless it were to refinance, it would have to devote 40 percent of its hard currency export earnings just to service its debts.)[8] With these serious economic problems, then, the East German regime is faced with the problem of how it will obtain the additional resources to pay the Soviet Union for the increasing costs of oil. (The Soviet Union has, since 1975, changed its own policies with regard to intra-CMEA price changes, particularly in oil, permitting it to readjust prices of its exports based on world prices for the preceding five years after than adhering to a fixed-price policy as previously practiced.)

There are, of course, ways to generate currency. One is to export arms to Third World countries on a cash rather than aid or grant basis. This is precisely what the Soviet Union has done; but the GDR's indigenous arms industry is too small for arms transfer to be a viable option. Offering one's services to the Soviet Union in military-related matters (among other things) is, however, an option open to the GDR. In this context, it is interesting to note that article 8 of the 1975 Soviet Union-GDR treaty of friendship, cooperation, and mutual assistance alludes to the fact that, in case of attack, assistance is no longer limited to Europe and that therefore the GDR could presumably be expected to render aid to the Soviet Union in other areas, for example, the Third World and, of course, Africa. [9] The treaty was signed in the same year that the price of Soviet oil exports to CMEA members was adjusted upward, causing the GDR's terms of trade with the Soviet Union to be substantially worsened. (All the Eastern European nations felt the shock of the worsening terms of trade from a low of 4 percent for Poland to the GDR's high of 25 percent). [10]

There are some other feasible economic reasons for East Germany's boldness in its African foreign policy. The GDR is probably also interested in building potential markets for its manufactured goods, which are not sophisticated enough for West European markets. Additionally, East Germany has cultivated relations with non-Socialist oil-producing nations in Africa, most notably Algeria, Libya, and, to some degree, Nigeria. The explanation for these interstate connections lies most plausibly in the GDR's search for new sources of oil. This aspect of GDR-African relations is more clearly understood when one considers that although the Soviet Union will supply East Germany with oil (and other energy-related products) through 1985, the amount will not meet the GDR's increasing needs; the Soviet Union has urged all its Eastern European neighbors to seek supplementary sources.

Finally, over recent years the Soviet Union has been pressing its Warsaw Pact allies to increase their annual monetary contributions to the alliance budget. It can be speculated that the GDR's increased military and security activities in Africa have been undertaken in partial compensation for direct financial contributions, which would be difficult to make given the GDR's hard currency and foreign debt problems. [11]

While it cannot be firmly established that East Germany is pursuing its new assertive policies in Africa and the Middle East as a sort of payoff for continued Soviet oil supplies and as a partial fulfillment of its Warsaw Pact obligations, economics, as in the case of Cuban involvement in Africa, cannot be discounted as a motivating factor. [12] Add to this the requirement for supplementary oil sources, and economic reasons assume increasing importance in East Germany's African policies.

The German Inferiority Complex

In the early 1970s, after nearly a quarter-century of pariah statehood, the GDR was finally accepted as a legitimate state in the global environment. International recognition did not, however, dispel the regime's chronic fears about its own sense of identity. The ambitious policies in Africa in the 1970s are, at least in part, motivated by a persistent inferiority complex. There are at least three reasons for the domestically highly publicized policy of the GDR in Africa: (1) it serves to increase the public's awareness and acceptance of a national political identity, thus reinforcing the East German regime's policy on delimitation from the FRG; (2) Africa provides the means for continuing the rivalry with the FRG, offering East German propagandists ample opportunity to attack the neocolonialism of the capitalist West

German state; and (3) East Germany's aid to selected African nations and to African national liberation movements serves to enhance the regime's prestige, which in turn could contribute to increased legitimacy. In combination, all three reasons might bolster regime stability and diminish the attraction the East German public still feels for its "other half."

CASE STUDIES: THE 1970s

Angola

The GDR reportedly signed a military agreement with Angola's Popular Movement for the Liberation of Angola (MPLA) in 1973 that provided for East German training of the forces of the MPLA as well as for GDR medical assistance to wounded personnel evacuated from Angola to the Congo, and thence to Berlin for the more serious cases.[13]
During the Angolan civil war, there were reportedly at least 700 East German military advisers working with the MPLA; there were also unconfirmed reports of East Germans flying MIG-21s. Since the MPLA victory, confirmed information, while available, is still limited about the exact nature of GDR activities in Angola, but it is generally agreed that the East Germans are involved in organizing civil and secret police forces and prison guards, setting up a country-wide communications system, port modernization (Luanda, Lopito, and Mocamedes), educational and health services, and piloting ships into the harbors at Luanda and Lopito. With regard to this last item, Neues Deutschland reported in 1978: "Nine GDR pilots have safely guided some 3,300 ships from almost 50 countries into the Angolan ports of Luanda and Lobito since 1976 . . . at the same time, young Angolans are being trained in this task."[14]
"Solidarity goods" shipments continue to arrive in Luanda, usually transported by special Interflug flights, and the GDR has sent a total of 6,000 four-wheel vehicles (mostly W-50 trucks) to the country. The exact nature of the solidarity goods is unknown, but it is usually reported by the East German news media as food, educational aid, and medical supplies and could include military-related items such as small weapons and communications gear; the military applications of the vehicles are obvious. That the GDR continues to provide direct military assistance, particularly in the form of advisers and, perhaps, even a small number of combat troops, can only be ascertained by unsubstantiated reports originating largely from South Africa and from occasional communiques from the Front for the Liberation of the Enclave of Cabinda (FLEC), which continues to fight against the MPLA. For example, this group issued a statement (unconfirmed) in

August 1979 alleging that three Cuban and two East German soldiers, identified as missile-launcher and heavy arms technicians, had been killed in Cabinda. [15]

Whatever the exact nature and extent of GDR military operations in Angola, its own highly publicized statements of solidarity donations and of economic, cultural, and educational assistance rendered illustrate not only a considerable East German interest in the country but also a considerable presence. The types of aid and assistance given, including perhaps most importantly the training of military, security, and police forces and organizational work with party cadres, are all consistent with GDR tasks in the division of labor on the African continent.

Shaba I and II

Washington Post columnist David Ottoway has said that Shaba II was, without a doubt, one of the best planned and executed operations seen anywhere in Africa for years. "The rebels were tough, determined and tenacious as if they had long been training for the assault. "[16]

Implicated in the Shaba II invasion in May 1978 (14 months after Shaba I, which failed, largely due to Western military action, as was the case in Shaba II) were first and foremost the Soviet Union and Cuba, but the GDR also had Western allegations directed at it. There is enough evidence from open-source literature to suggest that the GDR, not Cuba, was involved if not in the planning of Shaba II then certainly in the training of the FLNC. [17]

Following the return of the defeated Shaba I forces to Angola, fighting erupted among the various factions of the FLNC. Cuban forces were sent into the area in northeastern Angola to quell the disturbances. Once the fighting subsided, the Cubans were withdrawn and East German military advisers were sent in to train the FLNC forces. [18]

A noted journalist on African affairs, Colin Legum of the London Observer, reported in late May 1978 that the GDR had been assigned the task in May 1976 (presumably by the Soviets) of destabilizing the Mobutu regime. The main points of the plan to realize such an objective were: (1) To provide military equipment and training to the FLNC whose forces were based in Angola, principally at three bases: Luso, Texeira de Sousa, and Henrique de Carvalho. The military aid included Czech-made personnel carriers and Soviet surface-to-air missiles (SAMs), the latter to provide the FLNC with a strike capacity against the Zairian air force. SAMs were reportedly used on the first day of the Shaba I invasion but not during Shaba II, which was primarily a covert infiltration operation during its earlier stages; and (2) to create 45 pockets of continuing resistance inside Shaba itself, to be supplied from the three main FLNC bases in Angola. [19]

While the East German military contingent, consisting of 100 men under the leadership of Lieutenant General Helmut Poppe (General Hoffmann's righthand man on African affairs), was to ensure the combat readiness of the FLNC, they were under orders not to become involved in combat operations themselves, even at the risk of mission failure. The East Germans reportedly aided the retreat of the defeated FLNC force by providing tank cover from inside the Angolan border but did not engage in actual combat inside Zaire, as were their orders. [20]

There is additional evidence to lend further credibility to an East German role in the Shaba invasions:

First, East German and Soviet propaganda had flowed freely over the presence of the West German OTRAG in Shaba province after the text of the OTRAG-Zaire agreement was stolen from Zaire's embassy in Bonn. * One of Dr. Luts Kayser's (OTRAG's founding father) prime reasons for picking Shaba as the site for his rocket development was the relative security provided by the isolated, sparsely populated area west of Lake Tanganika. Any instability in the area would interfere with rocket testings; Shaba I and II provided that instability and eventually forced OTRAG out of the country in early 1979. The Soviet-GDR campaign against OTRAG was probably aimed not only at West Germany (although East Germany must have relished the opportunity to embarrass the Federal Republic in light of their sibling rivalry but also at the People's Republic of China (PRC), which was interested in purchasing OTRAG's launching services after its own test program ran into difficulty. The Soviet Union's payoff in the plan, then, was

---

*OTRAG has been much maligned by Western, Soviet bloc and African observers. Specifically, the GDR and Soviet Union accused the West German government (which was not connected with OTRAG) of testing cruise missiles. However, the Kayser rockets are not suitable for military purposes for the following reasons: (1) their fuel is highly explosive and cannot be stored in the rocket (also, refuelling takes eight hours); (2) continuing problems in the guidance and combustion systems make the rockets hazardous for launching anything, let alone expensive missiles; (3) the great weight of the standardized (vice-specialized) engineering components limits the size of the payload even the larger rockets can carry. Luts Kayser was, in fact, trying to develop an inexpensive rocket-launching capability in order to service the less fortunate nations of the world which cannot afford the more expensive programs of the United States and Soviet Union.

to thwart China's satellite program and perhaps also to embarrass the PRC because of its OTRAG connection.

Second, General Hoffmann, accompanied by Lieutenant General Poppe, visited Angola on May 8-12, 1978. The two were accompanied by Angola's defense minister, Henrique Teles Carreira, throughout their Angolan sojourn, and the group reportedly made a side-trip to the bases at Luso, Texeira de Sousa, and Henrique de Carvalho on May 8. [21] Neues Deutschland, which extensively covered General Hoffmann's Angola visit, failed to report these May 8 activities, thus giving the impression that the sensitivity of the visit three days before Shaba II precluded their inclusion in East German news coverage of General Hoffmann's visit.

Third, during the weeks before the attack on Shaba in May 1978, the Soviet Union, East Germany, and Poland bought all the available cobalt on the world market. The price tripled within a few days, and it would seem that these three countries knew exactly what they were doing and what was about to transpire in the cobalt-rich Shaba province.

Ethiopia and South Yemen

East Germany shifted in lock step with the Soviet Union and Cuba from Somalia to Ethiopia in 1977. Werner Lamberz's three visits to that country in 1977 (see Table 5. 3) would appear to indicate an increasing awareness of and commitment to the "Ethiopian revolution." South Yemen, which has close ties to the GDR, was included in the last two (June and December 1977) of these trips, while Somalia was visited in the first trip (February 1977) but not in the succeeding two, a good indicator as to where the GDR's interests lay (in conjunction, of course, with Soviet interests). The South Yemeni forces that fought in the Ogaden were reportedly trained by the GDR, [22] and East Germans may have actually been involved in combat in the Eritrean offensive in the spring of 1979. The Eritrean Liberation Front (ELF), complaining to the OAU in July 1979, stated in part that the massive offensive was launched by 50,000 troops from Ethiopia, while East German Defense Minister Heinz Hoffmann announced the dispatch of 1,500 military experts to help Ethiopia. [23]

GDR-Ethiopian military relations were solidified with the signing of a military cooperation agreement in Ethiopia in May 1979 (during General Hoffman's visit). Calling for the creation of a close relationship between the Ethiopian and GDR armed forces, General Hoffmann witnessed the signing of the agreement by Werner Fleischer, head of technology and armaments in the GDR Defense Ministry, and Colonel Abebe Wolde Mariam, chief of supply in the Ethiopian Defense Ministry. [24] Upon his return home, General Hoffmann stated in an interview

TABLE 5.3

GDR High-Level Visits to Africa, 1975-79

Date	Delegation Head	Countries Visited	Purpose/Salient Activities
March 1975	Horst Soelle, Minister for Foreign Trade	Algeria	Talks with Algerian officials on economic and scientific-technological cooperation.
April 1975	Klaus Willerding, Deputy Minister for Foreign Affairs	South Yemen/ Egypt	Talks on further development of bilateral relations. Also met with Mahmud Riyad, Arab League General Secretary.
June 1975	Bernhard Quandt, Central Committee and State Council Member	Mozambique	Independence day celebrations.
November 1975[a]	Werner Dorden, Special Ambassador	Angola	Independence day celebrations; FRG was not invited to this or to Mozambique's celebrations.
June 1976[b]	Guenther Kleiber, Politburo Member and Deputy Chairman, Council of Ministers	Angola	Agreements signed on cooperation for 1976-77 in the fields of culture, science, technology, and trade, and on air transport.
September 1976	Willi Stoph, Premier; Chairman, Council of Ministers	South Yemen/ Somalia	Talks on expanding all-around cooperation; Siad Barre paid tribute to the training of Somali "cadres" in the GDR, the sending of GDR experts to Somalia, and the work of the FDJ (Free German Youth) Brigade.
December 1976	Oska Fischer, Minister for Foreign Affairs	South Yemen/ Mozambique/ Tanzania/	Mozambique: Cultural treaty and "other" agreements signed;

Date	Delegation Head	Countries Visited	Purpose/Salient Activities
		Madagascar/ Kenya/ Ethiopia/ Egypt	Samora Machel noted that through this visit the GDR was again proving its militant solidarity with Mozambique. Ethiopia: Trade and cultural agreement signed.
February 1977	Werner Lamberz, Politburo Member; Secretary, SED Central Committee; also in charge of agitation and propaganda	Somalia/ Mozambique/ Ethiopia	Somalia: Agreement on cooperation (undefined) signed for 1977-78. Mozambique: Attendance at Third FRELIMO Congress; met with Joshua Nkomo (ZAPU), Robert Mugabe (ZANU), Oliver Tambo (ANC), and Sam Nujoma (SWAPO). Ethiopia: Talks on the further developing of relationships; visited a "political school" in Addis Ababa where revolutionary cadres are trained; talks on ideological orientation of the masses.
June 1977	Werner Lamberz	South Yemen/ Ethiopia/ Angola/Congo/Nigeria/ Zambia	Ethiopia: A number of agreements signed, aimed at the all-around strengthening of cooperation; visited training camps of the

(continued)

Table 5. 3, (continued)

Date	Delegation Head	Countries Visited	Purpose/Salient Activities
			People's Militia; handed over M600,000 of a solidarity donation; signed a protocol on long-term development of economic relations. Zambia: Signed protocol on cooperation which provides, inter alia, for developing the exchange of experiences between parties, for promoting the expansion of relations at the state level as well as between trade unions, women's, and youth organizations, and for granting support in training cadres.
October 1977	Hermann Axen, Politburo Member	Libya	Several cooperation agreements signed. Upon his return to the GDR, Axen noted that the GDR population's solidarity with Libya had practically opened the door in Libya, giving the GDR prestige and status.
November 1977	Konrad Naumann, Politburo Member	Algeria/ Guinea-Bissau, Cape Verde Islands	Attendance at Third Congress, PAIGC; brief stopover in Algeria en route.
November 1977	Wolfgang Rauchfuss, Minister for Material Management	Ethiopia	Talks on economic, communications, land and marine transport cooperation and assistance; talks on progress of the Ethiopi-

Date	Delegation Head	Countries Visited	Purpose/Salient Activities
			an revolution with politico-military affairs officials
December 1977	Horst Sindermann, Politburo Member; President, Presidium of the People's Chamber	Angola/São Tomé e Príncipe	Angola: Addressed the First Congress of the MPLA. São Tomé e Príncipe: Economic agreement signed; agreement on cooperation for 1978-80 signed.
December 1977	Werner Lamberz	South Yemen/ Ethiopia/ Libya	Ethiopia: More discussions on the deepening of relations. Libya: Working agreement signed which reportedly laid down the next steps for further development of bilateral relations.
March 1978	Werner Lamberz	Libya	Further discussions on bilateral relations; Lamberz killed in a helicopter crash on March 6.
May 1978	General Heinz Hoffmann, Minister for National Defense	Algeria/ Angola/ Guinea/ Congo	Reportedly witnessed training of African troops by East Germans. In a speech in Brazzaville, Hoffmann stated, "Let us make our comradeship in arms strong and unbreakable." Visited Shaba invasion forces' training bases on May 8.
Feb-	Erich Honecker	Libya/	Treaties of friendship

(continued)

Table 5.3, (continued)

Date	Delegation Heads	Countries Visited	Purpose/Salient Activities
ruary 1979	(first visit by the head of state/ head of party to Africa)	Angola/ Mozambique/ Zambia	and cooperation sign- ed with Angola and Mozambique, the lat- ter containing a mili- tary clause.
April 1979	Lt. Gen. Wolfgang Reinhold, Deputy Minister for De- fense and Chief of Air Force/Air Defense Command	Guinea- Bissau	"Working" meeting with armed forces officials.
May 1979[c]	General Hoffmann	Zambia/ Mozambique/ Ethiopia	Ethiopia: Military a- greement signed. Zambia: In Lusaka, General Hoffmann stated that the GDR would arm the front- line states to the teeth.

[a]Although no high-level GDR delegation visisted Angola prior to its independence on 11 November 1975, an Angolan delegation, led by Iko Carreira, MPLA Politburo member and subsequently Angolan Minister for Defense, visited the GDR from August 21-26, 1975. The MPLA dele- gation thanked the GDR for the political, moral, and material support re ered to the MPLA's struggle from the beginning. Discussions between the two sides centered around the further development and deepening of MPLA/SED relations. The MPLA delegation also met with Kurt Krueger General Secretary of the Solidarity Committee, and discussed further GDR solidarity support for Angola.

Date	Delegation Heads	Countries Visited	Purpose/Salient Activities
June 1979	Friedmar Calus- nitzer, Deputy Minister for Foreign Trade and Industry	Ethiopia	Negotiations concerning the deepening of coop- eration in foreign trade and industry; agree- ments signed on coop- eration in the construc- tion of "important" pro- jects as well as on long-term economic cooperation.
Sep- tember 1979	Willi Stoph	Angola	Attended funeral of President Antonio Agostino Neto.
Sep- tember 1979	Horst Dohlus, Politburo Candi- date Member	Ethiopia	Attended fifth anniver- sary of the Ethiopian revolution.
Novem- ber 1979	Erich Honecker	Ethiopia	Signed treaty of friend- ship and cooperation.

bFollowing Mr. Kleiber's return to the GDR, he was questioned by HORIZONT about the agreements. He responded by noting that the GDR would dispatch to Angola primarily advisors and experts in "vari- ous" fields, and that the GDR would continue to train cadres of superior and professional schools as well as specialists of Angola—a training pro- gram which, he stated, was initiated several years ago.

cPerhaps connected with this statement by General Hoffmann, the government of Zambia announced in early 1980 that it was purchasing 12 MIG-21s from the Soviet Union. It can be speculated (but not verified) that General Hoffmann and Kenneth Kaunda discussed this arms transfer deal and that Zambian pilots may be trained by East Germans.

with the East Berlin weekly journal <u>Horizont</u> that he had watched "thousands of the sons of former slaves and landless peasants practicing assaults with GDR machine guns and helmets" in the "Tatek" training base of the Ethiopian People's Militia. [25]

Like Angola, Ethiopia is also the recipient of quantities of East German solidarity goods. In essence, the GDR provides Ethiopia with essentially the same services as it does for Angola, including port modernization. GDR engineers are reportedly responsible for the modernization and expansion of the port of Assab and for the removal of war damage in Massawa. Their activities in Massawa also include construction of a dry dock, which will be capable of accommodating ships up to cruiser size. [26] The latter, of course, would benefit the Soviet navy in a great way by providing nearby repair facilities for its Indian Ocean units.

While the GDR appears to have cemented its relationships with both Angola and Ethiopia (it has treaties of friendship, cooperation, and mutual assistance with both, as well as with Mozambique), and its support for the African national liberation movements (with the exception now of Joshua Nkomo's ZAPU, which is in the minority in Robert Mugabe's new Zimbabwe government) sets it in good stead there, the dynamics of the region are such that today's solid friends can quickly become tomorrow's foes. The Soviet Union has been the victim of the uneven political scene in Africa, and the GDR experienced the same roller-coaster effects of foreign policy in Africa during its early involvement there. Then, too, recent events in the area, most notably the Zimbabwe settlement, which could have some positive effects upon Namibia (and perhaps even South Africa), serve to place constraints upon further East German inroads on the continent. It is these constraints to which we now turn.

PROSPECTS FOR THE FUTURE

The peaceful settlement in Zimbabwe and the cold shoulder given to the GDR by the new Mugabe government by not inviting the East Germans to its independence day celebrations has obviously limited at least near-term GDR relations with that country. Whatever the course of state relations between the two in the future, the end of fighting spelled the end of East Germany providing the guerrillas with solidarity and military assistance. While Zimbabwe and East Germany may at some point establish normal diplomatic relations, the East Germans and their Soviet comrades, if not the Cubans, have essentially been excluded from the main stream of Zimbabwe's political life.

Elsewhere, the resolution of conflict in Zimbabwe may give impetus to further attempts at a peaceful settlement in Namibia. In this case, however, the GDR's long support for the Southwest Africa People's Organization could portend a continuing East German influence in Namibia. But, as has been the case in many countries, once the fighting stops, economic development seems to take priority over ideology, and economic development implies seeking help from those most capable of giving it, that is, the Western nations. This is now the case in Angola, for example, which is seeking Western investment and capital. An irony of the Angolan situation is that the GDR's postmodernization efforts are being used by Angola to improve conditions for Western investments.

There is, of course, still the question of the continuing conflict in Namibia; but the Zimbabwe situation has demonstrated that enough pressure, from the right sources, and applied in the right direction can make a seemingly hopeless situation turn out favorably. The Zimbabwe lesson cannot be lost to the minds of the parties to the Namibia conflict.

East German involvement with the FLNC could present opportunities for a continued role in destabilizing the Mobutu regime in Zaire. Yet, to a great extent that situation has been defused, at least insofar as the Angolan-Zairian dispute goes. Their rapprochement appears to be holding up, and the FLNC rebels who were not repatriated to Zaire are currently reported to have taken refuge in Guinea-Bissau, having been expelled from Angola. There is no information to suggest, however, that the GDR continues its involvement with the FLNC. The problem here is that Zaire's internal problems, which seem to be proceeding from bad to worse, contribute to regime instability and offer opportunities for renewed violence, perhaps with external assistance, in that country.

The Angolan war continues unabated, providing many opportunities for a continued East German presence. Here again, though, there exists the possibility that the Zimbabwe settlement could positively affect the resolution of conflict between the MPLA and Jonas Savimbi's UNITA forces.

While this is all highly speculative, it does suggest that the potential exists for a tempering of conflict in southern Africa. If such a situation were to occur, the GDR's activities (as well as the Soviets' and Cubans') could be constrained and their influence diminished. The ultimate irony would be that, after years of increasing effort and expense, it would find itself in no better a position than it did in its original African experience.

East Germany is not without domestic problems that could militate against not only an exuberant foreign policy in Africa but also elsewhere in the Third World. While Erich Honecker had hoped to achieve at least an economically based legitimacy by raising standards of living, the progress the GDR has made (its per capita income, for example, is the highest in the Eastern bloc) has not dissipated continuing shortages of consumer goods. Furthermore, the new, relative open-door policy with the FRG constantly focuses the East German population's attention upon its more affluent neighbor. To alleviate this situation (and also to obtain hard currency), the regime has presided over an expanding network of intershops which offer Western goods not normally available elsewhere in exchange for hard currency (usually obtained from relatives in the West). Despite the regime's efforts to satisfy growing consumer discontent, the basic flaws in the economic system make for a very uncomfortable situation and could presage increasing domestic social unrest.

Domestic discontent has, in turn, led to a number of measures designed to control both the GDR population and visitors (particularly newsmen) from the West, signifying that the inherent lack of legitimacy continues to plague the regime. In April 1979, following West German television interviews with disgruntled East Berlin shoppers, severe new restrictions were placed on foreign reporters' movements and access to East German citizens. Then in August 1979 the regime revised the penal code providing for prison sentences for such offenses as denigration of the state and disturbing the Socialist way of life. [27] Richard von Weizacker, Bundestag vicespeaker, notes the conflict between West Germany's Ostpolitik—to obtain more openness and freedom of movement of ideas and information—and the East German aim of getting Western money and economic assistance. Both have succeeded to some extent, but the political price has been much higher for East Germans than for West Germans in terms of challenging their entire closed system. [28]

Because of its virtually complete control over its populace, the regime's authority is not likely to face a major challenge under present conditions. However, other variables could intervene that might affect the regime's stability and, in turn, its expanding foreign policy—a change in Soviet leadership (following Brezhnev's death), for example. There is, of course, a precedent for a challenge to the regime's authority. The insecurity felt in Eastern Europe after Stalin's death in 1953 as well as the depressed economy led to East German workers rioting in East Berlin and elsewhere; Soviet troops and tanks had to be called in to quell the disturbances.

While this is perhaps an extreme example of what might happen, there is no denying the current domestic unrest in the GDR. Whether or not it might affect the regime's ability to continue its expanding activities in Africa (and elsewhere in the Third World) is debatable. Yet some things are certain. First, the regime needs to take measures at home, particularly in the economy, to ease domestic discontent—or else run the risk of exacerbating the problem of its own stability. Also, opportunities afield, at least in Africa, seem to be narrowing. In combination, these two sets of conditions might compel the regime to rethink its foreign policy and to perhaps place more emphasis on domestic policy and/or to become involved more deeply in the parts of the Third World that offer new opportunities: the Caribbean basin (Nicaragua, Jamaica, and Grenada) or Asia (Vietnam, Cambodia, and Afghanistan).

East Germany and Cuba recently concluded a 25-year friendship treaty in which both countries pledged continuing support for the struggle of the people of the Third World. [29] This agreement could indicate an expansion of East German activities beyond Africa in the current decade. In fact, increased East German involvement in the Caribbean basin seems a likely possibility given the GDR's past relationship with the Sandinistas and its current ties with the ruling junta. East Germany has provided (and continues to provide) economic and medical assistance to Nicaragua, and Nicaraguan soldiers are being flown to East Berlin for medical treatment. This suggests a continuation of the pattern of involvement established first in Africa.

Recently a high-level Nicaraguan delegation, including the defense minister, visited East Berlin, where they concluded a number of cooperation agreements: trade, economic, cultural, and "other" unspecified accords. Continuing instability, not only in Nicaragua, but also elsewhere in Central America and the Caribbean region, could open up new doors and provide ample opportunities for a bold East Germany policy.

Afghanistan, too, provides increased opportunities for East German involvement. East Germany has been quick to offer solidarity aid to Babrak Karmal's government and, as is the case with Nicaragua, has been flying wounded Afghani soldiers to East Berlin for treatment. In addition, the GDR's involvement with Afghanistan may proceed, at some point, beyond mere economic and medical assistance. In early April 1980, General A. Epishev, chief of the Soviet Armed Forces Main Political Administration, suggested in Pravda that the Soviet Union might be calling upon its Warsaw Pact allies to send troops to Afghanistan. [30] While East Germany may not be overly enthusiastic about this possibility, particularly about the strain it might place on GDR-FRG relations, its choice in the matter might be limited, not only by the leverage Moscow normally maintains over it but also by its 1975 treaty commitment. Are the East Germans becoming Europe's Cubans?

NOTES

1. "Tanzania-Germany (GDR)," Africa Research Bulletin, February 1-28, 1965 (March 15, 1965): 246.

2. Arthur M. Hanhardt, Jr. , "German Democratic Republic," in Communism in Eastern Europe, eds. Teresa Rakowska-Harmstone and Andrew Gyorgy (Bloomington: Indiana University Press, 1979), p. 135.

3. Dale R. Herspring and Ivan Volgyes, "Political Reliability in the Eastern European Warsaw Pact Armies," Armed Forces and Society 6 (Winter 1980): 289.

4. Melvin Croan, "New Country, Old Nationality," Foreign Policy 37 (Winter 1979-80): 154.

5. L. H. Gann and Peter Duignan, The Rulers of German Africa, 1884-1914 (Stanford: Stanford University Press, 1977), pp. 107-8.

6. Ibid. , p. 112.

7. Edward Gonzales, as cited in William J. Durch, "The Cuban Military in Africa and the Middle East: From Algeria to Angola," Studies in Comparative Communism 2, nos. 1-2 (Spring-Summer 1978): 60.

8. Paul Marer, "East European Economies: Achievements, Problems, Prospects," in Communism in Eastern Europe, eds. Teresa Rakowska-Harmstone and Andrew Gyorgy, (Bloomington: Indiana University Press, 1979), pp. 274, 277.

9. "East Germany-Soviet Union—Conclusion of Treaty of Friendship, Cooperation and Mutual Assistance," Keesing's Contemporary Archives, January 16, 1976, p. 27525.

10. Marer, "East European Economies," p. 271.

11. Interview with Dr. Siegfried Georg, Ministry for Intra-German Relations, Bonn, Federal Republic of Germany, April 28, 1980. Dr. Georg believes the GDR's Warsaw Pact obligations to be a major motivating factor behind the GDR's military-security involvement in Africa.

12. Jiri Valenta, "The Soviet-Cuban Alliance in Africa and Future Prospects in the Third World," Cuban Studies (August 1980).

13. Elizabeth Pond, "East Germany's Afrika Korps," Christian Science Monitor, June 28, 1978. The signing of this agreement could not be verified by any other source, but it is well known that the GDR was providing medical assistance to the MPLA forces and that they were flown to East Berlin for treatment. Training of MPLA forces is not as well documented. However, since the NVA was training Congolese forces following the GDR's military agreement with that country, it is feasible that the MPLA may have also received some training, even prior to the large influx of Soviet military assistance in 1975. It is interesting to note that the GDR-Angolan treaty of friendship and cooperation of February 1979 does not contain a military clause, while that with Mozambique, also signed in February 1979, does. Specifically, articles 5 and 10 of the latter state, respectively, "In the inter-

est of strengthening the defense capability of the high contracting parties they will arrange the cooperation in the military sphere through
bilateral agreements," and, "Should a situation arise which threatens
or violates peace, the high contracting parties will immediately establish mutual contacts in order to coordinate their positions in order to
eliminate the danger that has emerged or to restore peace" ("Friendship, Cooperation Treaty," Neues Deutschland, February 26, 1979,
in FBIS-EEU, March 1, 1979, p. E-13.) In Ethiopia, a military treaty
was signed separately and prior to the treaty of friendship and cooperation of November 1979. Thus, the lack of any military clause in
the Angolan-GDR treaty lends credence to Pond's allegation that a
military treaty had already been signed in 1973.

14. "GDR Pilots' Activity in Angolan Ports Lauded," Neues
Deutschland, June 5, 1978, in FBIS-EEU, June 7, 1978, p. E-11.

15. "Clash with FLEC Forces," Africa Research Bulletin,
October 1-31, 1979 (November 15, 1979): 5441.

16. International Herald Tribune, cited in "Rebel Invasion,"
Africa Research Bulletin, May 1-31, 1978 (June 15, 1978): 4857.

17. Colin Legum to LCDR Shannon Butler, March 28, 1980.
Both authors are indebted to Mr. Legum for his advice and assistance.

18. Charles K. Ebinger, "Cuban Intervention in Angola: A Dis-
senting Opinion" (Paper presented at the African Studies Association
Conference, Los Angeles, November 1, 1979), p. 33. Mr. Ebinger's
information is derived from an interview with Diamang officials in
Lisbon in June 1977.

19. Colin Legum, "East Germans Set Up Zaire Attack," Observer, May 21, 1978.

20. David Lamb, "East Germans Gaining Influence in Black Africa," Sunday Peninsula Herald, May 11, 1980.

21. Legum, "East Germans Set Up Zaire Attack." Also reported
in William F. Robinson, Eastern Europe's Presence in Black Africa,
Radio Free Europe/Radio Liberty Background Report, no. 142 (Munich: June 21, 1979), p. 8.

22. Melvin Croan, "A New Africa Corps?" Washington Quarterly
3 (Winter 1980): 24.

23. "OAU Indifference," Africa Research Bulletin, July 1-31,
1979 (August 15, 1979): 5343.

24. "End of Ethiopian Talks," East Berlin ADN International
Service, May 31, 1979, in FBIS-EEU, June 1, 1979, p. E-1. Also
reported more extensively in Robinson, Eastern Europe's Presence
in Black Africa, p. 8.

25. "Defense Minister Discusses Africa Tour, Role of GDR,"
Horizont (East Berlin), no. 28 (1979): 3, in FBIS-EEU, July 13, 1979,
p. E-1.

26. Marine Rundschau (West Germany), no. 1 (1979): 55, in Naval Intelligence Support Center, NAVSCAN 8, no. 5 (March 1, 1979): 11.

27. Croan, "New Country, Old Nationality," p. 158.

28. Elizabeth Pond, "West German TV Sours East Germany on Detente," Christian Science Monitor, July 16, 1979.

29. Berlin AP release reprinted in the Moneterey Peninsula Herald, June 2, 1980.

30. John Darnton, "Soviet Bloc to Meet on Iranian and Afghan Policies," New York Times, May 1, 1980.

6

HUNGARY AND THE THIRD WORLD: AN ANALYSIS OF EAST-SOUTH TRADE

Scott Blau

HUNGARY, THE BLOC, AND THE THIRD WORLD:
AN ANALYSIS OF EAST-SOUTH TRADE

Hungary has scarcely any legacy of involvement in the areas of the globe now known as the Third World. Even at the height of Hungarian power following the Compromise of 1867 (which made it a partner with Austria in the "Central European Empire"), Hungary was sufficiently occupied with refractory nationalities on its northern, eastern, and southern borders to avoid the temptations that were enticing the other European powers into adventure and confrontation in Africa, Asia, and Latin America. Hungary's interests were quite parochial in scope compared to the sprawling imperial interests of England, France, and Germany.

The interwar period was no happier for Hungary's international position than the turn of the century had been. Indeed, the ravages of war and of peace—Trianon—reduced Hungary geographically to a fraction of its former size, relegating any vision of Hungary as a global power to a distant future. The best Hungarians could hope for (and there was no shortage of leaders to champion this aspiration) was a tight alliance with a great power willing to unleash Hungarian irredentism. Only two powers between the world wars showed such magnanimity: Mussolini's Italy and Hitler's Germany.

Against this background there is little cause for surprise at Hungary's limited contact with the Third World immediately following World War II. More striking is the fact that, after a lapse of three decades, Hungary's relations with the Third World remain very limited compared with its relations with other groups of countries. This is true for all types of relations, including trade, diplomacy, and military aid.

Though growth in these areas remains limited, and though their importance for Hungary remains equally circumscribed, Hungary is in fact involved in the Third World to a greater extent than ever before in its history. Trade is a good example of this. Whereas in 1950 less than one-twentieth of Hungary's total foreign trade was with the Third World, it has recently attained close to a tenth of that total. This modest level of trade does not rival Hungary's trade with Eastern or Western Europe, but it does reflect a decided recognition by Hungarian leaders of the value of relations with Third World countries.

This chapter focuses on Hungary's trade relations with the Third World. The first section explores those goals which the Hungarians have set for themselves in trading with the Third World and the political and economic limitations on their attainment. The next section documents the scope of this trade in general as well as with particular regions of the Third World: sub-Saharan Africa, Asia, the Middle East, and Latin America.

Types of Involvement

The rapid dissolution of colonialism in most of Africa in the late 1950s and early 1960s signalled the beginning of a conscious Third World movement. The "progressive" anticolonialist and anti-imperialist tendencies of this movement (as these terms are used in the Soviet lexicon), greatly increased the possibilities for friendly interstate contacts with Hungary. From 1959 through 1970, Hungary established diplomatic relations with no less than 40 underdeveloped nations around the globe.

Although Hungary has conducted trade with countries with which it does not have diplomatic relations and has relations with countries with which it conducts no significant trade, most often political recognition has paved the way for expanded economic contacts. For example, in 1960 Hungary's five largest trading partners in the Third World—Egypt, Iraq, Iran, India, and Argentina (accounting for approximately 60 percent of the total)—had previously established diplomatic relations with Hungary. These countries still figure prominently in Hungary's trade with the Third World, but Hungary presently conducts trade with a total of 86 Third World countries.

Trade is actually Hungary's most significant type of involvement in the Third World. A top Hungarian economist writing in the late 1960s on "The Perspectives of Our Relations with the Developing Countries" focused almost exclusively on trade relations and their economic importance. [1] The Hungarian foreign minister, on the other hand, when writing his observations on the political scene in Africa following a 1978 trip, had scarcely anything to say about the role Hungary might play politically. [2]

The emphasis on trade in Hungary's relations with the Third World contrasts with the types of involvement stressed by other Eastern European countries. Whereas the Hungarians have proffered only limited amounts of military aid and training, especially to Africa, the German Democratic Republic (GDR) has been the most active of the Eastern European countries in this field. In contrast, Romania has traditionally played a very active diplomatic role in the Third World, the goals of which will be examined in another chapter.

Goals

According to accepted doctrine in Eastern Europe, poor countries are the "natural allies" of Communism because of the rapacious exploitation they have suffered at the hands of the advanced capitalist countries. This is doubly true of those countries which have set out on a "noncapitalist road" of development. On this basis the countries of Eastern Europe, following the leadership of the Soviet Union, have usually sided with the Group of 77 and other informal Third World groupings, [3] particularly as long as criticism is directed at the advanced capitalist countries and there are no firm economic commitments to be made. Hungary, like the other countries in the region, has taken part in some of the concrete advances made on this new agenda. [4] Nevertheless, Hungary has rejected the notion that there is any North-South confrontation to be resolved, at least insofar as the consequent dialogue is conceived to include the Socialist countries of Eastern Europe with the "North." [5]

Behind these broader ideological considerations, Hungary's trade with the Third World seems to be firmly grounded in sound economic pragmatism. The expansion of Hungary's engineering exports is an oft-repeated goal, which, it is hoped, will help foster industrial progress in the developing countries and, incidentally, cultivate a rich harvest of expanded industrial capacity in Hungary itself. Their pragmatism has led the Hungarians at times to defy the more obvious political exigencies of their close ties with the other Eastern European countries. In sub-Saharan Africa especially, but also in other regions of the Third World, financial solvency of potential trading partners has played a greater role than their ideological solidarity in dictating the course of Hungary's trade.

It is not overemphasizing this point to suggest that the course of Hungary's trade with Third World countries over the last decade has been most influenced by the effect of soaring fuel costs on the balance of payments and foreign currency reserves of those partners. Higher fuel costs have undermined many countries' budgets, making them less desirable trade partners from Hungary's viewpoint because of their inability to purchase as much from Hungary as Hungary purchases from them. [6] Furthermore, the large proportion of primary products (raw materials, unprocessed agricultural goods, and so on) in Hungary's imports from the Third World, has led to a rapid deterioration in its terms of trade during the 1970s. * This is an additional force reinforcing the pragmatism of Hungary's trade goals in the Third World.

Pragmatism and national economic needs are certainly not absent from the goals pursued by the other Eastern European countries in their relations with the Third World. However, these considerations apparently loom much larger for Hungary than for East Germany or Romania. The GDR, as can be expected from its stress on military relations, pursues security goals, perhaps for the security of the entire bloc. Romania and Yugoslavia both strive more than Hungary to establish strong links with the outside world and thereby secure their international positions independently from the Soviet Union.

Industry and Power in Hungary

During the post-World War II era, Hungary's trade has grown at a very brisk pace, quadrupling from 1950 to 1975. This growth reflects important aspects of Hungary's economy, political structure, and political orientation. The economy has become industrialized since the end of World War II, or, more precisely, since the Hungarian Socialist Worker's Party secured unchallenged control of the country. Consequently, as an increasing proportion of domestic production has originated in industry, the demand for foreign raw material has soared. Simultaneously, the necessity of marketing industrial goods abroad has arisen. Hungary has not been alone in this. The trade of other Eastern European countries has also grown as a result of speeded industrialization and the adoption of the Soviet path to development (see Table 6.1).

Hungary's dearth of natural resources coupled with its industrialization has decisively influenced the growth of its trade both with the Third World and worldwide. In order to provide for its industrial needs economic extroversion has proved necessary, perhaps more than elsewhere in Eastern Europe. In any case, for Hungary an out-

---

*According to official price indexes in <u>Külkereskedelmi statisztikai évkönyv, 1978,</u> by 1978 Hungary's exports to the Third World as a whole had lost half the purchasing power they had possessed in 1970.

ward orientation began early, as for example with the dependence of steel-making capacities on foreign—Soviet and Eastern European—supplies of iron ore and anthracite.

The Hungarian economy greatly depends on foreign markets to achieve levels of domestic production high enough to utilize at least the minimum economies of scale available in any particular branch. [7] This is why the Hungarians have become interested in opening export opportunities in the Third World, as mentioned in the previous section.

Whether Hungary turned abroad in order to meet domestic demand for imports or to expand its export possibilities, the result has been the same: the Hungarian economy has become highly trade-oriented, or, as economists put it, trade-dependent. At present nearly one-half of domestic production is exported, with a slightly higher inflow of imports. [8] The Third World has been a subsidiary market for Hungary's exports as well as a source of materials to feed the flames of Hungarian industry. The specific products involved will be discussed in some detail in later sections of this chapter.

The Maturing Bloc System

Hungary's position in the political and economic context of the Eastern bloc has also limited its trade options and steered the choices made by Hungarian decision makers. Before the 1960s there was little independence in Hungarian policy regarding its contacts with the Third World—or anywhere else for that matter. Nevertheless, Hungary did trade with the outside world and even with developing countries, notably Egypt, Indonesia, and Argentina, which exchanged cotton, rubber, and leather, respectively, and other primary products for goods processed by Hungarian industry.

The oppressive international atmosphere that marked those early years of the bloc began to dissipate during the Khrushchev era, when dramatic changes were occurring within the Soviet Union. These internal changes led in turn to changes in the international role of the Soviet Union within the bloc system. The monopoly on political initiative held by the Soviets gave way to a tentative, though unequal, sharing of decision making among the bloc's members.

Actually, in the "new," post-Stalinist bloc, direct Soviet participation in domestic decision making in Eastern Europe became redundant. An increased sense of domestic authority and legitimacy based on the strength of industrialization has encouraged national authorities in each Eastern European country to make decisions which, though taken independently, are not far out of line with previous decisions in which the Soviets had been actively and directly involved. The bloc was maturing into a self-regulating system.

TABLE 6.1

Eastern European Trade with Major Regions in 1975
(index of turnover: 1960 = 100)

Country	Soviet Union	CMEA5	MDC	LDC	World
Bulgaria					
Turnover	52.5	19.0	17.0	7.2	100.0
Balance	-147.3	-31.1	-698.3	233.3	-593.4
Index	523.8	405.5	582.1	1338.4	526.7
Czechoslovakia					
Turnover	32.5	32.4	22.3	7.0	100.0
Balance	-123.5	-175.6	-450.6	166.7	-564.6
Index	256.9	335.3	314.1	181.6	278.3
East Germany					
Turnover	35.7	29.5	25.9	4.4	100.0
Balance	-378.1	218.9	-843.4	-39.4	-996.3
Index	239.7	387.2	342.9	311.2	296.8

Note: Vanous defines the regional categories as follows: CMEA5 consists of members of the CMEA in Europe, excluding the Soviet Union (there are five because the individual country does not trade with itself); MDC, or "more developed countries," the advanced capitalist counties of Western Europe (including Turkey), the United States, Canada, Japan, South Africa, and Oceania; LDC consists of non-Socialist, non-MDC countries.

The turnover figures are percentages and along with the balance figures are based on current, 1975 SDRs. The trade turnover index,

The bloc is self-regulating in the sense that trade relations among the members create a set of incentives as well as constraints which tend to guide their relations with the outside world. The fact that Hungary has conducted and continues to conduct a very large proportion of its trade within the bloc does not bear testimony to "Soviet imperialism." Rather, it shows the self-sustaining nature of the socioeconomic transformations that took place in Eastern Europe following World War II. The erosion of hierarchical decision making within the bloc provided opportunities also for the expansion of trade with all regions and in particular with regions outside the bloc. Not all the countries took advantage of these growing possibilities. Hungary's

Country	Soviet Union	CMEA5	MDC	LDC	World
Hungary					
Turnover	36. 3	27. 1	27. 4	5. 7	100. 0
Balance	-28. 9	-182. 8	-576. 0	-65. 7	-797. 9
Index	470. 3	359. 6	400. 3	453. 2	393. 7
Poland					
Turnover	28. 1	21. 2	41. 3	6. 5	100. 0
Balance	54. 9	253. 1	-2442. 9	224. 0	-1872. 5
Index	474. 6	455. 3	624. 9	457. 2	508. 5
Romania					
Turnover	18. 6	18. 9	39. 1	16. 2	100. 0
Balance	116. 7	-53. 6	-387. 3	277. 9	-0. 3
Index	232. 4	377. 5	785. 7	1628. 4	485. 2

however, is based on deflated 1975 volume. The adjustments were made according to indexes published by the Hungarians in their Statistical Yearbook of Foreign Trade, which are given by region and composition of trade. This means that the trade of all the Eastern European countries was adjusted using Hungarian price indexes.

Source: Jan Vanous, Project CMEA-FORTRAM: Data Bank of Foreign Trade Flows and Balances of CMEA Countries, 1950-1975 (Vancouver: University of British Columbia, 1977).

trade with the Soviet Union, for instance, grew both in volume and at a pace which has surpassed Hungarian trade with all other regions. For Romania the opposite has been true. Czechoslovakia's and East Germany's trade with the Soviet Union has lagged behind their trade with other regions, though the bulk of their trade still remains in the bloc (see Table 6.1 for details).

The percentage of total trade conducted within the bloc varies from country to country, from the high level maintained by Bulgaria to the low of Romania. [9] However, the significance for all these countries, including Romania, [10] of trade within the bloc is beyond doubt. First of all, they all depend on the bloc, and particularly on the Soviet

Union with its vast material resources, for essential supplies of primary products, often at prices more favorable than can be found on outside markets. Secondly, all make ample use of the protected market available for the export of those goods produced by domestic industry, which face numerous financial, political, and economic handicaps on capitalist markets.

The bloc market is a more congenial place for these countries to do business precisely because it is not a market in the laissez-faire sense. Trade is conducted between centrally planned economies and, despite efforts to the contrary (largely by the Hungarians), currencies remain inconvertible and bilateralism dominates.

These incentives and constraints within the bloc discourage renegade national economic policies. Thus Hungary obediently fulfills its intrabloc obligations and actively participates in the regional division of labor, at the cost, it must be assumed, of expanding contacts with the Third World. However, the high degree of autonomy demonstrated by Romania in its contacts outside the bloc clearly demonstrates that the system is not foolproof.

SCOPE OF TRADE WITH THE THIRD WORLD

Identifying the Main Regions

The poorer, less developed nations of the planet comprise far from a homogeneous grouping, due to their varying sizes, positions, populations, resources, and of course their relations with the richer nations. One convenient method by which to categorize this amalgam of well over a hundred countries is according to the continents on which they are situated. There are important historical reasons why this is a sensible approach. For example, the colonial background of an African nation is more similar to that of another African country than to any Latin American country. The same is true of the distinctive history of development in Asia. Yet, for some purposes, and the analysis of Hungary's trade with the Third World can be included here, a threefold categorization is still inadequate.

If a general categorization of the Third World is based on regions, then it is very useful to squeeze the countries of the Middle East and North Africa out of their respective continents and into a fourth region. (Creating the category "Middle East" for Tables 6.2 and 6.3 involved "squeezing," that is, subtracting Hungary's trade with its major Middle Eastern and North African partners from their respective continents and estimating the remainder on the basis of the very complete country-by-country aggregate statistics published in 1978 by the Hungarians.) As Table 6.2 shows, the four regions take

TABLE 6.2

Hungary's Trade with Major Third World Regions
(millions of forints)

Regions	1960	1965	1970	1974	1978	Percentage Share Third World	Percentage Share World
Africa							
Exports	376.1	980.3	1161.8	1164.9	2655.3	12.7	1.1
Imports	351.7	930.1	1624.6	3070.6	4357.2	16.7	1.4
Balance	24.4	50.2	-462.8	-1905.7	-1701.9		
Index	100.0	262.5	382.9	409.1	753.6		
Middle East							
Exports	1312.8	2757.6	4050.3	8632.1	15220.9	72.8	6.3
Imports	996.9	1766.6	3050.0	8292.5	8192.6	31.4	2.7
Balance	315.9	991.0	1000.3	339.6	7028.3		
Index	100.0	195.9	307.4	440.4	690.1		
Asia							
Exports	642.7	2188.4	1976.7	3136.2	1609.9	7.7	0.7
Imports	932.0	2074.4	2169.6	3285.7	3339.7	12.8	1.1
Balance	-289.3	114.0	-192.9	-149.5	-1729.8		
Index	100.0	270.7	263.3	287.3	246.5		

(continued)

Table 6.2, (continued)

Regions	1960	1965	1970	1974	1978	Percentage Share	
						Third World	World
Latin America							
Exports	1087.2	404.8	879.4	2001.2	1421.7	6.8	0.6
Imports	1133.5	1927.2	3637.0	4909.0	10201.6	39.1	3.4
Balance	-46.3	-1522.4	-2757.6	-2907.8	-8779.9		
Index	100.0	105.0	203.4	217.7	404.8		
Third World							
Exports	3418.8	6331.1	8068.2	14934.4	20907.8	100.0	8.7
Imports	3414.1	6698.3	10481.2	19557.8	26091.1	100.0	8.7
Balance	4.7	-367.2	-2413.0	-4623.4	-5183.3		
Index	100.0	190.7	271.5	329.4	501.8		

Note: Export and import figures for 1960, 1965, 1970, and 1974 are converted from their original denomination in the devisa-forint accounting unit to simple forints, in which all trade has been denominated since 1976. This was done on the basis of volume indexes published by the Hungarians. The "foreign trade rate of exchange" at the end of 1978 was 35.78 forints to the dollar. Thus Hungarian exports to the entire Third World in 1978 were approximately $584 million.

The "index" figures for 1974 and 1978 are based not on the current figures but on trade turnover adjusted for prices according to the composition of trade with each region as shown in Table 6.3. Therefore, they do not correspond to the import and export figures here.

Sources: Külkereskedelmi statisztikai évkönyv, 1973 and 1978; Statisztikai évkönyv, various years.

178

greatly varying proportions of Hungary's exports and provide differing levels of imports.* The net balance with the Middle East, surprisingly, shows a very hardy surplus in 1978, but not strong enough to offset the weighty negative imbalance of Hungary's exchanges with Latin America.

It is this trade balance situation that most recommends the detachment of North Africa from the sub-Saharan nations doing trade with Hungary. This and more can be said of the distinct content of relations between Hungary and the Middle East, on the one hand, and between Hungary and the countries of Asia proper on the other. Hungary's trade with the latter shows both a deteriorating balance and volume. Trade with the Middle East and North Africa, in contrast, has outpaced all the other regions of the Third World, even when adjustment is made for spiraling prices.

Composition of Trade

There are many reasons why Hungary's trade with the four regions of the Third World—and within those regions as well—is so varied. Political affinity, raw materials and food demand, marketing opportunities, and even such mundane considerations as transportation costs all play a role and are worthy of closer consideration, as will be attempted in the remainder of this chapter. There is no single cause, but many purely economic considerations are reflected in the composition of Hungary's exports and imports with those regions, as reported in Table 6. 3.

Category 1 in Table 6. 3 is for fuels. Besides the very small exports of heating oil, primarily to the Middle East, and the more substantial imports of crude oil from the same region, there is little of significance traded under this category with the Third World. Before 1970, Hungary did not depend on any source of crude outside the Eastern bloc. By 1978, 20 percent of its crude imports originated in Iraq and Iran, and in spite of the probable disturbance of Iranian ship-

---

*Data in Tables 6. 2 through 6. 11 are given in millions of current forints, except for indexes and percentages where indicated, and are based on trade according to country of origin and destination, not of sale and purchase. In all tables, "Exports" refers to Hungary's exports, "Imports" to Hungary's imports, and "Balance" to the balance of that trade obtained by subtracting the import value from the corresponding export value. The "Index" is for the volume of trade turnover, 1960 = 100.

TABLE 6.3

Composition of Hungary's Trade
with Major Third World Regions in 1978
(percentages)

Regions	1	2	3	4	5	Total
Africa						
Exports	0.0	21.4	39.8	34.1	4.7	100.0
Imports	0.0	10.9	0.2	0.0	88.9	100.0
Middle East						
Exports	0.1	22.7	23.4	17.6	36.3	100.0
Imports	64.1	22.5	0.0	6.4	7.0	100.0
Asia						
Exports	0.0	67.9	20.4	10.4	1.3	100.0
Imports	0.0	47.5	0.3	29.4	22.7	100.0
Latin America						
Exports	0.0	52.6	38.5	6.0	3.0	100.0
Imports	0.0	11.3	0.3	1.0	87.4	100.0
Third World						
Exports	0.1	25.4	29.0	20.1	25.4	100.0
Imports	19.9	21.9	0.4	6.3	51.5	100.0

Note: The five-category Hungarian trade breakdown is as follows: (1) energy carriers (fuels) and electric power; (2) raw materials, semi-processed goods, and components; (3) machines, vehicles,
and other capital goods; (4) consumer goods; and (5) basic food industry goods, live animals, and food.

The figures listed for each region are based on summing up the
value totals with the major partners within that region as presented
in Tables 6.5, 6.7, 6.9, and 6.11, respectively. They are thus based
on a sample, but a sample usually of well over 75 percent of exports
or imports of the individual region. The Third World figures, though,
are based on totals published in the Külkereskedelmi statisztikai
évkönyv.

Source: Külkereskedelmi statisztikai évkönyv, 1978.

ments since the ouster of the Shah, this percentage is likely to rise. Trade activities in this category are examined in more detail in the section on the Middle East and North Africa.

The second category officially covers "raw materials, semi-processed goods, and components, and is thus actually three categories in one. In general, Hungary's imports from the Third World listed under this category are of the first type, "raw materials," whereas its exports are predominantly "processed goods and components." For example, Hungary's export and import trade with Asia in 1978 was largely conducted in this second category. A closer look reveals that the Asian countries supply Hungary with basic raw materials, such as rubber from Malaysia and Indonesia and iron ore from India, in exchange for processed metals and basic pharmaceutical compounds. Pharmaceuticals, along with other basic chemicals and compounds, accounted for 37.8 percent of Hungary's category 2 exports to the Third World and 9.5 percent of total exports to the Third World in 1978. [11] Equally important are exports of processed metal products such as rolled steel, piping, and aluminum.

To no one's surprise, Hungary imports few machines (category 3) from the Third World. Only Brazil, Nigeria, Iran, and India provide any at all. In exports, though, Hungary has put much at stake on its ability to provide machines and capital goods to speed the industrialization of the Third World. These exports account for close to a third (29 percent) of Hungary's exports to the Third World and constitute the largest single category. Major exports include equipment for complete factories, hospitals, and laboratories. Other types of machines, both light and heavy, such as transformers and cranes, along with vehicles, particularly buses, make up the balance of exports in this category. [12]

Trade in category 4 goods, manufactured consumer goods, is, after category 1, the least significant in Hungary's trade with the Third World. Four-fifths of imports in this category are textile articles originating in Asia or the Middle East. These include both finished articles of clothing for men's shirts and women's dresses and unfinished bolts of cotton and wool cloth. Exports include, in addition to a similar selection of textiles processed in Hungary, other consumer manufactures such as televisions, light bulbs (which Hungary exports to 55 developing countries), and prepared medicines.

Half of Hungary's imports from the Third World are food products (category 5), such as coffee and tropical fruits, as well as fodder for cattle husbandry and oil seeds for the vegetable oil industry. These products dominate the imports from Africa and Latin America. As for exports, category 5 products account for less than one-twentieth the total to most regions. The Middle East is the one region in the Third World to which Hungary exports more food than metal products or machines. In recent years Hungary has very successfully promoted the export of beef, poultry, and some vegetable products, such as tomato puree to the wealthy (by Third World standards) Middle Eastern and North African countries, and has shaped this trade into a hard currency-earning proposition. [13]

The background, growth, and composition of Hungarian trade in commodities and technologies with the four regions of the Third World, and in particular the main trade partners in these regions, will be examined in detail in the next sections. [14]

Sub-Saharan Africa

During the 1970s the sub-Saharan region was a constant battleground for the political interests of East and West. In the Ogaden to the east, Angola to the west, and around Zimbabwe to the south, outright hostilities broke out, pitting forces receiving direct or clandestine support from the East or West. Confrontation in the economic sphere has been far less virulent; the Eastern European countries and the Soviet Union have an uphill battle against the well-worn patterns of African trade with former colonial powers in Western Europe. Hungary has striven to overcome these obstacles, and the choice of a "noncapitalist path" in Angola and Ethiopia has aided the effort, but trade remains at very low levels, in spite of strong growth of trade in percentage terms and a healthy export turnover of "technical and intellectual" goods, that is, licenses, plans, and research services, destined for Africa.

Hungarian trade with sub-Saharan Africa was insignificant prior to 1960, the year which marked the final collapse of European colonialism in much of Africa. The establishment of steady and significant trade relations with Hungary was led by Sudan, Ghana, and Nigeria, followed at the end of the decade by Uganda and later by others. With the exception of Ghana it appears that, once established, trade relations have provided a firm base for future growth. Table 6.4 lists Hungary's eight most important trade partners in Africa as of 1978.

Although Hungary's imports from sub-Saharan Africa account for a mere 1.5 percent of total imports from all countries, they are significant from the point of view of the Hungarian food industry and to a lesser extent the nonfood raw materials demand of Hungarian in-

TABLE 6.4

Value and Shares of Trade with Africa
(millions of forints)

Country	1976	1977	1978	Percentage Share		
				Region	Third World	World
Angola						
Exports	24.3	198.7	160.1	6.4	0.8	0.1
Imports	363.5	1060.1	0.0	0.0	0.0	0.0
Ethiopia						
Exports	114.7	157.5	271.4	10.9	1.3	0.1
Imports	22.9	8.7	17.9	0.4	0.1	0.0
Guinea						
Exports	31.0	37.2	10.5	0.4	0.1	0.0
Imports	346.2	485.2	452.2	10.5	1.7	0.2
Ivory Coast						
Exports	47.6	41.6	83.1	3.3	0.4	0.0
Imports	652.3	67.5	896.7	20.8	3.5	0.3
Malagasy						
Exports	1.0	196.0	7.3	0.3	0.0	0.0
Imports	252.8	186.6	465.0	10.8	1.8	0.2
Nigeria						
Exports	430.2	1322.7	1161.6	46.7	5.7	0.5
Imports	200.6	921.7	1508.0	34.9	5.8	0.5
Sudan						
Exports	340.4	279.8	190.2	7.6	0.9	0.1
Imports	314.0	360.0	354.8	8.2	1.4	0.1
Uganda						
Exports	7.2	21.6	0.1	0.0	0.0	0.0
Imports	118.9	153.8	343.6	8.0	1.3	0.1

Note: Since 1976 Hungary's trade has been denominated in domestic forints at a "foreign trade rate of exchange." The year-end 1976, 1977, and 1978 foreign trade rate of the forint to the dollar was 41.30 ft, 40.604 ft, and 35.78 ft, respectively.

Source: Külkereskedelmi statisztikai évkönyv, 1978.

dustry (see Table 6.5). Imports from each of Hungary's major partners in Africa follow the general pattern of near complete reliance on a small selection of food products or of basic raw materials. The most extreme cases of this were Angola in 1977 and Uganda in 1978, both of which sold Hungary only coffee. Nearly the same can be said of Hungary's imports from all the sub-Saharan countries, although they had slightly broader selections: in 1978, 94.4 percent of imports from Nigeria were cocoa, 99 percent from Sudan were cotton, 85.5 percent from the Ivory Coast were coffee, and 95.7 percent from Malagasy were the same.

These figures on imports show the fundamental weakness and lack of diversity of African industry, but these imports have provided the basis for a reverse flow of significant and diversified exports from Hungary. About 60 percent of those exports are modern industrial machines and products destined for the capital sectors of the purchasing countries. The rest are largely textile products such as cotton materials, thread, and finished clothing. Nigeria has taken the lead in purchasing complete packages of equipment for hospitals and laboratories (as well as prepared pharmaceuticals to go with them). Ethiopia, which is the second largest importer of Hungarian goods in Africa, buys buses (which are Hungary's strongest machine export, though the largest share of them go to other Eastern European countries and to the Soviet Union), and cotton cloth and heavy tent canvas. These patterns hold true for the other countries of the region as well.

In addition to being the most important trade partner for Hungary in Africa, Nigeria is also the most important purchaser of Hungary's technological exports in the region. Throughout the 1970s, Nigeria has been a constant client of TESCO (Organization for International Technical and Scientific Cooperation), previously the largest supplier of Hungarian technology to the Third World. CHEMOKOMPLEX (Hungarian Company for the Foreign Trade of Machines and Equipment for the Chemical Industry) now rivals TESCO, and in Africa it sold a license for a chemical plant to Kenya in 1978. The only other purchase in 1978 of this type of export by a country in sub-Saharan Africa was for ore-processing equipment plans by Togo from the firm Tatabánya.

At present there are five countries in sub-Saharan Africa which, according to the Hungarian foreign minister, have openly declared their intentions to follow a Socialist and Marxist-Leninist path: Angola, Benin, Ethiopia, Congo, and Mozambique.[15] With Benin and the Congo, Hungary does not have significant or regular trade contacts. With Angola no distinct import pattern seems yet to have emerged, though Hungarian exports are similar to those with Ethiopia in level and composition. As of 1978, Mozambique had begun to import from Hungary, without exports in return.[16] Hungary's trade offensive in Africa does not seem to have as much a political edge as a financial one: the overriding

TABLE 6.5

Composition of Trade with Africa in 1977
(percentages)

Country	1	2	3	4	5	Total
Angola						
Exports	0.0	21.8	30.5	38.9	8.8	100.0
Imports	0.0	0.0	0.0	0.0	100.0	100.0
Ethiopia						
Exports	0.0	12.0	32.6	55.4	0.0	100.0
Imports	0.0	100.0	0.0	0.0	0.0	100.0
Guinea						
Exports	0.0	0.0	9.0	91.0	0.0	100.0
Imports	N.A.	N.A.	N.A.	N.A.	N.A.	100.0
Ivory Coast						
Exports	0.0	17.6	25.6	53.7	3.1	100.0
Imports	0.0	6.3	0.0	0.0	93.7	100.0
Malagasy						
Exports	0.0	95.7	4.3	0.0	0.0	100.0
Imports	0.0	1.7	0.0	0.0	98.3	100.0
Nigeria						
Exports	0.0	23.2	50.3	20.3	6.2	100.0
Imports	0.0	4.9	0.7	0.0	94.4	100.0
Sudan						
Exports	0.0	22.7	1.5	75.8	0.0	100.0
Imports	0.0	100.0	0.0	0.0	0.0	100.0
Uganda						
Exports	0.0	100.0	0.0	0.0	0.0	100.0
Imports	0.0	0.0	0.0	0.0	100.0	100.0

Note: "N.A." indicates data is not available. Hungary's imports from Guinea account for 10.5 percent of imports from Africa. According to Berznai, Hungary's purchases from Guinea consist of coffee, palm oil, and high quality iron ore; Aurel Bereznai, "Hungary's Presence in Black Africa," Radio Free Europe Research, Background Report, no. 75 (April 1979): 14. Export figures for Angola are for 1977.

The five-category Hungarian trade breakdown is as follows: (1) energy carriers (fuels) and electric power; (2) raw materials, semi-processed goods, and components; (3) machines, vehicles, and other capital goods; (4) consumer goods; and (5) basic food industry goods, live animals, and food.

Source: Külkereskedelmi statisztikai évkönyv, 1978.

concern of Hungarian trade policy makers seems to be the solvency of partners rather than ideological solidarity. This is particularly important as long as Hungary is unable to export in quantities sufficient to offset its imports from the region.

The Middle East and North Africa

The countries of this region present a far more variegated picture in terms of Hungary's trade than do the countries of sub-Saharan Africa. In scarcely a decade, the oil-producing countries in this region have undergone a metamorphosis from the object of exploitation by the Seven Sister oil conglomerates to the subject of attention and deference by the greatest powers. In some ways this is analogous to the effect of decolonization in Africa, but because of the key importance of oil to all industry everywhere in the world and because of the success these countries have had in shifting financial resources to their favor, the change, at least in the short run, has been more influential on the course of world markets and world politics.

Of course, not all the countries in the Middle East and North Africa have been endowed with ample supplies of crude, and therefore they do not have the same financial reserves at their disposal or the same stature in international politics. But in general they are better off than their counterparts in other regions of the Third World. For Hungary, the proximity of this region and its general financial strength, as well as political fraternity with certain key countries, have made it the best market in the Third World for Hungarian exports as well as an auxillary source of petroleum.

Hungary's trade with this region stretches back to the early 1950s and the establishment of close ties between Egypt and the Soviet Union, even prior to Nasser's rise. Throughout the 1950s Hungary's trade with Egypt was among the largest in volume for any of Hungary's partners in the Third World. Since 1960, however, much has changed, although the top spot held by Egypt for trade in the region was surrendered only in the mid-1970s, to Iraq. [17] By 1978, Egypt's key role was in eclipse as Iran, Syria, Libya, Algeria, and Lebanon attracted competing or superior portions of Hungarian trade. Simultaneously, the importance of the entire region in Hungary's total turnover with the Third World grew from 38.3 percent in 1970 to 49.8 percent in 1978 (see Tables 6.2 and 6.6).

In terms of Hungary's exports, the Middle Eastern and North African countries are clearly the most important in the developing world, taking close to three-quarters of Hungary's exports destined to that grouping. From 1970 to 1978, the share of agricultural products in these exports rose from 16 to 36 percent, while the share of

TABLE 6.6

Value and Shares of Hungarian Trade
with the Middle East
(millions of forints)

| | | | | | Percentage Share | |
Country	1976	1977	1978	Region	Third World	World
Algeria						
Exports	1128.7	1906.1	1652.4	10.8	8.1	0.7
Imports	282.3	385.6	376.3	4.6	1.4	0.1
Egypt						
Exports	425.2	422.8	539.1	3.5	2.6	0.2
Imports	1031.7	574.2	807.5	9.9	3.1	0.3
Iran						
Exports	2209.7	2418.3	2067.3	13.5	10.1	0.9
Imports	2675.6	1196.7	1296.2	15.8	5.0	0.4
Iraq						
Exports	3570.0	2988.7	3667.0	24.0	17.9	1.5
Imports	3099.9	2800.1	4722.1	58.2	18.4	1.6
Kuwait						
Exports	1187.2	1823.4	1655.2	10.8	8.1	0.7
Imports	0.0	0.0	27.3	0.3	0.1	0.0
Lebanon						
Exports	174.5	1126.4	1437.3	9.4	7.0	0.6
Imports	17.0	44.7	139.6	1.7	0.5	0.0
Libya						
Exports	447.2	1026.7	2200.7	14.4	10.7	0.9
Imports	0.0	0.0	0.5	0.0	0.0	0.0
Morocco						
Exports	159.0	157.5	196.1	1.3	1.0	0.1
Imports	224.3	269.6	453.2	5.5	1.7	0.2
Syria						
Exports	1504.3	1076.6	746.5	4.9	3.6	0.3
Imports	137.6	215.7	244.9	3.0	0.9	0.1

Source: Külkereskedelmi statisztikai évkönyv, 1978.

machines and investment goods shrank in the face of competition from advanced capitalist countries. [18] As Table 6.7 shows, Algeria and Libya are the only countries to which Hungary sends a higher proportion of machines and capital goods than any other category of products. Major items in 1978 included barges to Libya and commercial ovens to Algeria.

For Egypt, Iran, Morocco, and Syria, category 2 exports from Hungary hold the highest proportion. Within this category, basic steel and aluminum products, such as hot-rolled steel and cold-draw wire, predominate. For all but Egypt, Iran, and Syria, at least a quarter of Hungary's exports are in category 5. For Lebanon, the percentage is over three times that, 83 percent. The major item is meat, both beef and fowl, and to a lesser extent eggs, cheese, and milk. One important vegetable export is tomato puree.

The Middle East is the only region from which Hungary imports oil, and from only two countries, Iraq and Iran. Together in 1978 they provided a little over one-fifth of Hungary's total oil imports, the Soviet Union providing all the rest. Nevertheless, crude oil accounted for about 65 percent of Hungary's imports from the Middle East. At the end of 1979, the Adria Pipeline from the Yugoslavian port of Omisalj to refineries in Hungary and Czechoslovakia was inaugurated. If Hungary is able or obliged to raise the money for purchases, the share of non-Soviet crude in domestic consumption is likely to rise. [19] The bulk of the remaining imports consists of cotton (from Iran and Egypt), phosphate (from Algeria), and other raw materials such as leather from Syria.

In addition to being Hungary's largest export partner in goods, the Middle East is also the biggest purchaser of Hungarian technology in the Third World. Iraq led all others, buying a total of 171 million forints' worth in 1978 (equivalent to approximately one-twentieth of Hungarian exports in goods to that country), 154 million of which went to oil prospecting by CHEMOKOMPLEX. Algeria, Libya, and Tunisia all purchased plans from TESCO for their building industries. Iran purchased 41 million forints' worth of planning for Hungarian "model farms."

Political considerations seem to have played a more direct role in the evolution of trade with the Middle East and with North Africa than with sub-Saharan Africa. For example, the decline in the relative position of Egypt and the corresponding rise in the role of Iraq, Libya, Syria, and Algeria seem to reflect the reorientation of these countries in respect to the United States and the Soviet Union. There is no doubt either that, for the time being, trade with Iran has suffered with the fall of the Pahlavi dynasty with which Hungary, as well as other Eastern bloc countries, enjoyed cordial economic relations. In any case, Hungarian partners in the Middle East and North Africa are far more

TABLE 6.7

Composition of Trade with the Middle East in 1978
(percentages)

Country	1	2	3	4	5	Total
Algeria						
Exports	0.2	9.1	45.0	6.6	39.1	100.0
Imports	0.4	56.9	0.0	0.0	42.7	100.0
Egypt						
Exports	0.0	64.9	14.7	16.6	3.8	100.0
Imports	0.0	57.4	0.0	24.8	17.8	100.0
Iran						
Exports	0.2	55.9	6.4	29.9	7.6	100.0
Imports	32.8	46.1	0.2	15.1	5.8	100.0
Iraq						
Exports	0.0	26.9	36.2	13.4	23.5	100.0
Imports	99.6	0.0	0.0	0.0	0.4	100.0
Kuwait						
Exports	0.0	5.4	19.0	22.6	53.0	100.0
Imports	0.0	0.0	0.0	0.0	0.0	100.0
Lebanon						
Exports	0.0	11.2	0.7	4.8	83.4	100.0
Imports	1.5	22.7	0.0	42.9	32.9	100.0
Libya						
Exports	0.0	1.7	29.4	19.8	49.1	100.0
Imports	0.0	0.0	0.0	0.0	0.0	100.0
Morocco						
Exports	0.0	48.6	17.8	9.6	24.0	100.0
Imports	0.0	77.5	0.0	0.0	22.5	100.0
Syria						
Exports	0.1	41.4	15.5	38.5	4.6	100.0
Imports	0.2	67.8	0.0	25.8	6.2	100.0

Note: The five-category Hungarian trade breakdown is as follows: (1) energy carriers (fuels) and electric power; (2) raw materials, semi-processed goods, and components; (3) machines, vehicles, and other capital goods; (4) consumer goods; and (5) basic food industry goods, live animals, and food.

Source: Külkereskedelmi statisztikai évkönyv, 1978.

financially solvent and able to pay for Hungarian products than other
Third World countries, as the strong overall balance in Hungary's
favor shows.

Asia

Asia is the least consequential region of the Third World in
terms of Hungary's trade. It is inaccessible, not a particularly good
market for Hungarian products, and of uncertain political friendship.
Compared to the dynamic changes that have swept Africa and the Middle East, the developing countries of Asia represent something of a
backwater as far as Hungary's trade is concerned (see Table 6.8).

TABLE 6.8

Value and Shares of Trade with Asia
(millions of forints)

Country	1976	1977	1978	Region	Percentage Share Third World	World
Bangladesh						
Exports	65.4	82.4	114.1	8.2	0.6	0.0
Imports	106.4	81.2	72.5	2.2	0.3	0.0
Hong Kong						
Exports	152.5	25.3	40.6	2.9	0.2	0.0
Imports	280.8	387.0	292.4	8.8	1.1	0.1
India						
Exports	826.4	1020.6	704.5	50.5	3.4	0.3
Imports	1263.4	1523.6	973.0	29.2	3.7	0.3
Indonesia						
Exports	137.6	76.4	142.6	10.2	0.7	0.1
Imports	42.3	704.5	759.4	22.8	2.9	0.3
Malaysia						
Exports	3.2	5.0	13.7	1.0	0.1	0.0
Imports	618.6	678.7	781.2	23.4	3.0	0.3
Pakistan						
Exports	142.7	337.4	188.8	13.5	0.9	0.1
Imports	215.9	247.4	229.9	6.9	0.9	0.1

Source: Külkereskedelmi statisztikai évkönyv, 1978.

TABLE 6.9

Composition of Trade with Asia in 1978
(percentages)

Country	1	2	3	4	5	Total
Bangladesh						
Exports	0.0	33.7	39.2	27.1	0.0	100.0
Imports	N.A.	N.A.	N.A.	N.A.	N.A.	100.0
Hong Kong						
Exports	0.0	36.0	2.8	23.9	37.3	100.0
Imports	0.0	0.0	0.0	100.0	0.0	100.0
India						
Exports	0.0	78.3	16.2	5.6	0.0	100.0
Imports	0.0	41.9	1.0	46.4	10.6	100.0
Indonesia						
Exports	0.0	61.0	39.0	0.0	0.0	100.0
Imports	0.0	29.6	0.0	0.0	70.4	100.0
Malaysia						
Exports	0.0	45.0	21.1	33.9	0.0	100.0
Imports	0.0	98.4	0.0	0.6	1.0	100.0
Pakistan						
Exports	0.0	56.1	16.7	27.2	0.0	100.0
Imports	0.0	4.5	0.0	88.5	7.0	100.0

Note: The five-category Hungary trade breakdown is as follows: (1) energy carriers (fuels) and electric power; (2) raw materials, semi-processed goods, and components; (3) machines, vehicles, and other capital goods; (4) consumer goods; and (5) basic food industry goods, live animals, and food.

"N.A." indicates data not available.

Source: Külkereskedelmi statisztikai évkönyv, 1978.

The strongest economy of this region, India, has been one of Hungary's chief trade partners in the Third World since the early 1960s. In recent years, though, trade with India has declined, as has the share of this region in total turnover with Hungary. Nevertheless, India's trade with Hungary continues to stand out not only because of its volume, still unrivalled by other countries in Asia, but also because of its composition, which from the Hungarian point of view might be considered quite "up to date," meaning that Hungary as an industrial country is able to export industrial products while India provides basic raw materials and consumer manufactures. Almost half of Hungary's exports to India in 1978 consisted of chemicals for the manufacture of pharmaceuticals. In return, India supplies Hungary with iron ore, ferro-manganese, and leather, as well as a number of finished textile goods such as shirts and dresses.

The array and volume of goods from other Asian partners is much more limited. From Malaysia, Hungary buys crude rubber, as it has for at least 20 years, but little else. From Indonesia the main import is coffee, though substantial importation of raw materials such as rubber continues. From Hong Kong and Pakistan finished textiles and prepared clothing are the principal imports.

In 1978, Hungary's exports to the same region were less than one-half of imports, leaving Hungary with a trade deficit just a bit larger than its deficit with Africa. Half of Hungary's exports to this region were bought by India and are described above. The remaining exports to the other countries of the region consisted of metal products, machines, and some specialities of Hungarian consumer goods export industry, such as lightbulbs.

Over the last decade India has also been a regular customer for Hungary's technological exports, buying plans for chemical plants and oil prospecting services from CHEMOKOMPLEX. In 1978, Pakistan bought a license from PANNÓNIA (export company of the Csepel Steel and Metal Works) for a textile mill.

In what ways and to what extent political undercurrents within the bloc may have influenced the course of Hungary's trade with Asia is not clear. Certainly, India's friendship with the Soviet Union has been warmer at other times, and it is possible that Hungarian trade with the former was influenced by the cooling of relations. Yet the commodity content of Hungarian-Indian trade is such as to lend doubts as to the long-term stability of the relationship, even without overt political pressures. That is to say, the dependence of Hungary on its export of machines has not proved as powerful a mechanism for the promotion of trade with Third World countries, in this case with India, as the Hungarians had hoped.

Latin America

Latin America is the last region and most remote to be considered. In many ways it is also the most advanced, or at least the most Western, in the Third World. In keeping with Hungary's efforts elsewhere, it has actively pursued trade contacts with this region, in spite of numerous setbacks for the assumption of power by friendly forces.

Hungary has had strong trade ties with Latin America since the advent of the Hungarian People's Republic. Peronist Argentina was

TABLE 6. 10

Value and Shares of Trade with Latin America
(millions of forints)

Country	1976	1977	1978	Region	Percentage Share Third World	World
Argentina						
Exports	115. 7	114. 9	91. 5	7. 1	0. 4	0. 0
Imports	130. 8	342. 3	827. 1	8. 2	3. 2	0. 3
Brazil						
Exports	222. 7	338. 3	483. 6	37. 3	2. 4	0. 2
Imports	5579. 1	8522. 1	6359. 2	62. 8	24. 5	2. 1
Ecuador						
Exports	3. 7	6. 3	15. 4	1. 2	0. 1	0. 0
Imports	615. 5	1338. 0	962. 8	9. 5	3. 7	0. 3
Guatemala						
Exports	5. 8	3. 3	8. 2	0. 6	0. 0	0. 0
Imports	2. 3	478. 5	520. 6	5. 1	2. 0	0. 2
Mexico						
Exports	119. 1	123. 4	131. 7	10. 2	0. 6	0. 1
Imports	235. 1	323. 2	391. 4	3. 9	1. 5	0. 1
Peru						
Exports	264. 1	375. 6	143. 5	11. 1	0. 7	0. 1
Imports	957. 9	1586. 3	555. 6	5. 5	2. 1	0. 2

Source: Külkereskedelmi statisztikai évkönyv, 1978.

Hungary's most important Third World partner in the early 1950s and
remained among the leading traders through most of the 1950s and
1960s. Hungarian trade with Argentina then, as with all major Latin
America partners now, was imbalanced to Hungary's disfavor (see
Table 6. 10).

Latin America, like Africa, is a source of raw materials and
foodstuffs for the Hungarian food industry (see Table 6. 11). The scale
of deliveries, though, is much larger. The greatest bulk of imports
from Latin America consist of coffee and oil seeds for the vegetable
oil industry in Hungary. Brazilian supplies destined for Hungary are
over six times greater than the value of sales by the next largest supplier in the region, Ecuador. Seventy-five percent of Hungary's imports from Brazil consist of supplies for the vegetable oil industry.

TABLE 6.11

Composition of Trade with Latin America in 1978
(percentages)

Country	1	2	3	4	5	Total
Argentina						
Exports	0.0	67.2	20.5	12.3	0.0	100.0
Imports	0.0	32.0	0.0	2.1	65.9	100.0
Brazil						
Exports	0.0	36.6	55.5	3.2	4.7	100.0
Imports	0.0	5.3	0.5	0.8	93.4	100.0
Ecuador						
Exports	N.A.	N.A.	N.A.	N.A.	N.A.	100.0
Imports	0.0	0.0	0.0	0.0	100.0	100.0
Guatemala						
Exports	0.0	0.0	0.0	100.0	0.0	100.0
Imports	0.0	0.0	0.0	0.0	100.0	100.0
Mexico						
Exports	0.0	87.7	8.9	3.0	0.4	100.0
Imports	0.0	73.7	0.0	7.7	18.6	100.0
Peru						
Exports	0.0	68.3	20.8	9.4	1.5	100.0
Imports	0.0	49.7	0.0	0.0	50.3	100.0

Note: The five-category Hungarian trade breakdown is as follows: (1) energy carriers (fuel) and electric power; (2) raw materials,
semi-processed goods, and components; (3) machines, vehicles, and
other capital goods; (4) consumer goods; and (5) basic food industry
goods, live animals, and food.
   "N.A." indicates data not available.
   Source: Külkereskedelmi statisztikai évkönyv, 1978.

Brazil is, in fact, Hungary's largest supplier in the entire Third
World. Unfortunately for Hungary's payment position with this "Latin
giant," Brazil is only the tenth largest purchaser of Hungarian exports.
   Guatemala is the second largest supplier of coffee to Hungary
in the Third World, next to the Ivory Coast. This product accounts
for all the imports from Guatemala, Nicaragua, and El Salvador, and
about half, along with cotton, of imports from Peru, and a large proportion from Ecuador. Argentina and Ecuador are important suppliers
of tropical fruit.

Hungary's exports to Latin America are the smallest to any Third World region, accounting for about 0.6 percent of exports to the entire world. In 1978 Hungary's most important export to Brazil, also the largest purchaser of Hungarian goods in the region, was one floating crane at the cost of 115 million forints. Other exports included numerous chemical compounds and small machines, such as medical X-ray machines. The principal exports to Mexico, the third largest purchaser in Latin America, were basic pharmaceutical chemicals.

Finally, Latin America is the smallest market in the Third World for Hungary's "technical and intellectual" exports. The largest purchase in the last few years was a license for the manufacture of locomotive components by Argentina from the engineering firm for the railways, Ganz Mávag.

In the early 1970s, Chile was one of Hungary's partners in Latin America but commanded only a very small percentage of the region's trade. Since the brutal crushing of the Allende regime and with the fading radicalism of the Peruvian military leadership, there has been little of political interest for Hungary in Latin America (outside of Cuba). Instead, Hungary cheerily purchases almost a quarter of its total Third World imports from an anti-Communist military regime in the region. Perhaps "cheerily" is not quite correct: with the right hand Hungary buys from Brazil, but with the left it chides Brazil for its participation in an "imperialist, political, military bloc" along with Argentina, the United States, and South Africa. [20]

CONCLUSION

In each of the three years 1976, 1977, and 1978, Hungary's trade turnover with the Third World has been close to a tenth of total trade: its highest level in proportion to total trade for the entire post-World War II era. In contrast, Romania conducts a far larger share of its trade with those regions, while the GDR has a smaller share than Hungary. Furthermore, though the Hungarian economy is very small, it is highly trade-dependent. Ten percent of its trade represents a figure of around 5 percent of GNP for the turnover of trade with the Third World. Although one must regard such calculations very suspiciously, they do indicate that Hungary's trade with the Third World is more than negligible.

The growth in trade with the Third World can be partly explained by increasing pressures within the bloc to turn toward the South to satisfy growing demand for primary goods, which previously had been amply supplied by the raw materials and fuel sources of the Soviet Union. The increased purchasing power of oil-exporting nations seeking to buy Hungarian foodstuffs as explored above in the section on the Middle East and North Africa has also contributed to this increase of trade. The renunciation in 1976 of the devisa-forint in favor of the domestic forint at a foreign trade rate of exchange and the simultaneous renegotiation of trade with many Third World partners into hard-currency settlement clearing agreements is another significant factor. [21]

In spite of the recent growth of Hungary's trade relations with Third World countries around the globe, its significance for the domestic economy is limited. To some extent, this is because the assumption of power by a Soviet-oriented Communist party as well as speeded industrialization have had a profound effect on the capability of the economy and on the willingness of the polity to engage in trade with the Third World. Industry has yet to prove itself dynamic enough to compete with advanced Western firms even on Third World markets; nor is the economy as a whole yet strong enough to allow the granting of trade credits at a level sufficient to support the expansion of this trade.

Another restraining factor has been the bloc international system. For example, over 80 percent of Hungary's engineering exports, machines, go to the member countries of the Council of Mutual Economic Assistance (CMEA). This, as others have noted, is one reason why there have been insufficient incentives for the Hungarians to produce machines competitive with capitalist goods. Contracts arrived at through negotiations by central authorities or foreign trade organizations do not exert pressure on the quality of output equivalent to contracts won in a competitive situation. Thus, Hungary finds itself conducting its most dynamic trade with the poor countries of the earth not so much by offering them the fruits of its industrial development but fruits packed into preserves. This is the chief characteristic of exports to the Middle East.

The weight of linkages within the bloc also exerts itself on imports. Although Hungary now imports substantial quantities of crude oil for domestic refining from Iraq and Iran, a full 80 percent of domestic needs continue to be supplied by the Soviet Union. In fact, the Soviet Union alone provides over 40 percent of fuel and raw materials and the other bloc countries an additional 15 percent. These are relatively secure sources and, with skyrocketing commodity prices, cheaper than outside the bloc. This circumstance is also an incentive to maintain imports within the bloc rather than turning toward more expensive and unreliable Third World sources.

The intrabloc system is thus a rather cozy environment which acts as a disincentive on member countries to trade outside the bloc. Trade with the Third World is not the same desperate hunt for new markets, supplies, and profits that characterizes the expansion of capitalist firms into all regions of the Third World. On the contrary, there are good (though increasingly scarce) sources of raw materials and reliable markets for industrial production.

The timidity of Hungary's relations with the Third World reflects patterns of activities within the bloc in another fashion as well. Hungary has embarked internally on economic reforms of a depth and long-term success unprecedented in Eastern Europe. Meanwhile its foreign policies have passively followed the Soviet lead. This contrasts with Romanian deviations from the Soviet path, which are limited mainly to foreign relations. Thus, it seems possible to identify a trade-off in the Hungarian case between internal autonomy and external fidelity. To the extent that this holds true, Hungary could not be expected to embark on any bold initiatives in its trade and other relations with the Third World unless the domestic reforms were to be abandoned.

For the time being, the future of Hungary's trade with the Third World will continue to reflect the industrial capabilities of the nation's economy as well as the integrative forces of the bloc market. Trade with the Third World will grow, especially as oil imports grow and the expansion of food exports is institutionalized. That trade will reflect political preference, as it has in the past, when friendly nations are most financially secure, but in general will probably gravitate toward any solvent Third World country regardless of its political persuasion.

The outlook by region, then, is clearly weighted toward the expansion of contacts with the Middle East and North Africa. The stabilization of the economies of the "people's republics" in Africa during the 1980s may lead to increased shares of Hungarian trade for them as well. But, again, it is their economic, not political solvency that is crucial. It is unclear whether the decline of trade with Asia will halt: it will probably be some time before Hungary's trade with Socialist Southeast Asia could counteract falling trade levels with the other countries. Finally, trade with Latin America, and in particular with Brazil, is not likely to remain stable unless Hungary brightens its payments picture elsewhere in order to pay for imports.

NOTES

1. Jozsef Bognar, Studies in Developing Countries 4 (1968).
2. Frigyes Puja, "Afrikai tapasztalatok," Külpolitika (February 1978).
3. Some details of how the Eastern bloc has acted in UNCTAD are revealed in Gosovic, "UNCTAD: North-South Encounter," International Conciliation 568 (May 1968).
4. For example, in February 1977 Hungary acceded to the Fifth International Tin Agreement of 1975. See K. Kvassinger, "Az ötödik nemzetkozi önegyezmény," Világgazdaság 9, no. 67 (1977).
5. J. Nyerges, "Az V. UNCTAD—magyar szemmel," Külgazdaság 23 (April 1979).

6. See ibid. , and Aurel Bereznai "Hungary's Presence in Black Africa," Radio Free Europe Research, Background Report 75 (April 1979): p. 9.

7. For example, such calculations have apparently influenced the decision to concentrate on buses and heavy-duty axles in the automotive sphere. Imogene Edwards and Robert Fraser, "Internationalization of the East European Automotive Industries" in East European Economies Post-Helsinki (U. S. Congress Joint Economic Committee: U. S. Government Printing Office, 1977), pp. 401-2.

8. According to Statisztikai évkönyv, 1977, in 1977 exports were 46. 9 percent of net national products. As is true of other countries with similar levels of trade dependence, Hungary's economy is relatively small. Based on a population scarecely over 10 million, its GNP is modest, a third of the Polish, about half of the Czechoslovak and East German, but only about 20 percent larger than the Bulgarian. See Thad Alton, "Comparative Structure and Growth of of Economic Activity in Eastern Europe," East European Economies U. S. Congress, p. 224.

9. In 1975, according to Jan Vanous's figures for Bulgaria, 74. 6 percent of exports and 68. 7 percent of imports were conducted either with the Soviet Union or other Eastern European countries. For Romania the figures were 38. 2 percent and 36. 7 percent, respectively. Jan Vanous, Project CMEA-FORTRAM: Data Bank of Foreign Trade Flows and Balances of CMEA Countries, 1950-1975 (Vancouver: University of British Columbia, 1977).

10. For example, according to the Chicago Tribune, November 23, 1979, in 1979 Romania signed a contract with the Soviet Union for the delivery of 350,000 metric tons of Soviet crude oil (out of an annual consumption of around 26 million tons), becoming the last Eastern European country to take advantage of this source.

11. Külkereskedelmi statisztikai évkönyv, 1978. See also J. Tihanyi, "Vegyiáru-külkereskedemünk a CHEMOLIMPEX tevékenységének tükrében," Világgazdaság 8, no. 196 (1976).

12. See Árpad Orosz, "Gépipari exportunk és a fejlödö országok," Külgazdaság 23 (April 1979).

13. Radio Free Europe Research, Hungarian Situation Reports: "Important Role of Meat Exports in Hard Currency Earnings," no. 23, (December 1979); "An Unheralded Hard Currency Earner: The Specialized Agricultural Group," no. 4 (February 1980); "Qadhafi's Libya: A Valuable Source of Hard Currency," no. 17 (July 1978).

14. Unless otherwise indicated in the text or footnotes, data are from the Hungarian Foreign Trade Statistical Yearbook (Külkereskedelmi statisztikai évkönyv), published in Budapest by the Central Statistical Office. Excluded from consideration are nontrade economic relations, such as technical training by the Hungarians, the export of Hungarian specialists, aid grants, and joint production projects.

15. Puja, "Afrikai tapasztalatok."

16. According to Bereznai, Hungary has a special noneconomic assignment in Mozambique from the Political Consultative Committee of the Warsaw Treaty Organization: "The Hungarians are to give military assistance to Mozambique, train their officers in Hungarian military academies, and help train military medical personnel." Bereznai, "Hungary's Presence," p. 20.

17. See Zs. Rostoványi, "A magyar-arab gazdasági kapcsolatok," Külgazdaság 23 (May 1979).

18. Whereas the Arab countries are buying more investment goods with their oil wealth, a shrinking proportion is being purchased in Eastern Europe or the Soviet Union, ibid.

19. "Adria Pipeline Ready: Whose Oil Will it Carry?" Radio Free Europe Reports, Hungarian Situation Report, no. 7 (January 1980).

20. Puja, "Afrikai tapasztalatok," p. 5.

21. "Economic Relations with Africa," Radio Free Europe Reports, Hungarian Situation Report, no. 2 (January 1979): 5-6.

7

POLAND AND THE THIRD WORLD:
THE PRIMACY OF ECONOMIC RELATIONS

Howard Frost

Interest in Polish foreign policy during the past several decades has centered around a limited number of issues, all of which concern European security and, implicitly, superpower conflict. Among these are the Oder-Neisse boundary issue, the Rapacki and Gomulka Plans to limit nuclear armaments in Europe, and the initiative for the European Conference on Security and Cooperation. This focus is partially justified because these issues have indeed been the ones of strategic importance to policy makers concerned with the balance of forces in Europe. Nevertheless, this emphasis has generated two problems. It has led to the neglect among the academic community of Poland's other foreign policy activities, and it has fostered analytical approaches to Polish foreign policy that tend to evaluate Poland's foreign policy initiatives by the criterion of how much these initiatives coincide with the interests of the Soviet Union or the West. James Morrison comments that the question too often asked has been whether Poland is an "obedient" or "independent" ally. [1] Efforts to argue in either direction have tended to obscure the less apparent dynamics of Polish foreign policy, such as Poland's relations with less developed countries (LDCs),* dynamics which are not directly tied to strategic superpow-

---

*The definition of less developed countries used herein includes

---

The views expressed in this chapter are the author's and do not necessarily reflect those of the Central Intelligence Agency.

er relations. These dynamics are nevertheless important, for it is they that inform Poland's relationships with secondary powers and developing countries. [2] Evaluation of these dynamics helps clarify perceptions of Polish policy makers of their country's role in international politics, since these dynamics are not particularly subject to pressures devolving from superpower conflict.

Since 1956, and especially since 1971, Poland has been expending its foreign policy activities. Poland has used the period of detente to increase its ties with West Germany, France, Scandinavia, and the United States, as well as with Britain, Austria, and other European countries. Poland has in addition been active during the past two decades in improving both its political ties and its trade with less developed countries. Prior to the mid-1960s, Poland had maintained relations with countries in Asia, Africa, and South America, but as new countries were created or as established LDCs reevaluated their links with Western nations, Poland increased its ties in all these regions. Poland's main interest in these areas has been trade; primarily it has sought markets for exports to improve its balance of payments. Although trade with the developing nations has been only a small part of Poland's total trade (in 1978, 6.9 percent of exports, 5.4 percent of imports), trade with LDCs in absolute terms has significantly increased along with improved diplomatic relations. Poland's exports to the developing nations almost tripled in value from 1960 to 1970, and almost quadrupled from 1970 to 1978. Poland's imports from developing countries doubled from 1960 to 1970, and more than quadrupled from 1970 to 1978. [3] Although in relative terms trade turnover with LDCs is still only a small portion of total foreign trade, these trends are indicative of increased Polish interest in economic entrees to the Third World.

What have been Poland's major approaches in pursuing relations with the Third World? The major factor in Poland's approach to LDC relations has been economic. In this sphere, trade and credit policies occupy the forefront as is the case with most Eastern European countries. [4] These credits are tied to equipment purchases and therefore do not create a drain on hard currency reserves. Poland also has strong scientific-technical and educational exchange programs; it sends numerous specialists to work in LDCs and receives Third World stu-

---

the following non-Communist countries: (1) all independent African countries, except the Republic of South Africa; (2) all independent countries of East Asia except Hong Kong and Japan; (3) all independent Latin American countries except Cuba; and (4) all countries in the Middle East and South Asia.

dents to its universities. While Poland is believed to supply arms to a number of Third World countries, these transfers are impossible to quantify because of the secrecy surrounding arms deals. It is known, however, that Poland gives at least rhetorical political support to liberation movements such as the Rhodesian Patriotic Front, SWAPO, the MPLA, and the PLO. [5]

Poland's approach to the Third World has therefore been one of pragmatism; it has pursued relations with LDCs that provide tangible, near-term benefits for itself. To the extent that information on Polish-Third World relations is available to Western analysts, it appears that Poland has not sought to establish itself as an independent actor among Eastern European nations as has Romania, nor has it sought extensively to solidify its international status as has East Germany. Consequently, policy makers in Poland have not expanded nearly as much effort publicizing political and military ties with LDCs as have their counterparts in Romania and the GDR. Trade and scientific-technical exchange have been the major factors informing Polish-LDC relations, and current trends suggest such will continue to be the case in the foreseeable future.

INTRODUCTION AND BACKGROUND FOR THE EVALUATION OF POLISH-LDC RELATIONS

To examine Poland's interaction with the Third World, I will briefly discuss Polish perceptions of relationships with Socialist and Western political systems, since dealing with Third World countries often necessitates interaction with countries that have neither Socialist governments nor planned economies. I will also look at recent Polish domestic economic developments to determine internal dynamics that have an impact on foreign policy. Turning to the actual conduct of relations with LDCs, Poland's instruments of foreign economic policy will be presented as will the goals and objectives of relations with the Third World. Finally, I have included short case studies of Poland's relations with selected regions of the world.

Basic Polish Foreign Policy Perceptions

Poland's associations with the Soviet Union and with the CMEA nations need only be referenced briefly to note that they are major factors affecting the conduct of Polish foreign policy. Regardless of the extent of Polish overtures to Western countries, its position in the Socialist camp is a primary determinant of its foreign policy. [6]

In addition to well-publicized political ties, Poland and the Soviet Union have extensive economic ties as well. [7] The Soviet Union is Poland's largest trading partner, receiving 35 percent of Poland's 1978 exports and supplying 31 percent of Poland's imports during the same year. In 1976, Poland received a $1.3 billion low-interest loan from the Soviet Union as well as guarantees for the delivery of low-cost foodstuffs, capital machinery, and consumer goods. [8]

The Polish leadership also values its ties with the West, basically to maintain peaceful strategic and economic relations. Mieczyslaw Rakowski, a Party theorist writing in a 1972 edition of Nowe Drogi, notes that broader contacts with the West are advantageous if not essential for Poland's economic growth. [9] In 1978, for example, Western countries provided markets for about 30 percent of Poland's exports and supplied approximately 38 percent of its imports. [10] Foreign affairs commentator Ignacy Krasicki summarizes Poland's position in relation to the two systems with his comment that the "effectiveness of our policy in the West depends upon our position in the socialist system." [11]

Recent Internal Developments

What are some of the internal dynamics that bear upon current Polish foreign policy and, in particular, on foreign policy towards LDCs? In the political and economic spheres, the regime's main goals in the 1970s were the modernization of industry and improvement of the standard of living, especially the availability of consumer goods. Gierek pursued the first goal basically through the importation of chiefly Western technology. Labor productivity ratios increased through this modernization, [12] but so also did the country's gross hard currency debt, which is currently estimated at $21 billion. [13] (The trade deficit with the West alone tripled between 1974 and 1977 to about $3 billion. [14]) Much of this amount is slated for repayment within the next several years, and it is obvious, given Poland's current economic problems, that the government will have difficulty avoiding substantial rescheduling of the country's debts. [15] Close to 74 percent of Poland's present hard currency earnings from exports of goods and services must be used to pay off the interest and amortization of this debt, so it is clear that Poland will continue to seek expanded export markets. [16] Another problem has been created by the rapid economic growth Gierek instituted in the early 1970s, which had led by 1973 to a 7.5 percent annual growth rate in real GNP and a 10.8 percent growth rate in domestic net material product (produced national income). [17] Financing the foreign debt has necessitated slowing the growth rate and diverting a greater percentage of GNP from capital investment to debt servicing. To stabilize the economic situation, then First Deputy Finance Minister Marion Krzak stated in 1977 that the government was charting national income growth to be approximately 7-8 percent through 1982; the 1981-85 plan slates annual national income growth at 2. 7-3. 4 percent. Moreover, while the share of investment in the national income during the 1970s reached a high of 28. 1 percent, the 1981-85 plan calls for investment to be held at 20 percent, again, chiefly to improve the debt picture. [18] While ameliorating the foreign debt, however, this diversion of investment will retard potential export production.

The standard of living has improved during the last decade, as has industrial productivity. Real income increased 46. 4 percent from 1970 to 1978, or an average of 4. 9 percent per year. [19] The availability of consumer goods improved as well during this period of growth but not enough to satisfy the Polish consumer, as the frequent shortages of these items readily attested. Whatever initiatives to develop profitable operations industrial managers may have exercised during the early 1970s, the government in the 1976-80 plan has reassumed many of these prerogatives, and its investment directions currently create significant shortages in the consumer products market and in the area of housing construction. The standard of living therefore has not increased with the same rapidity in the last half of the decade as in the first. [20] (Real income, in fact, decreased 2. 7 percent in 1978, and increased approximately 1. 9 percent in 1979. [21])

In addition to planning recentralization and the often poor management of the slowdown in GNP growth rate, Poland has several other major factors contributing to its economic problems. In 1979 Poland obtained 17 percent (3. 3 million metric tons) of its oil from nonbloc sources, but by the mid-1980s Polish policy makers project that the country will have to purchase 13 to 14 million metric tons of oil annually outside the bloc at a cost of around $15 billion per year. [22] (This estimate is in 1980 dollars and probably does not take oil price inflation into account.) This oil issue portends not only greater hard currency expenditures but also the probable slowdown of industrial growth as policy makers attempt to pursue conservation measures in energy-intensive sectors of the economy.

Another problem concerns the management of the price structure for foodstuffs. The populace has actively opposed increases which the government has considered essential to decrease the heavy subsidies of this sector. Balancing the political pressure created by popular antipathy to major food price increases with the economic pressures created by continued subsidies will be a major challenge for the current leadership.

What are the implications of these economic dynamics for Polish foreign trade? Considering the debt, the current recentralization in industrial management, and increasing energy needs, it is clear that

Poland's major economic problems will not improve in the short term. The implications for foreign trade are that the government must find import substitutes and increase exports for hard currency, especially exports to Western creditors. As Poland pursues its search for export markets, it is inevitable that these markets will largely be sought among Western nations. Current economic realities in the Third World preclude all but a few LDCs as primary targets for Polish export strategy because of the inability of the majority of these countries to purchase in hard currency the quantity or quality of exports Poland needs to sell. While trade with the Third World will probably increase as part of an overall attempt to develop export markets, it is unlikely that significant increases will occur in this sector of Polish trade. The Gierek leadership emphasized increased commerce with the Socialist countries during the 1980s as an important direction for foreign trade. [23] Nevertheless, Poland's development of exports competitive in hard currency markets will be a major goal in the management of its foreign trade. The ability of the regime to channel funds to develop such competitiveness and to solve other economic problems without further exacerbating discontent among the populace through unwise fiscal policies especially in light of the 1980 strikes will be an important factor in the regime's continued tenure. What the new Kania leadership will do remains to be seen.

CONDUCT OF POLISH-THIRD WORLD RELATIONS

Foreign Policy Instruments

As indicated earlier, Polish relations with the developing countries generally take place on the levels of economic, scientific-technical, and educational cooperation. Like other Eastern European countries, Poland initiates and conducts its relations with the Third World principally with bilateral agreements. Although this modus operandi differs from that used by Western countries, the use of bilateral agreements is common to the Socialist countries for several reasons. First, it allows them to plan their international economic relations together with their domestic economic developments and therefore better coordinate the two. Second, pursuit of economic relations with LDCs through bilateral agreements permits the Socialist countries a visible presence in the LDC, a presence which would not be as significant if the assistance were channeled through multilateral organizations such as U.N. bodies. This practice clearly identifies the source of the assistance, which redounds to the political advantage of the donor. [24] Finally, these bilateral agreements are usually formed with the state, not the private sector of LDC economies. Such has been the case because of the interests both in strengthening Socialist institutions in LDCs and in avoiding potentially adverse publicity that could result from cooperation with capitalist enterprises. [25]

From the inception of their trade relations with the Third World through the early 1970s, Eastern European countries established bilateral trade agreements on the basis of barter arrangements that used clearing accounts to settle imbalances in goods. [26] During the 1970s, most new agreements with LDCs were established on the basis of convertible currencies, which permitted greater flexibility for the partners in the context of their trade relations with the rest of the world. In addition, some previous clearing agreements were converted during that period to a hard currency basis. While by 1975 some countries such as Czechoslovakia and the GDR still pursued the majority of their trading relationships with the Third World on the basis of clearing agreements, Poland conducted more of its trade on the basis of hard currency agreements than any other Eastern European country. [27]

Poland's economic relations with less developed nations have usually involved one or more of the following basic facets: credits, joint venture arrangements, and scientific-technical or educational assistance. To stimulate trade, credits have been offered for both commodity purchases and industrial plants. Polish authorities term the extension of credits a "more effective" form of assistance than "direct financial help," on account of both Poland's limited supply of hard currency and the greater potential for political bonds created by making a long-term repayment schedule part of the package. [28] Poland has pursued an intensive marketing of credits since 1960, with a break from 1967 to 1970 when internal political problems of credit recipients forced a slowdown and reassessment of credit policies.

Credits Poland offers are of basically three types. Government credits are frequently offered for purchases of capital goods provided for in contracts concluded with Polish (state-owned) foreign trade agencies. These credits are extended for a period of up to ten years at up to 4.5 percent interest. They may be repaid in hard currency, in raw materials traditional for the LDC, or in goods produced in the factories built with Polish assistance. Trade credits, the second type, offer commercial interest rates (up to 8 percent) with repayment schedules of up to eight years. The third type, bank credits, are granted through negotiations with the Polish State Bank. This type is not frequently used, and little has been publicized about their structure. [29]

While Poland has found that clearing arrangements are beneficial in the case of LDCs just initiating economic relations, problems can occur with this type of arrangement over long periods of time because of trade imbalances. Polish economists have noted that LDCs will usually reduce imports if they observe an imbalance of trade in Poland's favor. Such fluctuations are of little advantage to either partner because of the problems these reactions create for long-term planning, and these problems have been an important factor leading to the increased interest in hard currency agreements. To circumvent further the problem of trade imbalances, Polish policy makers have been investigating the possibilities of multilateral trade exchanges, in which an LDC with a deficit balance with one Socialist country and a surplus with another can settle the differences through a cooperative exchange between the two Socialist countries. This cooperation would be pursued through the International Bank for Economic Cooperation on the basis of the transferable ruble. [30] The extension of credits, however, will continue to be an important instrument of Polish foreign trade as it has become accepted as a useful way to improve Poland's exports and imports as well as to stimulate internal industrial growth. [31]

Another instrument of economic cooperation is the joint venture. Joint ventures, Poland's only form of capital investment in the Third World, have focused on African countries. The major factors inhibiting the use of joint ventures, other than the hard currency problem, are the lack of experience and information among Polish foreign trade managers about technical and marketing opportunities in developing countries and the inability of foreign partners to raise the financial and technical resources to carry out their role in the enterprises. [32] Polish economists view these joint companies as advantageous in effectively penetrating the markets of their trade partners and in providing greater flexibility in changing market situations. Furthermore, given labor shortages in certain industries, it is often more practical for Poland to build and operate a plant in a Third World country than build and operate the same plant in Poland. [33]

Foreign trade negotiators consider the establishment of a joint marketing company a significant policy option when the following conditions obtain: (1) there are major obstacles to using other market channels, such as when only a single importer can be found; (2) Poland has a sufficiently large supply of goods to offer; and (3) there are feasible prospects for trade expansion that would compensate for costs incurred in establishing and operating the company. [34] The basic goal of such companies is the promotion of exports that are not likely to be sold commercially by other means, and these enterprises occasionally run deficits for three years before becoming profitable. [35] Joint companies have evolved as important channels for Poland's export of technology. Through these operations, Poland can sell not only sophisticated equipment but also the services of technicians to accompany these projects to operate the equipment or train local labor in its operation. [36]

Another factor in this outlook on participation in joint ventures is that Poland's level of technology for export is not as advanced as that of most Western countries; Polish economists admit this gap and realize that Poland's joint venture offer would not be as competitive if negotiators pressed for controlling interest. Consequently, the Poles generally contribute up to 49 percent of the capital for a joint venture so that the LDC can have controlling interest in the operation. [37] Because of this lack of technology, Poland, as well as other Eastern European countries, has also pursued joint ventures in LDCs with Western firms. In these arrangements, the Polish firm usually participates as the subcontractor and the Western firm as the general contractor, whereas the reverse is generally the case involving partnerships between Western firms and firms of other Eastern European countries. Through such arrangements, Poland is able to gain an important entree into an LDC economy without expending large amounts of hard currency for advanced technology to be used in the plant. This technology is usually contributed by the Western partner as its share of the arrangement. In addition, there are numerous fringe benefits for Poland in these ventures, such as increased business opportunities and political contacts with Third World partners. [38] Polish-LDC joint ventures include engineering, hardware equipment, pharmaceutical and textile firms, a fishing company, and an industrial construction partnership. [39] Polish-LDC joint ventures involving Western firms include a nylon plant operated with a West Germany company and a fertilizer plant operated with a Japanese firm. [40]

A third type of relation with LDCs is scientific-technical cooperation. This cooperation is usually established in the context of two- or three-year agreements, which are negotiated either by the Polish Ministry of Science, Higher Education and Technology, the Polish Academy of Sciences, or various research institutions subordinate to government ministries. These agreements usually provide for Polish specialists to study, teach, or work abroad and for foreign students to study at Polish educational centers. Poland's scientific and technical cooperation began in 1957, after the advent of serious economic relations with the Third World, when agreements on education, science, and technology were established with several countries in the Middle East and Asia. As many new countries, especially in Africa, gained their independence in the 1960s, Poland's scientific and technical cooperation expanded. Agreements formed with these new countries provided for exchange of scholars to study and teach, the exchange of scientific publications, and the pursuit of joint research projects. This initiative continued in the 1970s as cooperative agreements increased both numerically and geographically to include countries in Africa, the Middle East, and Latin America. [41]

Involved with the industrial aspects of scientific and technical exchange are Polish specialists who train foreign nationals to operate firms which their country has bought from Poland. Generally the in-

clusion of these experts and the offer of training is part of the con-
tractual agreement between Poland and the LDC for the plant purchased. These specialists and engineers are usually managed through
Polservice, a foreign trade enterprise which exports engineering and
consulting services and personnel. [42] In 1968, 458 experts were employed in LDCs in Africa, Asia, and Latin America, but by 1976, this
total had increased to 1,279. Most of these specialists abroad have
been involved in either engineering, medicine, or agriculture, and
usually the number of experts in a country varies both with the technical services that country has purchased from Poland and the technical expertise of that country's industry. The number of contracts for
specialists in the Third World has grown significantly since 1970, with
the number in 1975 exceeding the total number concluded between 1965
and 1973. Because of the favorable terms Poland has established for
technology transfer, it is likely that contracts for professional industrial specialists will continue to be substantial. Many of Poland's Third
World trade partners, however, are uninterested in contracting for
specialists because of the low level of technology these countries currently possess or are capable of receiving in the near future. Polish
specialists, therefore, will probably continue to serve in those LDCs
which have a developed industrial base. [43]

Polish programs for students to pursue training and academic
study began in 1961 and have increased rapidly since then. Between
1960 and 1975, about 1,300 students (approximately 55 percent from
Africa, 40 percent from Asia, and 5 percent from Latin America) and
3,500 trainees (approximately 77 percent from Africa, 22 percent
from Asia, and 1 percent from Latin America) participated in Polish
educational programs. Just as the types of trade with Poland certain
countries pursue are reflected in their contracts for Polish specialists,
so also are these types reflected in the specialization of students who
are sent to study in Poland. For example, India and Egypt, which import mining and metallurgical plants, send to Poland mostly students
specializing in mining, while countries like Morocco, Iraq, Syria, and
Pakistan, which import food-processing plants, send students who
specialize in food technology. Just as was true with the specialists,
trends in the 1970s towards increased cooperation in this area suggest
that the educational programs Poland offers will continue to be an important part of its cooperation with less developed countries. [44]

General Perceptions and Evaluation of Interaction with LDCs

Basically, Polish foreign policy analysts recognize that, for
various reasons, some LDCs choose a capitalist developmental path
while others do not. They do not rule out cooperation with the former

countries because of the principle that economic cooperation between Socialist and capitalist states can be pursued to mutual advantage. Most tend to agree with Soviet economist Oleg Bogomolov, who has remarked,

> It is clear that in a situation in which there are two basically opposing social systems, one cannot talk about the economic integration of socialist and capitalist countries. However, economic cooperation between the two, a cooperation beneficial to both parties, is possible. Such cooperation is an objective requirement of the present, the necessity of which was solemnly confirmed at the Helsinki Conference. It is connected with a general improvement in the international situation. Such cooperation will not, of course, lead either to the eradication of oppositions between socialism and capitalism or to suppression of the class struggle in the international arena. [45]

Moreover, Polish foreign affairs analysts recognize the political instability of Third World countries as an important factor in Socialist-Third World economic relations, and they accept that good relations may not be possible with strongly capitalist LDCs. Nevertheless, given the political appeal to many LDC leaders of trading with Socialist nations, foreign policy observers note that detente and peaceful coexistence provide an appropriate context for capitalist and Socialist competition for markets and influence over LDC developments. [46] As Gierek commented in a 1978 article, "[Peaceful coexistence] can become a reality only when its principles are accepted by all the countries. Socialism is strong enough to engage in peaceful competition on the basis of the principles of peaceful coexistence, and to demonstrate its superiority in the course of that competition."[47]

The benefits for Poland that policy makers perceive from LDC trade are basically twofold—economic and political. First, they realize that Poland's main advantage in trading with LDCs rests, as it does with Western countries, in the acquisition of raw materials such as fuel, minerals, and agricultural goods to support the domestic economy. [48] Vice Minister of Foreign Trade Stanislaw Dlugosz, for example, has commented that the goals of Polish foreign trade are to accelerate the modernization of domestic industry, improve the balance of payments, and provide high-quality imports for domestic markets. [49] In addition, Poland was able to obtain through earlier clearing agreements with LDCs valuable imports without expending scarce hard currency reserves. If it were not for the clearing arrangements Eastern European countries established, it is unlikely that their trade with LDCs would have advanced to the extent it has. [50]

Political goals Poland hopes to achieve through LDC trade are to "consolidate the socialist community" and to increase Socialist influence abroad by establishing stable economic and political relationships. [51] The terms of these agreements, which Poland would like to see continued and improved, are those of long-term agreements at fixed prices, nondiscrimination in trade terms, decreased tariffs, mutually advantageous terms for both partners, and "full respect for national sovereignty."[52] Although Polish foreign trade specialists realize that often only a partial convergence of international economic aims is possible between Socialist and developing countries, they frequently espouse the goal of international division of labor, which to them consists of relaxed trade restrictions, multilateral economic cooperation, simplification of trade negotiations, and pursuit of various other measures to increase foreign trade. [53]

Concerning advantages LDCs can derive from trading with Poland, foreign trade specialists have noted that the initial benefits of trade include the strengthening of the LDC's material resource base, the improvement of its financial standing, and the diversification of its economy, all of which would contribute to the LDC's economy becoming less vulnerable to changes in international economic markets.[54] This stability in turn would be expected to bolster the stability of the LDC government, making the country not only a stronger member of the international community but also a more dependable trading partner. [55] For those LDCs which have chosen to follow a Socialist developmental path and those considering such a direction, another benefit of trade with Poland is the availability of an alternative to dealing with capitalist trading partners. [56] Obviously these benefits affecting the stability of LDC partners would be advantageous for Poland as well as the Third World country itself. As Stanislaw Dlugosz comments in a 1975 article, the strengthening of Third World countries contributes to Poland's consolidation of its position in the international economic system and helps improve Poland's internal economic, scientific, and technical potentials. [57]

In spite of these advantages to both partners, there are still numerous impediments to broader economic and political relations between Poland and the LDCs. These impediments have basically two sources: problems involving LDC political infrastructures and problems involving continued Western investment in LDCs. Regarding the political infrastructure of many LDCs, Polish foreign policy specialists have noted that the lack of strong political and economic institutions handicaps LDC abilities to receive and export both capital-intensive and advanced industrial goods. Professor Michal Dobroczynski remarks in discussing African problems that LDCs in the postcolonial period have been characterized by insufficiently crystallized political and economic organizations and that this condition unfortunately makes changes of governments and major fluctuations in LDC political systems relatively simple. Polish foreign policy specialists note that the transition to governmental stability is a complex process for LDCs and one in which trade relations with Socialist countries do not necessarily result in the growth of Socialist political institutions.[58]

Another difficulty affecting Poland's relations with the developing countries has been the previous and continuing involvement of Western investment. Because Western countries, especially former colonial ones, maintain strong economic ties with LDCs, the competitive position of Socialist countries is often weak. Whether one assumes that Western investment is present in an LDC because of neocolonialist ties or because the LDC finds it more attractive than Socialist investment, it is still a major problem for Socialist countries to counter. [59] While there have been substantial indications that LDCs have found the terms of economic agreements with Socialist countries at least as favorable, if not more so, than those offered by Western countries, the Socialist countries have also encountered difficulty competing with Western countries for markets of some commodities. [60] Additionally, cooperation with Socialist countries may be used primarily to serve a political function; it can be touted by LDC leaders for domestic consumption, say, to convince their populace and others of the "Socialist" character of their regime. LDC leaders have also used Socialist aid offers as bargaining chips to obtain increased Western aid. For example, the growth in U.S. trade with India during its second five-year plan (1966-70) has often been linked with the substantial growth of Soviet aid during that same period. [61] Professor Boguslaw Jasinski notes that policy makers should recognize this potential problem and take it into account in trade dealings with the LDCs. [62] It is logical to conclude, then, that if an LDC is using its Socialist aid primarily for political purposes, the Socialist country's assistance agreement could easily be scaled down or abrograted if the LDC leadership finds it can achieve its political goals satisfactorily without the continuation of such aid. To summarize, cooperative arrangements between Poland and its LDC partners, like those of its Socialist neighbors with their partners, are not without significant obstacles. These arrangements are subject to almost as many of the same difficulties that Western-LDC relations encounter. Whether individual Polish-LDC agreements, and Socialist-LDC relations on the whole, will stabilize and improve depends upon the resilience, creativity, and determination of the partners involved.

Dynamics of Current Polish-LDC Relations

Having looked at some of the general parameters within which Polish-LDC relations operate, specific observations can be made about

Polish initiatives in the Third World. I will examine this question in the context of Poland's relations in Asia, Latin America, and Africa.

Historically, Poland's most fruitful economic relations have been with Asian countries. Polish trade with these countries began when most of these countries were still colonies, but it grew rapidly after World War II, when the industrial bases of these countries expanded and improved because of the war effort. Poland, like most nations, concentrates its efforts on countries with a similar industrial infrastructure, and the Asian countries, because of their maturity in this area, have been a significant channel for Polish investment. [63] The volume of trade with Asian countries almost tripled from 1960 to 1970 and again from 1970 to 1978, with 1978 trade amounting to approximately 2.4 billion zlotys, or 44 percent of total Polish-LDC trade. [64] Asian countries purchase numerous capital goods from Poland, such as ships, power station equipment, sugar mills, and chemical plants, and Poland purchases from them raw materials such as foodstuffs, fodder, mineral ores, textiles, and palm oil. Asian countries currently export to Poland more industrial goods than do countries in other regions of the world, including machine tools, rolling stock, textile machines, and automobile accessories. In addition, Polish foreign trade specialists comment that there are numerous possibilities for expansion of cooperation with countries in that area through the use of joint ventures. [65]

According to Polish analysts, Asian countries also stand to profit from Polish trade initiatives because of their geographic location; Poland and Japan have a flourishing trade, and Polish ships make frequent stops in Asian countries en route to Japan. Among its current trading relationships with Asian countries, those Poland has with Iran, Iraq, India, and Turkey are currently the most productive, constituting approximately 71 percent of Polish trade in that area in 1978. [66] Poland also has scientific and technological agreements with these four countries as well as with Afghanistan, Indonesia, Bangladesh, Malaysia, and Laos. [67]

On major political issues affecting the area, Poland has generally taken anticolonial and anti-Western stands. It has opposed the U. S. military presence in Vietnam, opposed Chinese initiatives in Asia, supported the Indian side during conflicts with Pakistan in 1965 and 1971 (though trying to maintain satisfactory relations with Pakistan), and supported both the Vietnamese invasion of Cambodia and the Soviet invasion of Afghanistan (the last reservedly). [68]

Latin American countries currently take second place among Poland's trading partners, accounting for approximately 30 percent of Polish-LDC trade in 1978. Poland has long been involved with Latin American states, though economic exchanges have begun relatively recently. Poland's informal contacts with Latin American countries began

TABLE 7.1

Polish Imports from Selected Developing Countries of Asia
(millions of zlotys at current value)

Country	1960	1970	1971	1972	1973	1974	1975	1976	1977	1978	1979
Bangladesh	N.A.	N.A.	N.A.	6.3	29.7	16.0	29.3	17.8	21.9	50.7	33.5
Cyprus	0.4	1.6	3.0	8.7	12.4	12.1	1.3	1.3	7.3	8.3	—
India	32.7	133.2	118.0	187.9	208.5	266.5	344.7	383.1	411.2	216.8	220.4
Indonesia	2.2	8.7	4.0	7.2	20.4	32.1	19.4	4.2	19.7	0.2	34.0
Iran	14.0	23.2	21.3	24.4	34.3	37.0	45.4	104.5	168.9	278.8	307.3
Iraq	0.4	0.1	1.1	1.1	3.0	4.8	5.1	2.9	8.4	366.8	781.9
Jordan	1.8	—	—	—	—	—	1.5	7.8	14.5	18.3	10.6
Kuwait	—	—	—	6.7	—	—	—	1.7	—	—	0.2
Lebanon	1.7	3.5	9.2	7.5	11.5	8.7	20.0	0.2	15.6	23.0	12.3
Malaysia	14.4	2.5	3.5	12.4	16.0	55.5	47.7	33.0	71.3	20.7	38.5
Nepal	—	0.6	3.8	2.5	—	0.2	3.4	5.6	3.9	3.5	—
Pakistan	30.1	83.8	84.0	77.6	37.6	26.3	55.3	35.4	5.5	15.8	29.5
Singapore	—	10.2	16.8	6.6	9.8	24.8	43.8	48.1	31.8	42.0	26.4
Sri Lanka	1.0	24.4	15.8	8.4	15.2	31.4	21.6	11.9	21.5	19.6	—
Syria	7.9	12.7	6.4	11.2	7.8	32.9	4.8	13.2	7.0	3.4	4.1
Thailand	0.3	4.0	5.2	4.2	4.6	10.3	8.4	16.9	11.3	4.5	2.0
Turkey	14.4	31.3	38.3	20.5	26.6	31.5	42.3	39.4	50.5	114.5	153.7
Total	121.3	339.8	330.4	393.2	437.4	590.1	693.0	727.0	860.3	1186.9	1654.4

Note: "N.A." indicates data not available. Dash indicates zero or negligible amount. Trade with Bangladesh is included with Pakistan until 1972.

Source: Rocznik Statystyczny Handlu Zagranicznego, 1974–1979 (Statistical Handbook of Foreign Trade).

214

TABLE 7.2

Polish Imports from Selected Developing Countries of Africa (millions of zlotys at current value)

Country	1960	1970	1971	1972	1973	1974	1975	1976	1977	1978	1979
Algeria	–	17.9	25.2	11.9	9.5	99.3	129.8	135.8	37.8	10.9	40.1
Angola	–	–	N.A.	N.A.	N.A.	N.A.	N.A.	20.8	53.4	22.4	N.A.
Egypt	45.1	78.2	112.8	146.2	129.3	113.6	184.8	100.9	86.7	54.6	97.7
Ethiopia		0.1	2.1	0.1	0.8	8.8	8.3	6.3	10.1	7.9	N.A.
Ghana	3.9	7.4	5.4	12.4	6.3	9.2	39.3	1.5	0.8	–	N.A.
Ivory Coast	–	6.1	7.4	3.4	4.5	8.5	1.7	6.5	5.3	16.1	7.0
Libya	–	3.1	0.3	–	0.1	6.4	1.0	1.7	–	–	276.8
Morocco	11.4	49.4	47.1	51.9	62.0	277.1	353.3	205.0	119.2	155.5	170.1
Nigeria	–	0.9	–	–	0.5	–	–	–	–	–	–
Sudan	2.7	13.6	31.2	12.8	11.1	19.1	14.2	22.1	24.9	18.3	23.8
Tunisia	3.5	19.0	21.5	31.9	13.9	30.1	51.4	26.8	29.2	24.1	21.0
Uganda	–	17.0	6.5	10.0	13.3	11.1	N.A.	N.A.	N.A.	N.A.	N.A.
Total	66.6	212.7	259.5	280.6	251.3	583.2	783.9	533.4	367.4	309.8	636.5

Note: "N.A." indicates data not available. Dash indicates zero or negligible amount.
Source: Rocznik Statystyczny Handlu Zagranicznego, 1974–1979 (Statistical Handbook of Foreign Trade).

TABLE 7.3

Polish Imports from Selected Developing Countries of Latin America
(millions of zlotys at current value)

Country	1960	1970	1971	1972	1973	1974	1975	1976	1977	1978	1979
Argentina	78.0	73.6	60.1	46.3	71.5	50.0	65.7	32.5	72.6	53.3	60.3
Bolivia	–	–	4.1	2.7	6.7	17.0	22.6	18.3	–	38.1	N.A.
Brazil	105.0	76.1	79.8	98.8	112.0	144.3	212.7	329.3	604.8	747.5	335.9
Chile	2.1	–	8.0	5.3	18.4	57.3	N.A.	N.A.	N.A.	N.A.	N.A.
Colombia	3.1	12.2	34.7	34.8	27.9	57.5	44.7	96.0	91.4	105.5	42.2
Equador	0.1	0.2	10.3	2.3	0.6	7.3	2.5	–	1.4	13.4	79.2
Jamaica	–	2.9	2.9	–	0.7	2.6	3.6	5.2	4.6	4.1	–
Mexico	0.1	1.0	2.1	5.0	14.8	26.0	7.7	13.0	3.2	4.5	N.A.
Peru	0.4	53.2	34.1	38.9	16.1	89.1	64.7	75.0	69.5	101.1	226.5
Uruguay	6.5	5.6	3.2	1.7	45.2	10.7	14.8	5.0	2.8	5.8	N.A.
Venezuela	–	–	–	–	0.1	7.1	4.3	1.4	6.3	3.1	N.A.
Total	195.3	224.8	239.5	235.8	314.0	468.9	443.3	574.7	856.6	1126.4	744.1

Note: "N.A." indicates data not available. Dash indicates zero or negligible amount.
Source: Rocznik Statystyczny Handlu Zagranicznego, 1974–1979 (Statistical Handbook of Foreign Trade).

TABLE 7.4

Polish Exports to Selected Developing Countries of Asia
(millions of zlotys at current value)

Country	1960	1970	1971	1972	1973	1974	1975	1976	1977	1978	1979
Bangladesh	N.A.	N.A.	N.A.	N.A.	N.A.	25.8	8.4	5.0	31.4	34.3	29.3
Cyprus	0.3	2.3	2.1	2.1	4.1	8.5	5.7	10.3	10.8	16.0	N.A.
India	24.7	124.9	171.6	132.9	152.3	311.8	358.2	113.3	177.5	171.3	230.2
Indonesia	64.2	5.2	4.5	4.7	10.9	110.8	119.6	16.2	17.5	28.0	30.4
Iran	22.9	19.7	17.0	28.3	40.2	160.1	201.5	253.6	223.6	197.5	100.9
Iraq	5.2	110.1	105.6	107.3	64.1	136.8	192.4	229.0	210.6	209.1	291.5
Jordan	1.9	27.7	13.2	4.3	5.2	5.4	8.8	13.0	17.4	24.5	—
Kuwait	1.1	11.2	7.7	7.0	15.9	19.7	25.5	65.2	107.1	93.1	84.4
Lebanon	6.7	11.7	17.5	30.2	40.3	54.4	73.4	27.8	69.8	72.0	76.0
Malaysia	2.9	0.8	5.1	2.2	6.7	4.1	9.8	9.1	6.6	4.3	48.9
Pakistan	8.7	63.1	84.1	64.3	52.9	36.1	64.3	29.1	32.5	51.8	36.4
Saudi Arabia	0.7	7.4	5.0	7.3	8.6	9.7	18.3	27.8	31.4	51.5	54.2
Singapore	0.6	3.8	4.1	4.6	10.8	22.9	9.8	13.2	9.3	17.8	24.5
Sri Lanka	0.5	12.6	14.0	9.0	11.6	8.7	2.6	N.A.	2.5	3.8	N.A.
Syria	1.7	19.7	16.9	8.6	9.2	48.0	47.3	41.0	49.6	41.4	109.0
Thailand	4.7	12.7	7.5	9.1	14.3	86.2	34.5	19.3	22.7	29.9	34.0
Turkey	30.2	69.2	20.1	30.9	47.7	31.4	114.8	120.6	130.3	156.2	246.1
United Arab Emirates	N.A.	0.6	N.A.	N.A.	N.A.	3.7	8.1	13.3	28.3	25.0	N.A.
Total	177.0	497.7	495.4	459.7	502.9	1084.7	1303.0	1006.8	1178.9	1227.5	1295.4

Note: "N.A." indicates data not available. Dash indicates zero or negligible amount. Trade with Bangladesh is included with Pakistan until 1972.

Source: Rocznik Statystyczny Handlu Zagranicznego, 1974–1979 (Statistical Handbook of Foreign Trade).

217

TABLE 7.5

Polish Exports to Selected Developing Countries of Africa (millions of zlotys at current value)

Country	1960	1970	1971	1972	1973	1974	1975	1976	1977	1978	1979
Algeria	0.4	6.8	5.2	17.5	19.4	110.9	117.7	145.3	189.7	119.7	130.4
Angola	—	—	N.A.	N.A.	N.A.	N.A.	—	1.0	27.7	113.3	N.A.
Egypt	34.2	121.4	76.2	79.2	116.3	142.5	109.7	83.6	123.0	145.3	114.2
Ethiopia	0.3	3.6	N.A.	N.A.	N.A.	N.A.	3.3	N.A.	4.9	4.7	N.A.
Ghana	0.1	8.4	7.6	4.5	8.9	24.2	6.0	6.4	10.5	7.9	N.A.
Ivory Coast	—	3.7	2.8	2.1	1.9	1.6	1.9	10.3	23.7	15.2	16.8
Kenya	—	5.4	4.8	12.3	10.3	6.4	3.0	1.8	3.8	7.2	N.A.
Liberia	—	11.7	10.8	10.7	16.0	20.6	13.4	14.2	15.4	15.4	N.A.
Libya	0.7	39.6	27.2	32.2	78.1	147.1	303.2	392.9	343.0	352.4	400.1
Morocco	11.6	49.5	25.8	49.5	42.5	83.6	111.9	177.0	88.2	61.6	113.5
Nigeria	0.1	16.8	17.4	19.0	17.9	27.8	63.8	68.6	134.3	104.1	56.7
Senegal	—	0.7	1.3	2.0	1.3	2.5	11.7	7.4	10.7	7.3	N.A.
Sierra Leone	—	3.2	4.0	5.9	8.7	10.0	75.6	—	2.7	4.7	N.A.
Sudan	4.8	27.5	15.6	17.1	14.1	20.1	13.5	11.3	16.6	47.7	50.8
Tunisia	3.8	28.7	24.2	14.9	10.3	14.6	33.2	20.2	33.3	35.3	42.1
Total	56.0	467.2	222.9	256.9	345.7	611.9	797.4	940.0	1027.5	1044.5	924.6

Note: "N.A." indicates data not available. Dash indicates zero or negligible amount.
Source: Rocznik Statystyczny Handlu Zagranicznego, 1974–1979 (Statistical Handbook of Foreign Trade).

TABLE 7.6

Polish Exports to Developing Countries of Latin America
(millions of zlotys at current value)

Country	1960	1970	1971	1972	1973	1974	1975	1976	1977	1978	1979
Argentina	33.5	40.0	35.7	40.8	26.9	56.2	108.6	77.0	103.5	48.9	60.3
Bolivia	–	–	–	0.6	–	1.0	1.2	10.0	4.2	2.7	N.A.
Brazil	79.7	86.0	156.3	135.4	53.2	108.3	270.7	354.5	382.3	234.0	335.9
Colombia	0.3	34.7	5.8	85.1	18.9	29.5	9.9	138.2	142.6	151.8	42.2
Ecuador	0.2	8.7	6.9	2.4	2.9	2.5	3.8	1.6	42.4	43.0	79.2
Mexico	0.9	2.2	2.2	1.6	1.9	2.8	43.7	34.5	9.3	14.1	N.A.
Panama	0.7	1.6	1.7	1.4	3.5	55.2	5.2	29.3	6.5	9.4	N.A.
Peru	–	2.0	3.5	2.0	9.1	12.4	7.6	24.1	4.4	58.8	226.5
Uruguay	1.5	0.1	1.1	0.4	2.4	0.4	12.2	7.3	8.1	8.7	N.A.
Venezuela	6.1	8.0	5.6	4.2	3.8	5.4	10.2	22.2	30.9	15.8	11.5
Total	122.9	183.8	218.8	273.9	122.6	273.7	472.9	698.7	734.2	587.2	755.6

Note: "N.A." indicates data not available. Dash indicates zero or negligible amount.
<u>Source</u>: Rocznik Statystyczny Landlu Zagranicznego, 1974–1979 (Statistical Handbook of Foreign Trade).

TABLE 7.7

Polish Imports from Selected Developing Countries,
by Industrial Group and Country of Sale, in 1979

Country	Total	Fuels and Energy	Industrial Products						Processed Goods	Agricultural Products
			Metallurgical Products	Electrical Machinery	Chemicals	Wood and Paper Products	Light and Manufactured Goods			
Aggregate	54,014.8	8,298.0	6,385.6	20,134.1	6,641.2	1,182.3	2,409.0	3,057.7	4,166.2
Asia									
Bangladesh	33.5	—	—	—	—	—	4.6	12.4	16.5
India	220.4	—	3.6	6.8	0.1	—	37.3	166.9	0.2
Iraq	781.9	780.4	—	—	—	—	0.8	—	0.6
Iran	307.3	282.8	—	0.3	1.4	—	17.8	—	4.2
Lebanon	12.3	—	—	—	—	—	—	1.2	11.1
Malaysia	38.5	—	14.5	—	12.4	—	—	11.5	—
Pakistan	29.5	—	—	—	0.1	—	29.4	—	—
Singapore	26.4	—	—	1.0	21.3	—	1.7	2.4	—
Turkey	153.7	—	5.0	—	12.8	—	51.8	47.3	36.9

Africa

Algeria	40.1	32.6	—	—	6.4	—	—	10.6
Angola	0.2	—	—	—	—	—	—	0.0
Egypt	97.7	—	—	0.9	—	86.2	10.4	0.2
Libya	276.8	276.8	—	—	—	—	—	—
Morocco	170.1	—	0.7	—	142.6	1.4	0.1	25.3
Sudan	23.8	—	—	—	—	23.8	—	—
Tunisia	21.0	—	—	—	20.7	—	0.2	—
Latin America								
Argentina	178.0	—	—	—	6.1	74.5	47.0	50.5
Brazil	1,324.3	—	152.7	—	12.5	63.8	746.4	307.4
Colombia	98.2	—	—	—	—	13.3	—	84.9
Peru	103.8	—	—	—	—	—	36.5	—

Note: Aggregate totals include trade with developed and developing countries. Dash indicates zero or negligible amount.

Source: Biuletyn Statystyczny (February 1980): 37–38.

TABLE 7.8

Polish Exports to Selected Developing Countries,
by Industrial Group and Country of Sale, in 1979

Country	Total	Fuels and Energy	Industrial Products						Agricultural Products
			Metallurgical Products	Electrical Machinery	Chemicals	Wood and Paper Products	Light and Manufactured Goods	Processed Goods	
Aggregate	50,140.7	7,486.8	3,447.5	24,616.9	3,760.0	1,179.9	4,283.7	3,056.5	1,294.9
Asia									
Saudi Arabia	54.2	—	0.0	19.7	0.1	—	17.4	16.2	—
Bangladesh	29.3	—	6.1	15.0	1.5	—	0.1	—	—
India	230.2	0.2	76.5	96.9	49.8	0.0	0.0	0.0	—
Indonesia	30.4	—	6.7	5.4	16.0	1.0	0.6	0.8	—
Iran	100.9	—	27.7	30.3	9.8	6.9	17.1	7.7	—
Iraq	291.5	0.1	26.0	242.9	4.1	7.9	10.4	0.0	—
Kuwait	84.9	—	4.3	6.6	2.1	0.1	59.5	10.0	—
Lebanon	76.0	—	—	15.8	1.7	0.0	10.9	25.0	21.8
Pakistan	36.4	—	1.2	23.0	8.2	0.1	—	3.5	—
Singapore	24.5	—	1.9	5.8	5.7	0.2	5.0	3.1	0.0
Syria	109.0	—	6.9	83.7	6.8	0.0	10.2	0.2	0.0
Thailand	34.0	—	1.3	14.6	14.3	—	2.8	0.6	0.0
Turkey	246.1	—	—	239.0	6.2	0.0	—	—	—

Africa									
Algeria	130.4	—	—	53.7	26.1	36.2	2.6	10.0	5.2
Angola	46.0	—	—	35.5	0.0	1.6	2.8	0.0	0.3
Egypt	114.2	—	5.5	76.2	11.1	2.8	15.2	2.1	7.9
Libya	400.1	—	1.6	342.5	1.3	0.6	6.0	40.0	2.1
Morocco	113.5	0.4	1.8	41.3	45.1	—	0.7	0.1	—
Nigeria	56.7	—	—	29.1	5.5	0.3	—	18.7	—
Sudan	50.8	—	—	46.6	0.6	0.0	3.0	—	—
Tunisia	42.1	1.1	0.1	2.9	32.3	—	0.2	0.0	2.3
Latin America									
Argentina	60.3	8.9	—	37.8	11.4	0.3	0.1	1.0	—
Brazil	335.9	213.5	4.1	98.1	19.4	—	—	0.8	—
Ecuador	79.2	—	4.0	73.4	1.5	0.0	—	0.1	—
Colombia	42.2	—	4.6	18.0	2.4	—	8.5	8.7	—
Peru	226.5	—	—	113.4	0.6	—	—	112.5	—

Note: Aggregate totals include trade with developed and developing countries. Dash indicates zero or negligible amount.

Source: Biuletyn Statystyczny (February 1980): 37–38.

in the early nineteenth century when many emigrants, mostly peasants and small landowners, left Poland for Latin America during periods of domestic strife (1830-31, 1848, 1863, and post-1905). Most of the Latin American countries that recognized the Second Republic of Poland after World War I also recognized the PPR in the post-World War II period, but relations made little progress because of the Cold War. Relations improved in the mid- and late 1960s, and by 1978, Poland's trade exchange with Latin America amounted to approximately 1.7 billion zlotys. Of this trade, 88 percent was with four South American countries: Brazil, Argentina, Columbia, and Peru.[69] Poland pursues economic cooperation with Latin America in the areas of railway transport (Argentina, Brazil, Colombia), fishing (Peru, Ecuador, Mexico), mining (Argentina, Brazil, Peru), auto plant construction (Ecuador, Colombia), power plant construction (Ecuador), and industrial plant construction (Bolivia).[70] Poland has also been involved in pulp and paper production in Venezuela and zinc refining in Bolivia.[71]

In addition, Poland has scientific agreements with Argentina, Bolivia, Equador, Mexico, Chile, Peru, Venezuela, and Panama.[72] Poland has also attempted cultural exchanges with Latin American countries, but Latin American countries have shown little interest in this area of cooperation.[73]

Concerning major international issues, Poland has supported Mexico's initiatives both for nuclear-weapon-free zones in Latin America and Europe and for the Charter of Economic Rights and Duties of Nations. Poland also supported the establishment of the Allende government, and it has pursued strong political and economic ties with Cuba.[74]

Africa, which in 1978 was the source of 26 percent of Poland's trade turnover with the LDCs, is potentially a very important politi- and economic frontier. From the pre-World War II period through the 1950s, Polish relations with African nations were limited; in the postwar period, Egypt was the only African country with which Poland had exchanged missions. In the early 1950s, Poland also had a legation in Ethiopia, but international tensions during this period were not conducive to the establishment of relations with many African countries. With the coming to independence of numerous African states in the early 1960s, however, and with the abatement of the Cold War, Poland proceeded to recognize most of these new states.[75] By 1975, Poland had established relations with 35 African countries, and by 1979 that total had increased to 43 of the 55 countries.[76] In addition to the Cold War, a number of other factors have inhibited Poland's interaction with African LDCs, including the instability of the governments, the poor balance-of-payments situation affecting many African nations, and the lack of diversity in the economies of these states. [77] Indeed, Poland's main trade in the 1960s and early 1970s was with Egypt, Libya, and Morocco, countries which had more developed industrial bases than most of the other African countries. This observation on the importance of similar industrial bases for foreign trade could be applied to North Africa as a whole. * The value of Polish trade with North African nations in 1970 amounted to about twice the trade with sub-Saharan nations and approximately three times that with sub-Saharan nations in 1978. Through the late 1960s and early 1970s, Polish trade with North Africa proceeded at this greater pace because of the commodities requiring advanced production technology which Poland desired to import and because of the capabilities of those countries' economies to absorb the technologically advanced goods Poland had to offer. Of these two regions of Africa, Egypt and Morocco then headed the list of Poland's most important North African trade partners, while Nigeria, Ghana, and Uganda headed the list of most important sub-Saharan trade partners. [78]

In addition to trade, Poland has also pursued other types of economic relations with African countries. Currently, Poland has eight joint ventures operating in Africa: four in Nigeria dealing with exporting and importing, pharmaceuticals, and fishing; one each in Kenya and Ghana involving hardware; one in Ethiopia dealing with metal tools; and one in Guinea involved with fishing. [79] There are still some marketing problems currently precluding establishment of further joint ventures, but Polish trade specialists expect these problems to be resolved. [80]

Among other types of economic assistance, Poland has extended credits to Egypt (for power stations, foundries, other factories), Tunisia (for mining and textile equipment), Ghana (for a sugar cane mill), and Nigeria and Ethiopia (for textile factories.)[81]

Poland has also pursued scientific and educational cooperation with African nations. It has signed scientific-technical agreements with Angola, Ghana, Guinea, Kenya, Libya, and Morocco. [82] In the field of educational exchange, Polish-African relations have been in the forefront among other LDC regions. In 1976, over 60 percent of the Polish specialists employed on industrial contracts in the Third World were in three African countries—Libya, Algeria, and Nigeria. Such is the case because of the significant technical and engineering services imported by these countries. [83] Nevertheless, the occupational range of Polish specialists in Africa is broad, extending from

---

*North Africa here includes Algeria, Libya, Morocco, Mauritania, Sudan, Tunisia, and Egypt.

TABLE 7.9

Polish Imports by SITC Commodity Classes
(millions of zlotyz at current value)

Import	1975	1976	1977	1978
Total (developed and developing countries)	41,650.7	46,070.9	48,558.4	50,938.4
(Non-Socialist) developing countries	2,024.6	1,954.7	2,322.1	2,721.1
Percentage	4.9	4.2	4.8	5.3
Food products, beverages, and tobacco	3,874.3	5,110.6	5,531.7	5,983.8
Developing countries	515.1	716.5	1,058.8	1,167.0
Percentage	13.3	14.0	19.1	19.5
Raw materials (except raw materials made into food products)	4,910.8	4,711.3	5,193.6	5,327.1
Developing countries	936.5	708.4	639.0	621.8
Percentage	19.1	15.0	12.3	11.7
Mineral fuels	3,816.2	4,548.8	5,647.8	6,541.6
Developing countries	182.0	139.8	217.8	618.7
Percentage	4.8	3.1	3.9	9.5
Chemicals	3,067.5	3,191.2	3,650.8	3,908.7
Developing countries	24.7	15.1	20.8	59.3
Percentage	0.8	0.5	0.6	0.7
Machinery and transport equipment	15,712.4	17,998.8	18,060.6	18,936.3
Developing countries	10.2	17.3	12.1	7.1
Percentage	0.06	0.1	0.07	0.04
Other industrial commodities	10,269.5	10,510.2	10,473.9	10,240.9
Developing countries	356.1	357.6	373.6	247.2
Percentage	3.5	3.4	3.6	2.4

Source: Based on Rocznik Statystyczny Zagranicznego 1979
(Statistical Handbook of Foreign Trade), pp. 46-48.

TABLE 7.10

Polish Exports by SITC Commodity Classes
(millions of zlotys at current value)

Import	1975	1976	1977	1978
Total (developed and developing countries)	34,160.7	36,600.3	4,074.8	44,685.0
(Non-Socialist) developing countries	2,921.0	3,036.2	3,457.9	3,391.5
Percentage	8.6	8.3	8.5	7.6
Food products, beverages, and tobacco	2,902.9	3,166.8	3,396.6	3,552.7
Developing countries	200.9	354.0	316.7	362.8
Percentage	7.0	11.2	9.4	10.2
Raw materials (except raw materials made into food products)	1,291.3	1,475.8	1,934.8	2,000.7
Developing countries	103.2	106.7	223.4	163.5
Percentage	8.0	7.2	11.5	8.2
Mineral fuels	6,849.1	6,614.1	6,685.9	6,958.8
Developing countries	272.9	367.2	388.7	316.2
Percentage	4.0	5.6	5.8	4.5
Chemicals	2,603.5	2,501.4	2,384.3	2,424.0
Developing countries	557.4	271.3	241.8	223.9
Percentage	22.2	10.8	10.1	9.2
Machinery and transport equipment	13,054.5	14,818.8	16,826.5	19,102.9
Developing countries	1,043.0	1,127.9	1,273.5	1,727.3
Percentage	8.0	7.6	7.6	9.0
Other industrial commodities	7,459.4	8,023.4	9,519.7	10,645.9
Developing countries	723.6	809.1	1,013.8	597.8
Percentage	9.7	10.1	10.6	5.6

Source: Based on Rocznik Statystyczny Zagranicznego 1979
(Statistical Handbook of Foreign Trade), pp. 46-48.

doctors, engineers, and economists to businessmen, urban planners, and pilots. [84] Opportunities for Africans to be trained in Poland have also been significant. Of the total number of Third World students and trainees who graduated from Polish institutions from 1960-75, those from Africa constituted 55 percent. Most of the students from Africa pursue medical or engineering disciplines, but there is also representation in the fields of economics, agronomy, and the humanities.[85]

Concerning important political issues affecting Africa, Poland has been a long and persistent supporter of independence for and liberation struggles of African nations. This general focus has manifested itself in several ways—in support for independence drives of particular countries, for the goals of SWAPO, the MPLA, ZAPU (Zimbabwe African People's Union), and the PLO, for the Ethiopian revolution, and for the Arab cause against Israel. [86]

In conclusion, Polish relationships with African nations are expanding, albeit slowly. Poland has been relatively successful in pursuing relations with African nations because of its sensitivity to their concerns about national sovereignty. While trade with African nations is not extensive, it is improving by degrees in spite of often volatile domestic political situations in Africa and the frequent backwardness and lack of hard currency reserves characteristic of African LDCs. Trade, therefore, is probably the main vehicle for the advancement of Polish-African relations, but current trends suggest that this advancement will be slow.

CONCLUSIONS

While Polish political relations with the Third World are progressing satisfactorily, Poland has no major cause, such as Romania and East Germany do, for expending significant time and effort garnering world support. The main dynamic of Poland's interaction with the Third World will continue to be economic for the near future. The major problems facing Poland are its tremendous hard currency debt, its strong consumer pressures, and its often poorly managed economy. Whether Poland can offset its financial problems through trade with LDCs and developed countries will depend upon its ability to export products non-Socialist nations would be interested in purchasing. Although Poland frequently cannot compete successfully with developed countries for LDC markets, it has been able to market successfully certain types of manufactured goods, such as machinery and ships, as well as raw materials, such as foodstuffs and coal. In addition, it has likely been a significant supplier of arms to Third World nations. Still, LDCs, which traditionally have not had significant hard currency reserves, will probably not develop as a primary market for Polish exports. Policy makers will undoubtedly target developed countries as markets for Polish exports, for it is these countries which have the hard currency to purchase Polish commodities in the quantity and quality Poland needs to export them to alleviate its debt problem. Poland will be able to find strong markets among more developed Third World countries as it has in the past, but total trade turnover with LDCs is unlikely to witness a significant increase in the foreseeable future.

NOTES

1. See James Morrison, "The Foreign Policy of Poland," in The Foreign Policies of Eastern Europe: Domestic and International Determinants, ed. James Kuhlman (Leyden: A. W. Sijthoff, 1978), pp. 129-32.

2. For a useful compilation of Polish-language analyses of foreign affairs involving the Third World, see Wlodzimierz Kostecki, "Studies on the Developing Countries at the Polish Institute of International Affairs," Studies on the Developing Countries (Warsaw) 1 (1972): 156-64.

3. Central Intelligence Agency, Handbook of Economic Statistics 1979 (Washington, D. C.: Central Intelligence Agency, 1980), pp. 106-7.

4. Deepak Nayyar, "Economic Relations between Socialist Countries and the Third World: An Introduction," in Economic Relations Between Socialist Countries and the Third World, ed. Deepak Nayyar (Montclair, N. J.: Allanheld, Osmun, 1977), p. 5.

5. Roman Stefanowski, "Poland's Presence in Black Africa," Radio Free Europe-Radio Liberty Background Report, no. 50 (March 1, 1979), p. 10; Foreign Broadcast Information Service, "Foreign Minister Wojtaszek Comments on Middle East," Daily Report on Eastern Europe April 18, 1979; and U. S. Arms Control and Disarmament Agency, World Military Expenditures and Arms Transfers, 1968-1977 (Washington, D. C.: U. S. Arms Control and Disarmament Agency, 1979), pp. 113-55.

6. "Ceremonial Session of the PPR Sejm," Current Digest of the Soviet Press 26 (August 14, 1974): 5.

7. Emil Wojtaszek, "Poland's Foreign Policy and European Security Problems," International Affairs (Moscow) no. 8 (August 8, 1978): 19.

8. "Soviet Aid Package for Poland Includes $1. 3 Billion Loan," Washington Post, November 20, 1976.

9. Mieczyslaw Rakowski, "Szanse na wielki pokoj" (The Chances of a Great Peace), Nowe Drogi (November 1972), quoted in Adam Bromke, "Polish Foreign Policy in the 1970s," Canadian Slavonic Papers 15 (Spring-Summer 1973): 202.

10. C. I. A. , Handbook, pp. 106-7.

11. Ignacy Krasicki, "Nasze miejsce w sojuszu" (Our Place in the Alliance), Zycie Warszawy, January 26, 1971, quoted in Adam Bromke, "A New Political Style," Problems of Communism 21 (September-October 1972): 15.

12. Zbigniew Fallenbuchl, "The Polish Economy in the 1970s," in Eastern European Economies Post-Helsinki, Report of the Joint Economic Committee, 95th Cong. , 1st sess. , 1977, pp. 846-51.

13. U. S. Government figures, 1980 (unpublished).

14. Geoffrey Smith, "Can Marxism Stand Prosperity?" Forbes 7 (January 1977): 44-45.

15. Radio Free Europe, Situation Reports on Poland, nos. 1, 2 (January 9, 21, 1980).

16. Jane Hallow, "The Economic Consequences of Mr. Gierek," Euromoney (December 1979): 35.

17. C. I. A. , Handbook, p. 26; and Fallenbuchl, "Polish Economy," p. 837.

18. Smith, "Can Marxism," p. 44; and Foreign Broadcast Information Service, "PAP Reports Eighth PZPR Congress Guidelines," Daily Report on Eastern Europe, October 30, 1979.

19. Central Statistical Office, Maly Rocznik Statystyczny 1979 (Concise Statistical Handbook) (Warsaw: Central Statistical Office, 1978), p. 67.

20. Fallenbuchl, "Polish Economy," pp. 852-64.

21. Central Statistical Office, Maly Rocznik Statystyczny, p. 67; and "Report of the Main Statistical Office on the Development of the National Economy and on the Fulfillment of the National Socioeconomic Plan in 1979," Trybunu Ludu (Warsaw) February 10, 1980, (Washington, D.C.: JPRS 75458, April 8, 1980), p. 45.

22. Radio Free Europe, Situation Reports on Poland, no. 25 (November 27, 1979).

23. Radio Free Europe, Situation Reports on Poland, no. 21 (September 27, 1979), and no. 1 (January 9, 1980).

24. U. S. Congressional Research Service, The Soviet Union and the Third World: A Watershed in Great Power Policy? CP-367, 95th Cong. , 1st sess. , 1977, p. 60; and Nayyar, "Economic Relations," pp. 4-5. For further information on the organization of Poland's foreign affairs and foreign trade bureaucracies, see Morrison, "Foreign Policy of Poland," pp. 139-41; Tadeusz Sodowski, "The Law of Foreign Trade in the Polish People's Republic," Law and Contemporary Problems 37 (Summer 1972): 510-12; T. Antoniewicz, "The Structure of Poland's External Trading System," Polish Foreign Trade, no. 9 (September 1974): 32-33; Central Intelligence Agency, Directory of Officials of the Polish People's Republic (Washington, D. C. : Central Intelligence Agency, 1979), pp. 13-18; Jerzy Gambit, "The Polish

Economy: Models and Muddles," Survey 17 (Summer 1971): 76; and
Fallenbuchl, "Polish Economy," p. 856.

25. See Congressional Research Service, Soviet Union and the
Third World, p. 67.

26. The trade agreements Eastern European countries formulate
with their partners generally specify trading objectives and delineate
the needs of the partners. These agreements also provide that trade
balances outstanding at the end of each period be settled in exports
and imports of mutually agreed products or in local currencies. While
the principle agreement may extend from five to 20 years, annual
protocols are negotiated on commodities and trade levels. Nayyar,
"Economic Relations," pp. 4-5.

27. United Nations, Conference on Trade and Development,
Multilateralization of Payments in Trade Between Socialist Countries
of Eastern Europe and Developing Countries, (TD/B/703), 1978, pp.
2-5, 13-18. According to a 1977 UNCTAD report, in 1975, 76 percent
of the value of Polish-LDC trade turnover was conducted on the basis
of hard currency agreements, compared with 71 percent for Hungary,
61 percent for Romania, 55 percent for Bulgaria, 41 percent for the
GDR, and 37 percent for both Czechoslovakia and the Soviet Union.
The accuracy of these figures, however, is questionable, given the
inevitable gaps in the reporting of such information. United Nations,
Multilateralization of Payments in Trade, p. 15.

28. Waldemar Markiewicz, "Poland's Economic Cooperation
with the Developing Countries: A Current Analysis and Prospects,"
Studies on the Developing Countries (Warsaw) 3 (1973): 8-9; see also
Congressional Research Service, Soviet Union and the Third World,
pp. 61-62.

29. Jozef Nowicki, "Mutual Economic Relations of Poland and
Developing Countries of Africa," Studies on the Developing Countries
(Warsaw) 2 (1972): 23-24; and U.S. Government figures, 1980 (unpub-
lished).

30. Markiewicz, "Economic Cooperation," pp. 8-10; and United
Nations, Multilateralization of Payments in Trade, pp. 4-8, 27-32.

31. Artur Bodnar and Maciej Deniszcyk, "External Factors Affecting the Economic Development of Poland up to the Year 2000" (reprinted from Handel Zagraniczny, 1971) Soviet and East European
Foreign Trade 8 (Spring-Summer 1972): 176-77.

32. Halina Kaczmarczyk-Araszkiewicz, Jerzy Cieslik, and Rys-
zard Rapacki, "Transfer of Technology from Poland to Developing
Countries," Economic Papers (Warsaw) 6 (1977): 89.

33. Pompiliu Verzariu, "Communist Countries Are Strengthening Commercial Ties with the Third World," Business America 3
(February 25, 1980): 9.

34. Nowicki, "Mutual Economic Relations," pp. 25-27.

232 / EASTERN EUROPE AND THE THIRD WORLD

35. Ibid.

36. Kaczmarczyk-Araszkiewicz, Cieslik, and Rapacki, "Technology Transfer," p. 80; and Verzariu, "Commercial Ties," p. 8.

37. Kaczmarczyk-Araszkiewicz, Cieslik, and Rapacki, "Technology Transfer," pp. 92-96; and Boguslaw Jasinski, "Factors Stimulating and Limiting Trade Exchange between the Socialist Countries and the LDCs," Economic Papers (Warsaw) 7 (1978): 45.

38. Verzariu, "Commercial Ties," p. 9.

39. Jasinski, "Factors," p. 87; and Stefanowski, "Poland in Black Africa," pp. 4-5.

40. Verzariu, "Commercial Ties," p. 9.

41. Jacek Machowski, "Poland's Cooperation with Foreign Countries in the Field of Science and Technology," Studies on International Relations (Warsaw) 10 (1978): 96-100.

42. Kaczmarczyk-Araszkiewicz, Cieslik, and Rapacki, "Technology Transfer," pp. 83-84.

43. Nowicki, "Mutual Economic Relations," p. 26.

44. Kaczmarczyk-Araszkiewicz, Cieslik, and Rapacik, "Technology Transfer," pp. 86-88.

45. Stanislaw Dlugosz, "The Evolution of Foreign Trade," (reprinted from Handel Zagraniczny, 1976) Soviet and East European Foreign Trade 13 (Spring 1977): 47-48.

46. Marian Dobrosielski, "Problems of Contemporary International Relations," Studies on International Relations (Warsaw) 3 (1974): 12-15, 18. For historical examinations of Eastern European and Polish involvement in the Third World, see Jerzy Prokopczuk, "Poland's Relations with Asian, African and Latin American Countries," Studies on the Developing Countries (Warsaw) 1 (1972): 4-12; William Robinson, "Eastern Europe's Presence in Black Africa," Radio Free Europe-Radio Liberty Background Report, no. 142 (June 21, 1979), pp. 2-5; and Stanislaw Dlugosz, "Polish Foreign Trade," Studies on International Relations (Warsaw) 5 (1975): 9.

47. Edward Gierek, "The Right to Live in Peace," World Marxist Review 21 (June 1978): 8.

48. Dlugosz, "Polish Foreign Trade," p. 18.

49. Nayyar, "Economic Relations," p. 11.

50. Ibid.; and Dlugosz, "Polish Foreign Trade," p. 19.

51. Markiewicz, "Economic Cooperation," pp. 5-6, 10.

52. Dlugosz, "Evolution of Foreign Trade," pp. 44-53; and Dlugosz, "Polish Foreign Trade, p. 7.

53. Markiewicz, "Economic Cooperation," pp. 5-6; Michal Dobroczynski, "Africa's International Trade: A Forward Look," Studies on the Developing Countries (Warsaw) 6 (1974): 85-88; and Jerzy Piotrowski, "New Developments in Asian, African and Latin American Countries and Their Influence on International Relations," Studies on the Developing Countries (Warsaw) 7 (1975): 143-44.

54. Jozef Nowicki, "Economic Growth and Social Progress: Facts About, and Prospects for Developing Countries," Studies on the Developing Countries 5 (Warsaw) (1974): 32-33; and Dlugosz, "Evolution of Foreign Trade," p. 46.

55. Stefanowski, "Poland in Black Africa," p. 4; and Jasinski, "Factors," p. 141.

56. Dlugosz, "Polish Foreign Trade," p. 21.

57. See Dobroczynski, "Africa's International Trade," pp. 85-86; Nowicki, "Economic Growth," pp. 30-31; Markiewicz, "Economic Cooperation," p. 9; and Dlugosz, "Polish Foreign Trade," p. 11.

58. Yerzy Prokopczuk, "The Development of the Third World. Principal Aspects, Theory and Practice," Studies on the Developing Countries, 3 (Warsaw) (1973), pp. 134-35.

59. Kaczmarczyk-Araszkiewicz, Cieslik, and Rapacki, "Technology Transfer," pp. 92-96.

60. Robinson, "Eastern Europe in Black Africa," p. 12; and Jasinski, "Factors," pp. 44-45.

61. Pramit Chaudhuri, "East European Aid to India," in Economic Relations Between Socialist Countries and the Third World, ed. Deepak Nayyar (Montclair, N.J.: Allanheld, Osmun, 1977), p. 151.

62. Jasinski, "Factors," p. 34.

63. Ibid., p. 42.

64. Central Statistical Office, Rocznik Statystyczny 1979 (Statistical Handbook) (Warsaw: Central Statistical Office, 1979), pp. 306-8.

65. Markiewicz, "Economic Cooperation," pp. 11-13.

66. Ibid.; and Central Statistical Office, Rocznik Statystyczny, pp. 306-8.

67. Machowski, "Cooperation with Foreign Countries," p. 106.

68. Radio Free Europe, Situation Report on Poland 3 (January 21, 1972): 1-4; Wojtaszek, "Poland's Foreign Policy," p. 20; and Stefan Olszowski, "Main Trends of Polish Foreign Policy," International Affairs, (Moscow), no. 10 (October 1972): 3-4.

69. Central Statistical Office, Rocznik Statystyczny, pp. 306-8.

70. Kaczmarczyk-Araszkiewicz, Cieslik, and Rapacki, "Technology Transfer," p. 82; and Waldemar Rommel, "Poland and Latin America," Studies on the Developing Countries (Warsaw) 7 (1975): 7-22.

71. Markiewicz, "Economic Cooperation," pp. 14-15.

72. Machowski, "Cooperation with Foreign Countries," p. 106.

73. Rommel, "Poland and Latin America," pp. 23-26.

74. Ibid., pp. 7-21; and Prokopczuk, "Poland's Relations," pp. 16-17.

75. Edward Palyga, "Poland's Diplomatic Relations with African

States, 1928-1977," Studies on the Developing Countries 9 (Warsaw) (1978): 124-41.

76. Stefanowski, "Poland in Black Africa," pp. 12-13 (Appendix I).

77. Dobroczynski, "Africa's International Trade," p. 97; and Stefanowski, "Poland in Black Africa," pp. 3-4.

78. Nowicki, "Mutual Economic Relations," pp. 11-12.

79. Ibid. , pp. 25-26; Kaczmarczyk-Araszkiewicz, Cieslik, and Rapacki, "Technology Transfer," pp. 88-89; and Stefanowski, "Poland in Black Africa," pp. 4-5.

80. Kaczmarczyk-Araszkiewicz, Cieslik, and Rapacki, "Technology Transfer," pp. 4-5.

81. Nowicki, "Mutual Economic Relations," pp. 23-24.

82. Machowski, "Cooperation with Foreign Countries," p. 106.

83. Kaczmarczyk-Araszkiewicz, Cieslik, and Rapacki, "Technology Transfer," p. 84.

84. Ibid. , pp. 86-88; and Stefanowski, "Poland in Black Africa," pp. 5-6.

85. Stefanowski, "Poland in Black Africa," pp. 5-6.

86. Ibid. , pp. 10-11; and Piotrowski, "New Developments," pp. 139-42.

8

ROMANIA AND THE THIRD WORLD: THE DILEMMAS OF A "FREE RIDER"

Michael Radu

Of all the Eastern European countries, with the possible exception of Yugoslavia, Romania is the most active in the South, both politically and economically, and there are indications that such activity will continue to increase during the next few years. As of July 1980, Romania had diplomatic relations with 137 states, economic ties with 143, and cultural relations with 140, while the Romanian Communist party (RCP) had party-to-party relations with 280 other parties throughout the world, ranging from Christian-Democrats and Conservatives to Marxist-Leninists. President Ceausescu of Romania has signed treaties of friendship and cooperation with Portugal, Khmer Rouge Kampuchea, and ten developing countries during the past seven years, more than any other Communist state. According to the Romanian media, the developing countries' share in the country's foreign trade turnover, about 25 percent in 1979, will reach 30 percent by the end of 1980, a far larger share than for any other Eastern European state. These figures themselves provide an interesting picture of the extent of Romania's involvement in the South and of the degree of acceptance it enjoys in that area. Both these factors are related to Romania's position as a "free rider" within the Eastern political subsystem, a position which implies a peculiar set of constraints and opportunities for the policy makers in Bucharest. At this point, before proceeding to an analysis of Romania's position with respect to the South, it might be useful to provide a brief description of how Romania has arrived at this position.

BACKGROUND ON ROMANIA'S FOREIGN POLICY

After being "liberated" by the Red Army in 1944, Romania rapidly became one of the most loyal and submissive Soviet client states in Eastern Europe, with one of the most rigidly orthodox Communist regimes anywhere, an orthodoxy which is still very much a reality today. Unlike most other Eastern European regimes established after World War II the one in Bucharest never had to face any serious internal challenge on the order of the event of 1953 in East Berlin, 1956 in Hungary, 1968 in Czechoslovakia, or 1970 in Poland. The relative ease with which the RCP established and strengthened its grip over the country made its leadership more confident of their ability to survive without direct support, a conviction shared by Moscow as well, which explains the early withdrawal of the Soviet troops from Romania, in 1957-58. It also explains why the Soviet Union was and still is willing to tolerate Romanian manifestations of particularism in foreign policy: the cause of Marxism-Leninism has never been in danger in that country. To all these reasons one may always add the relatively insignificant strategic location of Romania.

One of the last Eastern European states to implement even token de-Stalinization, Romania has paradoxically became the least orthodox in its foreign policy since the late 1950s and early 1960s, with the first signs of this peculiarity becoming apparent at the time of the Sino-Soviet break. At that time, the leadership of the RCP, under Gheorghiu-Dej, felt strong enough to adopt a neutral position between Moscow and Beijing, for a variety of internal and external reasons. Internally, the persistence of Stalinist structures made it uncomfortable for the Party to go along with the often erratic "liberalization" measures demanded by Khrushchev and made it feel closer to the Maoist admirers of Stalin. Externally, close relations with China allowed Romania to demonstrate to Moscow that it was of greater importance than the Kremlin had hitherto realized and that, therefore it could and it should play a more active role in intrabloc affairs than before. While such a position was not devoid of risk, Bucharest correctly considered those risks to be limited as long as its internal orthodoxy could not be questioned. Moreover, by subtly underlining its differences with the Soviet Union, or by taking highly visible symbolic stands against the general consensus of the Warsaw Pact, the RCP, especially under Ceausescu, did manage, at least temporarily, to increase its legitimacy internally and externally. Once the critical period of establishing Romania's maverick status passed and the new status was gradually accepted in Eastern Europe, a process which ended approximately at the time of Gheorghiu-Dej's death in 1965, Nicolae Ceausescu, his successor and the present Romanian leader, was able to introduce a new dynamism in his country's foreign policy. He expanded Bucharest's expressions of its autonomy from intrabloc to extrabloc issues, but only after a delay of a few years. That delay was due to Ceausescu's post-succession problems and to the invasion of Czechoslovakia, and those factors limited Ceausescu's personal involvement in foreign policy. Between 1965-1970 he limited himself to yearly travels to Moscow and to repeated visits in other Eastern European capitals, while the foreign policy team, led by Prime Minister Maurer and Foreign Minister Corneliu Manescu (a team he inherited from his predecessor) continued to expand Romania's ties with both the West and the South.

As a small country, Romania does not have the capability for an active policy in all areas of the world simultaneously and must assess her priorities according to more immediate interests. Thus, the period between 1960 and 1968 was one of reassessment of Romania's position within the Eastern subsystem of the international political system, followed by an active rapprochment with the West, which culminated with De Gaulle's visit to Bucharest in 1968 and included the establishment of diplomatic relations with West Germany as well as with a reorientation of trade away from complete dependence on the Council of Mutual Economic Assistance (CMEA) and toward the European Economic Community (EEC). Since 1970, Bucharest has become increasingly active in the developing countries, and in 1972 Ceausescu began his long series of visits to Africa, Latin America, the Middle East, and Asia. The foreign policy establishment of Romania was rather suddenly changed, with the old Gheorghiu-Dej era group being pushed aside and replaced by insignificant figures whose major qualification has been their personal loyalty to the president, who has become less and less willing to delegate any powers. As Ceausescu's grip on power became increasingly absolute in the early 1970s, he came to be more and more the only real decision maker in Bucharest, aided by a group of young party apparatchiks promoted by him, the most prominent of whom being the current foreign minister, Stefan Andrei.

Throughout the period from 1970 to 1980, relations with China and Yugoslavia have been strengthened, and an increasing similarity between their views and those of Romania become apparent in their policy toward the developing countries. The foreign leader Ceausescu met most often, sometimes twice a year, was Tito, and China became an increasingly important trade partner of Romania, while all three tended to vote similarly in the United Nations on issues related to the South.

Romania's relations with the South are closely linked to a general foreign policy that reflects the structure of the Romanian political and economic system. Economically, Romania is at the same time one of the most rigid centrally planned states in the world and one of the least developed countries in Europe, with a per capita GNP that places her in the same category with Turkey, Cyprus, Albania, and Malta. The costly and inefficient industrialization drive of the last ten years has yet to show concrete changes in the standard of living, but it has clearly aggravated the dependence on an inefficient agriculture, thoroughly collectivized, and on imports of raw materials and technology. One of the most spectacular and painful examples of the latter is the fact that until 1970 Romania was self-sufficient in oil, while by 1978 it imported half of her needs (13 million metric tons), and imports of coal, iron ore, and bauxite also increased sharply during the same period. Although almost half of the labor force is still engaged in agriculture, that sector is consistently unable to satisfy either internal or external demand, and Romanian industry is completely unable to compete with either the West or the advanced CMEA members, such as East Germany and Czechoslovakia.

Politically, Romania is almost unique in Eastern Europe in terms of the epic proportions of the cult of personality (the only possible comparison is Albania). All of the important levers of power are in the hands of President Ceausescu and his close collaborators, among whom his family plays a disproportionately large role (The prime minister, Ilie Verdet, is a relative of the president, while Ceausescu's wife, Elena, is de jure the third-ranking Politburo member and de facto the second most powerful figure in the country). All major and most minor decisions in all fields are taken by the president. This fact is probably the best explanation for the enormous importance given to summit meetings, the only occasions on which foreign policy decisions of any importance are made. The fact that Ceausescu has visited over 70 states since coming into power and has received in Bucharest more than 80 foreign heads of state or government clearly demonstrates the personalized character of Romania's foreign policy. The RCP itself is under the absolute control of the secretary general, and no individual or group has thus been able to establish a competing power base within it. Purges and periodic shuffles are the main methods used to prevent that from happening.

While Romania is one of the founding members of both the Warsaw Pact and CMEA and is thus economically and militarily tied to the Soviet Union, the regime in Bucharest has also declared (in 1972) Romania to be a "Socialist developing" country, thus creating a basis for its claim to be a bridge between the East and the South. The ideological framework created by the RCP for rationalizing and legitimizing its widespread ties with the developing countries, and its perception of them and of their role, is certainly worth elaboration here, since it can facilitate the understanding of the dilemma facing Romania as it attempts to navigate between internationalist solidarity and the solidarity of the poor.

THE IDEOLOGICAL FRAMEWORK

The political pragmatism that resulted in closer and closer relations with the South under the leadership of Maurer and Manescu in
the late 1960s began to be incorporated into the official RCP line after
the 1967 National Conference, but only with the 1972 National Conference did it receive a consistent and clear ideological formulation. That
event came only months after Ceausescu's first extended visit to the
developing world: Central Africa, Congo, Zaire, Tanzania, Zambia,
Sudan, and Egypt. Ever since that time, the RCP, through its leader
and main ideologue, has always stressed that whatever ideological innovations it may introduce are applicable to it alone and do not have
relevance for other Communist parties; however, it has also emphasized that it considers it both its right and duty to interpret Marxism-
Leninism for the peculiar conditions of Romania. In other words, while
stressing its right to define its own ideology, the RCP has also taken
care to reassure Moscow that it does not intend to "export" its ideological innovations to other parties in Eastern Europe.

The RCP has redefined and extrapolated the Leninist definition
of conflicts as being "antagonistic" or "nonantagonistic" to the sphere
of international relations in general and to the South in particular. The
difference between these two types of conflict was, in Lenin's opinion,
that the first was irreconcilable while the second type was negotiable,
that the first had to be settled by force while the second could be settled by compromise. The RCP, on the other hand, has tended to ex-
trapolate the notion of "nonantagonistic" conflict from the social arena
(that is, peasants vs. workers) to the international arena. Thus, conflicts between Communist states (China and the Soviet Union, Kampuchea and Vietnam) or between various developing countries are defined
as basically "nonantagonistic," to be solved through negotiations and
compromise only. While the Soviets admit no compromise (and neither
do the Chinese) between "revisionism" and Marxism-Leninism, or between "reactionary" and "progressive" developing countries, the RCP
has not used the word "revisionism" since the 1950s, when it applied
it to Tito, and rejects the very distinction between "progressive" and
"reactionary" regimes in the South, a distinction which provides the
basis for Soviet involvement in support of various radical regimes
and groups there. In the words of a Romanian commentator:

> The emphasis placed on dividing the developing countries
> into "progressive" and "moderate" ones and opposing them
> to each other in international relations runs counter to the
> unanimously recognized principle of peaceful coexistence
> of countries with different social and political systems,
> feeding instead the theory of the spheres of influence, which

is used to weaken the unity of the developing countries in
the international arena. [1]

This position is very similar to that of the Yugoslavs, reflecting once
again the similarity of viewpoint between Belgrade and Bucharest concerning the role and character of the Nonaligned Movement. As the
Yugoslav Foreign Minister Vrhovec has stated:

> If we were to . . . permit the application of ideological
> criteria, it would mean the division of the movement [the
> Nonaligned Movement] into a "progressive" part linked
> to one bloc and a "conservative" part linked to the other
> bloc. . . . Such distinction jeopardizes the meaning and
> content of active peaceful coexistence as one of the vital
> determinants of the policy of nonalignment. [2]

The very foundation of the RCP ideology, its demand that every
Communist party be free to choose its own way of applying Marxism-
Leninism, is linked to a rather particular assessment of the international situation as a whole. Although Bucharest does occasionally admit the existence of international conflicts, as Ceausescu put it, "Imperialism is much weaker than most people would say, and to overestimate its strength would lead to panic."[3] As a result, Romania
considers there to be no need for any "center" of the international
Communist movement and believes that, even if there still are dangers of war and conflict, they should be dealt with in other forums,
especially at the United Nations, thus interposing a universal organization between intrabloc relations and international relations as a
whole. Ceausescu has been quite specific and open on this point:

> An important role in mobilizing public opinion against any
> transgression of international principles is incumbent on
> the United Nations Organization. Membership of a country
> in a military bloc does not signify its being exempted from
> the rules of international law or being absolved of respon-
> sibility before the community of world peoples. [4] (Empha-
> sis added.)

Ceausescu likes to consider his main contribution to the development of contemporary Marxist theory to be the idea he expressed
for the first time at the 1972 National Conference of the RCP, that
Romania, "while having passed the stage of being an underdeveloped
country, continues to be a developing country,"[5] whose aim is to create a "multilaterally developed socialist society."[6] While the claim
that Romania is structurally similar to the developing countries goes

far beyond Yugoslavia's political attachment to the Nonaligned Movement and, as a result, to the most general interests of the South, the impact on Romania's relations with the developing countries, and especially with the Group of 77, is similar: in both cases a Communist country has gained wide acceptance as a legitimate ally and friend of the nonaligned countries, becoming de facto members of their group. In Romania's case, that acceptance by the South has materialized in her becoming a full member of the Group of 77, an observer at the Nonaligned Movement's meetings, a member of the General Agreement on Tariffs and Trade (GATT), the International Monetary Fund (IMF), and the World Bank. Interesting for another aspect of Romania's approach to some developing countries is the fact that it was the Latin American states that had the most important role in Bucharest's admission as an observer at the Colombo meeting of the Nonaligned Movement. Taking into consideration the repeated claims of Romania to be culturally related to Latin America because of her Romance language and Latin cultural inheritance, it becomes clear that at least some of those claims did receive a degree of acceptance south of the Rio Grande. The fact that Romania has by far the closest political and cultural relations with Latin America of all Eastern European states was, however, the most important factor in that decision.

The difficulty of convincing the developing countries that Romania is in a situation similar to their own in terms of development and that it therefore has essentially similar interests is perhaps less of a problem for Bucharest than is the need to convince Moscow that being a "Socialist developing" country does not mean a weakening of its links with either the Warsaw Pact or the CMEA. For this reason, the RCP has taken pains always to point out that there is no contradiction between Romania being a developing country and a Socialist one at the same time, [7] while also declaring that her position in the world is such that "we have been and are paying special attention to the development of relations with the countries which have taken the road to the affirmation of independence,"[8] that is, with the South as a whole. One way of reassuring Moscow is to take a "progressive" attitude toward some internal developments in the developing countries—nationalizations, expulsion of multinational corporations—at least formally. Moreover, the RCP considers that "unity among all national progressive forces, the military included"[9] is absolutely necessary to overcoming underdevelopment, although the predominance or even existence of Communist parties is not an essential condition for attaining that goal. This is the position the Soviet Union has had during the 1960s. The relationship between socialism and development, however, has been defined by Romania in terms very similar to the present Soviet position; that relationship is a necessary one, in the long term, because socialism "is the only way [original emphasis] to overcome underdevelopment. "[10] On the other hand, Romania's ties with those developing countries which are not Socialist has been justified by the "observance of every people's right to be full master of its own destiny, to build its future as it wishes. "[11] In an even more confusing, or vague, rationalization, the relationship between socialism and nonalignment was described as based on the fact that "socialism and nonalignment have the same vision of the new principles that are to underlie the future relations among all states of the world. There is a relationship of interaction [sic] between socialism and nonalignment. "[12] This stops statements short of proclaiming a "natural alliance" between East and South, a claim so manifest in Cuban, Soviet, and East German declarations, but is vague enough to allow any interpretation. Although the RCP has occasionally stressed its preference for radical developing countries, it has its own definition of such countries, and it has always balanced such preferences with pragmatic policies. On the one hand, Ceausescu stated:

> We particularly strengthen solidarity and collaboration with the countries which choose the socialist development path, as Guinea, the Congo, Angola, Mozambique, Somalia, Ethiopia, Algeria and others. At the same time, we think it necessary to intensify our links with all developing countries, starting from the need to do our utmost to strengthen solidarity among all developing countries. [13]

On the other hand, he also managed to always find common interests between Romania and countries like Zaire (with whom Romania has a standing treaty of friendship and cooperation) and Ivory Coast. Moreover, coming only a few months after a clash with Moscow over the level of military spending of the Warsaw Pact, that statement clearly expressed the dilemma inherent in Bucharest's position relative to the South: on one hand it must placate its allies, and on the other it needs to protect its political and economic interests in the developing countries. At the Twelfth Congress of the RCP in November 1979 the dilemma was still not resolved as was reflected by Ceausescu's report: "We are establishing links with those [developing] countries as part of our general anti-imperialist and anti-colonialist policy of free, independent, and prosperous self-affirming peoples. "[14] He also made it clear that Romania's relations with the developing countries are an integral part of her general foreign policy, which was determined primarily by her membership in the "Socialist community. " The congress's resolution also made it clear that the order of priorities in Romania's external affairs was to be, in descending order, the Socialist countries, the developing countries, the nonaligned states, and the West. [15] The distinction made between developing and nonaligned states, a distinction which has become a rule in the Romanian media since the late 1970s, is quite interesting, especially when it is defined as that between countries which "after liberating themselves from colonialism, have set out on a course of self-reliant social development"[16] and those nonaligned states priased for their role "in the struggle against the old policy of domination and oppression, for overcoming the policy of blocs, for detente and peace in the world. "[17] What this seems to signify is that in the RCP's opinion the radical countries are the only ones "developing," whereas the nonaligned states have a more limited, political impact in strengthening detente.

Romania's position toward the Nonaligned Movement as an institution can be summed up as being based on a stated commonality of interests, including opposition to military blocs, support for the New International Economic Order (NIEO), respect for national sovereignty, and equality among states, regardless of size, level of development, and social system. [18] In RCP's view, Romania is "objectively"[19] a participant in the Nonaligned Movement's struggle for the implementation of the above principles, and that fact should legitimize her persistent attempts to become a member, her membership in the Warsaw Pact and the CMEA notwithstanding. Romanian theorists, however, do accept the fact that Romania first had to establish a large network of bilateral ties with most of the nonaligned countries in order to be accepted as a valid partner of the Nonaligned Movement itself. [20]

While there are indications that Romania is becoming somewhat more careful in her support for the Nonaligned Movement on questions sensitive to the Soviet Union, it is also important to note that the RCP's opposition to the classification of developing countries along ideological lines has recently stiffened: such distinctions are now considered "premature and inappropriate" and a "subjective classification," harmful because it may turn the developing countries against one another, thus depriving them of their greatest asset, their solidarity. [21] Ceausescu's message to the Havana Conference mentioned above seems to be one more indication of Bucharest's unhappiness with the polarization of the Nonaligned Movement manifested at Havana.

If the ideological approach of the RCP to the problems of development and to the Nonaligned Movement seems rather ambiguous in some instances, because of the conflicting needs to assuage Soviet suspicions of heresy and to ensure Romania's continuous acceptance as another developing country by the South, the actual political stands adopted by Bucharest in the South go a long way toward clarifying that ambiguity in most instances.

POLITICAL RELATIONS

Romania has treaties of friendship and cooperation with the following developing countries: Argentina (1973), Costa Rica (1973), Guinea (1974), Gabon, Zambia, Angola, Mozambique, Burundi, and Sudan (1979), and Zaire (1980). This very list demonstrates the peculiar character of Romania's policy toward the South as well as the erratic and personal character of her decision-making process. Regarding the latter, there were few if any reasons for Ceausescu to sign the treaty with Burundi, a small, poor African state with which Romania has no significant trade or commonality of interests. However, his personal taste for ceremonial shows and his conviction that formal documents are the way to improve his and his country's international image were decisive factors. Although Argentina is and traditionally was an important Latin American trade partner of Romania, that fact probably weighed no more than Ceausescu's personal friendship with Juan Perón, a relationship established at the time when the former and future president of Argentina, then in exile in Spain, was a regular patient at a Bucharest clinic.

The other treaties, however, are much more significant for the general orientation of Romania's policy in the South, as are those with Portugal—the only such treaty ever signed between a NATO and a Warsaw Pact member—and the Khmer Rouge. The latter treaty, signed during Ceausescu's trip to Phnom Penh in 1978, is the only standing treaty between the Khmer Rouge and a Warsaw Pact member, and the fact that the RCP newspaper, Scinteia, published Khieu Samphan's message of congratulations on the occasion of Ceausescu's reelection as president in March 1980 seems to indicate Romania's continuous willingness to condemn indirectly the Vietnamese occupation of Kampuchea. That the dislike between Bucharest and Hanoi is reciprocal was demonstrated by the fact that Vietnam sent the lowest-level delegation of all Communist countries to the RCP's Twelfth Congress in November 1979.

Regarding the other treaties mentioned above, those with Angola and Mozambique may seem rather natural in view of those countries, close ties with the Soviet Union and the Eastern European countries, and so is the one signed with Guinea, although in that case again Ceausescu's friendship with Sékou Touré has played a role. For a Communist state to sign a treaty with Gabon, Costa Rica, or even Sudan (after that country's break with Moscow in 1974, and given its close ties with Egypt) is a very important development, however, as is the case of Zaire. Zambia, a country hopelessly overwhelmed by the radicalization of Southern Africa, is probably somewhere in between the two groups and is also a significant recipient of Romanian credits and technical aid (advisers, mining experts, teachers). The main reason such anti-Communist states as Zaire, Gabon, and Sudan were willing to sign formal treaties with Romania is their attempt to maintain some channels of communication to the Soviet Union and Eastern Europe open and an economic interest manifest in their acceptance of Romanian credits, investments, and joint economic ventures. In addition, Romania's excellent relations with Egypt may have played a role in the Sudanese decision, while Bucharest's close ties with Dakar and good relations with Abidjan probably attracted Sékou Touré, who at that time was beginning to reopen his ties with both the West and his pro-Western neighbors: Senegal and Ivory Coast.

The treaties with Sudan, Guinea, and Zaire, as well as Romania's good relations with Somalia, also demonstrate the importance of Romania's close ties with China, a supporter and friend of all those countries. The Chinese connection, and Romania's carefully cultivated image as an independent country, are the most plausible explanation of her being considered a legitimate partner by anti-Soviet states as well. Egypt and Somalia are the most spectacular cases of such attitudes, as both countries have expelled the Soviet and Eastern European advisers and broken relations with most Eastern European states and with Cuba, at the same time increasing their ties with Beijing. Egypt is even more important in this case than Sudan or Somalia, both of whom are more or less under its influence, and it was in Cairo that Ceausescu managed one of his most successful diplomatic ventures. As the only Communist state maintaining an embassy in Tel Aviv, it seems that Romania had played such an important role as an intermediary between Israel and Egypt that both Anwar Sadat and Menachem Begin have publicly expressed their appreciation to Ceausescu. Romania's use of her peculiar position between East, South, and West, was previously demonstrated in the role it attempted to play as a mediator between Washington and Beijing during the Nixon years. The fact that in 1979 Ceausescu was able to visit Libya and Egypt on the same trip is also a demonstration of Romania's ability to play the role of a neutral and disinterested partner of all developing countries, a "true" champion of compromise and peaceful resolution of conflicts. While all these actions demonstrated the advantages of being a "free rider" between China and the Soviet Union, as well as between East and South, the issues of Kampuchea and Afghanistan seem to indicate that there are also some pitfalls in such a position and that in some particular circumstances intrasubsystemic pressures on Romania may have both advantageous and damaging effects on her policy toward the developing countries.

As previously noted, Romania has a standing treaty of friendship and cooperation with the Khmer Rouge[22] and never accepted the legitimacy of the Vietnamese-imposed regime of Heng Samrin in Phnom Penh. At the U.N. General Assembly vote on the issue of

Kampuchean representation in November 1979, Romania cast the first anti-Soviet vote of any Warsaw Pact member, supporting the representative of the Khmer Rouge as the legitimate Cambodian delegate. While it is true that the Romanian media has maintained a careful low profile in reporting the events in Indochina ever since, it also avoided supporting the Vietnamese or condemning the Chinese attack on Vietnam in 1979, while deploring the conflict between fraternal Communist countries. Romanian insistence on maintaining relations with the Khmer Rouge, however, goes back to the period of the Lon Nol government, which the Soviet Union recognized while Bucharest gave complete support to Ceausescu's friend, Norodom Sihanouk, and to his Beijing-based government in exile. By supporting the Khmer Rouge at the United Nations, Romania not only continued a tradition of friendship toward the Pol Pot group and underlined her willingness to support China's friends, but it also provided a concrete proof of her respect for the consensus of the Nonaligned Movement, a majority of which also supported Pol Pot. Once more, Bucharest demonstrated its ability to assess Moscow's reactions accurately, and although it is hard to believe that the Soviets appreciated Romania's stand on that issue, it is also clear that they did not consider the topic important enough to react strongly. When the danger for such a reaction exists, however, Romania immediately perceives it and shifts her position accordingly by adopting a position that is clearly intended to assuage Soviet displeasure. The position adopted by Romania in the issue of the Soviet invasion of Afghanistan is most significant in this respect.

The initial Romanian reaction to the Soviet invasion of Afghanistan in late December 1979 was a matter-of-fact description of the events in <u>Scinteia</u> without any elaboration or interpretation of an official character. In his New Year's address in the aftermath of the invasion, Ceausescu did not mention Afghanistan, and during the following two weeks no mention whatsoever was made of the U.S. reaction or of the Security Council debates on the topic. Only on January 14, 1980, when the U.N. General Assembly voted to condemn the Soviet invasion, did the Romanians decide to take a position on the issue. In a statement reproduced in all major Romanian newspapers and journals,[23] the Romanian ambassador to the United Nations, Teodor Marinescu, declared that his government could not support the majority resolution because it would "damage detente" and increase international tensions but that it also could not condone interference in the internal affairs of a nonaligned country, as this represented a violation of the principles of international law and of Romania's foreign policy. As a result, the Romanian delegation declared itself absent at the time of the vote. Rumors at the United Nations, however, had it that Bucharest had initially tried, unsuccessfully, to attract support for a draft resolution very close to the Soviet version of events.[24] In light of later developments, those rumors seem to have been founded on fact.

Between January 14 and April 27, 1980, there was total silence in the Romanian media on developments in Afghanistan, and no mention of them was made in any of Ceausescu's speeches. On April 27, however, the text of a congratulatory message sent by Ceausescu to Babrak Karmal on the occasion of the second anniversary of the initial Afghan coup of 1978 was published by Scinteia. The message expressed "wishes of good health and sincere congratulations" to Karmal and "to the friend Afghan people success on the progressive, democratic development of their country." It also expressed the conviction that "relations between the RCP and the People's Democratic Party of Afghanistan, as well as between Romania and Afghanistan, would develop further to the benefit of both peoples, of the policy of peace, detente, independence and progress."[25] Significant for the light it sheds on the difference between Romania's ties with Afghanistan and other Marxist regimes in the South and its ties with non- or anti-Marxist governments is the fact that a message sent the same day by Ceausescu to the president of Togo, Gnassingbe Eyadema, on the twentieth anniversary of Togo's independence was phrased differently. It also expressed a desire for better relations between the two countries and peoples, but this time "in the interest of peace, national independence, security in the entire world, for the instauration of a New International Economic Order"[26] (emphasis added). The terms "progress" and "detente" were not used in the message to pro-Western Togo but were replaced instead with demands for the NIEO and expressions of support for national independence, two issues of small importance in the case of Soviet-occupied Afghanistan, a country undergoing a process of economic integration into CMEA, where it has received observer status.

The development of Romania's position on Afghanistan from an embarrassed detachment to a stand increasingly similar to that of the most loyal Soviet allies was further demonstrated at the Warsaw Pact summit meeting of May 1980. The declaration issued at the end of that meeting, which was signed by Ceausescu as well as by all the other leaders of the alliance, clearly and unequivocally supported the Soviet stand: that a "political settlement" in Afghanistan was possible only in return for a cessation of any support for the guerillas, and that only after that condition had been met would Soviet troops withdraw.[27] A similar statement on the Afghan issue was incorporated into the joint Romanian-Bulgarian declaration signed by Ceausescu and Zhivkov in Bucharest on June 7, 1980,[28] and the joint declaration signed by Ceausescu and Honecker of the GDR on June 27, 1980.[29] The fact that Romania agreed to support the Soviet position and did so in documents signed with the Soviet Union's closest allies is a clear demonstration of Romanian inability to withstand strong pressures from Moscow in cases where Soviet interests are threatened. On June 17, 1980, Prime Minister Verdet of Romania met with Afghan Politburo member and Deputy Prime Minister Ali Kishtmand at the CMEA meeting in Prague, [30] a further demonstration of Romania's coming back into line on Afghanistan. This development was subsequently demonstrated by the Romanian media's increasingly frequent repetition of the Soviet position and Bucharest's support for it. As a prominent Romanian commentator described it in Lumea;

> Regarding Afghanistan, regardless of the [different] opinions on the cause of the events, Romania considers that it should be acted toward a political solution, which would bring the cessation of any outside support for the antigovernment forces, and at the same time to the withdrawal of the Soviet military units. [31]

In other words, while supporting the Soviet stand, Romania still does not wholeheartedly accept the Soviet version of the initial cause for intervention in Afghanistan, but it does not consider any settlement other than one proposed by Moscow to be realistically feasible and, in particular, is not prepared to support Islamic and Western demands for prior Soviet withdrawal for fear of seriously upsetting the Kremlin.

In the case of Kampuchea, Romania supported the Khmer Rouge for her own reasons as well as for reasons related to China's interests, which were perceived by Bucharest, correctly as it turned out, to be more vital for Beijing than Moscow's interest in legitimizing Heng Samrin's regime. In the Afghan issue, however, the roles were reversed, and Romania finally and after hesitation sided with the Soviet Union. These two circumstances clearly define the two most important sets of restraints under which Romania's foreign policy has to operate. It would be inaccurate, however, to overestimate Romania's ability to exercise autonomy on many other topics of importance to the developing countries or her consistency in demonstrating that autonomy.

One of the methods most frequently and consistently applied by Romania in courting the developing countries as a group is the support it gives to their position on such global issues as the NIEO and the Law of the Sea Conference, as well as on various regional issues, ranging from support for various "liberation" movements in Namibia, Zimbabwe, and South Africa, to demands for a Palestinian state and calls for the neutralization of the Eastern Mediterranean and Indian Ocean.

In her support for African "liberation" movements, Bucharest has attempted, as in the case of Cambodia, to follow the unstable consensus of opinion of the states of the region. In 1974, when the Organization of African Unity (OAU) recognized all three Angolan movements—MPLA (Movimento de Libertação de Angola), FNLA (Frente Nacional de Libertação de Angola), and UNITA—as "legitimate" representatives of the Angolan people, Romania did the same and received the leaders of all three of them in Bucharest, with a somewhat greater warmth for the FNLA chief, Holden Roberto. [32] The reason for that show of preference was FNLA's close relationship with both Zaire, an important trade partner of Romania, and China. After the Angolan civil war ended in the apparent victory of the Cubans and their MPLA allies, it took almost two years for relations between Luanda and Bucharest to become friendly, but ultimately, in 1979, Ceausescu visited Angola and signed a treaty of friendship and cooperation with the late Agostino Neto.

Romania adopted a similar position toward the Patriotic Front in Rhodesia, where, after the OAU threw its support behind both Mugabe and Nkomo, Bucharest did the same, while demonstrating a more pronounced sympathy for Mugabe. The latter visited Romania twice, as compared with the one visit paid by Nkomo, and Romania sent Politburo member and Deputy Prime Minister Gheorghe Radulescu to Salisbury for the April 1980 independence festivities. This visit was all the more significant in light of the fact that China was the only other Communist state to be represented at such a high level, whereas the Soviet Union and Cuba sent low-ranking delegations and the GDR, Poland, and Czechoslovakia were not even invited. Moreover, while Mugabe was lavishly praised by the Romanian media on that occasion, Nkomo was seldom mentioned. [33] Given the fact that Mugabe's brand of Marxism-Leninism and political preference are pro-Chinese rather than pro-Soviet, Romania's good relations with the new Zimbabwe seem to be one more instance of her use of the "Chinese connection" in various parts of the developing world. In the case of Rhodesia, however, there were some previous actions of Romania, always denied by Bucharest, that would have upset her African friends. Indeed, there were consistent reports in the Western press before 1979 that Rhodesian chrome had found its way to the United States through a lucrative chain of sanction-busters that included South Africa, Israel, Romania, and the Soviet Union. To what extent such reports were accurate is very difficult to assess, but the fact is that Romania does have some relations with South Africa, as demonstrated by the sending of Romanian patients to undergo cardiac operations at the Groote Shuur Hospital in Capetown, the invitations extended to both Barnard brothers to visit Romania, and the publication in Romanian of two of Christiaan Bernard's books.

When support for some "liberation" movements, such as the Eritrean and Western Saharan ones—ELF (Eritrean Liberation Front).

EPLF (Eritrean People's Liberation Front), and POLISARIO, respectively—might conflict with Romania's close relations with the governments they are fighting against (in those cases Ethiopia and Morocco), and when there is no regional consensus on whether to recognize them or not, Bucharest has usually chosen either to ignore them or to condemn them in barely veiled terms. Bucharest has never recognized the Eritrean movements, paying no attention to them even before the present Marxist military regime took over in Addis Ababa, mostly because it had continuously good relations with Ethiopia under both Haile Selassie* and Mengistu. [34] Bucharest has been able to use the convenient pretext that the OAU has never recognized those movements, just as it has not recognized the POLISARIO, once again to the advantage of Romania, which has excellent trade relations with Morocco. On the other hand, Romania was the first European state to recognize the PAIGC-declared "independence" of Guinea-Bissau in 1973, and the second country to be visited by the leader of São Tomé e Príncipe, Manuel Pinto da Costa, after independence in November 1975. (The first state was Gabon, the long-time protector and supporter of the MLSTP [Movimento de Libertação de São Tomé e Principe].)

By limiting herself to deploring such conflicts between developing states as those between Ethiopia and Somalia, Angola and Zaire, or Tanzania and Amin's Uganda, Romania has managed to reinforce her image as a friend of the developing countries and a supporter of the peaceful resolution of their differences. It is this image which has enabled Bucharest to be the only Eastern European country to have good relations with both sides in such conflicts. Another factor reinforcing Romania's image as a nonideological and pragmatic friend of the developing countries as a group has been Bucharest's consistent unwillingness to establish or break relations with a developing country as a result of radical regime changes in that country. While it is true that Romania's relations with Israel and especially their upgrading at embassy level after 1967 prompted some Arab countries like Syria, Sudan, and Iraq to break diplomatic relations with Bucharest,

---

*Romania's relations with Ethiopia were established in the interwar period, and the then Romanian foreign minister, Nicolae Titulescu was one of the most ardent supporters of sanctions against Italy for its attack on Ethiopia. Ties were reestablished in the early 1960s and culminated in Haile Selassie's visit to Bucharest in 1964. Two years later, in the first high-level Romanian visit to sub-Saharan Africa, Chivu Stoica, then Romania's nominal head of state, visited Addis Ababa.

those relations were later reestablished. After Allende's overthrow, which occurred exactly when Ceausescu was scheduled to visit Chile, Romania not only maintained her embassy in Santiago but used it as a means of obtaining the release of prominent leftists from the military junta's jails, among whom was Allende's foreign minister, Clodomiro Almeida. Once again, significantly, the only other Communist state to maintain an embassy in Chile after 1973 was China. Given the Eastern European and Soviet investments in Chile between 1970 and 1973, Romania's continued presence there may also be interpreted as a guarantee that at least some of those investments are still protected.

As President Ceausescu put it, "It is not pluralism which these [developing] countries need now, but one national force, capable of leading the struggle for full liberation, independence, and welfare."[35] In most cases, that force is considered by the RCP to be the sole ruling party, which may not be Communist and in most cases is not even radical. Following this approach, the RCP has established party-to-party relations with ruling parties as diverse as Bokassa's now defunct MESAN (Mouvement de l'Evolution Sociale de l'Afrique Noire), Mobutu's MRP, TANU in Tanzania, PAIGN in Cape Verde and Guinea-Bissau, FRELIMO (Frente de Libertação de Moçambique) in Mozambique, MLSTP in São Tomé e Príncipe, and MPLA-PT in Angola. Delegations of those parties are regularly invited to RCP congresses and national conferences, and RCP delegations participate in the most important conventions and congresses of those parties. The aim of these contacts has been to increase the RCP's prestige throughout the world, to add weight to the political benefits of Romania's ties with governments of the developing countries, and to strengthen the influence of "anti-imperialist" forces, regardless of their precise ideology or lack thereof. As the resolution adopted by the Twelfth RCP Congress stated:

> Our Party will continue to expand its relations with the
> Socialist and social-democratic parties, with all revo-
> lutionary, democratic and progressive organizations,
> with the anti-imperialist forces everywhere, consider-
> ing that it is essentially important to the development
> of international life in a new, democratic way.[36]

Ceausescu himself made a similar argument in his report to that congress, stating that the RCP's ties with "liberation" movements and ruling parties in the developing countries, the strengthening of "solidarity and collaboration with these forces," is an essential condition for the ultimate establishment of social and national justice throughout the world.[37] In short, party-to-party ties between RCP and ruling parties in the South are but one additional means for the promotion of the same political and ideological goals pursued at the governmental level.

The extent to which Romania's declared policy goals in the South have been translated into action has been limited by both her membership in the Warsaw Pact and her close ties with China, Yugoslavia, and North Korea, all of which have tended to adopt policies toward the developing countries that are at variance with or directly opposed to those of the Soviet Union and her Eastern European allies. As long as it can, Romania has usually preferred to ignore such differences by never mentioning the presence of Cuban or East German troops in Angola, Ethiopia, or South Yemen or by consistently playing down the importance of events in Indochina. On the other hand, however, Bucharest has generally followed up the establishment of political ties with developing countries with the development of economic relations, which are more significant than in the case of any other Eastern European country. This increased economic interdependence between Romania and the South has made Bucharest even less inclined to adopt political stands that might jeopardize its investments in such troubled countries as Zaire, Libya, Syria, Egypt, and Iran.

ECONOMIC TIES

At UNCTAD and Group of 77 meetings, Romania has consistently been in the forefront of support for the NIEO. Officially, and in the opinion of the Romanian economists, the NIEO is necessary because of the preeminently "neocolonialist" character of the present international economic system. [38] Although they seldom name any "neocolonialist" state, when they do the Romanian economists and theorists usually mention U. S. -Latin American and EEC-African economic relations as examples of an unequal and unjust partnership. Such attacks on the West notwithstanding, Romania is also the only CMEA member to have openly supported the recent demands expressed by the UNCTAD and the Group of 77 that developed Communist countries provide their fair share of aid to the South. [39] Given Romania's own membership in CMEA, such an attitude may, at a first glance, seem unexpected, but one always has to bear in mind that Romania considers herself a "developing" country and therefore excludes herself from such obligations. Moreover, her trade orientation is such as to give at least some credibility to Romania's claim that it is as dependent on Western or Communist advanced countries for technology, capital, and aid (see Tables 8. 4 and 8. 5).

Although the only significant oil producer in Eastern Europe, Romania is also the largest importer of OPEC (Organization of Petroleum Exporting Countries) oil. The fact that Bucharest is far from enthusi-

astic about Soviet attempts at economic integration within the CMEA
and that it has consistently attempted to diversify its trade and sources
of raw materials and capital by expanding economic relations with the
developing countries and the West were at the origin of Romania's
present predicament. Indeed, while more dependent on non-Communist sources of energy and technology than other Eastern European
countries, Romania does not have their relative advantage of being
able to obtain Soviet oil and raw materials at lower and stable prices.
Romanian oil imports increased from zero in 1965 to 2,291.4 thousand
metric tons in 1970 and 12,937 thousand metric tons in 1978;[40] iron
ore imports increased from 6,267.8 thousand metric tons in 1970 to
13,843 thousand metric tons in 1978, and coal imports increased from
728.3 thousand metric tons to 4,668.5 thousand metric tons during the
same period. [41] Almost all of these imports were from the South and,
in the case of some coal, from the West (the United States).

Given this dependence on raw materials from the developing
countries, it is natural that Romania's leading trade partners in the
South are the oil-producing countries (see Table 8.1), mostly OAPEC
(Organization of Arab Petroleum Exporting Countries) states, but also
Mexico, and states such as Brazil, Liberia, India, and Gabon, which
provide Romania with imports of iron, Mozambique (coal), and Guinea
and Guyana (bauxite). Bucharest has consistently manifested a strong
interest in establishing long-term agreements with its raw materials
suppliers, and it has established a large number of joint ventures in
those countries as a means of limiting price fluctuations and ensuring
stable supplies. [42] Its joint ventures with the developing countries, 30
in number by 1980, account for 85 percent of Romania's total contracts
with those countries, [43] and are almost invariably related to the ex-
tractive industries or oil refining. Although about two-thirds of those
joint ventures are with sub-Saharan African countries, [44] primarily
in the fields of forestry (the Ondo and Calabar factories of the Seromwood and Nirowi enterprises, Carombois, in Central Africa), and
metal extraction (Mocambo in Zambia, LRPC in Liberia, Somifer in
Gabon, and the Musongati nickel mine in Burundi), the largest such
enterprises are in the Middle East. The Banyas oil refinery in Syria
is by far the largest such venture Romania has in any developing country, and it is typical for the general pattern of such ventures: Romania
provided technology and 3,500 skilled workers and engineers in addition to part of the invested capital, receiving in return a share of the
refined products on a long-term arrangement.

For Romania, the main advantage of such ventures is the lower
price of the product and the long-term guarantee of supplies that they
ensure—20 years, for example, in the case of Mozambican coal and
Liberian iron. [45] In addition, by producing timber, veneer, or metals
in countries participating in the Lome I and II conventions between the

TABLE 8.1

Romania's Trade with Main Middle East Partners, 1960-78
(millions of lei valuta)

Country	1960	1965	1970	1975	1976	1977	1978
Algeria							
Turnover		6.2	78.2	408.4	214.2	457.7	516.5
Exports		1.0	51.8	178.6	205.8	416.0	290.7
Imports		5.2	26.4	229.8	8.4	41.7	225.8
Balance		-4.2	25.4	-51.2	197.4	374.3	64.9
Egypt							
Turnover	102.8	206.3	250.7	726.6	487.0	489.0	713.7
Exports	53.5	101.8	138.4	367.2	346.5	402.4	593.0
Imports	49.3	104.5	112.3	359.4	140.5	86.6	120.7
Balance	4.2	-2.7	26.1	8.2	206.0	315.8	472.3
Iran							
Turnover	0.7	7.1	349.2	1702.1	2434.2	2520.0	1901.7
Exports	0.7	3.7	200.6	811.2	928.1	1053.6	818.6
Imports	—	3.4	148.6	890.9	1506.1	1466.4	1083.1
Balance	0.7	0.3	52.0	-79.7	-578.0	-412.8	-264.5
Iraq							
Turnover	8.2	17.7	3.3	359.9	1012.1	1119.5	2111.4
Exports	8.0	16.8	3.3	325.1	156.5	82.8	147.8
Imports	0.2	0.9	—	34.8	855.6	1036.7	-1963.6
Balance	7.8	15.9	3.3	290.3	-699.1	-953.9	-1815.8
Kuwait							
Turnover	0.1	6.1	21.2	385.6	489.5	556.1	281.9
Exports	0.1	6.1	21.2	52.8	141.7	101.7	88.4
Imports	—	—	—	332.8	-347.8	-454.4	-193.5
Balance	0.1	6.1	21.2	-280.0	-206.1	-352.7	-105.1

Libya							
Turnover	0.3	19.0	87.2	933.3	1273.5	1116.6	1856.3
Exports	0.3	19.0	87.2	582.0	565.8	664.0	707.5
Imports	–	–	–	351.3	707.6	452.6	1148.8
Balance	0.3	19.0	87.2	230.7	–141.8	211.4	–441.3
Morocco							
Turnover	0.2	0.6	6.6	213.1	228.2	143.1	200.4
Exports	0.2	0.5	3.1	53.7	74.0	33.1	89.5
Imports	–	0.1	3.5	159.4	154.2	110.0	110.9
Balance	0.2	0.4	–0.4	–105.7	–80.2	–76.9	–21.4
Saudi Arabia							
Turnover	0.5	6.1	9.1	40.3	87.5	105.5	86.5
Exports	0.5	6.1	9.1	40.3	87.5	105.5	86.5
Imports	–	–	–	–	–	–	–
Balance	0.5	6.1	9.1	40.3	37.5	105.5	86.5
Syria							
Turnover	15.7	104.5	23.9	402.5	814.1	1184.7	889.9
Exports	10.7	46.2	18.1	305.9	776.9	1123.7	819.5
Imports	5.0	58.3	5.8	96.6	37.2	61.0	70.4
Balance	5.7	–12.1	12.3	209.3	739.7	1062.7	749.1
Total							
Turnover	128.5	373.6	829.4	5171.8	7040.3	7692.2	8558.3
Exports	74.0	201.2	523.8	2716.8	3282.8	3982.8	3641.5
Imports	54.5	172.4	305.6	2455.0	3757.5	3709.4	4916.8
Balance	19.5	28.8	218.2	261.8	–474.7	273.4	–1275.3

Note: Dash indicates no data available.

Source: Figures for turnover, exports and imports by country were taken from Anuarul Statistic al Republicii Socialiste Romania, 1979 (Bucharest: Directia Centralá de Statisticá, 1980), pp. 495–98; those for total and balance were computed by the author.

EEC and the African, Caribbean, and Pacific states (ACP), Romania is in a position to sell these products on Western markets at favorable prices, while simply as a CMEA member, despite its own special arrangements with the EEC, it would not be able to do so. This is especially true of joint ventures in sub-Saharan Africa, and it may explain the large number of such enterprises there. The same is also true in the case of many manufactures produced in developing countries with Romanian capital, expertise, and equipment and with cheap local labor. Romania has built textile mills in Sudan, Tanzania, and the Congo, [46] and a tractor assembly plant was built in Ghana in the late 1960s. In light of the preferential treatment the European Economic Community is expected to give to the industrial products of the ACP states under the Lome II clauses, such Romanian ventures have an even better chance of penetrating Western tariff and nontariff barriers since, even though Romania is a GATT member and a beneficiary of the most-favored-nation clause in its trade with the United States, it still faces some tariff and many nontariff barriers in the West, as well as accusations of dumping.

While claiming to be in solidarity with the developing countries, Romania does not consider itself under any obligation to provide them aid, using the familiar Eastern European and Soviet argument that it is in no way responsible for the South's poverty and the additional argument that, since it is itself a developing country, it does not have the resources needed to aid others. Even when Bucharest speaks of "direct aid," it is referring to investments in joint ventures or in Southern industries rather than to soft loans or grants. In terms of capital investment, Romania is the most heavily involved of all Eastern European countries, with the largest amounts invested in such countries as Nigeria (£2 million in timber operations), Liberia, and Zambia. However, in light of the benefits to Romania mentioned above, such reimbursable investment can hardly qualify as "aid."

The only form of aid offered by Romania to the developing countries, with the exception of small quantities of arms to various "liberation" movements, is in the field of personnel training and sending of technical experts. Thus, as of September 1979, over 15,000 Romanian technicians were working in the developing countries, with the largest number in Libya, while the same number of experts and more than 12,000 students from those countries were being trained in Romania. [47] Engineers from 70 developing countries—400 post-graduates and 500 students—were enrolled at the Ploiesti Oil and Gases Institute alone in 1979. [48] Of all students from the developing countries in Romania at that time, 51 percent were being trained in technical specializations. At the same time, the "Stefan Gheorghiu" Academy, linked to the RCP training programs, and the CEPECA (Central de Perfectionare a Cadrelor) international training center in Bucharest trains

cadres for political, administrative, and trade union activities. Over
1,200 Romanian teachers are employed in the developing world, most
of them in Africa and the Middle East.[49] Military personnel from African states and members of "liberation" movements are also trained
in Romania, at the Sibiu Military School.

It should be noted, however, that Romanian specialists working
in the developing countries are paid at least partially by those countries, in hard currency. This makes such assignments very attractive
to Romanians, since a period of one or two years of work in a country
like Zaire, Libya, or Algeria can be the opportunity of a lifetime to
earn the money for a house or a car.

During the past decade some developing countries, such as Guinea and the Congo, have begun to reassess their economic ties with the
Eastern Europeans and the Soviets and to insist on fewer joint ventures
and credits and more outright grants or soft loans. UNCTAD has also
begun to demand that Communist states provide more aid to the developing countries, while Middle East oil producers, even when friendly
to Warsaw Pact members, are unwilling to sell their oil at less than
OPEC prices or engage in clearing arrangements with the Eastern
Europeans. Romania is one of the Eastern European countries most
vulnerable to such developments, because of its relatively greater
dependence on raw materials from the developing countries and on
their markets for its industrial products. Moreover, Romania's trade
deficits with the West worsened and her hard currency reserves
shrank at the same time as her traditional trade surpluses with the
Soviet Union declined or even disappeared (see Table 8.4).

By 1978, Romania's trade situation had deteriorated to such an
extent that resistance among the top economists in Bucharest to the
expansion or even continuation of trade with the developing countries
began to appear. Opposition to the official trade policy seems to have
grown to such proportions that Ceausescu felt it necessary to become
publicly involved, declaring:

> There are some comrades from the economic sectors
> who forwarded proposals for limiting the actions of co-
> operation with developing countries (i.e., the joint ven-
> tures), instead of drawing the necessary conclusions
> from the mistakes made before. . . . Of course, there
> are a series of difficulties, but they should be solved.
> . . . We give great importance to joint ventures.[50]

The debate continued, however, and Lumea mentioned it again by emphasizing that "Romania will take no steps to limit cooperation with
the developing countries, but to intensify and diversify our work together."[57] The same journal also pointed out the political character

TABLE 8.2

Romania's Trade with Main Partners in Asia and Latin America, 1960–78
(millions of lei valuta)

Country	1960	1965	1970	1975	1976	1977	1978
Argentina							
Turnover	22.6	13.4	56.0	173.0	160.8	366.1	276.5
Exports	12.9	6.7	1.1	170.5	50.5	37.0	34.1
Imports	9.7	6.7	54.9	2.5	110.3	329.1	242.4
Balance	3.2	0.0	-53.8	168.0	-59.8	-292.1	-208.3
Brazil							
Turnover	24.8	57.7	66.0	267.5	637.8	293.5	198.3
Exports	17.5	27.2	34.9	105.3	392.5	136.1	56.7
Imports	7.3	30.5	31.1	162.2	245.3	157.4	141.6
Balance	10.2	-3.3	3.8	-56.9	147.2	-21.3	-84.9
Chile							
Turnover	—	—	3.4	27.7	21.6	23.6	36.6
Exports			*	27.7	5.0	4.5	5.1
Imports			3.4	—	16.6	-19.1	-31.5
Balance			-3.4	27.7	-11.6	-14.6	-26.4
India							
Turnover	89.7	93.4	187.8	510.8	507.0	291.4	426.9
Exports	69.3	40.5	96.1	331.9	215.1	112.1	252.7
Imports	20.4	52.9	91.7	178.9	291.9	179.3	174.2
Balance	48.9	-12.4	4.4	153.0	-76.8	-67.2	78.5
Malaysia							
Turnover	0.4	0.4	0.1	19.5	73.4	101.8	80.1
Exports	0.4	0.4	0.1	3.9	7.2	23.1	18.3
Imports	—		—	15.6	66.2	78.7	61.8
Balance	0.4	0.4	0.1	-11.7	-59.0	-55.6	-43.5

	(1)	(2)	(3)	(4)	(5)	(6)	(7)
Peru							
Turnover	*	4.3	5.7	138.8	102.5	135.0	85.9
Exports	*	*	0.2	67.1	22.8	41.5	3.6
Imports	*	4.3	5.5	71.7	79.7	93.5	82.3
Balance	*	-4.3	-5.3	-4.6	-56.9	-52.0	-78.7
Philippines							
Turnover		*	—	25.9	117.7	53.0	107.9
Exports				6.6	18.6	20.9	36.2
Imports				19.3	99.1	32.1	71.7
Balance				-12.7	-80.5	-11.2	-35.5
Singapore							
Turnover	*		92.4	157.1	166.9	127.3	136.0
Exports			2.7	73.1	12.2	51.1	42.6
Imports			89.7	84.0	154.7	76.2	93.4
Balance			-87.0	-10.9	-142.5	-25.1	-50.8
Thailand							
Turnover	1.0	0.2	1.1	13.8	24.3	61.6	100.1
Exports	1.0	0.2	0.4	11.6	12.5	37.3	73.2
Imports	—	—	0.7	2.2	11.8	24.3	26.9
Balance	0.2	0.2	-0.3	9.4	0.7	13.0	46.3
Total							
Turnover	138.5	169.4	412.5	1334.1	1812.0	1453.3	1448.3
Exports	101.1	75.0	135.5	797.7	736.4	463.6	522.5
Imports	37.4	94.4	277.0	536.4	1075.6	989.7	925.8
Balance	63.7	-19.4	-141.5	261.3	-339.2	-526.1	-403.0

*The value of trade is statistically insignificant.

Source: The figures for turnover, exports, and imports by country were taken from Anuarul Statistic al Republicii Socialiste Romania, 1979 (Bucharest: Directia Centrală de Statistică, 1980), pp. 495–99; those for total and balance were computed by the author.

TABLE 8.3

Romania's Trade with Main Sub-Saharan Partners, 1960–78
(millions of lei valuta)

Country	1960	1965	1970	1975	1976	1977	1978
Angola						
Turnover					18.8	27.9	96.3
Exports					11.2	27.9	59.5
Imports					7.6	–	36.8
Balance					3.6	27.9	22.7
Ethiopia						
Turnover		0.4	0.7	7.8	6.7	4.5	15.8
Exports		0.4	0.7	7.8	6.7	4.5	12.7
Imports		–	–	–	–	–	3.1
Balance		0.4	0.7	7.8	6.7	4.5	9.6
Ghana						
Turnover		32.6	6.4	19.4	44.3	74.7	61.0
Exports		22.8	3.0	2.4	22.4	39.5	38.9
Imports		9.8	3.4	17.0	21.9	35.3	22.1
Balance		13.0	-0.4	-14.6	0.5	4.3	16.8
Guinea						
Turnover			4.9	51.5	35.3	20.5	15.7
Exports			1.9	50.3	35.3	1.5	2.9
Imports			3.0	1.2	–	19.0	12.8
Balance			-1.1	49.1	35.3	-17.5	-8.9
Ivory Coast						
Turnover			0.9	6.3	18.3	31.9	32.5
Exports			0.9	2.9	1.3	5.4	2.1
Imports			–	3.4	17.0	26.5	30.4
Balance			0.9	-0.5	-15.7	-21.1	-28.3

Nigeria							
Turnover			16.3	54.1	30.5	139.7	207.0
Exports			16.3	54.1	30.5	129.9	104.4
Imports			—	—	—	9.8	102.6
Balance			16.3	54.1	30.5	120.1	1.8
Sudan							
Turnover	14.3	22.2	38.3	66.5	88.8	56.7	91.4
Exports	9.5	12.8	24.7	50.7	14.0	39.8	63.5
Imports	4.8	9.4	13.6	15.8	74.8	16.9	27.9
Balance	4.7	3.4	11.1	34.9	-60.8	22.9	35.6
Tanzania							
Turnover			0.5	9.5	7.7	4.9	3.3
Exports			0.5	3.7	4.6	2.6	2.7
Imports			—	5.8	3.1	2.3	0.6
Balance			0.5	-2.1	1.5	0.3	2.1
Zaire							
Turnover				14.4	130.9	52.1	130.8
Exports				3.9	28.1	1.9	12.7
Imports				10.5	102.8	50.2	118.1
Balance				-6.6	-74.7	-48.3	-105.4
Total							
Turnover	14.3	55.2	68.0	225.5	381.3	412.9	644.8
Exports	9.5	36.0	48.0	175.8	154.1	253.0	299.4
Imports	4.8	19.2	20.0	49.7	227.2	159.9	354.4
Balance	4.7	16.8	28.0	126.1	-73.1	93.1	-55.0

Source: The figures for turnover, exports, and imports by country were taken from Anuarul Statistic al Republicii Socialiste Romania, 1979 (Bucharest: Direcția Centrală de Statistică, 1980), pp. 497–98; those for total and balance were computed by the author.

TABLE 8.4

Romania's Trade with Selected Communist Countries, 1960–78
(millions of lei valuta)

Country	1960	1965	1970	1975	1976	1977	1978
Albania							
Turnover	16.1	33.6	39.3	81.2	104.9	104.4	112.3
Exports	11.7	18.5	18.7	42.7	46.8	31.1	44.7
Imports	4.4	15.1	20.6	38.5	58.1	-73.3	-67.6
Balance	7.3	3.4	-1.9	4.2	-11.3	-42.2	-22.9
China							
Turnover	341.6	291.0	803.3	2164.4	2240.4	2546.4	3600.6
Exports	200.0	159.8	431.2	1094.0	1236.8	1188.7	1707.1
Imports	141.6	131.2	372.1	1070.4	1003.6	-1357.7	-1893.5
Balance	58.4	28.6	59.1	23.6	233.2	-169.0	-186.4
Cuba							
Turnover	—	14.6	165.7	127.3	160.6	105.9	18.0
Exports		14.5	87.9	84.4	86.1	43.2	15.9
Imports		0.1	77.8	42.9	74.5	62.7	2.1
Balance		14.4	10.1	41.5	11.6	-19.5	13.8
East Germany							
Turnover	634.5	805.4	1235.3	2909.0	4253.7	5105.6	5556.8
Exports	323.4	430.4	634.8	1339.6	2079.5	2570.3	2731.6
Imports	311.1	375.0	690.5	1569.4	2174.2	2553.3	2825.2
Balance	12.3	55.4	-55.7	-229.8	-94.7	17.0	-93.6
North Korea							
Turnover	49.6	51.4	83.8	185.1	163.2	127.7	216.6
Exports	31.9	30.4	47.7	110.5	124.0	89.2	97.9
Imports	17.7	21.0	36.1	74.6	39.2	38.5	118.7
Balance	14.2	9.4	11.6	35.9	84.8	50.7	-20.8

Poland							
Turnover	263.7	492.1	886.1	2072.6	2730.6	2805.4	3342.4
Exports	125.2	269.7	425.3	1012.3	1156.0	1424.6	1833.4
Imports	138.5	222.4	460.8	1060.3	1574.6	1380.8	1509.0
Balance	-13.3	47.3	-35.5	-48.0	-418.6	43.8	324.4
Soviet Union							
Turnover	3284.2	5067.5	6177.7	9857.5	10863.7	13341.4	12989.9
Exports	1688.6	2630.6	3172.9	5278.9	5558.6	6686.8	6469.1
Imports	1595.6	2436.9	3004.8	4578.6	5305.1	6654.6	6520.8
Balance	93.0	193.7	168.1	700.3	253.5	32.3	-51.7
Vietnam							
Turnover	39.7	32.6	58.8	57.8	48.1	65.8	312.0
Exports	26.8	20.1	58.0	42.9	31.3	40.3	268.8
Imports	12.9	12.5	0.8	14.9	16.8	25.5	43.2
Balance	13.9	7.6	57.2	28.0	14.5	14.8	225.6
Yugoslavia							
Turnover	76.5	173.1	421.3	1209.8	1402.7	1390.7	1569.0
Exports	47.4	98.6	246.1	676.0	856.8	898.1	932.9
Imports	29.1	74.5	175.2	533.8	545.9	492.6	636.1
Balance	18.3	24.1	70.9	142.2	319.9	405.5	296.8
Total							
Turnover	4705.9	6961.3	9871.3	18664.7	21967.9	25593.3	27717.6
Exports	2455.0	3672.6	5122.6	9681.3	11175.9	12972.3	14101.4
Imports	2250.9	3288.7	4748.7	8983.4	10792.0	12621.0	13616.2
Balance	204.1	383.9	373.9	697.9	383.9	351.3	485.2

Source: The figures for turnover, exports, and imports by country were taken from Anuarul Statistic al Republicii Socialiste Romania, 1979 (Bucharest: Direcţia Centrală de Statistică, 1980), pp. 492–99; those for total and balance were computed by the author.

TABLE 8.5

Romania's Trade with Main Western Partners, 1960–78 (millions of lei valuta)

Country	1960	1965	1970	1975	1976	1977	1978
Austria							
Turnover	153.4	289.0	686.1	1492.8	1625.8	1622.1	1850.3
Exports	94.2	145.8	329.4	597.9	685.6	637.9	690.5
Imports	59.2	143.2	356.7	894.9	-940.2	-984.2	1159.8
Balance	35.0	2.6	-27.3	-297.0	-254.6	-346.3	-469.3
France							
Turnover	265.9	426.5	1037.6	1689.2	2156.9	2055.6	2421.4
Exports	116.9	131.2	364.0	747.9	890.9	867.4	941.9
Imports	149.0	295.3	673.6	941.3	1266.0	1188.2	1479.5
Balance	-32.1	-164.1	-309.6	-193.4	-375.1	-320.8	-537.6
Italy							
Turnover	251.8	707.3	1233.6	2273.4	1956.4	1882.5	2345.3
Exports	153.7	395.7	656.3	1123.6	1001.6	1050.9	1208.3
Imports	98.1	311.6	577.3	1149.8	954.8	831.6	1137.0
Balance	55.6	84.1	79.0	-26.2	46.8	219.3	71.3
Japan							
Turnover		189.5	193.9	1089.1	905.4	1514.2	1530.7
Exports		83.5	33.3	253.7	224.7	260.3	322.8
Imports		106.0	160.6	835.4	680.7	1253.9	1207.9
Balance		-22.5	-127.3	-581.7	-456.0	-993.6	-885.1
Netherlands							
Turnover	42.9	96.9	321.2	1019.1	1266.8	1261.6	1524.2
Exports	19.3	40.4	130.5	594.6	781.2	748.9	819.0
Imports	23.6	56.5	190.7	424.5	485.6	512.7	705.2
Balance	-4.3	-16.1	-60.2	170.1	295.6	236.2	113.8

Switzerland						
Turnover	118.1	129.0	404.0	2068.5	1339.5	1951.8	1752.3
Exports	66.7	56.6	149.7	712.2	510.7	563.2	613.7
Imports	51.4	72.4	254.3	1356.3	828.8	1388.6	-1138.6
Balance	15.3	-15.8	-104.6	-644.1	-318.1	-825.4	-524.9
United Kingdom						
Turnover	196.2	446.6	899.8	1503.4	1568.6	1645.0	1838.5
Exports	89.5	183.2	306.9	624.2	745.3	660.2	890.7
Imports	106.5	263.4	592.9	879.2	823.2	984.8	-947.8
Balance	-17.0	-80.2	-286.0	-255.0	-77.9	-324.6	-57.1
United States						
Turnover	41.6	70.6	439.1	1174.1	2319.5	2795.7	3888.6
Exports	3.8	15.8	80.5	485.5	944.1	1368.3	1726.7
Imports	37.8	54.8	358.6	688.6	1375.4	-1427.4	2161.9
Balance	-34.0	-39.0	-278.1	-203.1	-431.2	-59.1	-435.2
West Germany						
Turnover	539.2	1042.2	1957.7	5039.1	4644.4	5201.2	6231.4
Exports	262.6	379.4	999.7	2192.3	2623.9	2547.8	2931.6
Imports	276.6	662.8	958.0	2846.8	2020.5	2653.4	3299.8
Balance	-14.0	-283.4	41.7	-654.5	603.4	-105.6	-368.2
Total						
Turnover	1609.1	3397.6	7173.0	17348.7	17783.3	19929.7	23382.7
Exports	806.7	1431.6	3050.3	7331.9	8408.0	8704.9	10145.2
Imports	802.4	1966.0	4122.7	10016.8	9375.3	11224.8	13237.5
Balance	4.3	-534.4	-1072.4	-2684.9	-967.3	-2519.9	-3092.3

Source: The figures for turnover, exports, and imports were taken from Anuarul Statistic al Republicii Socialiste Romania, 1979 (Bucharest: Direcția Centrală de Statistică, 1980), pp. 492–99; the figures for total and balance were computed by the author.

265

of the Romanian decision to continue to expand her trade with the developing countries:

> Obviously, the expansion of our country's economic rela-
> tions with the developing countries is a political option
> which implicitly stands proof of Socialist Romania's con-
> sistent action to translate into life the demands for a
> stepped up collaboration among developing countries. . . .
> Secondly, Romania's policy promotes ample collaboration
> with each and every developing country, being free from
> any preference or reticence for one or another. . . .
> Thirdly, we start from a realistic evaluation of what re-
> sults cooperation with the developing countries has yield-
> ed, of what difficulties were encountered and what mis-
> takes were made. [52] (Original emphasis)

In a speech in June 1980, Ceausescu described the "new economic mechanism" and its implications for Romania's foreign trade in the 1980s and clearly indicated that the trade deficits with and debts to the West (see Table 8.5) would be dealt with by reducing imports of technology and industrial equipment from the developed states, increasing exports of manufactures to Communist and developing countries, limiting most imports from the South to fuels and raw materials, and stressing the importance of joint ventures. [53] This drive toward an expansion in exports to the East and the South could mean attaining the often expressed goal of making trade with the developing countries 30 percent of Romania's total trade turnover by 1980-81, but it may also mean an increased willingness to expand trade with the other CMEA members. Already, in 1979, Romania signed her first contract with the Soviet Union for the import of a small quantity of oil. The extent to which developing countries will be willing to buy increased quantities of usually poor-quality Romanian manufactures—other than four-wheel-drive vehicles and oil-drilling equipment—remains to be seen, and the prospects for Romania seem anything but encouraging.

CONCLUSIONS

Unlike East Germany, with her concentrated military and security involvement in a limited number of radical developing countries, or Yugoslavia, with her great impact on the politics of nonalignment but insignificant economic relations with the South, Romania has a widespread presence in almost all of the developing countries, at both the political and the economic level. By usually refusing to become involved in Third World conflicts or, except in the case of the "libera-

tion" movements in Southern Africa and a few other places, [54] even
to provided limited quantities of weapons or security advisers, Romania seems to have sought during most of the 1970s to be accepted
as a legitimate partner of the developing countries and to increase
her international legitimacy by cultivating an image of independence
and similarity of interests with the South as a whole. By the mid-1970s,
however, with the industrialization drive in full swing and relations
with the CMEA and the Soviet Union at a new low, Romania had become increasingly dependent on imports of oil and other raw materials
from the developing countries, while running increasingly large trade
deficits with the West and being forced to borrow growing amounts of
hard currency from Western banks and international organizations.
Hoping to take advantage of her relatively higher level of industrial
development and her good political relations with the majority of developing countries, Romania began a steadily increasing trade offensive in the South based chiefly on joint ventures and capital investments in primary industries.

Changes in the international political climate, such as the increased polarization of the developing countries along political lines,
as manifested at the Havana Conference of the Nonaligned Movement
in August 1979, and the deterioration of detente as a result of the invasion of Afghanistan, combined with ever higher oil prices and a reduced willingness and ability on the part of many developing countries
to pay for Romanian industrial products have all resulted in growing
difficulties for Bucharest's relations with the South. On the economic
plane, those difficulties do not seem to have been successfully solved
by Ceausescu's continuing insistence on forging ahead with those very
types of involvement which were instrumental in creating the present
situation—joint ventures are the best example—while Romania's self-
proclaimed status as a "Socialist developing country" has not brought
with it the extensive Western aid or trade advantages anticipated in
1972.

Politically, Romania represents one of the most interesting and
in many ways most successful cases of Eastern European involvement
in the South. The very fact that Bucharest has been able to maintain
and develop good relations with such a variety of developing countries,
which have often been engaged in bitter conflicts with each other or,
as in the cases of Chile, Israel, and Khmer Rouge Kampuchea, have
been ruled by governments opposed by the rest of the Warsaw Pact,
suggests that Romania does have a margin of autonomy that is completely absent in Poland, Hungary, Czechoslovakia, East Germany,
or Bulgaria. On the other hand, in cases such as Afghanistan, it is
clear that Romania's autonomy should not be confused with independence, since once sufficiently strong Soviet pressures have been
brought to bear, Bucharest has been forced to comply, sooner or

later, with the Warsaw Pact consensus. As a member of the Warsaw Pact and the CMEA on the one hand, and a "Socialist developing country" on the other, Romania is under constant and increasingly direct pressure from opposite quarters. It ultimately had to acquiesce to the Soviet attack on a formerly nonaligned country, but it also accepted Third World demands for increased economic aid from developed Communist countries, with the implication that it should not be included among them. The most favorable solution to these contradictory pressures is, in Bucharest's opinion, a strengthening of the Nonaligned Movement along the lines supported by Yugoslavia and an increased role for the United Nations. While it is true that Ceausescu has actively pursued these two goals, it is also true that the turn of events in the late 1970s was not favorable to their implementation. With the weakening of the Nonaligned Movement and the continuing inability of the United Nations to solve international conflicts, Romania's success in becoming accepted as an ally of the former and a very active participant in the latter's activities may be expected to grow less and less significant.

From the standpoint of the developing countries, Romania's role as a channel for communication with either Moscow or Beijing, important in the early 1970s, may now be of less significance in a situation where China herself is now active in almost all parts of the South and the Soviet Union is regarded as a threat by those developing countries which are not already aligned with it or under its domination. Moreover, in light of Castro's campaign to bring the Nonaligned Movement closer to Soviet interests, those members of the movement opposed to such moves may be more reluctant to support or encourage Romania's attempts to further legitimize her ties with the Nonaligned Movement. In economic terms, those Southern countries able to export important raw materials may become less willing to engage in joint ventures with Romania for their production and marketing instead of selling them on the international market for hard currency. Bucharest's importance as a source of capital will most likely decline in absolute terms, as it is increasingly difficult for Romania to obtain new Western credits for Third World investments for her own needs.

If one accepts as valid the argument that Romania's highly successful political offensive in the South was conditioned by the early 1970s atmosphere of detente, it is clear that the return to international polarization and East-West competition will also have an adverse impact on Bucharest's ties with the developing countries, and with the West as well. Some actions of the Romanian government, such as its hurry to take advantage of the U. S. embargo against Iran and its support for the Khomeini regime (after long years of close ties with the Shah), translated into significantly higher exports of food to Iran and higher imports of oil, and its delayed but nevertheless unmistakably clear acceptance of the Soviet stand on Afghanistan, as well as a growing Western disenchantment with Ceausescu's record on human rights, all seem to point toward a reassessment of Romania's foreign policy in the direction of closer ties with her allies, if not with the most radical developing countries. On the other hand, however, relations with China, North Korea, and Yugoslavia remain very good, and some degree of coordination of efforts appear to exist between those countries and Romania on such issues as Kampuchea and the steering of the Nonaligned Movement away from too close a relationship with the Soviet Union.

What makes it difficult, for the time being, to discern any clear long-term trends in Romania's relations with the developing countries, however, is the relatively brief length of the period since those relations first became important in its foreign policy and the increasingly intimate relationship between Ceausescu's personal rule and his country's foreign policy. As mentioned earlier, there are voices in Bucharest that do not support such close ties with the South, at least for economic reasons, and the extreme concentration of political power in Ceausescu's hands may mean that his foreign policy will ultimately depend on his personal political longevity. As long as he or his successors consider Romania's autonomy to be best served by close ties with the developing countries and consider such ties to be economically advantageous, the widespread Romanian presence in the South will continue and perhaps expand, but there are no clear signs as to how long that perception will continue.

NOTES

1. Marcel Dinu, "The Developing Countries: Unity in Action," Lumea, April 7, 1979.
2. Josip Vrhovec, "The Nonaligned Movement Today Is the Most Developed Form of Democratic Pluralism in International Relations," Yugoslav Information Bulletin (May 1979): 13.
3. Nicolae Ceausescu, "Expose at the Jubilee Meeting of the Grand National Assembly, November 29, 1968," in Romania on the Way of Building Up the Multilaterally Developed Socialist Society, Nicolae Ceausescu, vol. 3 (Bucharest: Editura Politica, 1969), p. 675.
4. Ibid.
5. Nicolae Ceausescu, "Report at the National Conference of the Romanian Communist Party, July 12, 1972," in Romania on the Way of Building Up the Multilaterally Developed Socialist Society, Nicolae Ceausescu, vol. 7 (Bucharest: Editura Politica, 1973), p. 428.
6. Ibid., p. 495.
7. Ibid., p. 497.

8. Ibid. , p. 519.

9. Ibid. , p. 521.

10. Nicolae Ecobescu and Sergiu Celac, Socialist Romania in International Relations (Bucharest: Editura Politica, 1975), pp. 59-60.

11. ——— Programme of the Romanian Communist Party for the Building of the Multilaterally Developed Socialist Society and Romania's Advance Toward Communism (Bucharest, Editura Politica, 1975), p. 202.

12. Nicolae Mielcioiu, "The Nonaligned Movement," Revue Roumaine d'Etudes Internationales, no. 3 (1976): 303.

13. Nicolae Ceausescu, "Exposition at the Joint Solemn Session of the CC of RCP, the National Council of the Socialist Unity Front and the Grand National Assembly, Dedicated to the Celebration of Sixty Years Since the Creation of the Romanian Unitary Nation-State," reproduced in Lumea, December 1-7, 1978, supplement.

14. Nicolae Ceausescu, "Report of the Central Committee of the Activity of the Romanian Communist Party in the Period between the Eleventh Congress and the Twelfth Congress and the Party's Future Tasks," Romania, Documents-Events, no. 67 (November 21, 1979): 111-12.

15. "Resolution of the Twelfth Congress of the Romanian Communist Party," Romania, Documents-Events, no. 70 (November 1979): 15-16.

16. Ibid.

17. Ibid.

18. Academia "Stefan Gheorghiu," Miscarea de nealiniere (The Nonaligned Movement) (Bucharest: Editura Politica, 1978), pp. 202-4.

19. Ibid. , p. 204.

20. Ibid. , p. 205.

21. Nicolae Calina, "Romania's Relations with the Nonaligned Countries," Revue Roumaine d'Etudes Internationales, no. 2 (1979): 210.

22. Romania's treaty of friendship and cooperation with the Khmer Rouge regime, signed during Ceausescu's visit to Kampuchea in April 1978 (reproduced in Lumea, April, 1978), oriented as it was toward the implementation of the NIEO and respect for national sovereignty, may be usefully compared with the treaty of friendship and cooperation signed between the GDR and the present Vietnamese-installed regime in Phnom Penh (reproduced in Foreign Affairs Bulletin [Published by the GDR Ministry of Foreign Affairs], no. 10 [April 2, 1980]: 1-3), which affirmed that the two parties were "guided by the desire to ensure optimum international conditions for the building of socialism."

23. Scinteia, January 15, 1980.

24. Radio Free Europe, Romanian Situation Report 1 (January 29, 1980): 5.

25. Scinteia, April 27, 1980.

26. Ibid.

27. "Declaration of the States Parties to the Warsaw Treaty," Foreign Affairs Bulletin (Berlin), no. 16-17 (June 2, 1980): 126.

28. Lumea, June 13-19, 1980.

29. Scinteia, June 28, 1980.

30. Scinteia, June 18, 1980.

31. Ion Madosa, in Lumea, June 13-19, 1980.

32. For a detailed analysis of Romania's relations with and support for the Angolan movements between 1970 and 1975, see Michael Radu, "Romania's Involvement in Colonial Angola," South African Journal of African Affairs, no. 3-4 (1979).

33. Scinteia, April 19, 1980; Lumea, April 13-20, 1980.

34. Mengistu Haile Mariam visited Bucharest in December 1978, and signed a Joint Declaration with Ceausescu, reproduced in Lumea, December 8-14, 1978. Although the documents mentioned the "traditional" ties between the two countries, it also praised the Ethiopian revolution as having brought an end to "feudalism" in Ethiopia.

35. Nicolae Ceausescu, "Expose on the activity of the Party and the whole people for the elimination of the consequences of the catastrophic earthquake of 4 March, the present economic and social development of the country, the international activities of our Party and State, and the world political situation," Bucharest, 1977, p. 75. It is significant that that statement came immediately after Ceausescu's return from a trip to Ghana, Ivory Coast, Nigeria, and Mauritania.

36. "Resolution of the Twelfth Congress of the Romanian Communist Party," p. 20.

37. Nicolae Ceausescu, "Report at the Twelfth Congress," p. 133.

38. Academia "Stefan Gheorghiu, Economia Mondiala: Tipologia economiilor nationale, (The World Economy: Typology of national economies) (Bucharest: Editura Politica, 1977), p. 62.

39. Nicolae Ceausescu, "Report to the Twelfth Congress," p. 127.

40. Directia Centrală de Statistică, Anuarul Statistic al Republicii Socialiste Romania (Statistical Yearbook of the Socialist Republic of Romania), 1978 (Bucharest: Editura Politica, 1979), p. 513.

41. Ibid.

42. "Romania and World Energetics (II)," in Lumea, February 23-March 1, 1979.

43. Lumea, March 9-15, 1979.

44. Ibid.

45. Central Intelligence Agency, Communist Aid to Less Developed Countries of the Free World, 1976 (Washington, D.C.: CIA, 1976), p. 63.

46. Lumea, March 9-15, 1979.

47. Romania and the Developing Countries, no. 8 (1979): 29.

48. Ibid. , p. 38.

49. Romania and the Developing Countries, no. 10 (1979): 12, 30.

50. Scinteia, August 3, 1978.

51. Lumea, March 9-15, 1979.

52. Ibid.

53. Scinteia, June 14, 1980.

54. According to Max Linger-Goumaz, "La république de Guiné Equatoriale. Une indépendence à réfaire," Afrique Contemporaine, no. 105 (September-October, 1979): 20, Romanian, North Korean, Cuban, and East German (?) personal bodyguards of the former president Macias Nguema of Equatorial Guinea attempted to restore him to power in the aftermath of the military coup of August 1979, which deposed and ultimately executed him. Although the information cannot be verified, good relations between Bucharest and Malabo did exist and Romania was negotiating the extension of credits to Macias Nguema's regime in the spring of 1979. Scinteia, April 20, 1979, mentioned the visit to Bucharest of Nguema's deputy prime minister. After the coup, however, there was almost no reaction in Bucharest. If the information provided by Liniger-Goumaz is correct, that occasion would be the first circumstance of Romanian military involvement in the South, including the use of security personnel.

9

YUGOSLAVIA AND THE THIRD WORLD

Michael M. Milenkovitch

This chapter will examine the motives that propelled Yugoslavia to seek formation of the Nonaligned Movement, its role within the movement, and the impact of the Nonaligned Movement on bipolar and multipolar global balances of power. Special reference will be made to the movement's relations with the two superpowers—the Soviet Union and the United States—over the 20-year period.

To understand the meaning of the principle of nonalignment (especially as envisioned by the Yugoslavs) and the changing role played by the nonaligned states (especially Yugoslavia), one can construct three stages of the nonaligned model. The first stage (1961-70) focuses on the movement's struggle to ease the Cold War and maintain strict neutrality between the two blocs (Soviet and Western) while promoting active peaceful coexistence and cooperation with both blocs as well as within the Nonaligned Movement. This is the era when harmony and peace reigned within the movement. The second stage (1970-79) represents attempts to reconcile discord and contradictions of the growing Nonaligned Movement. Many member states pursue dual objectives: adherence to the principle of sovereign independence and noninterference in internal affairs of nonaligned states while promoting cooperation with two blocs; and creation of a new coalition of states within the movement (the developing South) that begins to oppose and demand concessions from the developed industrial countries (the North), especially the United States.

The third stage of the Nonaligned Movement (since Castro's Cuba took over the role of directing the movement in September 1979) shows serious weakening or even abandonment by some nonaligned states of the principle of strict respect for territorial integrity of member states, growing ideological and political tolerance of Soviet global ex-

pansionism, and increasing hostility toward the West. The nonaligned
countries of the developing South now make even greater compensatory
demands from countries of the developed North (particularly the United
States, Western Europe, and Japan). Castro's address to the U. N.
General Assembly in the fall of 1979 best illustrates this new anti-
Western policy.

The most worrisome and destabilizing development is the polarization into both neutral and more openly pro-Soviet policies within the
Nonaligned Movement. Yugoslavia's confrontation with Cuba over the
seating of a legitimate Kampuchean delegation representing the Pol
Pot government, which was dislodged following the Vietnamese-armed
occupation, ended in compromise. Neither of the rival Kampuchean
delegations was seated at the Sixth Conference of Nonaligned States in
Havana in September 1979. Genuinely neutral Burma resigned in protest from the movement because it had abandoned its fundamental
practice of respect for the territorial integrity of its members.

The second Yugoslav attempt at Havana meeting to defend the
inviolability of territorial integrity of a member nonaligned state—Afghanistan—ended in failure. The Yugoslav demand to include in the
agenda the question of Soviet aggression against nonaligned Afghanistan was sidetracked due to Castro's skillful maneuvering. Consequently
the majority of nonaligned nations condemned the Soviet occupation of
Afghanistan by convening a special session of the U. N. General Assembly in January 1980. Despite his lip service, praising Tito as an
architect of nonalignment, Castro's absence at Tito's funeral underlined his personal dislike for Tito's more severe condemnation of the
Soviet interventionist policy in Afghanistan.

Cuba uses its chairmanship of the Nonaligned Movement to promote greater economic and political confrontation with the West and
especially the United States. For example, Castro's skillful manipulation of the Cuban refugees seeking asylum in Colombia's embassy in
Havana outmaneuvered the U. S. effort to resettle the majority of Cuban refugees throughout Central and Latin America. He stopped growing anti-Communist and anti-Cuban sentiments in Latin America by
organizing and successfully implementing an illegal but nonviolent invasion of the United States and sending over 100,000 Cubans, including
a criminal contingent. By doing this, Castro defused an explosive situation in Cuba and exported potential Cuban unrest and divisiveness
to the United States. By encouraging reunification of Cuban families
and through its successful implementation Castro not only humiliated
but also bypassed the American government. By such skillful moves
he also divided monolithically anti-Communist Cuban Americans who
left Cuba in the 1960s. This illegal but successful reunification of Cuban families will have transformed thousands of anti-Castro Cubans
into greatful pro-Castro sympathizers whose good will he can mobilize

for future moves at creating possibly a new domestic Vietnam syndrome among U. S. citizens. More importantly, Castro initiated a
precedent encouraging further massive illegal invasion of the United
States by many others from the Caribbean islands. This would only
create more headaches for the United States in its dealing with the
economically and political unstable Caribbean region.

After a painful and lengthy process of healing the wounds of the
Vietnamese debacle, the emerging stability in the United States was
unacceptable to the Soviet Union or Cuba. Attempts to label the United
States as the enemy of nonaligned nations were partially successful.
Associating the United States with unpopular causes like the racist
Rhodesian regime of Ian Smith apartheid in South Africa, and "Zion-
ist" Israel were insufficient to disrupt the cohesion within the United
States. The attempt to provoke the United States attack on nonaligned
Iran following the hostage affair also failed to divide the country. Finally, Castro's launching of another internal domestic Vietnam-type
confrontation of longer duration may well have succeeded. This is the
planned and forceful introduction of large numbers of more skillful
people into recession-struck America. These new emigres are eager
to find work at any cost at the expense of the less-skilled American
blacks. A growing resistance to the introduction of Spanish as a co-
equal language by other minorities, not to speak of many native-born
English-speaking Americans, will turn U. S. attention away from the
Cuban mercenary roles in Africa and the Middle East and Soviet global
expansionism, which encompasses Afghanistan, Africa, the Middle
East, and Europe. The reintroduction of a Vietnam-type syndrome
into the U. S. political arena is the most dangerous factor, and it will
affect the domestic and foreign policies of the United States for many
years to come if it becomes successful and is not recognized in time
and neutralized.

In addition, the Nonaligned Movement is destabilized by Cuba's
increasing support of the Soviet ideological offensive against the West,
a lukewarm condemnation (or outright refusal to condemn) Vietnamese
regional or Soviet global expansionisms, and the abandonment of fundamental principles of nonalignment with either bloc. A lack of strict
respect for territorial integrity of nonaligned member states also effectively abrogates the essence of nonalignment.

APPROACHES TO ASSESSING
THE NONALIGNED MOVEMENT

A review of the final declarations at six conferences of nonaligned countries, from the Belgrade meeting of September 1961 and
through the Havana meeting of September 1979, can provide a quick

overview of the fundamental changes within the movement. For comparative purpose, this chapter will touch only briefly upon the 1961 Belgrade, 1974 Algiers, and 1979 Havana meetings of nonaligned states.

In addition to the above-mentioned drift from genuine nonalignment with either power bloc, Eastern or Western, we see the emergence of a cumbersome, almost anarchistic grouping of developing states in the South, which creates confusion more often than cooperation on the most general principles of nonalignment. This growing polarization and instability within the movement has to be watched carefully since it will probably escalate and lead to the erosion of economic and technological cooperation between developed and developing nations. It may even contribute to destabilization of peace and order in the world. These were original justifications for the establishment of the Third World as a counterforce to the Cold War confrontation between the major superpowers.

Thus, to understand Yugoslavia's role in the Nonaligned Movement and the evolution of the movement over two decades, one must examine Yugoslavia's fluctuating relations with the Soviet and the Western blocs and take into account two decades of Soviet and Western policies toward Yugoslavia, in particular, and toward the movement in general. The self-interest of big and small states plays a crucial role in diplomatic attempts at improving their individual position within a complex world afflicted with ideological, economic, cultural, religious, and technological contradictions.

Another way to assess the future direction of the Nonaligned Movement is to conceptualize two variants of the Soviet Marxist-Leninist model (Khrushchev's and Brezhnev's) in addition to three chronological variants of the nonaligned model. For Yugoslavia and the Eastern European countries a number of Marxist-Leninist variants must also be added. In the case of Yugoslavia, one has to survey the changing Yugoslav views of nonalignment within at least four Yugoslav Marxist-Leninist variants of the model,* including the post-Tito one. For the

---

*At least six Titoist variants of the Marxist-Leninist model were used in Yugoslavia since the League of Communists of Yugoslavia (the LCY) seized power in 1945.

The first postwar variant (1945-48) was a purely Stalinist variant of the Marxist-Leninist model in which Tito took the Soviet road to socialism. The second, the emerging Yugoslav variant (1949-53), was a product of Tito's defensive strategy against Stalin's and Cominform's attempt to destroy Yugoslavia for defying the Soviet Union. For the first time Tito and his aides began to do the unthinkable—they embraced freedom of thought as the natural right of any Communist

Western world one can propose three major variants: (1) containment of Soviet communism (the Cold War); (2) detente; and (3) Soviet post-detente global expansionism (Afghanistan invasion, direct and indirect intrusion in Africa, the Middle East, and Latin America).

———————————

party. This promoted the concept of national communism. Such thinking was not extended to any political opposition. Freedom of thought or national communism were not part of the original monolithic Marxist-Leninist model; nor were any of its subsequent Stalinist, Khrushchevian, or Brezhnevian variants. On the contrary, monolithism within the party and proletarian internationalism remain underlying concepts of all the Soviet Marxist-Leninist variants.

In the second postwar variant Yugoslav Communists renounced allegiance and subservience to the CPSU and Stalin. The shortlived euphoria of unlimited freedom within the Party and the withering of the Party as a power source was celebrated by Tito at the Sixth Party Congress of 1952. However, a year later, it had to be reversed following Djilas's demand for a total democratization of the LCY. Djilas had suggested the creation of two competing Communist party factions that could alternate in power.

The third postwar variant (1954-65) began with the Party purges of liberals and the silencing of Djilas. The restoration of friendly relations with the Soviet Union in 1955 was replaced by a cooling of relations following the Hungarian Revolution of 1956 and the attempt to modify workers' self-management. This also marked the solidification of the Yugoslav brand of national communism, separate roads to socialism, and a partial recentralization of the Party.

The fourth Yugoslav variant (1965-71) started with an attack upon centralistic forces within the LCY (the Rankovic purge of 1966) and ended with a return to the Titoist variety of a Leninist democratic centralism within six more or less equal republican parties which often defied the federal Party, the LCY. The creation of a sophisticated self-management system, very alien to the state-operated and directed economy of the Soviet Union, was used as the main excuse to prove the existence of fundamental internal differences between Yugoslavia and the Soviet Union; nonalignment was a way of maintaining greater Yugoslav independence from Soviet foreign policy in a legal sense. At the same time, it allowed support at a very low risk of many Soviet foreign policy moves toward the Third World, especially of the national liberation wars in former colonies.

The fifth Yugoslav variant (1971-79) heralded a more complete abandonment of freedom of thought within the Party and intolerance for excessive nationalism in various republics, especially Croatia and

The use of various Marxist-Leninist, nonaligned and Western models is necessary if one is to understand the complexities of Yugo-

---

Serbia. At the tenth congress of the LCY (June 1974) the Soviets were jubilant that Tito had forced a return to a pure Leninist democratic centralism and moderate purges of leading liberal Communists in almost all republican parties, especially the Croatian, Serbian, and Vojvodina ones. However, the disappearance of freedom of thought within the Party was balanced by the gradual introduction of some controlled freedom within the BOALs (Basic Organizations of Associated Labor)—the heart of constant changing systems of workers' self-management. To make sure that freedom was not abused by direct producers or non-Communists, Party membership was increased (one of four working people are now Party members). The LCY was reorganized, and many new basic party organizations (BAPS) were created so that the LCY could control BOALs indirectly by its members as actively participating in the self-management process of decision making.

The sixth variant (1980, a post-Tito one) was created in part by Tito as a transitional phase for a relatively orderly de-Titoization or a gradual return to a decentralized collective leadership of the Party and the country. Tito himself realized that much greater stability within Yugoslavia would be achieved by distribution of power, after his demise. Tensions among nationalities would be reduced, and a greater tolerance of their differences could become possible through decentralization of power within the Party and the economy. This would give everyone a feeling of national unity once again, last experienced when the Stalinist shadow loomed over Yugoslavia in 1952. Almost everybody in Yugoslavia would agree that the post-Tito Yugoslavia of 1980 is a better place to live than any other Eastern European country.

One must keep in mind these six Marxist-Leninist variants when viewing the Yugoslav attachment and manipulation of nonalignment. Two roles were to be fulfilled: the external one was to protect Yugoslavia against any Soviet attempt to draw it back into the Soviet bloc; the internal one was to reassure the Yugoslavs that they were a part of all three worlds—the nonaligned, Western, and Eastern one. This was achieved without sacrificing Yugoslavia's genuine independence from either of the two superpowers. During Soviet-Yugoslav disputes, Yugoslav Marxism was one of the most successful challenges to an ossified Soviet Marxism. At times of more harmonious coexistence with the Soviet Union it remained one of the most permanent irritants to Soviet Marxism. Because of fundamental ideological and structural differences with the Western parliamentary systems Yugoslav Marx-

slav ideological motivations and practical needs. It also simplifies
and allows us to distinguish irrational from rational behavior toward
nonalignment.

Here, a model is used to analyze and focus upon major policies
and principles pursued in the self-interest of a particular nation-state
with respect to other states. Finally, it should offer information explaining specific political behaviors or interactions between nation-
states and their leaders in regard to specific policies that affect them
all. Models at their best try to replicate the reality of world politics
in a microcosm; at their worst, they can create a distorted picture of
reality and increase fear and conflict instead of promoting trust and
cooperation among nation-states.

Yet, only by examining the motives of all major states and groupings, their behavior, and historical background can one discern the
aims (real and imagined) of this very amorphous Nonaligned Movement,
its fundamental strengths and weaknesses. A survey of the Nonaligned
Movement's changing global role in the game of international geopoli-
tics in economic and technical cooperation or in confrontation with developing nations will help us understand the often disguised national
self-interest of individual members and Yugoslavia.

Defining the shifting national interests of some founding members like Yugoslavia, Indonesia, India, Egypt and Ghana is of para-
mount importance if one is to strike a balance between the utopia and
reality of nonalignment. Differences and fundamental contradictory
policies multiplied as the membership increased from 25 to 92 between
1961 and 1979. The Soviet and U. S. attitudes toward the nonaligned
members also shifted in the direction of greater respect as their numbers grew.

The increase in membership was accompanied by a redefinition
of nonalignment. From the inception of the movement in 1961, Tito's
Marxist-Leninist and often pro-Soviet ideological views allowed for
the admission of Castro's Cuba into the movement. Two decades later,
Cuba has been joined by such "nonaligned" members as Vietnam, Laos,
North Korea, Afghanistan, Angola, Ethiopia, Mozambique, Southern
Yemen, and Grenada.[1] In the United Nations, all of these states sup-
ported the Soviet Union's occupation of Afghanistan as noninterference

---

ism shows a degree of hostility towards the West and the United States
in theory and practice. The Yugoslavs view the United States as another superpower, a domineering force to be checked and modified by
the Nonaligned Movement. The Yugoslavs have similar reservations
about the Soviet Union, another superpower which is even a greater
domineering threat to them than the United States.

in the internal affairs of a sovereign state. The same views were expressed with regard to Vietnam's occupation of Kampuchea.

Thus, even in a cursory examination of the Nonaligned Movement we can uncover the growing contradiction between theory (the achievement of global peace and cooperation while maintaining strict sovereignty and noninterference in affairs of nonaligned states) and practice (the pursuit of often separate national policies that often go against basic theoretical and legal postulates of the movement). This growing disparity between theory and practice seriously weakens and compromises, when it does not completely destroy, the noble aims of the so-called nonaligned nations.

YUGOSLAVIA'S MOTIVES FOR NONALIGNMENT

Yugoslav national self-interest and determination to survive as an independent state in the bipolar world were major motives in promoting active peaceful coexistence between nonaligned and bloc nations. [2] The immediate cause for the policy of nonalignment was the sudden and dramatic attack upon Yugoslavia by the Soviet Union under Stalin and its economic and political isolation following its expulsion from the Soviet bloc in 1948. Although welcoming economic and military aid from the West, Yugoslavia could not align itself with the West because of fundamental ideological outlooks. The only rational option for survival as an independent nation was active peaceful coexistence. This implied the creation of loose political and closer economic cooperation between Yugoslavia and both the Eastern and Western power blocs which are headed by the Soviet Union and the United States. This goal was accomplished, following Stalin's death, with the normalization of Yugoslav-Soviet relations when Khrushchev visited Yugoslavia in May of 1955 and Tito visited Moscow in June of 1956.

The next parallel goal of Yugoslav foreign policy was the building of an association of nonaligned nations that would likewise want to preserve their national independence and lessen the chances of outside interference in their internal affairs by the two superpowers or other excolonial powers. The common denominators that the original nonaligned members possessed were underdevelopment and the corresponding need for economic and technical aid from nations of both blocs, which was to be obtained without getting politically incorporated into either bloc. This overall goal was easier to achieve when dealing with the West and more difficult to accomplish when dealing with the Soviet bloc and especially with the Soviet Union itself.

It was agreed that the survival of nonalignment is dependent upon the prevention of a global conflict between two major superpowers and defusing of the Cold War in the aftermath of the Suez crisis and the

Hungarian Revolution of 1956. Following the Soviet starting of the 1958 and 1961 Berlin crises, Tito, Nasser, and Nehru agreed to convene the First Conference of the Nonaligned Nations in September 1961. A relatively short, eight-page declaration summarizing the views of the 25 founding members* at Belgrade was preceded by an even shorter "Statement on the Danger of War and an Appeal for Peace."

The statement made an appeal to the United States and the Soviet Union

> to suspend their recent war preparations and approaches, take no steps that would aggravate or contribute to further deteriorations in the situation, and resume negotiation for a peaceful settlement of any outstanding differences between them with due regard to the principles of the United Nations Charter and continue negotiating until both they and the

---

*Afghanistan, Algeria, Burma, Cambodia, Sri Lanka, Congo, Cuba, Cyprus, Ethiopia, Ghana, Guinea, India, Indonesia, Iraq, Lebanon, Mali, Morocco, Nepal, Saudi Arabia, Somalia, Sudan, Tunisia, United Arab Republic (Egypt and Syria), Yemen, Yugoslavia.

Countries sending observers: Bolivia, Brazil, Ecuador.

National liberation movements: the Angolan National Liberation Movement, the United National Independence Party of Northern Rhodesia, the National Democratic Party of Southern Rhodesia, the Uganda National Congress, the Ruanda-Urundi National Union, the Uganda People's Congress, the African Independence Party of Guinea and the Cape Verde Islands, the Democratic National Union of Mozambique, the Nationalist Organizations of the Portugese Colonies, the Kenya African National Union, the United Front of South Africa, the African National Congress (South Africa), the Pan-Africanist Congress, the South African Indian National Congress, the Southwest African People's Organization.

Socialist parties: Malta Labor Party, Socialist Party of Italy, United Socialist Party of France, Socialist Party of Japan, Socialist Party of Sri Lanka, Democratic Socialist Party of Japan, Socialist Party of Uruguay, Socialist Party of Chile, National People's Movement of Argentina, Venezuelan Democratic Action Party, and German Peace Union.

Trade unions: Sohyo General Trade Union Federation of Japan.

Other organizations: the World Veterans' Federation, National Committee for a Sane Nuclear Policy (U.S.), Movement for Colonial Freedom, and Provincial Assembly of Rio De Janeiro.

rest of the world achieve total disarmament and enduring peace.

3. While decisions leading to war or peace at present rest with these Great Powers, the consequences affect the entire world. [3]

Stressing that "a new order based on cooperation between nations, founded on freedom, equality and social justice for the promotion of prosperity" will be periodically interrupted by "a conflict between the old established and the new emerging nationalist forces," the declaration of the heads of state calls also for the radical elimination of "the domination of colonialism-imperialism and neo-colonialism." [4]

The fundamental principles of the Belgrade Declaration of the Nonaligned States are noninterference in internal affairs, rejection of outside imposition of social or political systems by force, and "peaceful coexistence among states with different social systems" as well as "that peoples and Governments shall refrain from any use of ideologies for the purpose of waging cold war, exercising pressure, or imposing their will." [5]

Examining specific recommendations of the declaration it becomes clear that specific interests of each participating member are promoted against those nonaligned nations with whom they are in conflict. The Arab cause is promoted by support of the Palestinian and Algerian struggle "for freedom, self-determination and independence . . . the immediate evacuation of French armed forces from the whole of Tunisian territory." [6] The policy of apartheid in South Africa, Portugese suppression in Angola, tragic events in the Congo and the United States maintenance of Guantanamo military base in Cuba are wrongs to be righted.

On the international plane the call for disarmament, the resumption of the moratorium on the testing of all nuclear weapons, and elimination of foreign military bases are stressed. The call for the immediate establishment and operation of the United Nations Capital Development Fund, fewer strings attached to the aid for developing countries, and the admission of the People's Republic of China to U. N. membership have also been emphasized. [7] A modified version of Khrushchev's call for restructuring the office of the U. N. secretary general and the revision of the U. N. charter is also included in the declaration.

Tito's speech at the Belgrade Conference of the Nonaligned States in 1961 stressed even more precisely the Yugoslav vision of nonalignment: to strengthen Yugoslavia's independence with respect to the superpowers, especially the Soviet Union, and to maintain closer ideological identification with overall goals of Soviet foreign policy in regard to disarmament. In practice, this latter meant backing Khrushchev's proposals while defending the Soviet intention of transferring to East Germany the sovereignty over East Berlin and finally supporting Khrushchev's "troika system" for the three-headed secretary of the United Nations.

To balance his pro-Soviet stand, Tito called for "the elimination of differences between the economically less developed and highly developed regions in the world," demanding that those developed countries "which are spending, today, enormous resources on armaments" aid developing nations "without any political conditions." Tito pointed out that the Common Market in Western Europe and the Council of Mutual Economic Assistance in Eastern Europe are the most discriminatory organizations toward less developed countries.

Tito condemned "aggressive intervention in Cuba"[8] without making specific reference to the United States. Tito expressed his support for Patrice Lumumba of the Congo and the Indonesian claim to West Irian. He ridiculed Western fears of peaceful coexistence with the East. He also stressed that bloc divisions are harmful to the world and that nonbloc countries are a firmer guarantee against a global war confrontation. Tito's assessment of the colonial question was ideologically correct from the Marxist-Leninist viewpoint.

The question arises as to the Yugoslav motives opposing Soviet dominance over other nations while ideologically often agreeing with some of the major thrusts of Soviet foreign policy. The answer is complex and often illusive. Yet, Tito was an old Comintern apparatchik and a seasoned revolutionary who as a statesman dealt with Churchill and Stalin. He had learned well the lesson that small nations are expendable when it comes to global confrontations between Communist and non-Communist nations and in particular between superpowers. Even in 1961 he could anticipate the conversation that took place when Brezhnev met President Johnson before the invasion of Czechoslovakia in 1968. Zdenek Mlynar, a former Czech Party official reports Brezhnev's statement: "I asked President Johnson if the American Government still fully recognizes the results of the Yalta and Potsdam Conferences. I received the reply: 'As far as Czechoslovakia and Romania are concerned, it recognizes them without reservation; in the case of Yugoslavia it would have to be discussed'."[9] Thus, in order to gain greater freedom in carrying out internal policies that might be abhorrent to the Soviet ideologues (workers' self-management, nonalignment, and so on), "it is the least costly for Yugoslavia to agree sometimes with Soviet foreign policy goals, especially if the United States and the West do not respond when verbally abused by Yugoslav propaganda."[10]

This view is confirmed also by V. Micunovic, former Yugoslav ambassador to Moscow in 1956-58 and 1969-71. The following excerpt from the Serbo-Croat version of his <u>Moscow Diary,</u> which was omitted from his recently published abridged English edition, confirm Tito's willingness to trade off with the Soviet Union. Yugoslavs, in general, supported some Soviet foreign policy moves to gain economic and other concessions. Micunovic cites a secret letter from the Presidium of the CPSU to the Party organizations in the Soviet Union and Eastern Europe which shows Tito's greater dependence on and cooperation with the Soviet Union. Micunovic notes in his entry of September 7, 1956:

> The third section deals with international relations. First, it specifically stressed Tito's demand that the Russians explain to their comrades from East Germany Yugoslavia's inability to recognize DDR immediately because of its economic interests in West Germany; this recognition is to come soon, however. Secondly, Tito officially promised the Russians to cancel the American military aid to Yugoslavia later in 1956. Thirdly, Yugoslavia agreed with the Soviet foreign policy. Fourthly, the USSR, Czechoslovakia and East Germany agreed to aid Yugoslavia in the construction of its aluminum industry. [11]

Milovan Djilas singles out some of the pitfalls to Yugoslavia favoring nonalignment over more logical cooperation with Western Europe. One unrealistic approach to nonalignment by Yugoslav foreign policy makers is "the utopian belief that a 'nonaligned ideology' can be preserved if the blame for the world's ills is evenhandedly assigned to both superpowers. Another simplistic approach is to attribute any crisis to 'superpower rivalry'."[12] What Yugoslavs refuse to or cannot see because of their ideological blinds is that the real cause of world tension does not arise from the conflict between the two superpowers or their attempt to divide the world. It is "the global expansionism of the Soviet state"[13] that is the real reason for the Soviet occupation of nonaligned Afghanistan, according to Djilas.

Thus, in part, nonalignment was the result of the most rational foreign policy choice or an option that Yugoslavia wanted to pursue. The Stalin-Tito rift of 1948 predetermined a less desirable choice— the creation of the new political-ideological alignment outside of Yugoslavia's natural geopolitical sphere. Turning only to the West would have proved Stalin's charges that Yugoslav Communists are "Western lackeys." Even more important, Yugoslav Communists were and still are genuinely opposed in part to the Western system of government. The path of nonalignment, however, offered Yugoslavian communality of mostly political-ideological interests and cooperation with other developing nations and varieties of emerging national socialisms in

Egypt, India, and Indonesia, nations which recently gained independence from various colonial powers. Yugoslavs could not and did not want to join the Western European community of nations since they were also part of the other bloc. More importantly, as a Marxist-Leninist, Tito could not or would not abandon the suppression of freedom or one party monopoly of power without abandoning the entire Communist structure itself and with it, possibly, his personal and Communist rule. Thus, the only acceptable personal option was to look toward newly emerging countries of the Third World, where similar nondemocratic tendencies existed.

By this ingenious acrobatic as well as statesmanlike act, Tito forged direct bilateral ties with the most important emerging nations and their leaders in the first half of the 1950s (Nasser, Nehru, Sukarno, Nkrumah). By maintaining closer economic ties with Western Europe and close political ties with European Social Democrats, Tito in part tied himself to the West. By joining the Balkan Pact with Greece and Turkey in 1953, Tito tied Yugoslavia indirectly to NATO. At the time of Khrushchev's "Cannossa" trip to Belgrade in May of 1955, Tito was able and willing to resume cautiously friendly governmental cooperation with the Soviet Union. Soon afterwards he reestablished ties with the other Eastern European countries.

However, Yugoslavia remained relatively more reluctant to reestablish close ideological ties with the Soviet Union. Eventually (in June 1956) it partially allowed the possibility for "consultations on the basis of equality and respect for separate roads to socialism." The Soviets and their satellites had to pay a price for this "normalization" of ideological relations. All Eastern European leaders (save Hoxha of Albania) also apologized to Tito for calling him a "traitor to communism." Tito's concessions in regard to support of Soviet foreign policy did not mean that much since ideologically he would have done it anyway. The debit for the Soviet Union was that tolerance and acceptance of Titoism destabilized the de-Stalinization policy and encouraged unrest and pressure for greater independence within the Soviet bloc.

A temporary freeze in Soviet-Yugoslav relations, which followed the suppression of the Hungarian Revolution of 1956, ended by May of 1960 when greater harmony in ideological and political views ensued between Tito's Yugoslavia and Khrushchev's Soviet Union. The 1960 Paris summit fiasco and the subsequent U.N. session confirmed this new Yugoslav-Soviet detente. The ouster of Khrushchev in 1964 and especially the Soviet invasion of Czechoslovakia in 1968 caused a serious deterioration in Soviet-Yugoslav relations. But after the nationalist unrest in Croatia in the fall of 1971 and the subsequent recentralization of power, Tito wobbled closer toward the Soviet Marxist-Leninist model. Yet, at the same time, decentralization from below was pursued through further experimentation with the concept of workers' self-management. This allowed over a million Yugoslavs to become economic emigrants and work in the West. Thus in another pragmatic move the Yugoslavs resolved the problem of large-scale unemployment under socialism.

Tito's motives to favor nonalignment served the Yugoslav self-interest well. It was weakened on the global scale after Castro's takeover of the chairmanship of the movement in 1979. The policy of active peaceful coexistence (unlike the strict neutrality of the nineteenth century) created a natural counterbalancing force to exploit conflict between two blocs, playing one bloc against the other while promoting independence for nonaligned members. The nonaligned nations were able to receive aid from both blocs at a time, play one bloc against the other while preserving greater political independence from the Soviet bloc especially.

Tito's pursuit of nonalignment also resolved some important internal difficulties: (1) preserving the suppression of freedom and the monopoly of a one-party rule, and (2) maintaining a quasi-open society where most of its citizens (with the exception of a very few political dissidents) could travel freely to the West and, by becoming economic emigrants there, relieve growing unemployment at home, learn technical skills abroad, and then send remittances from the West thus increasing Yugoslavia's holdings of convertible currencies.

THE YUGOSLAV ROLE AND IMPACT UPON THE NONALIGNED MOVEMENT

Examination of Yugoslav motives for nonalignment shows that it was the most logical choice for Communist Yugoslavia following the sudden rupture of its ties with the Soviet bloc. Unable and unwilling to join the Western world and determined to maintain the sociopolitical system forged after a bloody revolutionary struggle, nonalignment offered the best of both worlds plus greater independence for Yugoslavia and perpetuity of power for the LCY.

The first meeting of the nonaligned nations at Belgrade in 1961, including Tito's speech, set the stage for a comparative survey of Yugoslav role and impact upon the Nonaligned Movement. Another dual role of the Nonaligned Movement to promote nonalignment with two blocs is countered by policy of open support of national liberation movements. [14] Being mostly pro-Marxist, these movements reinforce the anti-Western orientation of nonalignment and frequently make the movement into a mouthpiece for Soviet foreign policy, indirectly attacking the Western world. This approach also has its rewards for the movement. After coming to power, often with the direct aid of the Soviet Union or its satellites (for example, the Vietcong, Algerian, and Angolan revolutionary fronts), the liberation movements become new members of the Nonaligned Movement, giving it a more and more Marxist slant. Thus, with or without Yugoslav aid, these movements would later create new power centers within the movement of the nonaligned and alter its character. Many of the new members learned well how to synchronize Marxist-Leninist anti-Western rhetoric with their national interest. The West is castigated more for its past sins; the Soviet Union and China are not taken to task for their suppression of the Hungarian or Tibetan revolutions.

It is also interesting to note that out of six conferences of the nonaligned states five were held in countries which at that time were more pro-Soviet than pro-Western. * The seventh conference in 1982 will be held in Baghdad, Iraq, another pro-Marxist-oriented "nonaligned" state.

There is a certain continuity in the Yugoslav role within the movement in its bilateral era (1950s), when the membership was smaller and more genuinely neutral and the last two decades (1960s and 1970s), when the loose but growing Nonaligned Movement entered the global political arena as a more demanding pressure group seeking concessions and retribution, especially from the Western developed nations. The impact of the Yugoslav leadership gradually declined in the second period. The membership is increasingly from among newly emerging countries whose national interests and problems differ from Yugoslav ones.

One of the most important Yugoslav contributions to the Nonaligned Movement has been the successful example of Yugoslav defiance of the Soviet Union and criticism of the United States. It is a useful and popular example, since most of the members are smaller states or, if larger ones like India or Indonesia, still dependent heavily upon

---

*The First Belgrade Conference of Nonaligned States in September 1961 was attended by 25 members, 3 observer countries, 15 liberation movements, and 16 organizations. The second Cairo conference of October 1964 was attended by 47 members and 10 liberation movements. The third Lusaka conference of September 1970 was attended by 54 members and 9 liberation movements. The fourth Algiers conference of September 1973 was attended by 75 members, 8 observer countries, 3 guest countries, and 20 liberation movements. The fifth Colombo conference of August 1976 was attended by 86 members, 10 observer countries, 7 liberation movements, and 13 international organizations. The sixth Havana conference of September 1979 was attended by 92 members, 13 observer countries, 8 liberation movements, and 19 international organizations.

cooperation with superpowers and other nonaligned developed nations. The Yugoslavs demonstrated successfully how a nation can straddle the fence between the East and the West and try to get most for itself while giving the least to either bloc or making concessions in matters that are least costly to its national interest.

Nasser openly acknowledged Tito's warning that Egypt must never become indebted to the Soviets too much; otherwise they would try to gain total control over that country. Of the five original major nonaligned countries—Yugoslavia, Egypt, Indonesia, India, and Ghana—all but India rejected quite sharply the Soviet Union's arrogance and meddling in their internal affairs, despite an enormous amount of Soviet aid granted to those nations. And, in the case of the Soviet occupation of Afghanistan, four of them voted in the United Nations to condemn it, while India abstained.

Another Yugoslav contribution is the lesson of how to play more daringly a policy of defiance toward developed nations at first from a position of weakness (appealing to the guilt feelings of the West for its colonial exploitation) and demanding greater technical and economic aid from the rostrums at the United Nations. In the late 1960s and 1970s, when raw material shortages emerged, a more successful approach was used. Oil and other raw material shortages were utilized to the fullest, by practicing monopolistic policies (something they condemned the colonial countries for), to weaken the West economically and politically. The approach was so appealing that even the pro-Western oil states (Iran, Saudi Arabia, Kuwait, and so on) joined the Nonaligned movement and practiced with great success the punishment of the West (and especially the United States) for its support of Israel and its past domineering economic role in world trade. Unfortunately, the end result was that nonaligned states not only weakened the West but also destabilized the less developed countries that lacked oil. At the same time this policy strengthened the much more aggressive global expanionism of the Soviet bloc.

Thanks to their growing numbers, the nonaligned states are using their own numerical strength at the United Nations and other international meetings to demand more equal and just relations between the developed and less developed states. Although militarily less threatening, an economically more paralyzing confrontation between the developed North and the developing South is taking place. Even the Soviet Union is sometimes considered a Northern power which should share some of its wealth with the developing Southern hemisphere nations.

A cursory view of Tito's speeches at the fourth (Algiers) and sixth (Havana) conferences of the nonaligned states reinforced Yusoslav policies set at the first (Belgrade) conference examined earlier. Those recommendations of Tito's influenced in part the views of nonaligned nations.

Tito's address at Algiers in 1973 noted with great satisfaction the presence of the Vietcong, Bangladesh, and Cambodian delegations. He praised the spirit of detente between the two superpowers, emphasizing that Europe's "security is inseparably linked with independence."[15] Tito condemned "the policy of force and brutal interference in the internal affairs of other nations . . . in Southeast Asia, the Middle East, in various parts of Africa and Latin America." He warned against "reactionary forces attempting to tip the balance of power . . . by instigating terrorism and by engaging in interventions and provoking local wars."[16] He did not bring up the question of the Soviet occupation of Czechoslovakia in 1968, which the Yugoslavs condemned bitterly at the time. Thus he confirmed Brezhnev's cynical statement to Czech Communists in 1968 that no one would care what happened to them after the Soviet Red Army occupied them. According to Mlynar, Brezhnev told the Czechs: "So what do you think will be done on your behalf? Nothing. There will be no war. Comrade Tito and Ceausescu will say their piece, and so will Comrade Berlinguer. Well, and what of it? You are counting on the Communist movement in Western Europe, but that won't amount to anything for 50 years."[17]

Tito continued to pursue his double policy at the Algiers conference. He only asked for the cessation of foreign (U. S.) intervention in Kampuchea, but failed to notice North Vietnamese intrusions into Laos. He supported North Korea's drive to unify both Koreas. Tito called for increased development aid for developing countries, stressing that "the nonaligned countries are not asking anyone to grant them the right to participate on an equal footing in the solution of world problems. They have acquired this right through struggle and are firmly resolved to exercise it through unity, organizational capability and action."[18]

Tito's address at the sixth Havana meeting of nonaligned states in September 1979 demonstrated the continuity of his opposition to bloc policies and foreign domination, "all forms of political and economic hegemony," and his support for "the right of each and every country to freedom, independence and autonomous development."[19] Traditional support for anticolonial movements in Africa was offered to specific countries and liberation movements (Zimbabwe, Namibia, South Africa, Patriotic Front-SWAPO-The African National Congress, the PLO, and the front line states—Angola, Botswana, Mozambique, Tanzania, and Zambia). Tito expressed his worries about "the worsening of the crisis in Southeast Asia" without mentioning Vietnam as the aggressor or Kampuchea as an aggrieved party. The traditional double treatment for branding non-Marxist aggressors by name but omitting the names of Marxist or pro-Marxist aggressors continued through the sixth summit at Havana. In all fairness to Yugoslavia, it condemned by name both Vietnam and the Soviet Union for their aggression against

Kampuchea and Afghanistan at the United Nations. But in Havana Tito went so far as to find "disturbing the conflicts arising between some nonaligned states."[20] Tito stressed the need for preserving detente and urged "the two big powers to engage not in confrontation but in negotiations."[21] The support for SALT II and its spirit was emphasized as well as the need to preserve more numerous and often feuding members of the Nonaligned Movement as the hope for a better and peaceful world.

The present complexity and diversity of the Nonaligned Movement is also discernible when one compares the eight-page final declaration from the 1961 Belgrade founding meeting with the 59-page final declaration (plus ten pages of various final resolutions) of the sixth 1979 Havana meeting of the nonaligned states. A much stronger Marxist bias prevailed in 1979 than in previous declarations. Burma withdrew from the movement in protest against the abandonment of its genuine disassociation from both blocs. While condemning by name all the Western powers for one or another transgression or association with South African apartheid policies, Israeli expansionism, the declaration does not specify Vietnamese aggression against Kampuchea or Ethiopia's against Somalia. While condemning the U. S. military bases in Puerto Rico and Cuba, there is no mention of Soviet military bases in Cuba. Support for the Helsinki Accords and the demand that Mediterranean and Indian regions be turned into zones of peace are also stressed. The military junta of nonaligned Chile is condemned; similar behavior by the Argentinian military junta is not mentioned, but the claims of Argentina for the Malvinas Islands is supported.

Tito's valiant but ultimately ineffective efforts to prevent pro-Soviet forces from gaining greater influence over the Nonaligned Movement met with partial success and partial failure. Praised for his contribution to the movement, he was unsuccessful in gaining admission of the legitimate Kampuchean delegation at the conference; Castro failed to seat the Vietnamese puppet Kampuchean government but pushed through a lengthy declaration that sounded very much like any Comintern resolutions from the Stalin era. The Yugoslav strategy of nonalignment as a defense against superpower dominance and interference in affairs of nonaligned states suffered serious setbacks as many Soviet dominated "nonaligned" states attacked successfully other non-Soviet "nonaligned" states (Vietnam vs. Cambodia, Ethiopia vs. Somalia, South Yemen vs. North Yemen, and so on). Yugoslav condemnation of the open aggression against Kampuchea failed to stop it; even more severe protests against Soviet occupation of Afghanistan in the United Nations were fruitless. In the end, Cuban manipulation of the movement up to now has prevented the nonaligned countries from even meeting to discuss that question. Brezhnev's words directed at the defiant Czech Communists of 1968 sound even more ominous now that nobody else speaks with Tito's prestige. Brezhnev certainly will pay far less heed to protests by Comrade Ceausescu and Comrade Berlinger than to objections of the late Tito.

YUGOSLAV TRADE WITH NONALIGNED COUNTRIES

While political systems or ideologies show discontinuity over time, trade, which often does not recognize ideological or political variations, is a continuous process. This is especially true if one includes normal and illicit trade as a global activity among nation-states. Trade also plays an important role behind Yugoslav maneuvering within the Nonaligned Movement. A brief review of that trade is therefore in order; it shows that Yugoslav trade with nonaligned states has increased by 300 percent between 1973 and 1978. However, this is not all that significant when compared with overall Yugoslav foreign trade indebtedness abroad.

Western Europe, particularly the Common Market countries, the Soviet Union, and particularly the Eastern European COMECON countries are Yugoslavia's major trading partners. The United States, while important, is not as vital a trade partner. The picture changes markedly when one examines Yugoslavia's credit situation in relation to foreign countries. [22] In 1978, the overall Yugoslav debt exceeded $11.3 billion. Most of these credits were extended by the West (67 percent) Of this amount, 15 percent was granted by the United States, 12 percent by Great Britain, and 22 percent by other Western European countries, with West Germany being the largest creditor. Only 16 percent of the total amount credited to Yugoslavia came from the Soviet Union and Eastern Europe. International organizations accounted for 12 percent of credits. Thus, only 5 percent of credits was obtained from OPEC countries.

A more detailed examination shows that Yugoslav trade with developing countries was not a significant factor in overall foreign trade. In 1973 it amounted to $279 million in exports and $562 million in imports. This stands in contrast to exports of $1 billion and imports of $1.3 billion in 1978, representing a growth of around 300 percent. Moreover, in recent years, Yugoslav deficit in the balance of trade with developing countries has had a tendency to decrease.

In 1978, the export and import figures for Asia, the Arab countries, Africa, and Latin America showed that most of the trade exchanges involved the Arab countries ($571 million in exports; $670 million in imports), followed by the Asian countries ($230 million in exports; $215 million in imports). Next came trade with the African developing countries ($136 million in exports; $266 million in imports). The Latin America's share was $111 million in exports; $221 million in imports.

Among the Arab countries the bulk of the trade was with Algeria, Iraq, Egypt, Libya, Morocco, and Kuwait. Iran, India, Indonesia, Burma, and Pakistan were among the remaining larger trade partners. For example, in 1978, 82 percent of all exports and 79 percent of all imports with developing countries were with the above-mentioned states. Crude oil, phosphates, and tropical fruit are major import items, with capital goods or construction projects (ports or various industrial projects) being major Yugoslav export items.

A deficit of over $200 million was incurred with Brazil, Ecuador, Cuba, Mexico, Peru, and El Salvador. A surplus resulted in exchanges with two major Latin American trading partners—Panama and Venezuela. In 1978, 70 percent of all Yugoslav exports to Latin America went to Panama and Venezuela, and 79 percent of all Latin American imports came from those two countries. The reason for the trade deficit with Latin America was due to large-scale Yugoslav imports of bananas and coffee in 1978.

It was most painful for Yugoslavia that 41.5 and 47.2 percent of its total imports from the developing countries in 1977 and 1978, respectively, represented the financing of necessary crude oil imports. Iraq, another Socialist country, is Yugoslavia's major supplier of crude oil.

The abandonment of the clearing system of payments in trade with developing countries marked a new phase, when convertible currencies and higher forms of interbank cooperation facilitate the free flow of goods between them. Closer cooperation, joint ventures, and construction activities are some of the new means of cooperation between Yugoslavia and developing nations.

The article, "Yugoslavia's Views on a New International Economic Order"[23] best illustrates the typical Yugoslav dilemma between ideological dogma and modern economic-technical realities. It has been a favored Yugoslav tenet that a widening economic gap between developed and developing countries "constitute a growing threat to world peace."[24] "Neocolonialism, technological colonialism and transnational companies" have been consistently blamed for this situation. At the same time, the Yugoslav government is reluctant to accept the fact that energy crises and inflationary price spiral are causes of severe socioeconomic dislocations in developed nations, which in turn will harm the nonaligned developed countries. Only in an oblique way do the Yugoslavs recognize that the need for solving the energy, raw materials, and food crises will not be accomplished through "a confrontation between the developed and developing countries."[25]

IN LIEU OF A CONCLUSION

Since both the Nonaligned Movement[26] and post-Tito Yugoslavia will be undergoing further radical changes in theory and practice during the 1980s, it is appropriate here to offer some observations rather than definitive conclusions. These radical changes will be more or less controlled if the forces of order in the world and individual countries prevail over those of anarchy and total self-interest. Future developments will be determined in part by the changing balance of power—from superpower dominance to a multipolar balance of power, wherein some large nations (mainly the Soviet Union and the United States) will remain dominant militarily, while others, like Japan and West Germany, will wield increasingly greater economic power. For a short period of time, more economic power and even military power will be distributed among some Third World countries rich in raw materials—especially the oil-rich states.

The ideological hostility, the differing economic-technical developments and standards of living in the "three worlds," and the geographical maze denoting the complex relationships between so-called East-West and North-South nations will make more sense if one interprets reality by means of appropriate variants of the three basic models: the Marxist-Leninist, the Western, and the nonaligned. Only by frequent comparison of the statements and actions of individual nations within the framework of the variants can one guess if the anarchical tripartite relations between the three worlds are evolving toward conflict or cooperation. Commitment to the principle of coexistence seems to be on the decline among a growing number of the Third World countries as well as among some Communist countries, such as the Soviet Union, Vietnam, and Cuba.

Thus, armed with approaches to assess the Nonaligned Movement, one can examine Yugoslavia's future motives for nonalignment. Despite the passing of Tito, the chief Yugoslav architect of nonalignment who personally created a greater global role for himself through nonalignment and who secured Yugoslav independence with respect to the Soviet Union during his long reign, nonalignment will remain one of the major Yugoslav foreign policy goals. Yugoslavia's national self-interest, its determination to remain outside of the Soviet bloc, and its pursuit of the idea of workers' self-management (an adaptation of anarchosyndicalist, Marxist humanist concepts) can best be achieved if Yugoslavia maintains its nonaligned status relative to both superpowers, continues to establish economic-technical ties with the West, and propagates modified Marxist-Leninist ideological views within the nonaligned world. In these ways Yugoslavia pleases in part both the West and the East while maintaining in its own eyes and those of the nonaligned world the status of a proud and independent country.

Serving as a role model, Yugoslavia offers each new nation in the Third World an example of how to adapt the best ideas and economic-technical approaches from abroad while maintaining many of the traditional ways of life at home and without being incorporated into the embrace of one or another foreign power. Yet, by her intolerance of dissent and her ideological orientation toward Marxism-Leninism, Yugoslavia fails to offer any clearcut solution to the issue of individual freedom.

Additional contradictions between Yugoslav theory and practice resulted in valiant efforts to merge the best from the Eastern planned economies and the Western free enterprise system. The result is the hybrid known as "market socialism." While opposing for dogmatic ideological reasons Western "transnational (multinational) corporations," Yugoslavs seem to encourage so-called joint ventures, primarily with Western free enterprises.

The idea of workers' self-management is another major Yugoslav invention that has evolved, with many changes, over three decades into a major updated version of the nineteenth-century anarcho-syndicalist approach. It was designed to curb as much as possible the role of the state and management in the running of enterprises. Workers are encouraged not only to work but also to participate in managing their factories with some real power over those managers who want to ensure that enterprises will be profitable and efficient. This particular approach to resolving a major question of Marxism—how to reduce exploitation and alienation of workers, whether in capitalist countries or in state-owned enterprises in the Soviet Union and other Socialist countries—is a genuine challenge to the system of Soviet state-capitalist monopolies. This bold and often frustrating Yugoslav experiment challenges all variants of the Soviet Marxist-Leninist model and is a major irritant to Soviet ideologues and government leaders.

On the other hand, Yugoslav rigidity on the issue of intolerance of dissent within or outside the LCY and the constitutional provision inscribing the LCY as the only guiding sociopolitical force in the nation prevents more dynamic and experimental adjustment for this multinational, unevenly developed country. To be sure, the constant shifting of power from the center to the periphery and back within the LCY and the state is a much smarter approach than anything the ossified Soviet Marxist-Leninist variants offer. Nonetheless, it discourages incentives and imagination as well as personal efforts by individuals to make the country a more prosperous and stable community.

The Yugoslav ability to shift power smoothly from the top to the bottom as shown by its "centralization and decentralization" drives—however manipulative it may seem—makes the Yugoslav variants of the Marxist-Leninist model appealing to developing countries, since one of those variants seems to be adaptable to each of those countries at a particular stage in its development. Yugoslavia offers more variants of developmental and foreign policy approaches toward the developed countries of the East and the West than all other Eastern European variants of the Marxist-Leninist model combined. Why is this so? Because over a period of almost four decades Yugoslavia encountered and in part successfully coped with the problems of the rich vs. poor (developed parts of Yugoslavia vs. developing parts), nationalist rivalries, cultural and religious conflicts, and even the problem of a one-party dictatorship or "closed society" vs. a one-and-a-half party system, or "half-open society." No other Eastern European country was allowed by the Soviet Union to experiment in this way. Hungary and Czechoslovakia were severely punished when they dared: Albania never freed itself from its own Stalinist past. Thus Yugoslavia is a bridge of a sort between the East and the West. It is also a link, albeit a weak one, between the North and the South.

Even in the domain of Marxist-Leninist ideology, Yugoslavs made giant strides. The birth of Marxist humanism, curbed by Tito after 1971, provided in theory and later in practice the fundamental criticism of dogmatic Leninist approaches to socioeconomic problems of modern mankind by incorporating indirectly some of the best ideas of Marxist thought, which had been suppressed by Lenin and Stalin because of their irrelevance to the Soviet Union at the time of the October Revolution of 1917. Although Tito suppressed the Marxist humanist practice of traditional Western approaches to theory and practice (and even purged some leading Marxist humanists and banned their journal Praxis), he incorporated the idea of workers' self-management as a consequence of the existence of a humanist movement.

One can hope that the post-Tito variant of the Marxist-Leninist model will once again encourage a renaissance of critical Marxism humanism since the collective leadership now shares the power that was concentrated in Tito's hands. The new redistribution of power from the top to Basic Party Organizations (BPOs) to control or coordinate the work of Basic Organizations of Associated Labor (BOALs) is another major decentralization effort which should infuse a Communist-controlled but nevertheless mass participatory democracy within the Yugoslav self-management system.

So despite some Marxist-Leninist ideological rigidity, an intolerance of freedom, and a one-party system, Yugoslavia offers, in contrast to other developing nations, several variants of how to cope with development. If will remain for some time a valuable, if not always the best, model. At worst, it is an alternative to outdated Soviet and rigid Eastern European models. The latter models may offer innovative approaches but are often inhibited by the fear of offending the Soviet Union.

By trading with nonaligned countries and training their students,

Yugoslavia encourages international cooperation and joint ventures on the basis of equality and respect of territorial integrity, making it more difficult for the Soviet Union to establish unequal relations with those nonaligned states. By struggling to remain independent, Yugoslavia offers an example of how to avoid being permanently embraced by the expansionistic Soviet Union. The Yugoslav way is one of many ways for the continued existence of a small, often inexperienced developing state, which, propelled by a desperate need for survival, seeks and embraces relationships with other expansionistic developed states.

Subtle but persistent conflict between Yugoslavia and the Soviet Union and its client states in the Nonaligned Movement will continue. This conflict became discernable especially during the Havana meeting. Out of the 27 speakers at the sixth conference who cited Tito, [27] none were from any of the nine Moscow client "nonaligned" states that supported the Soviet invasion of Afghanistan. * Obviously they could not quote Tito, who stated explicitly:

> We have opposed power politics and foreign interference in all form in which they manifest themselves. . . . We are also very worried by the worsening of the crisis on Southeast Asia, by the outbreak of armed conflicts and the use of force in dealing with existing disputes. This endangers the security and independence of that region and holds the threat of wider conflicts.
>
> Above all, we must reconcile outselves to the imposition of foreign will on peoples by military interventions. Such behavior is totally incompatible with the principles

---

*The growing pro-Soviet realignment of a significant number of "nonaligned" states is clear when one views how nonaligned member states voted in regard to the Soviet invasion of Afghanistan at the U. N. General Assembly session of January 14, 1980. The vote was 104 states condemning Soviet invasion; 18 abstaining; 12 absent or not voting; 18 supporting the Soviet invasion.

When one sorts out how 89 nonaligned member states voted, it is quite shocking to find that nine "nonaligned" states supported the Soviet invasion of nonaligned Afghanistan (Afghanistan, Angola, Cuba, Ethiopia, Grenada, Laos, Mozambique, South Yemen, and Vietnam); 24 nonaligned states abstained or did not vote (among them, Algeria, India, Nicaragua, Syria, North Yemen, Zambia, Libya); and 56 condemned the Soviet invasion (among them were Kampuchea, Egypt, Ghana, Indonesia, Iran, Iraq, Somalia, Tanzania, and Yugoslavia).

of the Charter of the United Nations and the policy of non-alignment. Thus, here, again, we see a way out of the crisis in the withdrawal of all foreign troops from the territories of other countries and in respect for the independence, security and peaceful development of all countries in the region. [28]

The validity of the Yugoslav model will be tested ultimately by the ability of post-Tito Yugoslavia to preserve its economic stability and remain independent from the superpowers, especially the Soviet Union. It is a difficult task to achieve in a multinational, unevenly developed, and religiously and culturally fragmented country. It is a task for a divinity in the present world seething with nationalistic and religious revivalism. But perhaps the Yugoslavs will pull it off; the prospect of being a Soviet colony is bleak for all of them.

NOTES

1. With the increase in the number of nations declaring their real or imagined adherence to Marxism, it becomes imperative to discern to what extent these nations emulate the new or old variants of the Marxist-Leninist models and how serious they are in their pursuit. To understand the basic Marxist-Leninist model one must grasp seven basic variants of the model used by Lenin's successors—Stalin, Khrushchev, and Brezhnev. This model is based on Lenin's insistence upon overcentralization and control of the Communist party from above and his well-known distaste for dissent in and out of the party. Rosa Luxemburg also prophetically forecast the harm that would befall the Party headed by a strong-willed and dogmatic dictator, and Djilas elaborated upon Luxemburg's warnings six decades later. Last but not least is the current Soviet official view of Marxism-Leninism. All the above led me to derive a framework that allows a definition of the major essential characteristics of the Marxist-Leninist model. The first Marxist-Leninist model is based upon the following major premises (Mao's and Pol Pot's are some later Eastern variants):

1. Marxist-Leninist theory and practice (as defined and modified by the CPSU or the specific Communist party or its leadership) is the basic guide for action for the Socialist government and thus would be implemented as a state policy in internal and external affairs.
2. All Communist parties must, like the CPSU, be elitist, monolithic, disciplined, conspiratorial (before the seizure of power) and remain closed or hold secret meet-

ings even after the seizure of power (where only those Party members that belong to a specific branch of the Party apparatus participate). The concepts of non-freedom—democratic centralism, self-criticism and <u>partiinost</u> govern the lives of each Party members.

3. The Communist Party (especially the top bodies and leaders) represents the 'vanguard' of the working class, of the peasantry and of the 'toiling intelligentsia,' in whose name it controls and administers the state and guides the people on the road to socialism and eventually communism.

4. The state ownership and control of industry through nationalization and central planning and more flexible ways of control over agriculture (controlled limited private land ownership, co-operative, collective and state farms) make it very difficult for anyone to either enrich themselves or escape some form of state supervision.

5. The permanent totalitarian or oligarchic rule of the CPSU over all aspects of social life precludes any organized opposition toward the Party and the state. By outlawing the private ownership of means or production, guaranteeing full employment and legalizing class divisions, the state controls not only economic independence but also social stratification or job selection, as well as the geographical distribution and domicile of each Soviet citizen. Even the freedom not to work, in jobs that the state offers to the individuals, is taken away.

6. The CPSU reign over society is the best guarantee to the workers and other working people that they, through the state ownership, will control all the means of production, and in turn will not be exploited as they were when private owners or corporations controlled the means of production.

7. The concept of the dictatorship of the proletariat, through growing centralization of power within the state apparatus (the state becomes stronger than the bourgeois state) and the democratic centralism and monolithism within the CPSU, guarantees the impossibility of take-over by any anti-socialist group.

8. Other Socialist revolutions, the Communist parties and progressive national and colonial movements directed against capitalist, imperialist or neo-colonialist forces or states must be fully supported (directly or indirectly). One may fight or co-operate with the capitalist

industrial states, but the remnants of Western imperialism and bourgeois ideology must be fought mercilessly.
The CPSU supports and demands adherence to 'proletarian internationalism'—a term that expresses its dominance or seniority over other Communist parties.

This description of the Marxist-Leninist model appeared in my
article, "Jugoslav Marxism: Retrospect and Prospect," Review (London) 2, no. 3 (1977): 247-48.
  2. The Conference of the Heads of State or Government of Non-
Aligned Countries (Belgrade: 1961), p. 252.
  3. Ibid.
  4. Ibid., p. 254.
  5. Ibid., pp. 255, 256.
  6. Ibid., pp. 257, 258.
  7. Ibid., pp. 161, 162.
  8. Ibid., p. 160.
  9. Zdenek Mlynar, "Invasion 1968," New York Times, February 5, 1980.
  10. Michael M. Milenkovitch, "Jugoslav Marxism: Retrospect
and Prospect," Review (London) 2, no. 3 (1977): 282.
  11. V. Micunovic, Moskovske Godine, 1956-1958 (Zagreb:
Liber, 1977), p. 129.
  12. M. Djilas, "Confusions About Afghanistan," New Leader,
February 25, 1980.
  13. M. Djilas, "Yugoslavia After Tito," New York Times, January 24, 1980.
  14. Z. Micic, The Movement and Policy of Nonalignment (Beograd: STP, 1979), pp. 26-27.
  15. Address by President Tito, Yugoslav Facts and Views (New
York), no. 80 (September 7, 1973): 2.
  16. Ibid., pp. 3-4.
  17. Mlynar, "Invasion 1968."
  18. Address by President Tito, p. 13.
  19. "President Tito's Speech," Socialist Thought and Practice
(Belgrade), no. 10 (October 1979): 4.
  20. Ibid., p. 12.
  21. Ibid., p. 8.
  22. "Yugoslavia's Credit Relations With Foreign Countries,"
Yugoslav Survey (Belgrade), no. 3 (August 1979): 63-74.
  23. "Yugoslavia's Views on a New International Economic Order,"
Yugoslav Survey (Belgrade), no. 3 (August 1979): 115-36.
  24. Ibid., p. 115.
  25. Ibid., p. 127.
  26. There were 96 full members listed at the sixth conference

of nonaligned states at Havana in September 1979: 93 members were sovereign states; one, Burma, withdrew from the movement. Three national liberation fronts were listed as members: Palestine Liberation Organization (PLO), Southwest African People's Organization (SWAPO), Namibia and Patriotic Front of Zimbabwe (ZANU, ZAPU). Here is the list of those countries and organizations that attended the Havana Conference as reported by Review of International Affairs (Belgrade), no. 707 (September 20, 1979): 5-10:

Member states: Afghanistan, Algeria, Angola, Argentina, Bahrein, Bangladesh, Benin, Bhutan, Botswana, Burma (resigned from the movement), Burundi, Cameroon, Cape Verde, Central African Republic, Chad, Colombia, Comoros, Congo, Cuba, Cyprus, Djibouti, Egypt, Guinea, Ethiopia, Gabon, Gambia, Ghana, Grenada, Equatorial Guinea, Guinea-Bissau, Guyana, India, Indonesia, Iran, Iraq, Ivory Coast, Jamaica, Jordan, Kampuchea (not seated at the conference), Kenya, North Korea, Kuwait, Laos, Lebanon, Lesotho, Liberia, Libya, Madagascar, Malayasia, Malawi, Maldives, Mali, Malta, Mauritania, Mauritius, Morocco, Mozambique, Nepal, Niger, Nigeria, Nicaragua, Oman, Pakistan, Panama, Peru, Qutar, Rwanda, São Tomé e Príncipe, Saudi Arabia, Senegal, Seychelles, Sierra Leone, Singapore, Somalia, Sri Lanka, Sudan, Surinam, Swaziland, Syria, Tanzania, Togo, Trinidad & Tobago, Tunisia, Uganda, United Arab Emirates, Upper Volta, Vietnam, Yemen Arab Republic, People's Democratic Republic of Yemen, Yugoslavia, Zaire, Zambia, Belize (British Honduras).

Countries sending observers: Barbados, Bolivia, Brazil, Costa Rica, Ecuador, El Salvador, Mexico, Urugay, Venezuela,

Parties and organizations sending observers: Socialist Party of Puerto Rico, African National Congress, Afro-Asian People's Solidarity Organization, Arab League, Islamic Conference, Pan African Congress of Azania, Organization of African Unity, United Nations.

Countries with guest status: Austria, Finland, Guatemala, Philippines, Portugal, Romania, Sweden, Switzerland, Spain, San Marino.

27. Yugoslav Survey (Belgrade), no. 4 (November 1979): 116.
28. Yugoslav Survey (Belgrade), no. 4 (November 1979): 124-26.

PART III
GENERAL PATTERNS OF INVOLVEMENT

10

PATTERNS OF EASTERN EUROPEAN ECONOMIC INVOLVEMENT IN THE THIRD WORLD

Roger Kanet

At the beginning of the 1980s the Eastern European members of the Council for Mutual Economic Assistance* find themselves in a precarious position in the international political and economic systems. On the one hand, in the early 1970s most of the Eastern European states introduced policies oriented toward rapid economic growth and modernization. To a substantial degree these policies succeeded, and by the middle of the decade economic growth rates in most of the Eastern European countries had risen significantly. However, along with this growth came a number of unforeseen problems with which the leadership of the CMEA states must now deal. For example, most of the CMEA states have been unable to expand exports to the international market to the degree originally envisioned in the economic development plans of the early 1970s. The result has been a growing hard currency balance-of-payments deficit which, for some countries at least, has reached serious proportions. Poland, for example, has been forced to cut back on imports from hard currency markets as a means of reducing the trade imbalance, even though this is likely to have long-term negative implications for continued economic growth. [1] A related problem has been the impact of inflationary pressures from

---

*For the purposes of the present discussion Eastern Europe includes Bulgaria, Czechoslovakia, the German Democratic Republic, Hungary, Poland, and Romania. Unless stated otherwise the terms Council for Mutual Economic Assistance (CMEA) and Warsaw Treaty Organization (WTO) also refer to the European members of the organization, minus the Soviet Union.

the world market on the economies of Eastern Europe. Throughout Eastern Europe, trade has become a much more important element of the national economy during the 1970s (see Table 10.1). By the mid-1970s exports comprised between one-fourth and one-half of total national income in the CMEA countries. At the very time that the economies of these countries have become more involved in foreign trade, prices on the world market for both raw materials and indus-

TABLE 10.1

Ratio of Exports of Eastern European CMEA Countries
to Total National Income
(percentage)

Country	1970	1976
Bulgaria	24	34
Czechoslovakia	18	26
German Democratic Republic	20	28
Hungary	29	52
Poland	16	25
Romania	18	23

Source: Oleg T. Bogomolov, "The CMEA Countries in the Changing International Economic Climate," in Partners in East-West Economic Relations: The Determinants of Choice, eds. Zbigniew M. Fallenbuchl and Carl H. McMillan (New York: Pergamon Press, 1980), p. 1; based on data collected by the Institute of Economics of the World Socialist System, USSR Academy of Sciences, Moscow.

trial products have risen extremely rapidly, with both a direct and an indirect impact on Eastern Europe. First of all, prices of imports of industrial goods from the West and of raw materials from the Third World have risen in line with increases in prices on the international market. Indirectly these price increases have had an additional impact because the Soviet Union, which continues to be the major supplier of raw materials (including petroleum) to Eastern Europe, has also raised its export prices for raw materials in line with increases on the world market.[2] For the most part, prices of exports of the products of the Eastern European states have not risen comparably, and the small European Socialist states have suffered a serious deterioration in the terms of trade.

In addition, however, the Soviets have made it clear during most of the past decade that they are unwilling or unable to continue to meet the rapidly expanding Eastern European demands for raw materials, in particular petroleum and petroleum products. Even though Soviet exports have continued to rise, the rate of increase has slowed drastically, and the Eastern Europeans have been forced to meet a growing percentage of their petroleum needs on the world market. [3]

For the Eastern European states, the developing countries of Asia, Africa, and Latin America are likely to become increasingly important economically as both a source of raw materials for the continued growth of the Socialist states' economies and a market for their industrial exports. Political factors, including support for Socialist-oriented revolution in the Third World, although still of great importance in determining their relations, are likely to become relatively less important than they have been in the past, except insofar as such revolutions are viewed as a means of assuring future access to raw materials and to markets.

THE POLITICAL ENVIRONMENT OF RELATIONS BETWEEN
EASTERN EUROPE AND THE DEVELOPING COUNTRIES

Since the 1950s the European Communist states, including the Soviet Union, have been expanding their political and economic contacts with the countries of the Third World. Generally the Eastern European states have followed the lead of the Soviet Union in the development of these contacts, although there have been indications of separate Eastern European motivations in establishing ties with the developing countries, especially in the cases of the German Democratic Republic and Romania. The leaderships of the Eastern European states share a common view with their Soviet counterparts concerning the role of the developing world in the historic struggle with the capitalist West. The mid-1950s witnessed a complete change in Soviet and Eastern European ideological pronouncements concerning the developing world. Formerly nationalist political leaders like Nehru in India, Nasser in Egypt, and Nkrumah in Ghana had been viewed as mere lackeys of Western imperialism. After Stalin's death and the major shift in Soviet attitudes represented by the trip of Khrushchev and Bulganin in Asia in 1954, it was argued that the national bourgeoisie could also play an important role in the collapse of the European colonial empires and in the development of progressive national states. [4]

The most important ideological reformulation in the mid-1950s was the development of the theory of peaceful coexistence and of the role of the developing countries as part of a worldwide "zone of peace." Initial Communist interpretations of the importance of the neutralist foreign policy of many Third World states were based on the assumption that these states would soon align themselves with the Communist world. Speaking at the Twenty-Second Congress of the CPSU in 1961, First Secretary Khrushchev stated that so-called neutralist states were not "neutral when it comes to the fundamental question of the day—the question of war and peace."[5] The failure of most Third World states to support Communist positions in international affairs led to a refinement of Communist theory as it related to the developing world. In 1960 the concept of "the state of national democracy" was introduced as a means of differentiating among Third World states and of paving the way for the gradual development of the necessary prerequisites for socialism in societies in which the proletariat was extremely weak. This new type of state was supposedly characterized by (1) the refusal to join military blocs or to permit foreign military bases on its territory; (2) a major effort to decrease Western economic influence in its economy; (3) the granting of democratic rights to progressive political parties, labor unions, and other social organizations, including the local Communists; and (4) the introduction of major social changes, especially agrarian reforms, in the interests of the people.[6]

In the first stage of the revolutionary process, local nationalists, even bourgeois nationalists, who are committed to the establishment of politically independent states throughout the developing world are seen as a progressive force and, therefore, worthy of support from the Communist states. The second stage of the struggle for liberation, which emphasizes the attempt to acquire economic independence, requires active participation of the most progressive forces in developing societies, that is, those committed to the development of scientific socialism.[7] The only means by which the developing countries can successfully achieve full economic development is by emulating the experience of the Communist states, according to the standard view of the European Communist states. As a result, the members of the CMEA have emphasized support for the expansion of those areas of the economy in Third World states that strengthen the "noncapitalist" aspects of the economy, for example, nationalization of industry and investment in the state-controlled sectors of the economy. The most important indicator of progress, however, is the foreign policy orientation of the individual Third World country. Support for positions taken by the Soviet Union and its allies are critical to the successful development of Third World states whose interests coincide objectively with those of the Socialist community.[8]

In sum, the political position of the European Communist states toward the developing world has been related primarily to the competition between capitalism and communism. Political and ideological support—as well as various forms of military assistance—have been granted overwhelmingly to those Third World states viewed as hostile to the West and/or likely to develop the foundations for future Socialist development. In addition, however, Romania and the GDR have sought to bolster their own international political positions by expanding relations with Third World countries. Romania has been interested primarily in strengthening its autonomy relative to the Soviet Union by emphasizing its position as a developing country and by expanding its ties with other developing countries. [9] An important result of this policy has been Romania's regular deviation from Soviet policy on a variety of issues related to the Third World, from the Arab-Israeli conflict and the 1977-78 war in the Horn of Africa to the question of the New International Economic Order.

The German Democratic Republic, on the other hand, has been especially concerned with establishing and strengthening its place as a recognized sovereign state independent from the Federal Republic. While this motive clearly played a more important role prior to East German recognition by the West in the early 1970s, it continues to influence GDR policies in the Third World where, after Cuba, it has become the most active Communist supporter of recent Soviet activities.[10]

Although economic factors have become more important for Eastern Europe in recent years, as we shall see below, political considerations continue to play a significant role in the expansion of those relations. Throughout the past 30 years the European members of the CMEA, with the important exception of Romania, have adopted a position on virtually every major and minor event or development in the Third World that parallels almost exactly that of the Soviet Union. [11] The area in which the coincidence of Soviet and East European policies has been most evident in recent years has been in their relations with the national liberation movements and revolutionary governments in sub-Saharan Africa. As they did in the early 1960s in Ghana, Guinea, and Mali, Eastern European governments have seemingly coordinated their political support and military assistance programs in a number of countries with those of the Soviet Union. In Mozambique, for example, Hungary has been supplying military assistance and training officers of the Mozambique military, while Romania has reportedly agreed to assist in the training of Mozambique's military forces in the use of Soviet weapons. [12] This form of military cooperation between the Soviet Union and its Eastern European allies can be traced back to 1947-48, when Czechoslovakia, with the support and encouragement of the Soviet Union, provided military equipment and training to the Israelis in order to support what the Soviets then viewed as the major challenge to Western influence in the Middle East. [13] Again in the mid-1950s, after a shift in Soviet Middle Eastern policy, Czechoslovakia functioned as a Soviet surrogate when it acted as the intermediary for the initial major shipment of Soviet military equipment to a developing country—this time Egypt. [14] More recently the most active of the Eastern Euro-

TABLE 10. 2

Arms Sales and Deliveries of the Soviet Union and
Eastern Europe to Non-Communist Developing Countries
(millions of current U. S. dollars)

	Agreements		Deliveries	
Year	Soviet Union	Eastern Europe	Soviet Union	Eastern Europe
Total	29,655	3,255	25,310	2,605
1955–68	5,495	810	4,585	745
1969	360	125	450	80
1970	1,150	50	995	80
1971	1,590	120	865	120
1972	1,635	150	1,215	70
1973	2,810	130	3,130	120
1974	4,225	530	2,310	165
1975	2,035	215	1,845	255
1976	3,375	215	2,575	315
1977	5,215	450	3,515	325
1978	1,765	465	3,825	325

Note: Significantly lower figures are given in Henrik Bischof,
"Militärbeziehungen zwischen den kommunistischen Staaten und der
Dritten Welt," Monatsberichte: Entwicklungspolitische Aktivitäten
kommunistischer Länder (Forschungsinstitut der Friedrich-Ebert-
Stiftung) (June 1977): 407. Bischof's figures do provide a breakdown
for Eastern Europe.

Source: Central Intelligence Agency, National Foreign Assessment Center, Communist Aid Activities in Non-Communist Less Developed Countries 1978: A Research Paper, ER 79-10412U, September 1979, p. 2.

pean states in the military field has been the GDR. It was estimated
in early 1979 that between 3,000 and 4,500 East German instructors
in police and security operations were working in various countries
in Africa and the Middle East. [15] In all of the cases of Eastern European military involvement in the developing world, there is clear indication of cooperation with one another and with the Soviet Union.

While military assistance and sales have comprised an increasingly important part of Soviet relations with the developing countries,

Armaments Agreements, 1955-76
(millions of current U.S. dollars)

Year	Czechoslovakia	German Democratic Republic	Poland	Total
1955	250. 0	—	—	250. 0
1956	95. 0	—	—	95. 0
1957	200. 0	—	15. 0	215. 0
1959	160. 0	—	—	160. 0
1967	19. 4	40. 0	—	59. 4
1972	10. 0	0. 5	—	10. 5
1973	75. 0	—	—	75. 0
Total 1955-76	809. 4	40. 5	15. 0	864. 9

Note: According to Bischof, military aid data for other Eastern European states to developing countries is not available.

they have remained relatively less important for Eastern Europe. Soviet deliveries of military equipment rose from an average of less than $400 million annually in the 1960s to more than $3,200 million since 1972; those of Eastern Europe increased from about $60 million to slightly more than $300 million during the same period (see Table 10.2). Soviet military assistance and arms trade have been associated with attempts to gain a presence in various Third World countries and regions—in particular such strategically important areas as the Eastern Mediterranean, the Horn of Africa, and Southern Africa. While Eastern European military assistance has been, in part at least, ancillary to that of the Soviet Union, it has also been motivated increasingly by financial considerations—as has that of the Soviet Union itself—since military equipment supplied to some developing countries is paid for in hard currency.

During the course of the past 25 years the political and military relations of the Eastern European states with the Third World have grown immensely. Eastern European states now maintain diplomatic relations with the vast majority of the countries of the developing world. To a considerable degree these relations are closely coordinated with those of the Soviet Union. Only the Romanians have deviated in their policies from those of the Soviets, and even they appear to have coordinated certain of their activities with their Soviet allies.

ECONOMIC RELATIONS BETWEEN EASTERN EUROPE
AND THE DEVELOPING COUNTRIES

Trade relations between the European Communist states and the developing countries have expanded more than nine times during the course of the past two decades. Between 1960 and 1977, for example, total trade turnover between the two groups of countries rose from almost $1 billion to more than $9 billion in current prices. However, as a percentage of the trade of the European Communist states, trade with the developing world has increased only slightly. While trade with the developing countries comprised 6.5 percent of total Eastern European trade in 1960, by 1970 it had fallen to 6.2 percent. In recent years it has risen to 7.9 and 8.1 percent in 1976 and 1977, respectively (see Table 10.3). More careful perusal of trade statistics, however, shows substantial differences in the relative importance of trade with developing countries for individual Eastern European states. While trade with developing countries made up 18.5 percent of total Romanian trade in 1977, for the GDR it comprised less than 5 percent of total trade.

In spite of claims by Communist states that they offer the developing countries markets for the products of their newly developed industries on terms considerably more favorable than those available in the West, trade between the two groups of countries looks very much like that between the West and the Third World. Exports from Eastern Europe consist primarily of industrial products, while imports continue to be dominated by traditional agricultural and raw materials products.[16] In 1973, for example, only 18.5 percent of the CMEA countries' imports consisted of manufactured goods, while such products comprised 24 percent of the imports of the Western industrial states from the developing countries.[17]

The growth of trade between the European Communist states and the developing world has been directly related to developments in the domestic economies of the Communist states and in trade relations with their other major trading partners. The fact that virtually all of the Eastern European countries are heavily dependent on imports of raw materials—especially energy—has meant that they have been interested in establishing stable, long-term agreements for the supply of petroleum and other raw materials with the developing countries.[18] For example, prior to 1978 Poland's trade with Iraq consisted almost entirely of exports. In 1978, for the first time, Polish imports from Iraq, which consisted almost entirely of oil, exceeded imports.[19] Before the overthrow of the Shah in Iran in early 1979, most of the Eastern European countries had signed agreements with Iran calling for expanded gas and oil imports. Kuwait, Libya, Mexico, and even Saudi Arabia have become the suppliers of increasing amounts of energy imports for the Eastern European countries.[20] This search for new supplies of petroleum and natural gas is the result of a twofold development during the past decade. First of all, the modernization drive in the domestic economies of all of the Communist states has resulted in a rapidly expanding domestic demand for new supplies of energy, especially for their expanding petrochemical industries. At the same time the Soviets have indicated that they cannot continue to meet these growing energy demands of their Eastern European "partners," particularly if they are to be able to continue exporting considerable amounts of oil and gas to Western Europe in order to cover the costs of Western industrial goods and technology.

Given their chronic lack of convertible currency, most of the Communist states have been attempting to cover the costs of imports of petroleum and other industrial raw materials through barter agreements. [21] Poland, for example, is presently building 20 major industrial projects in Iraq employing approximately 2,500 workers and specialists. In return Iraq will supply Poland with oil exports in the coming years. [22] This is a pattern that has been quite common in the trade between the European Communist states and many of the developing countries. For most of the Communist states trade relations with the developing countries have been conducted on the basis of bilateral clearing agreements, a form of barter in which currency is employed merely as an accounting device. In recent years, however, there has been a clear trend toward replacing such clearing agreements with agreements stipulating payment by multilateral clearing procedures, including the use of convertible currencies. [23]

Although economic and technical assistance has long comprised an important element of Eastern European activities in the developing countries (see Table 10.4), it has apparently become more closely tied to the economic concerns of the donor countries recently than was true in the past. Not only has Eastern European assistance been increasingly motivated by the desire to ensure future supplies of raw materials, it has also been closely coordinated with efforts to build up markets for Eastern European industrial and agricultural equipment in the Third World. This aspect of Eastern European economic assistance has been especially visible in Latin America, where approximately 17 percent of total Eastern European credits have been committed (see Table 10.5). Virtually all of these credits have been supplied in order to cover the export of various types of Eastern European industrial products to Latin America. It is important to recognize, however, the extremely limited nature of the economic assistance of the European Communist states. Not only has the total assistance been far less than that granted by Western industrial states, but aid as a percentage of GNP has also been far lower (.03 percent of GNP as compared with about .33 percent) (see Table 10.6).

The distribution of Eastern European economic assistance by re-

TABLE 10.3

Trade of Eastern European States with the Non-Communist Developing Countries (millions of current U. S. dollars)

Country	1960 Export	1960 Import	1965 Export	1965 Import	1970 Export	1970 Import	1975 Export	1975 Import	1976 Export	1976 Import	1977 Export	1977 Import
Bulgaria												
Total trade	572	633	1,176	1,178	2,004	1,831	4,691	5,408	5,382	5,636	6,351	6,393
With LDCs	20	15	56	41	130	86	504	222	496	250	662	389
% of total trade	3.5	2.4	4.7	3.5	6.5	4.7	10.7	4.1	9.2	4.4	10.4	4.5
Czechoslovakia												
Total trade	1,930	1,816	2,686	2,673	3,792	3,695	9,349	9,077	9,037	9,706	10,308	11,187
With LDCs	213	178	264	209	342	226	719	522	682	507	841	732
% of total trade	11.0	9.9	9.8	7.8	9.0	6.1	8.6	5.8	7.5	5.2	8.2	6.5
German Democratic Republic												
Total trade	2,208	2,195	3,070	2,810	4,581	4,847	10,088	11,290	11,361	13,196	12,025	14,334
With LDCs	93	96	139	125	192	189	444	497	509	620	565	717
% of total trade	4.2	4.4	4.5	4.4	4.2	3.9	4.4	4.4	4.4	4.7	4.7	5.0
Hungary												
Total trade	874	976	1,255	1,331	1,605	2,506	6,084	7,176	4,922*	5,528*	5,822	6,522
With LDCs	58	58	107	113	137	177	363	498	391*	523*	501	647
% of total trade	6.6	5.9	7.1	7.5	5.9	7.1	6.0	6.9	8.0	9.5	8.6	9.9

Poland												
Total trade	1,326	1,495	2,228	2,340	3,548	3,608	10,282	12,537	11,017	13,868	12,265	14,616
With LDCs	100	102	180	219	275	204	879	610	914	588	1,041	699
% of total trade	7.5	6.8	8.1	9.4	7.7	5.7	8.6	4.9	8.4	4.2	8.5	4.8
Romania												
Total trade	717	648	1,102	1,077	1,851	1,960	5,341	5,342	6,138	6,095	7,021	7,018
With LDCs	41	23	72	59	185	129	1,031	695	1,191	1,122	1,488	1,109
% of total trade	5.7	3.5	6.5	5.5	10.0	6.6	19.3	13.0	19.4	18.4	21.2	15.8
Total Eastern Europe												
Total trade	7,625	7,761	11,773	11,598	18,093	18,447	44,836	30,830	47,857	54,019	33,791	60,070
With LDCs	525	470	817	767	1,261	1,013	3,940	3,043	4,182	3,610	5,065	4,192
% of total trade	6.9	6.1	6.9	6.6	7.0	5.5	8.8	6.0	8.7	6.7	9.4	7.0

*In 1976 Hungary changed from foreign exchange forints to a new commercial rate.

Sources: Statisticheski godishnik na Narodna Republika Bŭlgariya, Statistická ročenka ČSSR, Statistisches Jahrbuch der Deutschen Demokratischen Republik, and Statisztikai Evkonyv, as reported in Aurel Bereznai, "Hungary's Presence in Black Africa," Radio Free Europe Research, RAD Background Report (Hungary), no. 75, (April 2, 1979): 7–8, 11; Rocznik statystyczny handlu zagranicznego, and Anuarul Statistic al Republici Socialiste Romania for the appropriate years. Exchange rates used in calculating dollar value of trade have been taken from Vienna Institute for Comparative Economic Studies, ed. , CMEA Data 1979, (Vienna: Vienna Institute for Comparative Economic Studies 1979), p. 307.

TABLE 10.4

Bilateral Commitments of Capital by Eastern European States to
Non-Communist Developing Countries

Donor Country	1954-67	1968	1969	1970	1971	1972	1973	1974	1975	1976	1977*	1954-77	1978
Bulgaria	102	35	30	82	55	40	43	117	17	8		529	x
Czechoslovakia	929	200	37	55	14	100	303	108	168	1,064	57	3,035	x
German Democratic Republic	542	8	134	125	25	23		46	277	105	77	1,362	x
Hungary	314	40	21	79	42	45	148	110	151	20	103	1,073	x
Poland	479	20	30	25	65	100	247	107	54	52	100	1,279	x
Romania	196	45	132	10	141	385	36	752	465	261	275	2,698	x
Total	2,562	348	384	376	342	693	777	1,240	1,132	1,510	612	9,976	
Total commitments, CIA estimates	2,165	220	403	196	484	915	605	914	511	773	397	7,584	1,502
Total deliveries, CIA estimates	675	125	105	145	190	170	220	230	245	370	460	2,940	365

*Preliminary U. N. figures.

Sources: United Nations, Department of International Economic and Social Affairs, Statistical Office, Statistical Yearbook (New York: United Nations, for the appropriate years); for CIA figures, Central Intelligence Agency, National Foreign Assessment Center, Communist Aid Activities in Non-Communist Less Developed Countries, 1978: A Research Paper, ER 79-10412U, September 1979, p. 11. Note that, although U. N. and CIA figures do not agree, the trends are similar.

314

gion illustrates an important difference in this assistance from that provided by the Soviet Union. While the Soviets have concentrated their aid on a relatively small number of countries in the Middle East, North Africa, and South Asia (almost 87 percent of their assistance from 1954 to 1978), Eastern European aid has been much more evenly distributed by both region and recipient country. Over the period 1954-78 the Middle East has received 41 percent of Eastern European aid commitments, Latin America 17 percent, sub-Saharan Africa 16 percent, and North Africa 10 percent.

There has been a very visible shift in the patterns of economic assistance granted by Eastern European states during the 1970s. Romania, for example, has replaced Czechoslovakia as the primary donor, while the GDR has fallen from second to fifth place on the list of Eastern European countries.[24] The growth in Romanian commitments of aid to Third World states is clearly related to the attempts by the Romanian leadership to strengthen its ties with developing countries, while the substantial reduction of East German assistance in recent years, at least in relative terms, has resulted from the significant growth in the cost of military support provided by the GDR.

Terms for Eastern European economic assistance have generally been quite favorable when compared with terms for commercial loans on the world market. Interest rates have been in the area of 2.5 to 3.0 percent, and repayment periods have ranged from 8 to 12 years.[25] However, it must also be noted that all of this assistance is provided in the form of credits to be used in the acquisition of goods produced in the donor country. When compared with terms provided by Western aid donors, which often include repayment periods of 25 to 40 years, Eastern European assistance does not appear nearly so generous. In addition, a number of Western aid donors have cancelled the debts of developing countries, and, besides providing long-term loans, Western states have distributed a substantial amount of assistance in the form of nonrepayable grants. Grants have played a very small role in the assistance of the CMEA member states and made up less than 1 percent of total aid through 1976.[26]

An important element of Eastern European assistance to developing countries has been the provision of economic advisers and technicians (see Table 10.7). Initially technical services were provided as part of the economic assistance program of the European Communist states. In recent years, however, a growing percentage of Eastern European technicians has been paid in hard currency for services unrelated to economic assistance projects. Of approximately 44,000 Eastern Europeans working abroad in 1978, almost half were in Libya and an additional 10,000 were in Algeria, Syria, and other Middle Eastern countries.[27] While the number of Eastern European technicians has risen, the number of technical personnel from the developing world

TABLE 10.5

Soviet and Eastern European Credits and Grants Extended
to Non-Communist Developing Countries
(millions of current U.S. dollars)

Country	1954-1978		1977		1978	
	Soviet Union	Eastern Europe	Soviet Union	Eastern Europe	Soviet Union	Eastern Europe
Total	17,088	9,086	402	397	3,707	1,502
Africa	3,989 (23.3)	2,350 (25.9)	31 (7.7)	154 (38.8)	2,010 (54.2)	627 (41.7)
North Africa	2,918 (17.1)	934 (10.3)	— (—)	35 (8.8)	2,000	110 (7.3)
Algeria	716	524	—	—	—	—
Mauritania	8	10	—	—	—	—
Morocco	2,098	170	—	—	2,000	89
Tunisia	96	210	—	35	—	—
Other	—	20	—	—	—	20
Sub-Saharan Africa	1,071 (6.3)	1,416 (15.6)	31 (7.7)	119 (30.0)	11 (0.3)	517 (34.4)
Angola	17	88	6	N.A.	1	76
Benin	5	N.A.	—	—	—	—
Cameroon	8	—	—	—	—	—
Cape Verde	3	1	—	—	3	—
Central African Empire	3	—	—	—	—	—
Chad	5	—	—	—	—	—

Congo	28	60	—	3	—	—
Equatorial Guinea	1	—	—	—	ng.	—
Ethiopia	105	95	—	23	—	45
Gabon	—	2	1	—	—	2
Ghana	94	105	1	—	—	—
Guinea	212	110	—	—	—	—
Guinea-Bissau	11	N.A.	—	—	6	—
Kenya	48	—	—	—	1	ng.
Madagascar	20	ng.	—	—	—	—
Mali	90	23	—	—	—	—
Mauritius	5	—	5	—	—	2
Mozambique	5	17	—	12	—	N.A.
Niger	2	—	—	—	—	—
Nigeria	7	80	—	—	—	—
Rwanda	1	—	—	—	—	—
Senegal	8	35	ng.	—	—	—
Sierra Leone	28	—	—	ng.	—	—
Somalia	164	6	—	62	—	24
Sudan	65	240	18	—	—	3
Tanzania	38	23	—	—	—	—
Uganda	16	—	—	—	ng.	—
Upper Volta	6	—	—	—	—	—
Zambia	9	62	—	—	—	12
Other	67	469	—	19	—	352

(continued)

317

Table 10.5, (continued)

Country	1954–1978		1977		1978	
	Soviet Union	Eastern Europe	Soviet Union	Eastern Europe	Soviet Union	Eastern Europe
East Asia	261 (1.5)	552 (6.1)	— (—)	— (—)	— (—)	170 (11.3)
Burma	16	173	—	—	—	140
Cambodia	25	17	—	—	—	—
Indonesia	214	292	—	—	—	—
Laos	6	4	—	—	—	—
Philippines	—	66	—	—	—	30
Latin America	964 (5.6)	1,500 (16.5)	30 (7.5)	90 (22.7)	15 (0.4)	244 (16.2)
Argentina	220	204	—	—	—	—
Bolivia	69	52	—	15	—	—
Brazil	88	621	—	—	—	200
Chile	238	145	—	—	—	—
Colombia	211	81	—	—	—	10
Costa Rica	15	12	—	10	—	—
Ecuador	n.g.	19	—	—	—	—
Guyana	N.A.	30	N.A.	20	—	—
Jamaica	30	36	30	8	—	28
Mexico	N.A.	35	—	35	—	—
Peru	25	216	—	1	—	—
Uruguay	52	31	—	—	—	—
Venezuela	N.A.	10	—	—	—	—
Other	16	17	—	1	15	6

Middle East	6,918 (40.5)	3,712 (40.9)	(—)	148 (37.3)	1,399 (37.7)	441 (29.4)
Cyprus	—	5	—	—	—	—
Egypt	1,440	890	—	95	—	—
Greece	8	N.A.	—	—	—	—
Iran	1,165	686	—	—	—	—
Iraq	705	493	—	50	—	—
Jordan	26	N.A.	—	—	—	—
Lebanon	—	9	—	—	—	—
North Yemen	143	13	—	3	38	—
South Yemen	204	66	—	—	90	6
Syria	768	954	—	—	1,200	150
Turkey	2,380	396	—	—	71	85
Other	79	200	—	—	—	200
South Asia	4,956 (29.0)	872 (9.6)	341 (84.8)	6 (1.5)	283 (7.6)	20 (1.3)
Afghanistan	1,263	39	—	—	—	—
Bangladesh	304	159	—	—	—	—
India	2,282	455	340	—	—	—
Nepal	30	—	1	—	—	—
Pakistan	921	126	—	6	225	—
Sri Lanka	158	93	—	—	60	20

Notes: Components may not add to totals because of rounding. Dashes indicate no data available. Figures in parentheses indicate percentages.

Source: Central Intelligence Agency, National Foreign Assessment Center. Communist Aid Activities in Non-Communist Less Developed Countries 1978: A Research Paper, ER 79-10412U, September 1979, pp. 7-10.

TABLE 10. 6

Net Development Assistance Dispersed, by Groups of Countries

Donor Group or Country	Millions of U. S. Dollars			Assistance as Percentage of GNP		
	1973	1977	1978	1973	1977	1978
Western industrial countries	9. 40	14. 70	19. 90	0. 03	0. 31	0. 35
OPEC countries	1. 30	5. 90	3. 70	1. 41	1. 96	1. 11
Eastern Europe	0. 22	0. 20	0. 28	0. 05	0. 04	0. 05
Soviet Union	0. 29	0. 31	0. 30	0. 03	0. 03	0. 03

Note: Figures are based on net dispersal of development assistance, which is determined by subtracting repayments on past development aid from current deliveries.

Source: Development Cooperation: Effects and Policies of the Members of the DAC: 1979 Review (Paris: OECD, 1979).

receiving training in Eastern Europe has fallen. By 1978 only 3, 300 technicians were resident in the Soviet Union and Eastern Europe—down from 4, 380 four years earlier (see Table 10. 8).

Another important aspect of long-term development assistance provided by both the Soviet Union and the Eastern European countries has been the education of substantial numbers of academic students from the developing countries. The numbers of such students have risen consistently, and by 1978 more than 18, 000 were studying in Eastern Europe—up from about 9, 000 in 1970 (see Table 10. 9). An interesting element of this program has been the focus on sub-Saharan Africa. Since the inception of the academic training program in the late 1950s and early 1960s, close to 40 percent of all students in Eastern Europe have come from Black Africa, even though less than 16 percent of total economic assistance has been committed to that region.

Eastern European academic and technical training programs for students from the Third World have had two major purposes. First, they help to provide the skilled personnel needed to modernize the economies of countries receiving economic assistance and to staff the projects and programs established with Eastern European aid. In this respect they represent an important component of the overall Eastern European aid programs. In addition, however, the academic training program in particular is geared to prepare a future elite that, at a minimum, is favorably disposed toward the European Communist states. [28]

TABLE 10.7

Soviet, Eastern European, and Cuban Economic Technicians Working in Non-Communist Developing Countries

	1970		1975		1977		1978	
	Soviet Union	Eastern Europe	Soviet Union	Eastern Europe	Soviet Union and Eastern Europe	Cuba	Soviet Union and Eastern Europe	Cuba
Total	10,600	5,300	17,785	13,915	58,755	6,575	72,655	12,525
Africa	4,010	3,150	5,930	10,290	34,390	5,900	43,805	11,420
North Africa	—	—	—	—	21,850	15	36,165	450
Sub-Saharan Africa	—	—	—	—	12,540	5,885	7,640	8,500
East Asia	100	60	25	30	125	0	85	0
Latin America	35	140	330	225	830	335	700	190
Middle East	6,455	1,950	8,375	3,370	20,010	330	23,890	915
South Asia					3,475	0	4,145	0

Note: Dashes indicate no data available.

Sources: Central Intelligence Agency, National Foreign Assessment Center, Communist Aid to Less Developed Countries of the Free World, 1975, ER 76-10372U, July 1976, p. 8; idem, Communist Aid to Less Developed Countries of the Free World, 1977, ER 78-10478U, November 1978, p. 9; idem, Communist Aid Activities in Non-Communist Less Developed Countries, 1978, ER 79-10412U, 1978, pp. 14-15.

TABLE 10.8

Technical Personnel from Developing Countries Receiving
Training in the Soviet Union and Eastern Europe

Year	Soviet Union	Eastern Europe	Soviet Union and Eastern Europe Combined
1965	—	—	2,000+
1970	1,020	530	—
1971	1,310	1,435	—
1972	1,355	975	—
1973	—	—	3,715
1974	—	—	4,380
1975	—	—	—
1976	4,250	—	—
1977	—	—	3,200
1978	—	—	3,300
Total 1954-78	—	—	48,000+

Note: Dashes indicate no data available.
Sources: Through 1974, annual publications of the Bureau of Intelligence and Research, U.S. Department of State, entitled Communist States and Developing Countries: Aid and Trade in. For 1975
through 1978, see Central Intelligence Agency, National Foreign Assessment Center, Communist Aid to Less Developed Countries of the
Free World, 1975, ER 76-10372U, July 1976; idem, Communist Aid
to Less Developed Countries of the Free World, 1977, ER-10478U,
November 1978; idem, Communist Aid Activities in Non-Communist
Less Developed Countries, 1978, ER 79-10412U.

In recent years a new form of economic cooperation has evolved
in the relations between the Eastern European states and their Third
World economic partners. During the 1970s, joint ventures were established in which the Eastern European state provided capital, equipment, and technical expertise, while the host country provided labor
and raw materials. [29] Romania is already involved in 30 such joint
ventures, 20 of which are in sub-Saharan Africa. These joint ventures
now account for 85 percent of Romania's contracts with developing
countries. [30] Other Eastern European countries are also involved in
the creation of joint ventures in the Third World, but on a much smaller scale than Romania. A noted Polish economist has referred to Pol-

TABLE 10.9

Academic Students from Developing Countries Being Trained in Communist Countries

Country of Origin	All Communist Countries			Soviet Union 1978	Eastern Europe 1978	China 1978
	1970[a]	1975[b]	1977[c]			
Total	21,415	27,275	40,345	26,445	18,560	260
Africa	10,990	14,895	20,780	13,635	9,755	160
North Africa	2,115	2,370	2,965	2,035	1,520	20
Sub-Saharan Africa	8,875	12,525	17,815	11,600	8,235	140
East Asia	650	335	20	25	10	0
Latin America	2,425	2,940	4,445	2,760	1,890	0
Middle East	5,770	6,270	11,320	6,615	5,525	15
South Asia	1,580	2,825	3,780	3,400	1,375	80

[a]Approximately 12,500 of these students were in the Soviet Union and the remainder in Eastern Europe.
[b]Approximately two-thirds of these students were in the Soviet Union and most of the remainder in Eastern Europe.
[c]More than 60 percent of the students were in the Soviet Union and most of the remainder in Eastern Europe.

Sources: For 1970 data, U.S. Department of State, Bureau of Intelligence and Research, Communist States and Developing Countries: Aid and Trade in 1970, p. 13. For the 1975–79 data, see Central Intelligence Agency, National Foreign Assessment Center, Communist Aid to Less Developed Countries of the Free World, 1975, ER 76–10372U, July 1976; idem, Communist Aid to Less Developed Countries of the Free World, 1977, ER 78–10478U, November 1978; idem, Communist Aid Activities in Non-Communist Less Developed Countries, 1978, ER 79–10412U.

ish achievements in this area as "rather modest," while a Hungarian research team has noted that "joint ventures set up with Hungarian participation have as yet had only a modest influence on the economies of the developing countries concerned."[31] Such projects provide a number of potential benefits to the Eastern European states. First of all, CMEA members are able to participate in such ventures with relatively lowly paid experts and with machinery and equipment that are often not competitive on the international market. In return they are able to acquire raw materials and, in some cases, gain indirect entry into the Western European market by "disguising their goods as Third World." This permits the products of the joint ventures to enter the European Community under the terms of the Lomé Convention.

Even though there has been relatively little effort to date to coordinate the economic relations of the individual European CMEA members with the developing world—as has clearly occurred in the military and political spheres—there are recent indications that the European Communist states plan to coordinate some of their economic activities in the developing countries in the future. Czechoslovak government officials announced in spring 1979 that the members of the CMEA envisage the joint supplying of complete industrial plants to Third World countries as a "new step" in economic cooperation. The primary purpose of this type of cooperation will be to pay for increased imports of fuel, energy, and raw materials from the developing countries.[32] The success of such a cooperative program will depend not only on the ability of the Communist states to compete effectively with Western suppliers of modern industrial equipment but also on the continued willingness of developing countries to enter into what are still essentially barter arrangements. Unless the Eastern Europeans are able to provide goods and materials competitive with those available from the West, it is likely that they will have to provide "commercial packages" that cover both exports and the provision of technical assistance.

An additional question concerns the likelihood that Eastern European investments in aid will pay off in future supplies of raw materials. The developing countries that are likely to be the most receptive to barter-type arrangements are the very ones that are the least developed and the least stable politically.[33] It is conceivable that the Eastern Europeans will find it difficult to continue to negotiate such agreements with those countries in the Third World which command the resources that they are seeking.

Finally, the Eastern Europeans, along with their Soviet allies, are learning that representatives of developing countries are unwilling to differentiate between capitalist and Socialist developed countries when making their demands for the establishment of a new world economic order. Although the Socialist countries have been willing to support, in principle, many of the demands of the developing world, they have refused to commit themselves to guaranteed prices for raw materials or to specific amounts of economic assistance.[34] The Eastern Europeans have "opposed some incorrect formulations, as for example those included in the recommendations of the Group of 77, and the untenable attempts to combine the capitalist industrial states and the socialist countries into a group of 'developed' states."[35] Only the Romanians, who have viewed themselves as part of the developing world and have, in fact, participated in the drafting of the various demands of the developing countries, has not spoken out against the specifics of the proposed new world economic order.[36]

SOME CONCLUDING REMARKS

What is clear from this very brief survey of Eastern European relations with the developing world is that most Eastern Europeans states are more interested in the potential role of the developing world in stabilizing and strengthening the economies of the CMEA members themselves than they are in most other matters relating to the Third World. The significant industrial growth that has occurred in most CMEA countries in the 1970s has resulted in a notable increase in both the need for raw materials and the availability of exportable industrial products. Some of the developing countries represent both potential suppliers of industrial raw materials and markets for a portion of the industrial exports.

However, in spite of Eastern Europe's growing economic interest in the Third World and the political stability that successful economic relations imply, the Eastern Europeans are still involved in supporting revolutionary movements and regimes in consort with the Soviet Union. However, these two sets of relationships are not necessarily contradictory, for military-political support for a revolutionary movement may well be viewed as a means of ensuring future favorable economic relations.

Overall Eastern European relations with the countries of the Third World have expanded markedly over the course of the past two decades. Political relations are now maintained with the majority of the independent states of Asia, Africa, and Latin America. In some isolated cases, Eastern Europe, in conjunction with the Soviet Union, has become the major supplier of economic and military assistance, for example, in several of the more "radical" African countries. Insofar as individual Eastern European countries have been able to have a political impact on the developing world, however, it has usually been in those areas where they have collaborated with their Soviet allies in providing support for "anti-Western" regimes or movements. Nevertheless, the available evidence seems to indicate that the Eastern

Europeans increasingly view the developing countries in relationship to their own economic needs and that policies toward the developing countries will be motivated even more than they have been in the past by economic, as opposed to exclusively political, factors.

NOTES

1. In 1977, 1978, and 1979 Polish imports from the West fell by 6. 6, 1. 9 and 0. 7 percent, respectively. In 1979 the deficit in Polish trade with the West was reduced to 4, 907 million exchange zloty compared with a deficit of 6, 654 million for 1978 and 9, 771 for 1975. See Rocznik Stastystyczny Handlu Zagranicznego, for the appropriate years. For a more complete discussion of these problems, see Roger E. Kanet, "Le Commerce extérieur polonais: les interrelations entre la politique économique interne et exérieure," Revue d'études comparatives est-ouest 24, no. 1 (1980): 40-46.

2. Since 1975, prices for trade within the CMEA have been based on a five-year floating average of prices on the international market. This has meant that, although prices of Soviet raw materials exports to Eastern Europe have risen, the increase has been more gradual and price increases have lagged behind those on the world market. For a discussion of pricing within the CMEA, see "Soviet-Eastern European Economic Relations, 1975-78," "Price Changes in Soviet Trade with CMEA and the Rest of the World Since 1975," pp. 263-90, both in Soviet Economy in a Time of Change: A Compendium of Papers, vol. 1, U.S. Congress, Joint Economic Committee (Washington, D. C. : Government Printing Office, 1979).

3. See Harry G. Trend, "Energy—The Key to East European Economic Development," Radio Free Europe Research (hereafter RFER), RAD Background Report (Eastern Europe), no. 93 (May 12, 1978). Romania, for example, has recently negotiated a trade agreement with Iran and has begun discussions on cooperation in the oil, gas, and petrochemical industries. Pars News Agency (Iran), as reported in the Christian Science Monitor, June 9, 1980.

4. See, for example, E. Varga, Osnovnye voprosy ekonomiki i politiki imperializma (posle Vtoroi Mirovoi Voiny), 2d ed. (Moscow: Gospolitizdat, 1957), pp. 339-40.

5. "Report of the Central Committee of the Communist Party of the Soviet Union," Pravda, October 18, 1961, translated in Current Soviet Policies IV: The Documentary Record of the 22nd Communist Party Congress, ed. Leo Gruliow (New York: Columbia University Press, 1962), pp. 48-49.

6. See Brosi Ponomarev, "O gosudarstve natsional 'noi demokratii," Kommunist, no. 8 (1961): 45-55. For a discussion of the ide-

ological position of Czechoslovakia on the Third World, which agreed totally with that of the Soviet Union, see Robert F. Lamberg, Prag und die Dritte Welt (Hanover: Verlag für Literatur und Zeitgeschehen, 1966), pp. 28 ff. For the position of the GDR, see Wolfgang Spröte and Gerhard Hahn, DDR-Wirtschaftshilfe contra Bonner Neokolonialismus: Studie über die wirtschaftliche und wissentschaftlichtechnische Unterstützung der Nationalstaaten durch die DDR und die staatsmonopolistische Föderung der neokolonialistischen Expansion des westdeutschen Monopolkapitals (Berlin: Staatsverlag der DDR, 1965), especially pp. 5-65.

7. See, for example, Marian Paszyński, "Nowy międzynarodowy ład ekonomiczny (Refleksje na tle IV Światowej Konferencji Handlu i Rozwoju)," Ekonomista, no. 1 (1977): 128-32.

8. See V. Berezin, Cooperation Between CMEA and Developing Countries (Moscow: Novosti Press, 1976), p. 5.

9. See Trond Gilberg, "Romania, Yugoslavia, and Africa: 'Nonalignment and Progressivism'" (unpublished paper, prepared for the Conference on Socialist States in Africa, Monterey, California, July 26-28, 1979). See also Chapter 8 on Romania by Michael Radu in the present volume.

10. For a discussion of GDR policy see Hans Siegfried Lamm and Siegfried Kupper, DDR und Dritte Welt (Munich-Vienna: R. Oldenbourg, 1976), especially pp. 203 ff. See also Chapters 4 and 5 in the present volume by Michael Sodaro and by Shannon Butler and Jiri Valenta.

11. In a recent study of Eastern European voting at the United Nations, Robert Weiner notes slight variations in voting on several issues related to the developing world. However, only Romania's position has deviated significantly from that of the Soviet Union and the other Eastern European states as a group. Robert Weiner, "East Europe at the United Nations," in Foreign Policies of East Europe: New Approaches, ed. Ronald H. Linden (New York: Praeger).

12. Aurel Bereznai, "Hungary's Presence in Black Africa," RFER, RAD Background Report (Hungary), no. 75, (April 2, 1979): 20; and Paul Gaftan et al., "Romania's Presence in Black Africa," RFER, RFE Background Report (Romania), no. 118, (May 23, 1979): 11. For a general discussion of Eastern European involvement in Africa, see Roger E. Kanet, "Eastern Europe and Sub-Saharan Africa," in The Communist States and Sub-Saharan Africa, ed. Richard F. Staar (Stanford: Hoover Institution Press).

13. See Arnold Krammer, The Forgotten Friendship: Israel and the Soviet Bloc, 1947-1953 (Urbana: University of Illinois Press, 1974), pp. 54 ff.

14. See Lamberg, Prag und die Dritte Welt, pp. 19 ff. For a recent discussion of the background of the Soviet-Czechoslovak arms

shipment, see Mohamed Heikal, The Sphinx and the Commissar: The Rise and Fall of Soviet Influence in the Middle East (New York: Harper & Row, 1979), pp. 57-60.

15. Elizabeth Pond, "E. Germany's Quiet African Role," Christian Science Monitor, February 22, 1979. In an earlier article, Pond noted that East German military and security training was occurring in Guinea-Bissau, São Tome e Príncipe, Angola, Mozambique, Ethiopia, and South Yemen, see "East Germany's 'Afrika Korps'," Christian Science Monitor, June 27, 1978. According to CIA estimates, only 1,300 Eastern European military technicians were operating in developing countries in 1978, while 10,800 Soviets were working abroad. See Central Intelligence Agency, National Foreign Assessment Center, Communist Aid Activities in Non-Communist Less Developed Countries 1978: A Research Paper, ER 79-10412U, September 1979, pp. 3-4. Estimates included in a cover story in Der Spiegel in early 1980 placed the number of East German military advisers in Africa, including North Africa, at 2,720. See "Honeckers Afrika-Korps: Hilfstruppe für Moskaus Machtstrategie," Der Spiegel 34, no. 10 (March 3, 1980): 43.

16. In 1970, 45 percent of CMEA exports, including those from the Soviet Union, consisted of machinery and equipment, while other industrial products made up an additional 25 percent of exports. See Jiri Elias, Die Aussenwirtschaftsbeziehungen des Comecon mit den Entwicklungsländern Unter besonderer Berücksichtigung Südasiens (Bern: Peter Lang, 1977), p. 114.

17. Siegfried Wenger, "Wirtschaftszusammenarbeit der RGW-Länder mit den Entwicklungsländern," Deutsche Aussenpolitik 21 (1976): 536.

18. Already in the early 1960s a Czechoslovak economist argued that economic cooperation and assistance have "great meaning for our industrially well-developed country which has an insufficient energy base." Vaclav Mondous, "The Socialist Countries and Their Relations with the National Liberation Movement of the Colonial Countries," Pravda (Plzeň), July 4, 1963; cited in and translated from the German of Lamberg, Prag und die Dritte Welt, p. 27.

19. In 1977 Polish exports amounted to 210 million exchange zloty and imports to 8.4 million. One year later the figures were 209 and 366 million, respectively. Główny Urząd Statystyczny, Rocznik Statystyczny 1979 (Warsaw: Główny Urząd Statystyczny, 1979), pp. 306-8.

20. See RFER, Czechoslovakia Situation Report, no. 7, (February 21, 1979); RFER, Poland Situation Report, no. 4, (February 27, 1979); and RFER, Romania Situation Report, no. 2, (February 9, 1979). For additional information on the energy situation in Eastern Europe, see Daniel Park, Oil and Gas in Comecon Countries (London:

Kogan Page; New York: Nichols, 1979); Jeremy Russell, Energy as a Factor in Soviet Foreign Policy (Westmead; Saxon House; Lexington, Mass.: Lexington Books, 1976), esp. pp. 89–130; and Jonathan P. Stern, Soviet Natural Gas Development to 1990: The Implications for the CMEA and the West (Lexington, Mass.: Lexington Books, 1980).

21. For a discussion of the hard currency debt of the Eastern European states, see Joan P. Zoeter, "Eastern Europe: The Growing Hard Currency Debt," pp. 1350–68, and Kathryn Melson and Edwin M. Snell, "Estimating East European Indebtedness to the West," pp. 1369–95, both in East European Economies Post-Helsinki, U.S. Congress, Joint Economic Committee (Washington, D.C.: Government Printing Office, 1977).

22. RFER, Poland Situation Report, no. 4 (February 27, 1979).

23. See Report of the Intergovernmental Group of Experts to Study a Multilateral System of Payments Between Socialist Countries of Eastern Europe and Developing Countries, UNCTAD Document TD/B/683, Td/B/AC.22/6, December 14, 1977. This document is reprinted in United Nations Conference on Trade and Development, Multilateralization of Payments in Trade Between Socialist Countries of Eastern Europe and Developing Countries: Selected Documents, TD/B/703 (New York: United Nations, 1978), pp. 1–10. The shift away from bilateral clearing is clearly visible in the following figures:

Percentage of Trade of European Socialist Countries
Conducted Under Bilateral Clearing Agreements

Country	1965	1970	1975
Bulgaria	80.9	75.1	44.9
Czechoslovakia	67.7	69.0	61.1
German Democratic Republic	81.3	84.0	56.2
Hungary	62.8	75.3	28.9
Poland	79.0	76.3	23.9
Romania	86.6	78.7	39.1
Total	74.8	75.9	42.5
Soviet Union	78.6	73.0	61.1

Source: Statistical Review of Trade among Countries Having Different Economic and Social Systems, Prepared by the UNCTAD Secretariat, TD/B/656/Add.1; reprinted in UNCTAD, Multilateralization of Payments in Trade Between Socialist Countries of Eastern Europe and Developing Countries: Selected Documents, TD/B/703 (New York: United Nations, 1978), p. 15.

24. The shift in assistance can be seen in the following figures:

Percentage of East European Economic Assistance Committed
to Developing Countries, 1954-70 and 1971-77

| | 1954-70 | | 1971-77 | |
Country	Percentage	Ranking	Percentage	Ranking
Bulgaria	6.8	6	4.4	4
Czechoslovakia	33.3	1	28.8	2
German Democratic				
Republic	22.0	2	8.8	5
Hungary	12.4	4	9.8	4
Poland	15.1	3	11.5	3
Romania	10.4	5	36.7	1
Total	100.0		100.0	

Sources: United Nations, Department of International Economic
and Social Affairs, Statistical Office, Statistical Yearbook (New York:
United Nations, for the appropriate years); and Central Intelligence
Agency, National Foreign Assessment Center, Communist Aid Activi-
ties in Non-Communist Less Developed Countries, 1978: A Research
Paper, ER 79-10412U, September 1979, p. 11.

25. See Miroslav Virius, "Ekonomická spolupráce zemí RVHP
a rozvojovými zemémi," Zahranicni obchod, no. 11 (1977), translated
as "Economic Cooperation Between CMEA Members and the Developing Countries," Soviet and East European Foreign Trade 15, no. 2
(1979): 82-84.
26. See Henrik Bischof, "Zum Stand der Wirtschaftsbeziehungen
zwischen kommunistischen Staaten und Entwicklungsländern," Monatsberichte: Entwicklungspolitische Aktivitäten kommunistischer Länder
(Forschungsinstitut der Friedrich-Ebert-Stiftung), (January 1977): 7-8.
27. See CIA, Communist Aid Activities 1978, p. 13.
28. For a discussion of the GDR's training programs see
"Honeckers Afrika-Korps," pp. 42-61.
29. See, for example, Pavel Šimerda, "Stand und neue Tenden-
zen in den aussenwirtschaftlichen Beziehungen der ČSSR zu den Entwicklungsländern," Osteuropa-Wirtschaft 24 (1979): 297-98.
30. Lumea, March 9-15, 1979, as cited in Chapter 8 in the
present book.
31. See Józef Nowicki, "Polish Economic Relations with Devel-

oping Countries in Africa," Osteuropa-Wirtschaft 21 (1976): 303;
Istvan Dobozi et al. , "Economic Cooperation Between Hungary and
the Developing Countries," in Economic Cooperation Between Socialist and Developing Countries, ed. Istvan Dobozi (Budapest: Hungarian
Scientific Council for World Economy, 1978), p. 125.

32. Czechoslovak Television, March 7, 1979, cited in H. G.
Trend, "COMECON Joint Investments in Third World as Payment for
Raw Materials?" RFER, RAD Background Report (Eastern Europe),
no. 55 (March 9, 1979). For an overview of research on the small
amount of East-West cooperation in industrial and raw materials projects in the Third World, see Carl H. McMillan, The Political Economy of Tripartite (East-West-South) Industrial Cooperation, East-
West Commercial Relations Series, Research Report, no. 12 (Otta-
wa: Institute of Soviet and East European Studies, Carleton University,
1980).

33. A recent example of the negative impact of political instability on Eastern European economic interests is visible in Iran. Soon
after the overthrow of the Shah the new government cancelled a contract with the Soviet Union—and several other Eastern and Western
European countries—that called for the construction of a second gas
pipeline from Iran to the Soviet Union. The Soviets were to receive
additional Iranian natural gas and, in turn, expand their exports of
gas to both Eastern and Western Europe. As noted above, however,
Romania has already signed a new cooperation agreement with Iran.
See note 3.

34. See Peter Knirsch, "The CMEA Attitude to a New Economic
Order," Intereconomics 14 (1979); 209. For a more complete discussion of this topic, see Jürgen Nötzold, "Die RGW-Staaten und der
Nord-Süd Dialog," Aussenpolitik 30, no. 1 (1979): 192-209; and E.
Böhm et al. , "Zur Rolle der sozialistischen Staaten im Nord-Süd
Dialog" (Paper presented to the HWWA-Institut für Wirtschaftsfors-
chung, Hamburg, August 1979). For an excellent treatment of Soviet
views, see Elizabeth K. Valkenier, "The USSR, the Third World, and
the Global Economy," Problems of Communism 28, no. 4 (1979): 17-33.

35. See Wenger, "Wirtschaftszusammenarbeit," p. 533. In an
interesting article the Polish economist Stanisław Polaczek has admitted that, although the Socialist states are not responsible for the
economic backwardness of the developing world, this does not mean
that they should not commit themselves to increased assistance. He
also discusses at some length the reasons that the proposals of the
Socialist countries concerning a new world economic system have
not always received a positive response in the developing world. See
Stanisław Polaczek, "Nowy Międzynarodowy Ład ekonomiczny a kraje
KWPG," Sprawy Międzynarodowe, no. 12 (1978); especially 68-69.
See also Marian Paszyński, "Kraje socjalistyczne w wielostronnej

debacie o światowych stosunkach ekonomicznych," Sprawy Międzynarodowe, no. 5 (1979); pp. 85-96.

36. See Dionisie Ghermani, "Bukarest und die 'Neue Weltwirtschaftsordnung,'" Wissenschaftlicher Dienst Südosteuropa 27, no. 3 (1978): 66-72; and Ion Barac and Dragoş Şerbaescu, "The Main Features of the Romanian Concept of the New International and Political Order," Revue roumaine d'études internationales 12 (1978): 343-54. For a collection of articles on the New International Economic Order by scholars from CMEA countries, see Eastern Europe and the New International Economic Order: Representative Samples of Socialist Perspectives, eds. Ervin Laszlo and Joel Kurtzman (New York: Pergamon Press, 1979).

11

POLICY PATTERNS OF EASTERN EUROPEAN SOCIALIST COUNTRIES TOWARD THE THIRD WORLD

Janos Radvanyi

Over the past two decades, five Eastern European countries—Bulgaria, Czechoslovakia, the German Democratic Republic (GDR), Hungary, and Poland—have contributed in fairly large measure to Moscow's successes in the Third World. The diverse activities of these Socialist regimes promoted closer ties with the emerging nations of Africa, Asia, and Latin America, and their concerted efforts tipped the international balance of power further toward the Kremlin-led Socialist bloc. In political, military, security, and Party matters, the "Five" followed the Soviet lead. In economic matters they acted on an individual basis, although they attempted to investigate possibilities of economic cooperation between the Soviet-dominated Council for Economic Mutual Assistance (CMEA) and the Third World countries.

Understandably, the Five regarded the Third World countries with a "progressive" or "Marxist"-orientation the most logical targets for their ideological and political influence. [1] They classified the rest of the Third World into two categories: nonaligned neutral countries and nonaligned Western-oriented countries, with solvent and nonsolvent economies. Regardless of political orientation, however, the Five saw the Third World countries with solvent economies as valuable markets for goods and new sources for industrial raw materials and oil supplies. For obvious reasons, they paid little attention to those Third World countries with nonsolvent economies.

The approach of the three other Eastern European Socialist countries—maverick Romania, lonely Albania, and nonaligned Yugoslavia—to the Third World was distinctly different. There is no evidence to suggest that President Nicolae Ceausescu of Romania ever coordinated his Third World policy with Moscow or with any of the other Eastern European Socialist governments. Yet the overall pattern of Romania's relations with Third World countries indicates that Bucharest has always been aware of its own limits and has carefully avoided a head-on collision with the Soviet bloc. [2] Hoxha's Albania, in sharp defiance of the Soviet Union and its Eastern European allies, has acted in accordance with its own interests to establish ties with the Third World. Of course, Yugoslavia, as cofounder of the Nonaligned Movement, has conducted Third World foreign policy that is decidedly independent of Eastern European policies and actions. Actually, Belgrade has directed its Third World affairs with the intent of creating an international political defense shield against possible Soviet bloc expansionism.

Although all available data indicate that neither Romania, Albania, nor Yugoslavia could influence or alter in the slightest the cooperation of the faithful Five with Moscow, it would be an oversimplification and certainly misleading to argue that the Five had no room for maneuver. [3] It would be equally misleading to state that Soviet decision makers always asked for unconditional collaboration from their Eastern European allies. An unwritten law presupposed the understanding that Eastern Europeans had freedom of action to the extent that such freedom served, or at any rate did not counter, Soviet national interests. This "law" also presumed that the Kremlin would give some operative consideration to Eastern European interests.

Close coordination was also an integral part of the policy-planning process and required the participation of the Party leaderships as well as a number of interactions on all sides and at all levels of Party and government bodies. Usually the highest-level policy coordination and consultation took place at Party congresses, Warsaw Pact political consultative committee meetings, or during bilateral discussions in the Crimea and elsewhere. At all these meetings Soviet Politburo members briefed their Eastern European counterparts, and Soviet Central Committee secretaries responsible for foreign affairs and economic, propaganda, and administrative (military and intelligence) matters exchanged views on operative problems with their Eastern European colleagues. If necessary, the Central Committee of the Communist Party of the Soviet Union's (CPSU) Department of International Relations and the Soviet Foreign Ministry provided additional guidance and information for Budapest, Warsaw, Berlin, Prague, and Sofia. The implementation of the policy decision rested with the Eastern European politburos and the appropriate government bodies (foreign ministries, foreign trade ministries, economic ministries, and others).

POLICY PATTERNS IN THE KHRUSHCHEV ERA

While the mechanism for interparty and interstate coordination and cooperation remained the same during two distinct periods—the Khrushchev and Brezhnev eras—the pattern of Eastern European policies toward the Third World changed considerably. In the 1960s reliance on the "national bourgeoisie" was the motto. In the 1970s the strategy focused on the support of radical elements in Asia, Africa, and Latin America.

During the Khrushchev era, the Five concentrated their efforts on South and Southeast Asia (specifically, Indonesia and India) and on the Arab Middle East, with emphasis on Egypt and, to a somewhat lesser extent, Syria. In contrast to the policy of the U.S. government, the Five (like the Soviets) accepted neutrality as the guiding principle of the newly emerging nations. As "unselfish protectors," they supported real and imaginary Third World grievances against former colonial rulers, as when the backed up Sukarno's claim to Dutch New Guinea and stood for the nationalization of the Suez Canal. They also lent "unflinching support" to most national liberation movements. Czechoslovakia's arms shipments during the Algerian struggle for independence and the establishment of rehabilitation centers all over Eastern Europe for wounded Algerian freedom fighters illustrate the importance that leaders in the Eastern European Socialist camp attached to the issue.

In retrospect, however, the mobilization of Third World nationalism was only partially advantageous for the Five. Their support of national liberation movements proved to be remarkably successful in arousing hatred against Western "imperialism" and "neocolonialism" and in weakening Western political and economic influence. In addition, such support created a climate within which the Eastern European Socialist regimes could operate and enhance their own political and economic influence. However, the formation of regional nationalist movements, particularly Pan-Africanism and Pan-Arabism, worked against the interests of the Five. [4] Moreover, Third World Marxism (such as Sékou Touré's African anarchosyndicalism) caused constant friction with the "scientific socialism" of Eastern Europe. Lastly, the nationists, persecution of local Communists resulted in severe setbacks for Socialist influence. For the sake of maintaining friendly state-to-state relations, Khrushchev and his Eastern European allies overlooked the brutal treatment of their comrades. They did not intervene when Nasser sent hundreds of Egyptian Communists to desert concentration camps or when the Iraqi Baathists ordered the execution of the first secretary of the Iraqi Communist party.

Another policy pattern of the Khrushchev era was the Eastern

Europe Five's subordination of their economic interests to political considerations. At the same time that they initiated unsound aid projects (construction of huge industrial complexes, roads, and bridges in Indonesia, India, and Egypt), they agreed to the postponement of credit payments and granted new loans to sympathetic Third World customers. Within three years, these ill-considered and ill-contrived economic activities accumulated such a heavy burden that the Eastern European governments had to curtail drastically future aid commitments. [5]

The presence of the Five in Black Africa remained marginal during the Khrushchev era. Although the Eastern European Socialist regimes greeted with enthusiasm the wave of independence that inundated Black Africa in the 1960s, they were not prepared to take advantage of the favorable situation. For example, there was no organizational backing. The international relations departments of the central committees of the Eastern European Communist parties usually had only one rapporteur in charge of African affairs, and the foreign ministries had only one political department for Asia, Africa, and the Middle East. On the economic front, with the exception of Czechoslovakia, foreign trade specialists were not available to conduct the necessary marketing. In addition, Eastern European industries could not supply Black Africa with the goods and services they had obtained from the West in the past and had acquired after independence. Yet the Kremlin made it clear to the Five that political and economic assistance had to be given to the newly emerging countries. Consequently, diplomatic and trade relations were expeditiously established, but the actual opening of the diplomatic and trade missions still depended on both the availability of personnel and budgetary considerations.

REEVALUATION IN THE BREZHNEV ERA

Following the downfall of Khrushchev in October 1964, no immediate change was seen in the pattern and direction of East European policies toward the Third World. Eastern European diplomats in Africa, Asia, and Latin America were still arguing that only economic cooperation with the Socialist bloc and the supply of modern military hardware made in the Soviet Union and Czechoslovakia could assure the independence and prosperity of the emerging nations. Otherwise, the Five continued to focus attention on the Arab Middle East, where two bloody wars took place in short succession. The Eastern European presence remained strong in India also, and trade activity expanded gradually in Burma and Sri Lanka. Although Eastern European and Soviet activities were reduced to routine diplomatic representation of interest in Indonesia, this change resulted not from a shift of

Soviet bloc priorities but from the fiasco of the abortive Communist coup there and the overthrow of President Sukarno. New opportunities arose for the Five in Sudan and Somalia. In Ghana, Hungarian economists were asked to oversee the establishment of a central planning board, and high officials of the Czechoslovak secret police helped organize Nkrumah's internal security and police forces. In Chile, the Five made a concerted effort to stabilize the Allende regime.

The general trend of economic activity during the first two years of the Brezhnev period followed the old line. Bilateral clearing agreements between the Eastern European Socialist regimes and Third World countries had little built-in flexibility because they stipulated payment in national currencies. Not surprisingly, the total trade turnover remained as insignificant as in the past. Meanwhile, the aid programs were closely tied to trade, and there the figures showed a downward trend. [6] The beneficiaries of the loans and credits were usually the state sectors of the Third World countries. In accordance with the nature of the loans, the funds were generally used to finance the construction of a particular industrial investment and to purchase equipment. [7] The recipient countries paid the cost of the advisers and technicians separately. Eastern European loans were higher than those of the Soviet Union by two or three points because the Five had to borrow the money at international money market rates.

Thus the continuation of the Khrushchevian pattern yielded insignificant trade benefits and failed to preserve the staying power of key pro-Soviet bourgeois nationalist leaders, as the overthrow of Ben Bella of Algeria (June 1965), Sukarno of Indonesia (September 1965), Nkrumah of Ghana (February 1966), and Keita of Mali (November 1968) clearly indicated. In addition, the complex indigenous socioeconomic forces at work produced more unpleasant surprises. In July 1971, Sudan President Nimeri restricted relations with the Soviets and the Five after an abortive Communist coup. A year later President Sadat expelled Soviet advisers from Egypt and reduced economic and scientific cooperation with the rest of the Socialist bloc. (Egypt's relations with Yugoslavia and Romania remained friendly, however.)

The Soviets responded to these setbacks by assessing the causes of their failures and contemplating future possibilities. Their policy review must have considered the growing Sino-Soviet rift and the U. S. - Chinese rapprochement as negative elements influencing Third World policy. The Soviets probably regarded Romania's foreign policy actions in Africa and Asia and the Ceausescu government's overtures to the nonaligned nations and the Group of 77 as mere nuisances. However, they must have viewed the successful integration of the five Eastern European Socialist regimes into the CMEA and the modernization and expansion of the military preparedness of the Warsaw Pact countries as supporting elements that would facilitate comebacks and new beginnings. Finally, the growing number of strong Marxist-Leninist parties operating in Asia and Africa must have given the Kremlin planners renewed hope for expanding Soviet influence.

What unfolded as a new Soviet policy toward the Third World during the Brezhnev era was a flexible diplomacy for detecting new eventualities and a new dynamism in supporting radical elements, such as the Arab Baathists in Syria and Iraq and radicals in Algeria. The most striking innovation was the decision to provide all-out support, including military assistance coupled with Soviet military advisers with Cuban combat troops and GDR security agents, for local Communist parties or fronts dominated by them seeking to gain state power.

As all available evidence suggests, the five Eastern European Socialist regimes joined the new Soviet venture with full force and speed. First and foremost, a concerted effort was made to support all pro-Soviet Marxist-Leninist parties in Angola, Mozambique, Congo-Brazzaville, Ethiopia, Afghanistan, and South Yemen that had seized power by force in the past five years. As a symbolic gesture of good will, such Eastern European party and government leaders as Erick Honecker of the GDR, Thodor Zhivkov of Bulgaria, and Pál Losonczi of Hungary visited their new-found allies and signed friendship and cooperation treaties that contained either open or secret clauses for military cooperation. But that was not all. Contrary to their activities in the past, the Five undertook some sort of military commitment to support radical Arab, pro-Soviet, and other friendly regimes. The GDR took the lead in the supply of arms. Czechoslovakia was next in line, and the total Eastern European arms shipments amounted to $1,180 million between 1973 and 1977, and reached a one-year record of $325 million in 1977. The concluded military agreements, which had amounted to $450 million in 1977, rose to $465 million in 1978. However, the value of the delivered equipment did not exceed the previous year's level. [8]

Arms exports turned out to be beneficial in reducing the huge nonmilitary trade deficits of the Soviet bloc countries and supplemented the East European national bank's hard currency earnings. Income from arms sales was often used to obtain strategically important raw materials. An important transaction in this category was the recent Soviet-Zambian agreement by which the government of Zambia sold its whole cobalt production in exchange for a $95 million purchase of Soviet military hardware. [9]

The Five played an active role in training Third World military personnel at Soviet and Eastern European military academies and other training facilities. In 1978 alone, 1,900 Third World military personnel (artillerymen, pilots, tank operators, and the like) received advanced training in the Soviet Union and Eastern Europe. The Poles

and the Hungarians trained Mozambique officers, and East German
and Czechs trained Ethiopian and Angolan servicemen. Also in 1978,
more than 10,800 Soviet and 1,300 Eastern European military advisers
instructed local units on site in combat techniques and provided maintenance services for the new weapons systems.[10] The East German
"Afrika Corps" of some 9,000 military and civilian advisers drilled
Palestinian commandos in South Yemen, offered substantial assistance
to guerrillas in Rhodesia and South Africa, and organized the security
and police forces in Congo-Brazzaville, Ethiopia, and Mozambique.[11]
Reportedly, East German security and civilian advisers were active
in great numbers in Kabul.

Equally as important as the military assistance programs were
the interparty cooperation agreements that the Eastern Europeans
concluded with African and Asian Marxist-Leninist parties or other
pro-Soviet parties. The Hungarian Socialist Workers' party, for example, signed such agreements with the Congolese Workers' party,
the Mozambique Liberation Front (FRELIMO), and the Popular Movement for the Liberation of Angola (MPLA). The Polish United Workers'
party also signed an interparty cooperation agreement with the MPLA.
Under the terms of these agreements, the contracting parties conducted regular consultations on the highest level. African and Asian Marxist-Leninist study groups visited Eastern European Party headquarters
to become acquainted with the system of Party control over government bureaucracy and to explore the overall working methods of the
Central Committees' departments for administrative affairs, agita-
tion and propaganda, science, public education and culture, and international relations. The agreements also provided ideological training
for Third World party cadres in the one- and two-year Party schools
in Eastern European capitals.

The East Europeans, in cooperation with Cuba's Fidel Castro
demonstrated some interest also in assuring a foothold in the Caribbean states and Central America. For instance East German, Bulgarian, Czechoslovak, and Polish party leaders discussed the possibility of extended political, economic, and cultural cooperation with
officials of Grenada. East Europeans established close ideological
ties with Guyana, but offered them only $70 million in economic aid,
in addition to Hungary's $10 million credit for consumer and capital
goods. Czechoslovakia, East Germany, and Poland negotiated commercial agreements and development assistance programs with Panama. Hungarian trade representatives signed a trade credit agreement
in Jamaica for consumer goods, medical equipment, pharmaceuticals,
and textiles. As in other parts of the Third World, in Central and
South America, too, the East Germans seemed to be the most active.
In May 1980 the Chairman of the GDR Council of State, Erich Honecker, while signing a treaty of friendship and cooperation with Castro

met Humberto Ortega, Commander-in-Chief of the Sandinista People's Army and member of the National Directorate of the Sandinista National Liberation Front of Nicaragua who was also visiting the Cuban capital. Meanwhile a Nicaraguan military delegation headed by Deputy Defense Minister and Chief of the General Staff, Commandante Guerrillero Joaquin Cuadra Lacayo, visited East Germany and Czechoslovakia to procure military hardware, especially automatic weapons.[12]

In other parts of Latin America East European governments were engaged in normal trade activities. Their importation of mineral and agricultural goods from countries like Argentina, Brazil, and Bolivia greatly exceeded their export deliveries and the galloping inflation in the region worsened this unbalanced situation. As of today the annual East European and Soviet deficit went beyond a billion dollars. The sale of East European machinery and equipment somewhat reduced this unfavorable trade balance but a satisfactory solution is not in sight.

As a departure from the past the Five introduced the principle of cost-effectiveness. By setting up mixed economic commissions and concluding long-range framework agreements with Third World countries, they hoped that economics in the service of political aims ultimately would pay off. The new framework agreements consisted of ordinary commercial or barter clauses and supplier-type credits. As a means of expanding trade, the Soviets and Eastern Europeans now declared their willingness to replace a great many of the clearing agreements with multilateral settlements, and the CMEA members' bank, the International Bank for Economic Cooperation, facilitated such multilateral settlements through a system of payments in convertible rubles.[13] Consequently, in the period 1970-75, trade in convertible rubles between the Eastern European Socialist regimes and Third World countries increased almost fivefold, while trade under clearing agreements only doubled.[14] This innovation, however, did not eliminate the old practice of expanding the Socialist bloc countries trade relations with Third World countries independently and often at each other's expense.[15]

Meanwhile, the economic aid program to the Third World, which was reduced to an all-time low commitment of $397 million in 1977, jumped to an unprecedented $1,502 million commitment in 1978.[16] This seesaw pattern reflects the rapidly changing political climate and power relations in the Third World. It also indicates the degree of difficulty Eastern European creditors experienced during the long years they had to uphold their part of the bargain. Almost all of the aid programs were used for industrial projects in the public sector and were warmly welcomed by Marxist-Leninist, radical left-wing, and sometimes even nonaligned Third World countries interested in expanding industrial state monopoly. A portion of credits was used in sub-Saharan Africa and North Africa, and the main beneficiaries in 1978 were Syria, Brazil, Burma, Angola, and the Philippines.

In exchange for long-term credits, the borrowers were often willing to contract raw material resources. At the same time members of CMEA attempted to coordinate their search for new markets and additional raw material and oil in the Third World. At present, however, it is not known whether or not joint CMEA investment programs got off the ground or whether OPEC countries would be interested in selling oil for complex industrial complexes as long as they can get payment in hard currency. [17]

Like economic aid programs, both technical service and academic study programs grew steadily during the Brezhnev era. In 1978 the Soviet bloc provided 72,000 specialists to the Third World countries. Moreover Eastern European personnel in Third World countries increased by 9,000 between 1976 and 1980, and could hardly keep up with the mounting demand. [18] While complaints about Cuban specialists were often heard, Eastern European qualifications were usually appreciated. Not surprisingly, the Eastern Europeans preferred to extend their services to oil-rich countries such as Libya, Iraq, and Kuwait, but they were also located in great numbers in sub-Saharan Africa and South Asia.

The technical service programs were lucrative as long as the Third World countries paid in hard currency for the assistance rendered. However, many specialists working on investment projects were compensated only through technical and scientific cooperation programs and were paid instead in local money. Even less profitable was the technical instruction of the 550,000 Third World nations who received training at Soviet and East European schools established mainly in the Middle East, South Asia, and lately in Afghanistan. It is worthwhile to mention that the Third World students trained in Eastern Europe numbered only around 18,560 in 1978, and the costs to the host countries amounted to between $3,000 and $5,000 per student per annum. [19]

SUMMARY AND CONCLUSION

The effects of Eastern European activities in the Third World are more visible today than ever before because the policies initiated under Brezhnev's leadership made possible the survival of the pro-Soviet Marxist-oriented regimes in Black Africa and Asia. The stabilization of Third World countries created a new alliance system whereby the Soviet Union, the five Eastern European Socialist countries, and selected Third World Marxist-oriented regimes were bound by bilateral friendship and cooperation treaties. The smooth functioning of the new system was assured by interparty cooperation treaties. The collaboration not only extended the radius of Eastern European activities but also helped the politically and ideologically inexperienced Third World Marxist leaders in doctrinaire party building, mass organization, propaganda, and foreign affairs.

Concomitant with expanding influence, the Five had to endure serious political setbacks, as had the Soviets, in Egypt, Somalia, and other parts of Africa. Yet there were cases when Eastern European relations with pro-Western Third World governments remained warm despite the hostile attitude of these governments toward Soviet policies in the area.

On the military front Eastern European aid programs effectively supplemented Soviet military sales agreements and other forms of military assistance. For example, Eastern European participation in the Ethiopian arms buildup in 1977 considerably boosted the morale of the beleaguered Marxist-oriented Ethiopian regimes and helped to outgun the invading Somali forces. In Angola and Mozambique, the closely coordinated Soviet bloc operation helped to subdue Western-supported guerrilla movements. Political and military assistance, however, was seldom supported by sizable economic aid, a practice that contributed markedly to the soaring difficulties of these countries. In Angola and Mozambique, for example, the situation deteriorated to the point where Marxist-oriented governments had to turn to the West for capital investments.

The Eastern European Socialist regimes—like the Soviet Union—seemed to be less successful in dealing with countries favoring nonalignment (in the proper sense of the word). For these countries they used various policy instruments, including economic and technical cooperation. The pattern and the selection of the recipients and the provision of the aid programs followed that of the Soviet Union, and consequently political consideration often superseded economic necessities. In addition, they offered limited investment credits, training programs, and scholarships, but they could not offset Third World displeasure at the low level of their aid commitments. To make matters worse, the Eastern Europeans participated in food assistance programs only on a small scale and refused to support infrastructure developments.

The GDR provided two-thirds of Eastern European aid to Third World countries; the Romanians contributed beyond the bounds of their ability. Czechoslovakia, Hungary, Poland, and Bulgaria kept their commitments to a relatively low level, and the needs of their own economies had distinct priority over Third World development assistance. An exception to this rule was the substantial economic support given to India, Morocco, and Turkey, where major Soviet foreign policy interest was at stake.

As in the past, the search for new market and commercial gains remained the major objectives of Eastern European governments in the Third World. The conclusion of ordinary commercial transactions and barter agreements partially served this purpose. Their interest in long-term mining and raw material processing cooperation as well as their offer to conduct geological surveys in selected Third World countries intensified as the Soviet Union started to cut back on Eastern European export quotas for iron, oil, and other important deliveries. For that very reason and because of the expected raw material shortages, Eastern Europeans started to look upon Asia, Africa, and Latin America as new market outlets and important sources of raw materials and crude oil. Inherent in this necessity was a subtle evolutionary change in the Eastern European perspective toward new economic possibilities. Yet as East-West trade had only slightly influenced the political behavior of the Eastern European countries, an extensive trade relation with the Third World would not be likely to bring Berlin, Budapest, Prague, Sofia, and Warsaw into the camp of the nonaligned nations. Nevertheless, the possibility that Eastern European economies will not depend exclusively on Soviet raw materials in the future in the long run might strengthen their independence within and outside the Soviet-dominated CMEA.

NOTES

1. See "Report of the Politburo to the 11th SED Central Committee Plenum, delivered by Erich Honecker, general secretary of the SED Central Committee, on 13 December 1979," FBIS-FEU-80-003.

2. A concise treatment of the question can be found in Robert R. King, "Romania and the Third World," Orbis 21, no. 4 (Winter 1978).

3. For further details of patterns of Eastern European policy, see János Radványi, Hungary and the Superpowers (Stanford, 1972), pp. 152-57.

4. For discussion of Pan-Africanism and Pan-Arabism, see Hugh Seton-Watson, The Imperialist Revolutionaries (Stanford, 1978), pp. 54-60.

5. According to a Central Intelligence Agency, National Foreign Assessment Center, July 1976 report, Eastern European aid agreements between 1954 and 1965 amounted to $1,719 million, and aid deliveries were only $487 million.

6. The total trade turnover of the Socialist countries of Eastern Europe with the Third World countries amounted to $5,209 million in 1965. "Statistical Review of Trade Among Countries Having Different

Economic and Social Systems, Prepared by the UNCTAD Secretariat"
(TD/B/656/Add. 1).

7. Eastern European credits and grants to Third World countries in 1975 amounted to $195 million in Africa, $150 million in Latin America, $35 million in East Asia, and $38 million in the Middle East and South Asia. As quoted in U.S. Congress, House, "A Watershed in Great Power Policy?" Doc. 95, 1st. sess. 1977, pp. 123-24.

8. Interestingly enough, Soviet military sales agreements, which reached a record $5,215 million in 1977, plunged to $1,765 million in 1978. For detailed figures, see Central Intelligence Agency, National Foreign Assessment Center, Communist Aid Activities in Non-Communist Less Developed Countries, 1978 (September 1979, p. 2.

9. For further details, see Congressman James Santini's interview in the San Francisco Chronicle, July 19, 1980.

10. CIA, Communist Aid, pp. 3-5.

11. Richard F. Staar, "Soviet Policies in East Europe," Current History (October 1979): 121-22.

12. Soviet Analyst V. 9m. 15 (July 23, 1980).

13. United Nations Conference on Trade and Development, "Report of the Intergovernmental Group of Experts to Study a Multilateral System of Payments between Socialist Countries of Eastern Europe and Developing Countries," TD/B/Ac. 22/6 (New York: United Nations, 1978).

14. Ibid. , p. 14.

15. The Hungarian journal Külpolitika (no. 1 [1977]: 132) reported at great length on the discussion of African specialists at a conference in Budapest in November 1976. According to the report the conference proposed to the governmental organization responsible for international economic relations and to the CMEA Secretariat that economic relations with the developing countries and the drawing up of joint agreements be coordinated more precisely. The participants considered it necessary to lay down the CMEA countries' common goals and principles, itemize programs for individual developing countries; elucidate the special interests of the different Socialist countries; and outline the system of implementation of the detailed program. As of now there is no evidence that the recommendations of the African specialists were accepted or realized.

16. CIA, Communist Aid, pp. 7-11.

17. For further details, see Radio Free Europe Research, RAD Background Report (Eastern Europe), no. 55 (March 9, 1979).

18. CIA, Communist Aid, pp. 13-16.

19. Ibid. , p. 17.

INDEX

Abebe, Wolde Mariam, 155
Abidjan, 19, 245
Addis Ababa, 44, 119, 249
Aden, 123, 129
Afghanistan, 4, 9, 11, 20, 24,
  26-28, 33, 34, 36, 42, 43,
  63, 66, 67, 78, 82, 94, 131,
  165, 213, 245-48, 257, 259,
  274, 275, 277, 279, 284, 288,
  296, 338, 341; People's Democratic Party (Communist) of,
  3-4, 247
Africa, 16, 17, 19, 20, 23, 24,
  26, 30, 31, 34, 38, 39, 45,
  55, 57, 60, 64, 65, 78, 79,
  82, 83, 86, 98, 106, 107, 109,
  110, 117, 119, 121, 122, 131,
  134, 142, 144, 145, 147, 149-
  53, 162-65, 169-71, 181-85,
  190, 192, 193, 197, 200, 208,
  209, 213, 225, 237, 275, 277,
  289, 291, 305, 308, 325, 333,
  335-38, 342, 343; Black, 116,
  119, 336, 337, 341; North, 77,
  87, 117, 123, 176, 179, 181,
  186, 188, 196, 197, 224, 225,
  312, 341; Portuguese, 30, 38;
  Southern, 7, 309; Southwest,
  116; (see also Namibia); sub-
  Saharan, 27, 30, 84, 92, 170,
  171, 179, 182, 184, 225, 254,
  307, 322, 341; West, 30
African National Congress (of
  South Africa), 117, 144, 289
Albania, People's Socialist Republic of (PSRA), 4, 11, 14,
  24, 27, 29, 33, 238, 285, 295,
  333, 334; economic relations
  with the Third World, 65-67;

level of economic development, 55-
  57; political relations with the
  Third World, 64-65; policy of self-
  reliance, 67-74; relations with
  radical Third World groups, 62-
  64; views on nonalignment, 59-61;
  views on superpowers, 57-59
Albanian Party of Labor (APL), 56,
  58, 62, 64, 65, 70, 73
Alexandria, 123
Algeria, 24-28, 31, 61, 65, 87, 98,
  126, 127, 142, 144, 151, 186-88,
  225, 243, 255, 291, 315, 337, 338
Algiers, 25, 126; 1974 Conference of
  the Nonaligned Movement at, 276,
  288, 289
Allende, Salvador Gossens, 27, 132,
  195, 224, 251, 337
Almeida, Clodomiro, 251
Alvarado, Juan Velasco, 94
Alwan, Hamid, 65
America, Central, 274; Latin, 26,
  41, 55, 57, 60, 65, 83, 86, 98,
  106, 132, 133, 169, 170, 179,
  181, 192-95, 197, 208, 209, 213,
  214, 224, 237, 241, 274, 277, 289,
  291, 292, 305, 311, 312, 325,
  333, 335, 336, 343; North, 133;
  South, 133, 200
Amin, Idi, 17, 22, 250
Amuzegar, Mahmoud, 128
Andrei, Ştefan, 237
Angola, 5, 9, 11-13, 16, 20, 24, 25,
  27, 28, 30, 31, 33-34, 36, 38-39,
  43, 82, 113, 115-22, 129, 137,
  144, 148, 152-55, 162, 163,
  182-85, 225, 243-45, 249-52,
  279, 282, 338, 341, 342; civil war,
  148, 152, 163

Arab League, 7, 47
Arafat, Yassir, 130
Argentina, 15, 27, 41, 61, 133, 170, 173, 193-95, 224, 244
ASEAN, 8
Asia, 55, 57, 60, 65, 78-79, 83, 86, 98, 106, 107, 130, 165, 169, 170, 176, 177, 179-81, 190-92, 200, 208, 209, 212, 213, 237, 291, 305, 306, 325, 333, 335-38, 341, 343; East, 26; South, 201, 312, 335, 341; Southeast, 67, 131, 197, 289, 296, 335
Assab, 162
Assad, Hafez al-, 125
Austria, 169, 200
Azania, 289 (see also South Africa)
Axen, Hermann, 127

Baghdad, 124-26, 287
Balkan Pact, 285
Ballsh, oil refinery in, 69
Baltic Sea, 145
Bangladesh, 27-28, 30, 285
Banyas, oil refinery in, 253
Barbados, 21
Barčák, Andrej, 102
Barnard, brothers, 249; Christiaan, 249
Basic Organizations of Associated Labor (BOALs), 278, 295
Bata Company, 78
Batanagar, 78
Bazargan, Mehdi, 128
Begin, Menachem, 245
Beijing, 6, 12, 28, 30, 32, 37, 41, 57, 59, 61, 64, 72, 236, 245, 248, 258
Belgium, 78
Belgrade, 11, 33, 38, 57, 240, 285, 334; 1961 Conference of the Nonaligned Movement at, 275, 276, 281, 283, 286, 288

Ben Bella, Ahmed, 25, 337
Benin, Republic of, 9, 23, 24, 31, 34, 45, 65, 184
Berlin, 134, 135; East, 92, 109, 111, 115-17, 125, 127, 128, 131, 133, 136, 137, 152, 162, 164, 165, 236, 281, 284, 334, 343; Wall, 108; West, 128
Berlin, Isaiah, 103
Berlinguer, Enrico, 289, 291
Bishop, Maurice, 21, 25
Bogomolov, Oleg, 210
Bohemia, Kingdom of, 77, 78
Bokassa, Jean Bedel, 22, 64, 108, 251
Bolivia, 7, 27, 61, 78, 82, 224
Bonn, 108, 135, 136, 154
Botswana, 8, 21, 27, 289
Brasilia, 7, 16
Bratislava, 101
Brazil, 7, 15-16, 26, 27, 41, 61, 62, 65, 78, 111, 132-34, 181, 193-95, 197, 224, 253, 292, 341
Brezhnev, Leonid, 36, 131, 164, 283, 289-91; Doctrine, 36, 43; Era, 335, 337, 341
Britain, 21, 78, 84, 200, 291 (see also England, United Kingdom)
Brno, 77
Bucharest, 11, 235-42, 244, 246, 248-50, 252, 254, 255, 257-9, 334
Budapest, 334, 343
Bulganin, Nikolai, 305
Bulgaria, 13, 94, 147, 175, 198, 206, 257, 338, 342
Bundestag, 164
Burma, 25, 27, 28, 30, 63, 87, 98, 274, 290, 292, 336, 340
Burnham, Forbes, 133
Burundi, 27, 65, 224, 253

Cabinda, 153
Cabral, Amilcar, 116
Cairo, 42, 245

Calabar, factory, 253
Cambodia (see Kampuchea)
Cameroon, 27, 28
Camp David, accords of, 63,
   123, 130
Canada, 174
Capetown, 249
Cape Verde, Republic of, 9, 19,
   30, 39, 117, 135, 251
Çarçani, Adil, 65
Caribbean Sea, 21, 31, 165, 369
Carombois, joint venture, 253
Carreira, Henrique Teles, "Iko,"
   155
Carter, Jimmy, 3
Castro, Fidel, 12, 13, 33, 34,
   84, 87, 88, 258, 273-75, 279,
   286, 290
Ceausescu, Elena, 238
Ceausescu, Nicolae, 19, 33, 235-
   38, 240, 242, 244-47, 249,
   251, 255-59, 289, 291, 333,
   337
Central Africa, Republic of, 27,
   64, 108, 239, 253
ÇEPECA, 256
Českomoravská Kolben-Daněk, 78
Ceylon, 31, 87 (see also Sri Lanka)
Chad, 27
Charter of Economic Rights and
   Duties of Nations, 224
CHEMOKOMPLEX, 184, 188, 192
Chile, 15, 25, 27, 41, 61-62, 65,
   132, 133, 195, 224, 251, 257,
   290, 337
China, People's Republic of, 4,
   6, 10-12, 14, 16, 17, 19, 23-
   34, 36, 37, 41, 42, 57-59,
   61-62, 64, 64-67, 69, 70, 72,
   74, 130, 154, 236-39, 245,
   248, 249, 251, 252, 258, 259,
   282, 287
Churchill, Winston, 283
CMEA, 4, 12, 13, 94, 98, 100,

113, 150, 174, 175, 196, 202, 237,
   238, 241, 243, 247, 252-54, 256,
   284, 303, 304, 306, 307, 310, 318,
   324, 325, 333, 337, 340, 341, 343
Cold War, 224
Colombia, 37, 61, 133, 224
Colombo, Conference of the Non-
   aligned Movement at, 241
Comecon (see CMEA)
Comintern, 284
Commonwealth, 18
Comoros, Republic of, 11, 21
Conakry, 19
Confederation of African Socialist
   States, proposed, 35
Congo, Bassin, 87
Congo (Léopoldville) 87, 282, 284
   (see also Zaire)
Congo, People's Republic of the, 9,
   23, 24, 27, 28, 34, 45, 117, 118,
   152, 184, 239, 242, 254, 338, 339
Congolese Workers' Party, 339
Costa Rica, 8, 244, 245
Crimea, 334
Croan, Melvin, 148
Croatia, 285
Cuba, 4, 5, 12, 13, 16, 19, 21, 27,
   28, 31, 33, 34, 38, 40-43, 84, 87,
   88, 93, 106, 147, 150, 153, 155,
   165, 195, 201, 224, 245, 249, 273-
   75, 279, 282, 284, 290, 292, 293,
   307
Cuba, Communist Party of, 35
Cultural Revolution, 26, 32
Czechoslovak Communist Party, 100
Czechoslovakia, 4, 13, 61, 113, 146,
   147, 175, 188, 206, 236-38, 249,
   257, 283-85, 295, 307, 312, 333,
   335, 336; aid to the Third World
   from, 83-88, 96-98, 342; arms
   supplies to the Third World, 83,
   84, 338, 339; early economic relations with the developing countries, 77-79; economic ties with

the Third World, 87-96, 100-
103; ideological approach to
the Third World, 79-82; position on CMEA relations with
the developing countries, 99,
100; support for Communist
front organizations, 82, 83
Cyprus, 27, 238

da Costa, Manuel Pinto, 250
Dakar, 245
Damascus, 125
Dar-es-Salaam, 7, 17, 144
Daud, Mohammad, 94
De Gaulle, Charles, 237
Deng Hsiaoping, 37, 60
Dergue, 20, 119, 120
Desai, Morarji, 131
Djilas, Milovan, 284
Dlugosz, Stanislaw, 210, 211
Dobroczynski, Michal, 211
Dollaku, Kristaq, 70
Dominica, 9
Dominican Republic, 61
Dubček, Alexander, 90, 98

East Germany (see German
Democratic Republic)
ECOWAS, 18
Ecuador, 27, 61, 62, 78, 133,
193, 194, 224, 292
EEC, 100, 237, 252, 254, 284
Egypt, 7, 15, 19, 25-27, 38, 42,
63, 65, 78, 83, 84, 87, 88,
107, 108, 111, 112, 123, 142,
144, 170, 173, 182, 186-89,
209, 224-25, 239, 245, 252,
279, 284, 288, 292, 305, 307,
335-37, 342
Elbasan, industrial complex, 69
El Salvador, 194, 292
England, 169 (see also Britain)
Epishev, A., 165
Eqbal, 128

Equatorial Guinea, 23, 28
Eritrea, 119
Eritrean Liberation Front (ELF),
155, 249
Eritrean People's Liberation Front
(EPLF), 250
Ethiopia, 9, 11, 13, 20, 21, 23, 24,
27, 28, 31, 33-36, 43, 44, 115-
21, 129, 137, 144, 155, 162, 184,
224, 225, 242, 249, 250, 252,
279, 290, 338, 339, 342
Europe, 36, 66, 78, 87, 135, 200,
224; Eastern, 24, 26-29, 31, 34,
43, 65, 116, 150, 164, 172-74,
235-39, 245, 252, 253, 284, 291,
303-5, 309, 310-12, 315, 320,
322, 324, 325, 335, 338, 339;
Western, 65, 101, 274, 289, 311
European Economic Community (see
EEC)
Eyadema, Gnassingbe, 247

Fazel, Khosrow, 66
Federal Republic of Germany (FRG),
106, 108, 109, 113, 121, 124, 127,
131, 134-36, 144, 145, 148, 151,
154, 164, 200, 237, 284, 291,
293, 307
Fierzë, plant, 69
Fischer, Oskar, 128, 129, 133
FLEC (Cabinda), 152
Fleischer, Werner, 155
FLNC (Congo), 148, 153, 154, 163
FNLA (Angola), 249
France, 5, 15, 18, 19, 23, 30, 78,
83, 87, 169, 200
FRELIMO, 20, 116, 251, 339
French Community, 87

Gabon, 9, 27, 28, 30, 244, 245, 253
Gambia, 27, 28
Gandhi, Indira, 130, 131
Ganz Mávag, 195
GATT, 79, 99, 241, 254

General Agreement on Tariffs and Trade (see GATT)

Geneva, 82

German Democratic Republic (GDR), 4, 13, 16, 27, 91, 171, 172, 175, 195, 202, 206, 238, 249, 256, 257, 305, 307, 308, 310, 312, 315, 333, 338; aid to the Third World, 112-14, 121, 342; ideological approach to the Third World, 109-11; influence in the Third World, 114-16, 134-37, 147; imports of oil by, 107, 123, 124, 150, 151; invasions of Shaba, role of, 153-55; quest for international legitimacy by, 107-9, 151, 152; relations with Angola, 152, 153; relations with Asian states, 130-32; relations with Black Africa, 116, 117, 121, 122, 142, 144, 145; relations with Ethiopia, 117-20, 155, 162; relations with Iran, 128, 129; relations with Latin America, 132-34, 164, 165; relations with the Middle East, 123-30; relations with Southern Africa, 162-64; relations with the Soviet Union, 145-48; role of the army, 148, 149; trade with the Third World, 111-14

Germany, 169

Ghana, 11, 24, 26, 27, 92, 108, 182, 225, 254, 279, 288, 305, 307, 337

Gheorghiu-Dej, Gheorghe, 236, 237

Gierek, Edward, 203, 210

Gizenga, Antoine, 87

Gomulka Plan, 200

Greece, 378

Grenada, 9, 13, 17, 20, 21, 25, 33, 132, 165, 279

Groote Schuur, hospital of, 249

Group of 77, 7, 8, 11, 12, 171, 241, 252, 325, 337

Guantánamo, U.S. base at, 282

Guatemala, 194

Guevara, Ernesto "Che," 13

Guinea, Republic of, 8, 9, 19, 20, 23, 27, 28, 65, 84, 87, 108, 185, 225, 242, 244, 253, 307

Guinea-Bissau, 9, 19, 20, 27, 28, 30, 116, 134, 148, 163, 250, 251

Guri i Kuq, mine at, 69

Guyana, 27, 133, 253

Habsburg Empire, 77

Haile Selassie, 120, 250

Hájek, Jiři, 90

Hallstein doctrine, 108, 121, 142, 144

Hammarskjöld, Dag, 87

Hanoi, 12, 13, 244

Havana, 12, 13, 30, 341; 1979 Conference of the Nonaligned Movement in, 25, 32, 33, 242, 257, 274-76, 288, 289, 296

Helsinki, Conference of, 210, 290

Heng Samrin, 245, 248

Henrique de Carvalho, 153, 155

Hitler, Adolf, 169

Hoffmann, Heinz, 125, 126, 130, 149, 155

Homs, oil refinery of, 89

Honecker, Erich, 116, 117, 119, 121, 122, 125, 127-31, 133, 163, 247, 338

Hong Kong, 29, 37, 192, 201

Horn of Africa, 117, 207, 209

Hoxha, Enver, 57-61, 68, 285, 334

Hoxha, Nedin, 65

Hua Guofeng, 37

Hungarian Socialist Workers' Party, 172, 339

Hungary, 4, 13, 94, 205, 236, 257, 295, 307, 333, 338, 342; composition of trade with the Third World, 179-82; foreign trade, 172,

173; Revolution of 1956 in, 281, 285, 287; Soviet bloc economy and, 173-76; trade with Asia, 190-92; trade with Latin America, 190-92; trade with the Middle East and North Africa, 186-90; trade with sub-Saharan Africa, 182-86

Husák, Gustav, 100

Hussein, Saddam, 125

Hyderabad, plant at, 89

India, 7, 11, 15, 17, 25-27, 41, 87, 88, 94, 96, 97, 111, 130, 131, 171, 181, 190, 191, 209, 212, 213, 253, 279, 285, 287, 288, 292, 305, 335, 336, 342

Indian Ocean, 15, 162, 248, 290

Indochina, 38, 39, 246, 252

Indonesia, 11, 19, 25, 27, 41, 61, 63, 84, 87, 131, 173, 181, 213, 279, 285, 288, 292, 335-37

International Bank for Economic Cooperation, 207, 340

International Bank for Reconstruction and Development (World Bank), 79, 241

International Monetary Fund, 79, 241

Iran, 3, 7, 26, 27, 62-66, 78, 79, 95, 97, 101, 111, 127-29, 171, 179, 181, 186-88, 196, 213, 252, 258, 275, 288, 292, 310

Iraq, 7, 10, 27, 28, 31, 61, 65, 84, 87, 89, 97, 108, 111, 124-26, 171, 181, 186-89, 196, 209, 213, 250, 287, 292, 310, 311, 341; Baath Party of, 335, 338; Communist Party of, 335

Irian, West (Dutch New Guinea), 284, 335

Islamic Conference, 7

Ismail, Abdul Fattah, 43, 130

Israel, 63, 83, 84, 125, 130, 228, 245, 249, 250, 257, 275, 288

Italy, 57, 68, 169

Ivory Coast, 9, 18, 19, 30, 184, 194, 242, 245

Jakub, Ibrahim Ibn, 77

Jamaica, 8, 17, 18, 29, 165

Japan, 174, 201, 213, 274, 293

Jasinski, Boguslaw, 212

Jawa motorcycles, 97

Johnson, Lyndon, 283

Jordan, 98

Kabul, 3, 4, 5, 43, 339

Kampuchea, 4, 11, 13, 14, 25, 26, 31, 39, 87, 107, 108, 131, 165, 213, 236, 239, 245, 246, 248, 257, 259, 274, 280, 289, 290

"Karl Marx" Memorial, in Addis Ababa, 119

Karmal, Babrak, 165, 247

Kaunda, Kenneth, 121

Kayser, Luts, 154

Keita, Modibo, 337

Kellezi, Abdyl, 68

Kenya, 8, 27, 137, 225

Keshtmand, Sultan Ali, 248

KGB, 146

Khieu Samphan, 244

Khmer Rouge, 10, 38, 235, 244-46, 248, 257

Khomeini, Ayatollah Ruhollah, 129, 258

Khrushchev, Nikita, 25, 38, 173, 236, 280, 285, 305, 306; era, 335, 336

Kleiber, Gunther, 124, 126

Korea, People's Democratic Republic of (North Korea), 11, 14, 27, 33, 34, 40, 41, 107, 252, 259, 379, 289

Kosovë, 56

Krasicki, Ignacy, 203
Kremlin, 36, 120, 135, 236, 248,
  333, 334, 336
Krzak, Marion, 204
Kuwait, 65, 95, 98, 130, 288,
  292, 310, 341

Lamberz, Werner, 117, 121,
  127, 129, 155
Laos, 5, 13, 14, 27, 31, 33, 39,
  213, 279, 289
Lazri, Sofokli, 63
League of Communists of Yugo-
  slavia (LCY), 286, 288, 294
Lebanon, 65, 112, 130, 186, 188
Leipzig, African Institute of the
  University of, 111
Legum, Colin, 153
Lenin, Vladimir Ilich, 239, 295
Lesotho, 21
Levant, 77
Lezhë, 70
Liberec, 77
Liberia, 21, 27, 28, 78, 253, 254
Libya, 7, 11, 15, 17, 21, 27, 28,
  31, 45, 65, 66, 98, 111, 117,
  121, 127, 136, 151, 186-88,
  225, 245, 252, 254, 255, 292,
  310, 315, 341
Lidice, freighter, 84
Li Hsien nien, 37
Lisbon, 38
Lopito, 152
Lomé, Conventions of, 22, 253,
  254, 324
Lon Nol, 246
López-Portillo, José, 133
Losonczi, Pál, 338
LRPC, joint venture, 253
Luanda, 15, 38, 152, 249
Lumumba, Patrice, 87, 284;
  University in Moscow, 97
Luso, 153, 155

Macao, 29, 37
Machel, Samora Moisés, 116
Macias Nguema, 22, 27
Madagascar, 9, 27, 28, 65 (see also
  Malagasy)
Malagasy, 184 (see also Madagascar)
Malawi, 21
Malaysia, 63, 181, 192, 213
Maldive Islands, 15
Mali, 11, 27, 28, 65, 83, 87, 142,
  307, 337
Malta, 27, 28, 238
Malvinas (Falkland) Islands, 290
Mănescu, Corneliu, 237, 239
Mao Zedong, 30, 32, 36, 37, 41
Marinescu, Gheorghe, 246
Masawa, 162
Maurer, Ion Gheorghe, 237, 239
Mauritania, 27, 28, 30, 225
Mauritius, 27, 28
Mediterranean Sea, 12, 15, 248,
  290, 309
Mengistu, Haile Mariam, 117-20,
  250
MESAN, 251
Mexico, 7, 27, 61, 62, 65, 97, 100,
  132, 133, 195, 225, 253, 292, 310
Micunovic, V., 283, 284
Middle East, 24, 26, 29, 42, 66, 84,
  106-8, 117, 123, 125, 129-31, 134,
  151, 170, 176, 179-81, 186, 187,
  188, 190, 195-97, 200, 208, 237,
  253, 255, 275, 277, 289, 307, 308,
  312, 335, 336, 341
Mittag, Günther, 127, 133
MLSTP, 250, 251
Mlynar, Zdenek, 283, 289
Mobutu, Sese Seko, 30, 153, 163,
  251
Mocambo, joint venture, 253
Moçamedes, 152
Mogadishu, 44, 119
Mohammed, Ali Nasser, 43

Mongolia, 5, 14, 107
Moravia, 77, 78; northern, 101
Morocco, 7, 26, 27, 42, 64-66,
    87, 98, 188, 209, 225, 250,
    292, 342
Morrison, James, 200
Moscow, 12, 15, 25, 41, 43, 84,
    92, 97, 107, 108, 110, 111,
    113, 116, 125, 137, 165, 236,
    237, 239, 241, 245-48, 258,
    280, 296, 333, 334
Moscow Diary, 284
Mozambique, 9, 13, 20, 21, 27,
    28, 31, 34, 38, 45, 82, 111,
    115-17, 119-22, 129, 134,
    135, 144, 148, 162, 184, 242,
    244, 245, 251, 253, 279, 289,
    307, 338, 339, 342
MPLA-PT, 5, 20, 24, 38, 39,
    116, 121, 152, 163, 202, 228,
    249, 251, 339
MRP, 251
Mugabe, Robert, 162, 249
Munich, 78
Murra, Prokup, 70
Musongati, mine at, 253
Mussolini, Benito, 169

Namibia, 63, 162, 248 (see also
    South West Africa)
Nase, Nesti, 65
Nasser, Kamal Abdel, 38, 83,
    108, 186, 281, 285, 305
National People's Army (NVA),
    145, 147-49
NATO, 4, 125, 127, 147, 244, 285
Naumann, Konrad, 119
Nehru, Jawaharlal, 38, 108, 281,
    285, 305
Nepal, 8, 26-28, 30
Netherlands, the, 78
Neto, Agostinho, 116, 249
New Delhi, 15, 130
New International Economic Or-

der (NIEO), 6, 8, 22, 60, 243,
    247, 248, 252, 292, 307
New Jewel (Joint Endeavor for Wel-
    fare, Education, and Liberation),
    ruling group of Grenada, 20
New York, 84
Ngjela, Kiço, 68
Nicaragua, 5, 10, 13, 63, 132, 133,
    136, 165, 194
Niger, 27, 28
Nigeria, 7, 18, 27, 39, 98, 111, 151,
    181-84, 225, 253, 254
Nimeiri, Mohammed al, 337
Nirowi, joint venture, 253
Nixon, Richard, 245
Nkomo, Joshua, 119, 162, 249
Nkrumah, Kwame, 24, 108, 285,
    305, 337
Nonaligned Movement, 7, 9, 11, 12,
    18, 25, 31-34, 36, 38, 90, 240,
    241, 243, 257-59
Nushi, Ksenofon, 63
Nyerere, Julius, 17, 121

OAPEC, 253
OAS, 7
OAU, 7, 17, 19, 38, 47, 155, 249, 250
Oceania, 174
October Revolution, 295
Oder-Neisse boundary, 200
Ogaden, 129, 148, 155, 182
Oman, 7; People's Liberation Front
    of, 129
Omisalj, 188
Ondo, factory at, 253
OPEC, 18, 123, 252, 255, 291
Oran, 84
Ostpolitik, 164
Ostrava, 77, 78
OTRAG, 149, 154, 155
Ottoway, David, 153

Pahlevi dynasty, 188
PAIGC, 20, 116, 250, 251

Pakistan, 3, 27, 28, 30, 89, 109, 130, 192, 209, 213, 292
Panama, 41, 133, 224, 292
Pannónia, 192
Paraguay, 7, 61
Paris, 30, 285
Patriotic Front (of Rhodesia), 202, 289
Peking (see Beijing)
Péron, Juan Domingo, 244
Persian Gulf, 7
Peru, 27, 61, 94, 98, 133, 195, 224, 274, 292
Philippines, 27, 61, 63, 130, 131, 341
Phnom Penh, 244, 245
Pinochet, Augusto, 133
PLO, 63, 65, 123, 129, 130, 202, 226, 289
Ploieşti, Oil and Gases Institute of, 254
Plzeň, 77, 78
Poland, 5, 13, 94, 113, 146, 150, 155, 236, 249, 257, 303, 310, 311, 333, 342; bilateral relations with the developing countries, 205; economic ties with the Soviet Union, 202, 203; foreign policy of, 200-2; internal economic situation of, 203-5; perception of ties with the Third World, 209-11; Polish exports to the developing countries, 208-9; trade with African states, 224-28; trade with Asian states, 213; trade with Latin America, 213, 224; trade with the Third World, 206-8, 211, 217, 224-29
Polisario, 127, 250
Polish United Workers' Party, 339
Pol Pot, 11, 22, 246, 274
Pomerania, 149
Poppe, Helmut, 154, 155

Portugal, 38, 78, 109, 130, 235, 244
Potsdam, Conference of, 283
Prague, 77-78, 87, 95, 97, 98, 102, 247, 334, 343
Prussia, 149
Prvni Brněnská Strojírna, 78
Puerto Rico, 290
Pyongyang, 11

Qaddafi, Moamar, 127

Rădulescu, Gheorghe, 249
Rakowski, Mieczyslaw, 203
Ranchi, factory at, 88, 89
Rapacki Plan, 200
Rauchfuss, Wolfgang, 128
Red Army, 235, 289
Reddy, Neelam Sanjiva, 131
Rhodesia, 81, 116, 148, 249, 339 (see also Zimbabwe)
Rio Grande, 241
Rjeka, 101
Roberto, Holden, 249
Roman Empire, Holy, 77
Romania, 5, 10-12, 14, 19, 26, 27, 29, 33, 34, 40, 41, 106, 107, 171, 172, 175, 176, 195, 202, 206, 283, 305, 307, 312, 322, 333, 334, 337; aid to the developing countries, 256, 257, 342; internal disputes over economic ties with the Third World, 257, 266; internal political structure, 235-38; joint ventures in the developing countries, 252, 253, 256; "liberation movements" and, 248-51; Nonaligned Movement and, 243; relations with Afghanistan, 246-48; relations with Kampuchea, 245, 246, 248; role in the South, 257-59; status as a developing country, 241-43; support for NIEO, 252; trade with the Third World, 235-37; treaties with

developing countries, 244-46;
views on Third World con-
flicts, 239-41
Romanian Communist Party
(RCP), 235-43, 251
Rwanda, 27, 28

Sachsen, 149
Sadat, Anwar al, 42, 123, 245,
337
Sal Island, 20
Salisbury, 249
SALT, 290
Sanaa, 130
Sandinistas, 5, 133, 136, 165
Santiago, 251
São Tomé e Príncipe, 9, 27, 28,
30, 39, 117, 250, 251
Saudi Arabia, 7, 43, 61, 95,
288, 310
Savimbi, Jonas, 163
Scandinavia, 200
Schmidt, Helmut, 121
Schneider-Creusot, firm, 78
Senegal, 9, 23, 27, 28, 35, 36
Seoul, 40
Seromwood, joint venture, 253
Seychelles, 7, 9, 27
Sibiu, Military School of, 257
Sierra Leone, 18, 27, 28, 30
Sihanouk, Norodom, 246
Šik, Ota, 90
Silesia, 149
Simango, Uria, 116
Sindermann, Horst, 117, 126,
128, 130
Shaba, invasions of, 30, 149,
153-55
Shah of Iran, 63, 64, 95, 128,
129, 181, 258, 310
Shehu, Mehmet, 69, 70
Shiite sect, 63
Shkodër, 70
Skoda factory, 78

Smith, Ian, 275
Socialist International, 36
Socialist Unity Party (SED) of East
Germany, 108, 114, 116, 117,
121, 123-27, 133, 136, 146
Sofia, 334, 343
Soilih, Ali, 11, 22
Somalia, 9, 10, 19, 23, 26-28, 42,
44, 117-19, 121, 129, 162, 242,
245, 250, 290, 337, 342
Somifer joint venture, 253
Somoza, Anastasio, 133
South Africa, Republic of, 21, 63,
148, 152, 162, 174, 195, 201,
248, 249, 275, 282, 339
Soviet Union, 3-6, 9-17, 19, 21,
23-34, 38, 40-46, 57-59, 61,
62, 66, 67, 69, 72, 79, 80, 84,
85, 88, 92-94, 98, 101, 102,
106, 107, 111, 116, 120, 123,
124, 130, 137, 145-48, 150,
151, 154, 155, 162, 165, 171,
172, 173, 174, 182, 184, 186,
188, 192, 195, 196, 200, 202,
203, 206, 236, 238, 239, 245-
49, 252, 257, 267-69, 273, 275,
279-87, 291, 293-97, 304-9, 312,
315, 320, 325, 336, 338, 341-
43
Spahiu, Xhafer, 70
Spain, 78, 244
Spanish Sahara (Western Sahara),
127
Sri Lanka, 8, 27, 28, 336 (see also
Ceylon)
SSD (State Security Service, of the
GDR), 146, 147
Stalin, Joseph, 107, 164, 236, 280,
283, 284, 295, 305
"Stefan Gheorghiu" Academy, in
Bucharest, 256
St. Lucia, 9, 21
Stoph, Willi, 128, 129
Štrougal, Lubomír, 101

St. Vincent, 11
Subandrio, 11
Sudan, 9, 19, 23, 27, 28, 38, 42, 65, 87, 92, 108, 144, 182-84, 225, 239, 244, 245, 250, 256, 337
Suez Canal, 335
Sukarno, Ahmed, 11, 25, 285, 335, 337
Surinam, 21
SWAPO, 117, 121, 144, 163, 202, 228, 289
Swaziland, 21
Syria, 8, 9, 26-28, 65, 84, 87, 89, 108, 111, 125, 126, 186, 188, 209, 250, 252, 253, 315, 335, 341; Baath Party of, 338

Tanganyika, 121, 144; lake, 154 (see also Tanzania)
TANU, 251
Tanzania, 7, 11, 17, 23, 24, 26-28, 35, 61, 65, 120, 121, 142, 144, 239, 250, 251, 256, 289
Tatabánya, 184
"Tatek," Ethiopian training base, 162
Teheran, 128
Tel Aviv, 245
Telli, Dialo, 84
Tesco Organization, 184, 188
Texeira de Sousa, 153, 155
Theodhosi, Koço, 68
Tibet, 287
Tirana, 11, 56-65, 67, 69, 72
Tiruchirapalli, plant at, 89
Tito (Josip Broz), 33, 67, 237, 239, 274, 279-81, 283-85, 289, 291, 293, 295, 296
Togo, 9, 23, 27, 30, 247
Touré, Ahmed Sékou, 20, 84, 108, 245, 335
Trianon, Treaty of, 169
Trinidad and Tobago, 21

Tripoli, 17, 127
Tunisia, 27, 65, 87, 98, 188, 225
Turkey, 174, 213, 238, 285, 342

Uganda, 7, 17, 182, 184, 225, 250
Ulbricht, Walter, 108, 145
Ulqinaku, Esma, 70
Ungelt, 77
UNITA, 163, 249
United Nations, 8, 14, 18, 33, 34, 47, 81, 91, 99, 131, 135, 205, 237, 240, 246, 267, 282, 285, 288, 289; Charter of, 283, 297; Conference on the Law of the Sea, at, 82, 248; FAO agency, 99; General Assembly of, 9, 59, 60, 245, 246, 274; ILO agency of, 99; programs of, 97, 99; UDF of, 282; UDP of, 136; UNCTAD meetings, 231, 252, 257; UNESCO agency of, 99; UNIDO program of, 99; WHO agency of, 99
United States, 5, 15, 16, 19, 21, 33, 58, 59, 63, 84, 129, 132, 148, 174, 188, 195, 201, 212, 213, 246, 253, 256, 273-75, 280-83, 287, 288, 290, 291, 293
University of "17 November" (Prague), 97, 98
Upper Volta, 18, 27
Uruguay, 7, 27, 61

Valdés, Raúl Vivò, 35
Venezuela, 27, 62, 132, 224, 292
Verdęt, Ilie, 238, 248
Verner, Paul, 149
Vickers Company, 78
Vienna, 78
Vietcong, 286, 289
Vietnam, People's Democratic Republic of, 5, 12-14, 31, 33, 34, 38, 40, 107, 131, 165, 213, 239, 244, 246, 275, 279, 280, 290,

293; South, 39, 108
Vitkovické Železárny, 78
Vrhovec, Josip, 240

Warsaw, 92, 334, 343; Pact, 13,
  91, 107, 110, 123, 136, 145-
  47, 151, 165, 236, 238, 241-
  47, 257, 267, 268, 334, 337
Washington, D.C., 5, 16, 36,
  245
Weizacker, Richard von, 164
West Germany (see Federal Re-
  public of Germany)
World Federation of Trade
  Unions, 83
World Peace Council, the, 115
World War I, 224; II, 169, 174,
  213, 224

Yalta Conference, 283
Yemen, Arab Republic of (North),
  7, 24, 27, 28, 42, 43, 65,
  87, 130
Yemen, People's Democratic Republic of (South), 9, 13, 20,
  24, 27, 28, 31, 33, 34, 42,
  43, 65, 108, 117, 123, 129,
  130, 155, 252, 279, 290, 338,
  339; Socialist Party of, 129
Yugoslavia, 5, 10, 11, 14, 23,
  27, 33, 34, 38, 40, 41, 56,

57, 59, 67, 68, 90, 172, 235,
  237, 252, 266, 268, 269, 333,
  337; activities in the Nonaligned
  Movement, 375-80; "model"
  for the developing countries,
  294-97; motives for participation in the Nonaligned Movement, by, 280-86; NIEO, and,
  292; place in the international
  system, 292-94; role in the Nonaligned Movement, 286-91;
  trade with the developing countries, by, 291, 292

Zaire, 17, 18, 27, 30, 61, 148,
  149, 153, 154, 163, 239, 242,
  244, 245, 249, 250, 252, 257
  (see also Congo Léopoldville)
Zambia, 21, 26-28, 35, 65, 66,
  117, 118, 120, 121, 136, 239,
  244, 245, 253, 256, 289, 338
Zandshabi, 128
ZANU, 65
Zanzibar, 121, 174
ZAPU, 117, 121, 144, 162, 228
Zetor tractors, 97
Zhivkov, Thodor, 247, 338
Zimbabwe, 63, 162, 163, 182,
  248, 249, 289 (see also Rho-
  desia)
Zlin, 78

ABOUT THE EDITOR AND CONTRIBUTORS

MICHAEL RADU is Research Associate at the Institute on East Central Europe, Columbia University, and a Ph. D. candidate at Columbia. He has published a number of articles on U. S. and Romanian policies in Africa and on Eastern European dissidence and human rights. Mr. Radu holds a M. A. in history and in philosophy from the Babes-Bolyai University, Cluj, Romania.

ELEZ BIBERAJ is a Ph. D. candidate at Columbia University.

SCOTT BLAU is a Ph. D. candidate at Columbia University.

SHANNON BUTLER, Lieutenant Commander (LCDR), United States Navy, has served as a Soviet naval operations analyst in Washington, D. C. , Western Europe, and South Korea. LCDR Butler now teaches at the U. S. Air Force Academy in Colorado Springs.

HOWARD E. FROST, III, is a Soviet affairs analyst with the Central Intelligence Agency. His publications include frequent contributions on Soviet energy and agriculture to intelligence journals as well as conference papers on Eastern European and Soviet foreign policy issues.

ROGER E. KANET is Professor of Political Science and a member of the Russian and East European Center of the University of Illinois at Urbana-Champaign. He has edited and contributed to The Behavioral Revolution and Communist Studies (with Ivan Volgyes), On the Road to Communism, The Soviet Union and the Developing Nations, Soviet Economic and Political Relations with the Developing World (Praeger, 1975) and is the author of a number of other books and scholarly articles.

MICHAEL M. MILENKOVITCH is Associate Professor at the Herbert H. Lehman College in New York. His publications include

The View from the Red Square: A Critique of Soviet Cartoons from Pravda and Izvestia, Milovan Djilas: An Annotated Bibliography (with D. Milenkovitch) Yugoslav Marxism: Retrospect and Prospect, and various articles and reviews.

VRATISLAV PECHOTA is a Visiting Scholar at the Columbia Law School. Between 1965 and 1968 he was principal legal adviser and head of Department in the Ministry of Foreign Affairs in Prague. In 1966 he was the chairman of the Sixth Legal Committee of the United Nations General Assembly. Professor Pechota is the author of The Quiet Approach: A Study of the Good Offices Exercised by the United Nations Secretary General in the Cause of Peace and of other books as well as numerous articles published in various law journals.

JANOS RADVANYI is Professor of History at Mississippi State University. Until 1967 he was Hungary's ambassador to the United States. Professor Radvanyi is the author of Delusion and Reality: Gambits, Hoaxes and Diplomatic One-Upmanship in Vietnam.

MICHAEL SODARO is Assistant Professor of International Affairs and Political Science at the Institute for Sino-Soviet Studies, The George Washington University. He is the author of "The French 'New Philosophers,'" "The Nouveaux Philosophes and Marxism," and of other scholarly papers and articles.

JIRI VALENTA is Associate Professor and Coordinator of Soviet and East European Studies in the Department of National Security Affairs at the Naval Postgraduate School, Monterey, California. He is the author of Soviet Intervention in Czechoslovakia, 1968: Anatomy of a Decision, and co-editor of Eurocommunism between East and West, and Communist States and Africa. Professor Valenta is also the author of numerous articles on Soviet foreign policy and comparative communism.